Veloce *Classic Reprint* Series

How to improve

Triumph
TR5
250 & 6

Other great books from Veloce –

Speedpro Series

4-Cylinder Engine Short Block High-Performance Manual – New Updated & Revised Edition (Hammill)
Alfa Romeo DOHC High-performance Manual (Kartalamakis)
Alfa Romeo V6 Engine High-performance Manual (Kartalamakis)
BMC 998cc A-series Engine, How to Power Tune (Hammill)
1275cc A-series High-performance Manual (Hammill)
Camshafts – How to Choose & Time Them For Maximum Power (Hammill)
Competition Car Datalogging Manual, The (Templeman)
Cylinder Heads, How to Build, Modify & Power Tune – Updated & Revised Edition (Burgess & Gollan)
Distributor-type Ignition Systems, How to Build & Power Tune – New 3rd Edition (Hammill)
Fast Road Car, How to Plan and Build – Revised & Updated Colour New Edition (Stapleton)
Ford SOHC 'Pinto' & Sierra Cosworth DOHC Engines, How to Power Tune – Updated & Enlarged Edition (Hammill)
Ford V8, How to Power Tune Small Block Engines (Hammill)
Harley-Davidson Evolution Engines, How to Build & Power Tune (Hammill)
Holley Carburetors, How to Build & Power Tune – Revised & Updated Edition (Hammill)
Honda Civic Type R High-Performance Manual, The (Cowland & Clifford)
Jaguar XK Engines, How to Power Tune – Revised & Updated Colour Edition (Hammill)
Land Rover Discovery, Defender & Range Rover – How to Modify Coil Sprung Models for High Performance & Off-Road Action (Hosier)
MG Midget & Austin-Healey Sprite, How to Power Tune – New 3rd Edition (Stapleton)
MGB 4-cylinder Engine, How to Power Tune (Burgess)
MGB V8 Power, How to Give Your – Third Colour Edition (Williams)
MGB, MGC & MGB V8, How to Improve – New 2nd Edition (Williams)
Mini Engines, How to Power Tune On a Small Budget – Colour Edition (Hammill)
Motorcycle-engined Racing Car, How to Build (Pashley)
Motorsport, Getting Started in (Collins)
Nissan GT-R High-performance Manual, The (Gorodji)
Nitrous Oxide High-performance Manual, The (Langfield)
Race & Trackday Driving Techniques (Hornsey)
Retro or classic car for high performance, How to modify your (Stapleton)
Rover V8 Engines, How to Power Tune (Hammill)
Secrets of Speed – Today's techniques for 4-stroke engine blueprinting & tuning (Swager)
Sportscar & Kitcar Suspension & Brakes, How to Build & Modify – Revised 3rd Edition (Hammill)
SU Carburettor High-performance Manual (Hammill)
Successful Low-Cost Rally Car, How to Build a (Young)
Suzuki 4x4, How to Modify For Serious Off-road Action (Richardson)
Tiger Avon Sportscar, How to Build Your Own – Updated & Revised 2nd Edition (Dudley)
TR2, 3 & TR4, How to Improve (Williams)
TR5, 250 & TR6, How to Improve (Williams)
TR7 & TR8, How to Improve (Williams)
V8 Engine, How to Build a Short Block For High Performance (Hammill)
Volkswagen Beetle Suspension, Brakes & Chassis, How to Modify For High Performance (Hale)
Volkswagen Bus Suspension, Brakes & Chassis for High Performance, How to Modify – Updated & Enlarged New Edition (Hale)
Weber DCOE, & Dellorto DHLA Carburetors, How to Build & Power Tune – 3rd Edition (Hammill)

RAC handbooks

Caring for your car – How to maintain & service your car (Fry)
Caring for your car's bodywork and interior (Nixon)
Caring for your bicycle – How to maintain & repair your bicycle (Henshaw)
Caring for your scooter – How to maintain & service your 49cc to 125cc twist & go scooter (Fry)
Efficient Driver's Handbook, The (Moss)
Electric Cars – The Future is Now! (Linde)
First aid for your car – Your expert guide to common problems & how to fix them (Collins)
How your car works (Linde)
How your motorcycle works – Your guide to the components & systems of modern motorcycles (Henshaw)
Motorcycles – A first-time-buyer's guide (Henshaw)
Motorhomes – A first-time-buyer's guide (Fry)
Pass the MoT test! – How to check & prepare your car for the annual MoT test (Paxton)
Selling your car – How to make your car look great and how to sell it fast (Knight)
Simple fixes for your car – How to do small jobs for yourself and save money (Collins)

Enthusiast's Restoration Manual Series

Beginner's Guide to Classic Motorcycle Restoration YOUR step-by-step guide to setting up a workshop, choosing a project, dismantling, sourcing parts, renovating & rebuilding classic motorcycles from the 1970s & 1980s, The (Burns)
Citroën 2CV, How to Restore (Porter)
Classic Large Frame Vespa Scooters, How to Restore (Paxton)
Classic Car Bodywork, How to Restore (Thaddeus)
Classic British Car Electrical Systems (Astley)
Classic Car Electrics (Thaddeus)
Classic Cars, How to Paint (Thaddeus)
Ducati Bevel Twins 1971 to 1986 (Falloon)
How to restore Honda CX500 & CX650 – YOUR step-by-step colour illustrated guide to complete restoration (Burns)
How to restore Honda Fours – YOUR step-by-step colour illustrated guide to complete restoration (Burns)
Jaguar E-type (Crespin)
Reliant Regal, How to Restore (Payne)
Triumph TR2, 3, 3A, 4 & 4A, How to Restore (Williams)
Triumph TR5/250 & 6, How to Restore (Williams)
Triumph TR7/8, How to Restore (Williams)
Triumph Trident T150/T160 & BSA Rocket III, How to Restore (Rooke)
Ultimate Mini Restoration Manual, The (Ayre & Webber)
Volkswagen Beetle, How to Restore (Tyler)
VW Bay Window Bus (Paxton)
Yamaha FS1-E, How to Restore (Watts)

Expert Guides

Land Rover Series I-III – Your expert guide to common problems & how to fix them (Thurman)
MG Midget & A-H Sprite – Your expert guide to common problems & how to fix them (Horler)

Essential Buyer's Guide Series
Triumph Herald & Vitesse (Davies)
Triumph Spitfire & GT6 (Baugues)
Triumph Stag (Mort)
Triumph Thunderbird, Trophy & Tiger (Henshaw)
Triumph TR6 (Williams)
Triumph TR7 & TR8 (Williams)

Great Cars

Austin-Healey – A celebration of the fabulous 'Big' Healey (Piggott)
Triumph TR - TR2 to 6: The last of the traditional sports cars (Piggott)

General

1½-litre GP Racing 1961-1965 (Whitelock)
AC Two-litre Saloons & Buckland Sportscars (Archibald)
Alfa Romeo 155/156/147 Competition Touring Cars (Collins)
Alfa Romeo Giulia Coupé GT & GTA (Tipler)
Alfa Romeo Montreal – The dream car that came true (Taylor)
Alfa Romeo Montreal – The Essential Companion (Classic Reprint of 500 copies) (Taylor)
Alfa Tipo 33 (McDonough & Collins)
Alpine & Renault – The Development of the Revolutionary Turbo F1 Car 1968 to 1979 (Smith)
Alpine & Renault – The Sports Prototypes 1963 to 1969 (Smith)
Alpine & Renault – The Sports Prototypes 1973 to 1978 (Smith)
Anatomy of the Classic Mini (Huthert & Ely)
Anatomy of the Works Minis (Moylan)
Armstrong-Siddeley (Smith)
Art Deco and British Car Design (Down)
Autodrome (Collins & Ireland)
Autodrome 2 (Collins & Ireland)
Automotive A-Z, Lane's Dictionary of Automotive Terms (Lane)
Automotive Mascots (Kay & Springate)
Bahamas Speed Weeks, The (O'Neil)
Bentley Continental, Corniche and Azure (Bennett)
Bentley MkVI, Rolls-Royce Silver Wraith, Dawn & Cloud/Bentley R & S-Series (Nutland)
Bluebird CN7 (Stevens)
BMC Competitions Department Secrets (Turner, Chambers & Browning)
BMW 5-Series (Cranswick)
BMW Z-Cars (Taylor)
BMW Boxer Twins 1970-1995 Bible, The (Falloon)
BMW Cafe Racers (Cloesen)
BMW Custom Motorcycles – Choppers, Cruisers, Bobbers, Trikes & Quads (Cloesen)
BMW – The Power of M (Vivian)
Bonjour – Is this Italy? (Turner)
British 250cc Racing Motorcycles (Pereira)
British at Indianapolis, The (Wagstaff)
British Café Racers (Cloesen)
British Cars, The Complete Catalogue of, 1895-1975 (Culshaw & Horrobin)
British Custom Motorcycles – The Brit Chop – choppers, cruisers, bobbers & trikes (Cloesen)
BRM – A Mechanic's Tale (Salmon)
BRM V16 (Ludvigsen)
BSA Bantam Bible, The (Henshaw)
BSA Motorcycles – the final evolution (Jones)
Bugatti Type 40 (Price)
Bugatti 46/50 Updated Edition (Price & Arbey)
Bugatti T44 & T49 (Price & Arbey)
Bugatti 57 2nd Edition (Price)
Bugatti Type 57 Grand Prix – A Celebration (Tomlinson)
Caravan, Improve & Modify Your (Porter)
Caravans, The Illustrated History 1919-1959 (Jenkinson)
Caravans, The Illustrated History From 1960 (Jenkinson)
Carrera Panamericana, La (Tipler)
Chrysler 300 – America's Most Powerful Car 2nd Edition (Ackerson)
Chrysler PT Cruiser (Ackerson)
Citroën DS (Bobbitt)
Classic British Car Electrical Systems (Astley)
Cobra – The Real Thing! (Legate)
Competition Car Aerodynamics 3rd Edition (McBeath)
Competition Car Composites A Practical Handbook (Revised 2nd Edition) (McBeath)
Concept Cars, How to illustrate and design (Dewey)
Cortina – Ford's Bestseller (Robson)
Coventry Climax Racing Engines (Hammill)
Daily Mirror 1970 World Cup Rally 40, The (Robson)
Daimler SP250 New Edition (Long)
Datsun Fairlady Roadster to 280ZX – The Z-Car Story (Long)
Dino – The V6 Ferrari (Long)
Dodge Challenger & Plymouth Barracuda (Grist)
Dodge Charger – Enduring Thunder (Ackerson)
Dodge Dynamite! (Grist)
Dorset from the Sea – The Jurassic Coast from Lyme Regis to Old Harry Rocks photographed from its best viewpoint (Belasco)
Dorset from the Sea – The Jurassic Coast from Lyme Regis to Old Harry Rocks photographed from its best viewpoint (souvenir edition) (Belasco)
Draw & Paint Cars – How to (Gardiner)
Drive on the Wild Side, A – 20 Extreme Driving Adventures From Around the World (Weaver)
Ducati 750 Bible, The (Falloon)
Ducati 750 SS 'round-case' 1974, The Book of the (Falloon)
Ducati 860, 900 and Mille Bible, The (Falloon)
Ducati Monster Bible (New Updated & Revised Edition), The (Falloon)
Ducati 916 (updated edition) (Falloon)
Dune Buggy, Building A – The Essential Manual (Shakespeare)
Dune Buggy Files (Hale)
Dune Buggy Handbook (Hale)
East German Motor Vehicles in Pictures (Suhr/Weinreich)
Fast Ladies – Female Racing Drivers 1888 to 1970 (Bouzanquet)
Fate of the Sleeping Beauties, The (op de Weegh/Hottendorff/op de Weegh)
Ferrari 288 GTO, The Book of the (Sackey)
Ferrari 333 SP (O'Neil)
Fiat & Abarth 124 Spider & Coupé (Tipler)
Fiat & Abarth 500 & 600 – 2nd Edition (Bobbitt)
Fiats, Great Small (Ward)
Fine Art of the Motorcycle Engine, The (Peirce)
Ford Cleveland 335-Series V8 engine 1970 to 1982 – The Essential Source Book (Hammill)
Ford F100/F150 Pick-up 1948-1996 (Ackerson)
Ford F150 Pick-up 1997-2005 (Ackerson)
Ford GT – Then, and Now (Streather)
Ford GT40 (Legate)
Ford Midsize Muscle – Fairlane, Torino & Ranchero (Cranswick)
Ford Model Y (Roberts)
Ford Small Block V8 Racing Engines 1962-1970 – The Essential Source Book (Hammill)
Ford Thunderbird From 1954, The Book of the (Long)
Formula 5000 Motor Racing, Back then ... and back now (Lawson)
Forza Minardi! (Vigar)
France: the essential guide for car enthusiasts – 200 things for the car enthusiast to see and do (Parish)
From Crystal Palace to Red Square – A Hapless Biker's Road to Russia (Turner)
Funky Mopeds (Skelton)
Grand Prix Ferrari – The Years of Enzo Ferrari's Power, 1948-1980 (Pritchard)
Grand Prix Ford – DFV-powered Formula 1 Cars (Robson)
GT – The World's Best GT Cars 1953-73 (Dawson)
Hillclimbing & Sprinting – The Essential Manual (Short & Wilkinson)
Honda NSX (Long)
Inside the Rolls-Royce & Bentley Styling Department – 1971 to 2001 (Hull)
Intermeccanica – The Story of the Prancing Bull (McCredie & Reisner)
Italian Cafe Racers (Cloesen)
Italian Custom Motorcycles (Cloesen)
Jaguar, The Rise of (Price)
Jaguar XJ 220 – The Inside Story (Moreton)
Jaguar XJ-S, The Book of the (Long)
Jeep CJ (Ackerson)
Jeep Wrangler (Ackerson)
The Jowett Jupiter - The car that leaped to fame (Nankivell)
Karmann-Ghia Coupé & Convertible (Bobbitt)
Kawasaki Triples Bible, The (Walker)
Kawasaki Z1 Story, The (Sheehan)
Kris Meeke – Intercontinental Rally Challenge Champion (McBride)
Lamborghini Miura Bible, The (Sackey)
Lamborghini Urraco, The Book of the (Landsem)
Lambretta Bible, The (Davies)
Lancia 037 (Collins)
Lancia Delta HF Integrale (Blaettel & Wagner)
Land Rover Series III Reborn (Porter)
Land Rover, The Half-ton Military (Cook)
Laverda Twins & Triples Bible 1968-1986 (Falloon)
Lea-Francis Story, The (Price)
Le Mans Panoramic (Ireland)
Lexus Story, The (Long)
Little book of microcars, the (Quellin)
Little book of smart, the – New Edition (Jackson)
Little book of trikes, the (Quellin)
Lola – The Illustrated History (1957-1977) (Starkey)
Lola – All the Sports Racing & Single-seater Racing Cars 1978-1997 (Starkey)
Lola T70 – The Racing History & Individual Chassis Record – 4th Edition (Starkey)
Lotus 18 Colin Chapman's U-turn (Whitelock)
Lotus 49 (Oliver)
Marketingmobiles, The Wonderful Wacky World of (Hale)
Maserati 250F In Focus (Pritchard)
Mazda MX-5/Miata 1.6 Enthusiast's Workshop Manual (Grainger & Shoemark)
Mazda MX-5/Miata 1.8 Enthusiast's Workshop Manual (Grainger & Shoemark)
Mazda MX-5 Miata, The book of the – The 'Mk1' NA-series 1988 to 1997 (Long)
Mazda MX-5 Miata Roadster (Long)
Mazda Rotary-engined Cars (Cranshaw)
Maximum Mini (Booij)
Meet the English (Bowie)
Mercedes-Benz SL – R230 series 2001 to 2011 (Long)
Mercedes-Benz SL – W113-series 1963-1971 (Long)
Mercedes-Benz SL & SLC – 107-series 1971-1989 (Long)
Mercedes-Benz SLK – R170 series 1996-2004 (Long)
Mercedes-Benz SLK – R171 series 2004-2011 (Long)
Mercedes-Benz W123-series – All models 1976 to 1986 (Long)
Mercedes G-Wagen (Long)
MGA (Price Williams)
MGB & MGB GT– Expert Guide (Auto-doc Series) (Williams)
MGB Electrical Systems Updated & Revised Edition (Astley)
Micro Caravans (Jenkinson)
Micro Trucks (Mort)
Microcars at Large! (Quellin)
Mini Cooper – The Real Thing! (Tipler)
Mini Minor to Asia Minor (West)
Mitsubishi Lancer Evo, The Road Car & WRC Story (Long)
Montlhéry, The Story of the Paris Autodrome (Boddy)
Morgan Maverick (Lawrence)
Morgan 3 Wheeler – back to the future!, The (Dron)
Morris Minor, 60 Years on the Road (Newell)
Moto Guzzi Sport & Le Mans Bible, The (Falloon)
Motor Movies – The Posters! (Veysey)
Motor Racing – Reflections of a Lost Era (Carter)
Motor Racing – The Pursuit of Victory 1930-1962 (Carter)
Motor Racing – The Pursuit of Victory 1963-1972 (Wyatt/Sears)
Motor Racing Heroes – The Stories of 100 Greats (Newman)
Motorcycle Apprentice (Cakebread)
Motorcycle GP Racing in the 1960s (Pereira)
Motorcycle Road & Racing Chassis Designs (Noakes)
Motorhomes, The Illustrated History (Jenkinson)
Motorsport In colour, 1950s (Wainwright)
MV Agusta Fours, The book of the classic (Falloon)
N.A.R.T. – A concise history of the North American Racing Team 1957 to 1983 (O'Neil)
Nissan 300ZX & 350Z – The Z-Car Story (Long)
Nissan GT-R Supercar: Born to race (Gorodji)
Northeast American Sports Car Races 1950-1959 (O'Neil)
Nothing Runs – Misadventures in the Classic, Collectable & Exotic Car Biz (Slutsky)
Off-Road Giants! (Volume 1) – Heroes of 1960s Motorcycle Sport (Westlake)
Off-Road Giants! (Volume 2) – Heroes of 1960s Motorcycle Sport (Westlake)
Off-Road Giants! (volume 3) – Heroes of 1960s Motorcycle Sport (Westlake)
Pass the Theory and Practical Driving Tests (Gibson & Hoole)
Peking to Paris 2007 (Young)
Pontiac Firebird (Cranswick)
Porsche Boxster (Long)
Porsche 356 (2nd Edition) (Long)
Porsche 908 (Födisch, Neßhöver, Roßbach, Schwarz & Roßbach)
Porsche 911 Carrera – The Last of the Evolution (Corlett)
Porsche 911R, RS & RSR, 4th Edition (Starkey)
Porsche 911, The Book of the (Long)
Porsche 911 – The Definitive History 2004-2012 (Long)
Porsche – The Racing 914s (Smith)
Porsche 911SC 'Super Carrera' – The Essential Companion (Streather)
Porsche 914 & 914-6: The Definitive History of the Road & Competition Cars (Long)
Porsche 924 (Long)
The Porsche 924 Carreras – evolution to excellence (Smith)
Porsche 928 (Long)
Porsche 944 (Long)
Porsche 964, 993 & 996 Data Plate Code Breaker (Streather)
Porsche 993 'King Of Porsche' – The Essential Companion (Streather)
Porsche 996 'Supreme Porsche' – The Essential Companion (Streather)
Porsche 997 2004-2012 – Porsche Excellence (Streather)
Porsche Racing Cars – 1953 to 1975 (Long)
Porsche Racing Cars – 1976 to 2005 (Long)
Porsche – The Rally Story (Meredith)
Porsche: Three Generations of Genius (Meredith)
Preston Tucker & Others (Linde)
RAC Rally Action! (Gardiner)
RACING COLOURS – MOTOR RACING COMPOSITIONS 1908-2009 (Newman)
Racing Line – British motorcycle racing in the golden age of the big single (Guntrip)
Rallye Sport Fords: The Inside Story (Moreton)
Renewable Energy Home Handbook, The (Porter)
Roads with a View – England's greatest views and how to find them by road (Corfield)
Rolls-Royce Silver Shadow/Bentley T Series Corniche & Camargue – Revised & Enlarged Edition (Bobbitt)
Rolls-Royce Silver Spirit, Silver Spur & Bentley Mulsanne 2nd Edition (Bobbitt)
Rover P4 (Bobbitt)
Runways & Racers (O'Neil)
Russian Motor Vehicles – Soviet Limousines 1930-2003 (Kelly)
Russian Motor Vehicles – The Czarist Period 1784 to 1917 (Kelly)
RX-7 – Mazda's Rotary Engine Sportscar (Updated & Revised New Edition) (Long)
Scooters & Microcars, The A-Z of Popular (Dan)
Scooter Lifestyle (Grainger)
SCOOTER MANIA! – Recollections of the Isle of Man International Scooter Rally (Jackson)
Singer Story: Cars, Commercial Vehicles, Bicycles & Motorcycle (Atkinson)
Sleeping Beauties USA – abandoned classic cars & trucks (Marek)
SM – Citroën's Maserati-engined Supercar (Long & Claverol)
Speedway – Auto racing's ghost tracks (Collins & Ireland)
Sprite Caravans, The Story of (Jenkinson)
Standard Motor Company, The Book of the (Robson)
Steve Hole's Kit Car Cornucopia – Cars, Companies, Stories, Facts & Figures: the UK's kit car scene since 1949 (Hole)
Subaru Impreza: The Road Car And WRC Story (Long)
Supercar, How to Build your own (Thompson)
Tales from the Toolbox (Oliver)
Tatra – The Legacy of Hans Ledwinka, Updated & Enlarged Collector's Edition of 1500 copies (Margolius & Henry)
Taxi! The Story of the 'London' Taxicab (Bobbitt)
Toleman Story, The (Hilton)
Toyota Celica & Supra, The Book of Toyota's Sports Coupés (Long)
Toyota MR2 Coupés & Spyders (Long)
Triumph Bonneville Bible (59-83) (Henshaw)
Triumph Bonneville!, Save the – The inside story of the Meriden Workers' Co-op (Rosamond)
Triumph Motorcycles & the Meriden Factory (Hancox)
Triumph Speed Twin & Thunderbird Bible (Woolridge)
Triumph Tiger Cub Bible (Estall)
Triumph Trophy Bible (Woolridge)
Triumph TR6 (Kimberley)
TT Talking – The TT's most exciting era – As seen by Manx Radio TT's lead commentator 2004-2012 (Lambert)
Two Summers – The Mercedes-Benz W196R Racing Car (Ackerson)
TWR Story, The – Group A (Hughes & Scott)
Unraced (Collins)
Velocette Motorcycles – MSS to Thruxton – New Third Edition (Burris)
Vespa – The Story of a Cult Classic in Pictures (Uhlig)
Vincent Motorcycles: The Untold Story since 1946 (Guyony & Parker)
Volkswagen Bus Book, The (Bobbitt)
Volkswagen Bus or Van to Camper, How to Convert (Porter)
Volkswagens of the World (Glen)
VW Beetle Cabriolet – The full story of the convertible Beetle (Bobbitt)
VW Beetle – The Car of the 20th Century (Copping)
VW Bus – 40 Years of Splitties, Bays & Wedges (Copping)
VW Bus Book, The (Bobbitt)
VW Golf: Five Generations of Fun (Copping & Cservenka)
VW – The Air-cooled Era (Copping)
VW T5 Camper Conversion Manual (Porter)
VW Campers (Copping)
You & Your Jaguar XK8/XKR – Buying, Enjoying, Maintaining, Modifying – New Edition (Thorley)
Which Oil? – Choosing the right oils & greases for your antique, vintage, veteran, classic or collector car (Michell)
Works Minis, The Last (Purves & Brenchley)
Works Rally Mechanic (Moylan)

www.veloce.co.uk

First published in 2003 by Veloce Publishing Limited, Veloce House, Parkway Farm Business Park, Middle Farm Way, Poundbury, Dorchester, Dorset, DT1 3AR, England. Fax 01305 250479/e-mail info@veloce.co.uk/web www.veloce.co.uk or www.velocebooks.com. Reprinted 2004, 2008, and 2016. This edition printed February 2017.
ISBN: 978-1-787111-40-0/UPC: 6-36847-01140-6

© Roger Williams and Veloce Publishing 2003, 2004, 2008, 2016 & 2017. All rights reserved. With the exception of quoting brief passages for the purpose of review, no part of this publication may be recorded, reproduced or transmitted by any means, including photocopying, without the written permission of Veloce Publishing Ltd. Throughout this book logos, model names and designations, etc, have been used for the purposes of identification, illustration and decoration. Such names are the property of the trademark holder as this is not an official publication.

Readers with ideas for automotive books, or books on other transport or related hobby subjects, are invited to write to the editorial director of Veloce Publishing at the above address.
British Library Cataloguing in Publication Data – A catalogue record for this book is available from the British Library.
Typesetting, design and page make-up all by Veloce Publishing Ltd on Apple Mac. Printed and bound by CPI Group (UK) Ltd, Croydon, CR04YY.

Veloce *Classic Reprint* Series

SpeedPro Series

How to improve

Triumph
TR5
250 & 6

ROGER WILLIAMS

VELOCE PUBLISHING
THE PUBLISHER OF FINE AUTOMOTIVE BOOKS

Veloce *SpeedPro* books –

978-1-903706-59-6

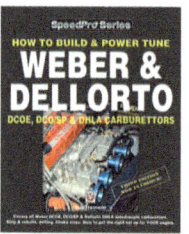
978-1-903706-75-6

978-1-903706-76-3

978-1-903706-99-2

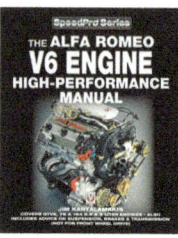
978-1-845840-21-1

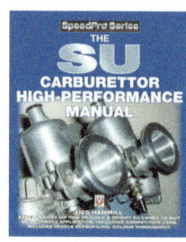
978-1-845840-73-0

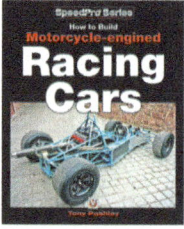
978-1-845841-23-2

978-1-84584-186-7

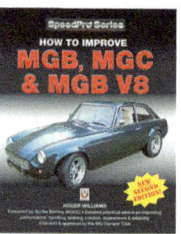
978-1-84584-187-4

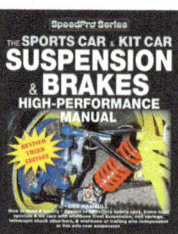
978-1-84584-207-9

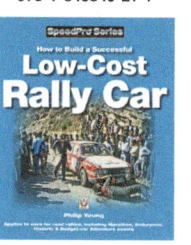
978-1-84584-208-6

978-1-845842-62-8

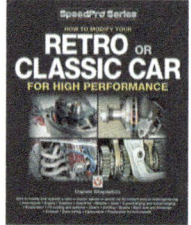
978-1-845842-89-5

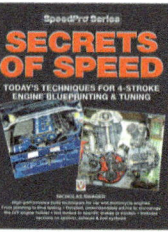
978-1-845842-97-0

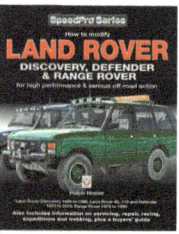
978-1-845843-15-1

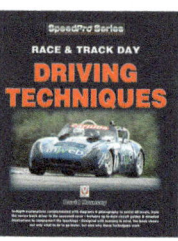
978-1-845843-55-7

978-1-845844-33-2

978-1-845844-38-7

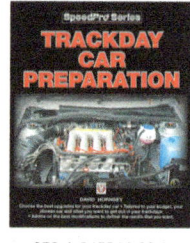
978-1-845844-83-7

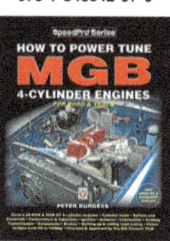
978-1-84584615-2

978-1-845848-33-0

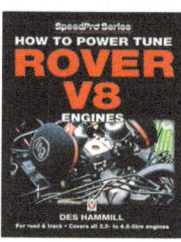
978-1-845848-68-2

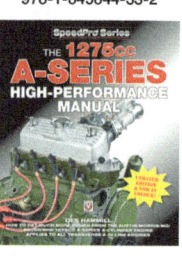
978-1-845848-69-9

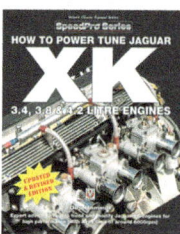
978-1-845849-60-3

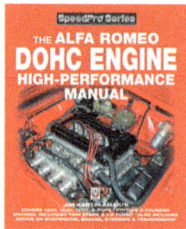
978-1-845840-19-8

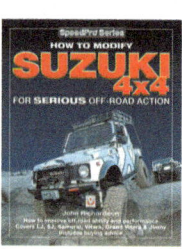
978-1-904788-91-1

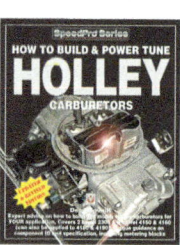
978-1-845840-06-8

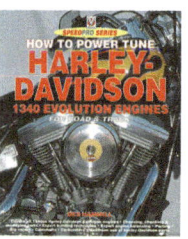
978-1-903706-94-7

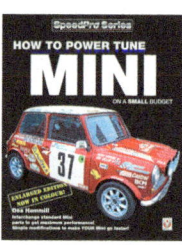
978-1-904788-84-3

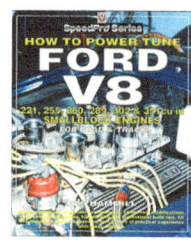
978-1-903706-72-5

978-1-78711-001-4

978-1-901295-26-9

978-1-84584-162-1

978-1-903706-80-0

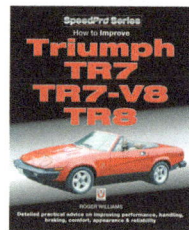
978-1-845840-45-7

978-1-903706-78-7

Contents

Acknowledgements & about the author

This book would never have been written without the help of a great number of people, both in terms of encouragement, and the provision of information, photographs and diagrams. While I appreciate every contribution, the full list is too extensive to mention everyone by name. I hope everyone who helped in the production of this book, to whatever extent, will accept my grateful thanks.

Having said that, I feel that I must single out a small number of absolutely crucial contributors for special thanks, without whom there really would have been no book. John Sykes of TR Bitz suggested this series of books, got me started with a huge initial contribution, and provided much by way of technical help and introductions along the way. Chris Conoley of Cambridge Motorsport, Daryl Uprichard of Racetorations, Neil Revington of Revington TR and Gary Bates of TRGB provided invaluable technical information, photographic opportunities, and were extremely generous with the time they set aside for me. Dan Masters provided much by way of photographs and information on the US scene, while Des Hammill and Geoff Bedding have been absolutely invaluable

with tuning and brake detail respectively.

I owe Darryl Uprichard & Peter Cox a particular vote of thanks for reading some of the key chapters and the many helpful suggestions that followed. My thanks also go to Peter for writing the Foreword.

These books would remain stillborn without the collective help of these professionals, for which I am most grateful.

ABOUT THE AUTHOR

Roger Williams was born in 1940 in Cardiff, brought up in Guildford, and attended Guildford Royal Grammar School. Aircraft became his first love and he joined the de Havilland Aircraft Company in 1957 as a production engineering apprentice and very quickly added motor cars to his list of prime interests. During the ensuing six years he not only completed his apprenticeship and studies, but built two Ford-based 'specials' and started on a career in the manufacturing engineering industry as a production engineer. Works managerial and directorial posts followed and these responsibilities, together with his family commitments, reduced his time

for motoring interests to exiting the company car park as fast as possible! Roger's business interest moved on to company doctoring, which he enjoyed for some ten years, specialising in turning round ailing engineering businesses.

In 1986 he started his own consultancy business and renewed his motoring interests. His company specialised in helping improve client profitability by interim management or consulting assignments, while his spare time was and continues to be devoted to motor cars or writing.

Roger has owned numerous MGBs, all of which he rebuilt over a period of some seven years, and he still retains two of his favourites – the V8 powered variants. More recently he has become involved with the Triumph marque and has restored a TR6 and, currently, a Stag. Roger is married and lives in France in retirement. He has two married daughters and is a Fellow of the Institution of Mechanical Engineers and a Fellow of the Institution of Engineering & Technology.

Roger has two MGB books and now four Triumph TR books in print.

Foreword by Peter Cox

In 1981, production of the TR range of Triumph cars was coming to an end. In all the time these cars were being produced, I doubt a single person at Canley gave any thought to the longevity of the marque. Had the subject come up during a Spares-Provisioning meeting, for example, those present would certainly never have considered a 25 year life span, let alone the 50 years some models have achieved. The cars are still going strong, though, thanks to their robustness and the enthusiasm of their owners, but also because of the excellent aftermarket spares and component businesses.

Because TR owners still expect their 25 to 50 year old classic to demonstrate sports car performance, and because keeping a TR on the road is no mean feat, considering their age, Roger Williams has written three comprehensive 'How to Restore' books covering TRs built from 1952 to 1976 and I recommend these to you. However, Roger would be the first to tell you that even a basic modern saloon/sedan has improved so much in the intervening years that the performance of most original TRs seems less than sporty by comparison. The good news is that with a little help from the TR aftermarket industry, and the guidance from Roger contained in

these companion volumes, your TR's performance can be enhanced.

The TR aftermarket industry, like the performance of the TR, is ever-changing. The 'old' Moss International has gone, but its legacy lives on in the form of a new and improved format TR5/250/6 catalogue. It contains not only exploded drawings and part numbers, but hints and information to help all owners maximise their car's performance and the enjoyment it gives. Nevertheless, more is required. The preparation of a new, improved and extended 'Performance' catalogue is in the hands of Moss Europe, but an independent book analysing the whole improvement market and its offerings is of immense value to almost every TR owner. The book needs to relate what is available to what the TR owner is considering, enabling an evaluation before handing over hard-earned cash.

The book is here and I think you will agree that Roger Williams has done an excellent job with these 'Improving TR' offerings. The differences between the four- and six-cylinder cars has made it essential for the earlier cars to be covered by a separate but companion volume that focuses upon the 'fours'. Moss's 'Performance' catalogue will incorporate new and exciting products,

many reflecting Roger's opinions. It will certainly reflect what is available, what works, and will be kept up to date as products get developed and customers' requirements change.

So who are the other contributors to the health and vigour of the TR aftermarket, and where does Roger come into it? In the UK, but in no deliberate order, we have Rimmer Bros, TR Bitz, Revington TR, Racetorations, TR Enterprises and Protek. These specialists contribute to the performance market and Roger's job has been to assess these suppliers and their parts. This is a daunting task considering there are numerous suppliers and models involved. How To Improve TR250, 5 and 6 is a book by an unbiased TR enthusiast dedicated to looking at the market place as it is today, and it will guide TR owners through the exciting range of products available at the time of writing. Follow its thoughts and guidance and you will have a good chance of ending up with the 'dream TR' you always hoped for rather than a nightmare you dreaded.

Pete Cox
December 2002

Introduction & Using this book

INTRODUCTION

Deciding on which topics to include, and the best order in which to present them, actually proved surprisingly difficult. To start with there are many reasons for wanting to improve your TR, and the objectives, priorities, acceptable cost, and extent of modification will vary almost with every reader. On purchasing this book, the majority of readers were probably thinking solely of improvements to performance and, perhaps, handling. There are many other considerations, of course, so I eventually concluded that modifications which improve the safety, reliability and 'maintainability' of the cars are as important as those that enhance performance.

The issue of 'originality' caused me no concern whatsoever when drafting this book. Many classic car enthusiasts feel, often very strongly, that their cars should be repaired and maintained strictly in accordance with the parameters of the original design. Though I very much respect this point of view, my opinion is that changes which enhance the car's safety, reliability and performance also increase the pleasure the car provides, so variations from originality are quite acceptable. Having said that, I would stop short of changes that permanently altered the basic shape

of the car to the point where it became unrecognisable, and also those which were difficult to reverse. TRs hold their value remarkably well, with only a very few exceptions. If you make extensive modifications which are very expensive to reverse, you are very likely to devalue it.

I have based the structure of this book on the premise that most readers already own, have recently bought, or are about to buy a very tidy and largely serviceable TR, and now wish to explore the available improvement options and the respective cost. As a result, many improvements will be explored from the position that they are part of a rolling improvement programme for an 'on the road' car. This presented me with a dilemma, however, for a rolling improvement programme requires that the sequence of improvements is correct, and that the balance is right too. It could have most unhappy consequences if a reader devoted all their time, attention and funds into upgrading the engine's performance, for example, but neglected to make commensurate changes to the suspension and brakes. I strongly recommend, therefore, that readers embarking on a rolling improvement programme make the changes in a

very specific order – the chassis and suspension first, brakes next, and the engine and gearbox last.

With regard to the 'balance' issue, I am very anxious that readers end up with cars where, for example, the braking improvements balance the changes made to the engine. This is not an exact science, of course, but I've tried to help you get the balance right by subdividing the modifications, as far as is practical, into the following categories:

- Fast road cars
- Ultra fast road cars
- Competitive cars

The first category is largely self-explanatory, but a few words about the other two may be helpful. Ultra Fast Road cars first. These occupy the niche between 'fast road' and 'competition', and meet the ever-growing interest in track days and club circuit-racing. Although these cars may not be raced in the usual sense of the word, they are, nevertheless, built to a very high specification indeed. Their cost will likely be significantly higher than the average fast road car and, while they will spend some of their time on the race track, they will need to be sufficiently tractable to be driven on the road as well.

Although 'Competitive' cars probably applies to a relatively small number of vehicles, it does cover quite a broad spectrum of competitive events. Those that want to rally their TR will need to have it extensively improved. Sprint cars, hill-climbing cars and, of course, straightforward race cars, will each require their own improvements. Despite this broad spectrum, and the inexactitude of these categories, I trust this book will offer some help and guidance!

USING THIS BOOK

As stated in the author's introduction, the purpose of this book is to guide you through the upgrading of a number of TR sportscars (all those produced with a separate chassis between 1952 and 1976, in fact). However, not only did the body shapes evolve during this period, but so did the technical specification. The chassis and its rear suspension changed from a simple ladder with a beam-axle to the more complex chassis required for the IRS cars. The engines also changed from four- to six-cylinder, while, simultaneously, the induction system on some cars changed dramatically. Consequently, whatever car you own, there will be chapters in this book that do not apply to you.

The book is not intended as a restoration, workshop, operations or spares manual. It is, instead, intended to supplement these invaluable sources of information. Consequently, you would be well advised to purchase the manual(s) relevant to your particular model before embarking upon a significant repair, modification or upgrade. If it's your plan to simultaneously restore and improve your car then you will need the relevant *How to Restore ...* TR book written by the same author.

All of the component/service prices are approximately those prevailing in the UK at the time of publication. These prices will be subject to normal market forces and will, of course, tend to rise with economic inflation. You would be well advised to allow for these factors when calculating your budget.

It's possible that the goods and services mentioned will become unavailable or altered with the passage of time. Dimensions given in the illustrations are in millimetres, unless otherwise noted, and line illustrations are not to scale. References to right side and left side are from the point of view of standing behind the car.

Important! During work of any type on your car, your personal safety must always be your prime consideration. You must not undertake any of the work described in this book yourself unless you have sufficient experience, aptitude and a well equipped workshop to ensure your personal safety.

The author, editors, publisher and retailer cannot accept any responsibility for personal injury, mechanical damage or financial loss, which results from errors or omissions in the information given. If this disclaimer is not acceptable to you, please immediately return your pristine, unused, book and receipt to your retailer who will refund the purchase price paid.

Veloce Publishing Ltd

Chapter 1
Initial checks

If you've had your TR for some time, this initial chapter should be of no more than academic interest. If, however, you've recently bought your TR, then read on. With any second-hand car there are a number of prudent things to do before you go blasting around the countryside or starting on improvements. You would be well advised to check the brake pads and shoes for wear, for example, check ALL fluids for levels and leaks, tyres for tread depth and sidewall damage, and generally attend to the car's service and lubrication needs. With TRs in particular, there are a number of additional tasks that you really would be wise to attend to. This first chapter will offer a summary of the more crucial safety checks and make one or two recommended mechanical checks. A more complete discussion on what to check before buying a TR can be found in the appropriate restoration guide published by Veloce.

The first point I want to make, however, involves purchasing spares. All the cars in question have enjoyed extensive lives, and many will have had second-hand (possibly reconditioned) parts fitted. While most will have had no adverse effect on the car's operation or reliability, not all these parts will have exactly matched the original specification of the car. Furthermore, the evolution process these cars underwent has resulted in, by way of an example, five different types of front brake caliper being used, with two different sizes of disc/rotor. Most of the early calipers can easily be identified, but the penultimate caliper looks very similar to the final metric replacement. If you are not alert to such possibilities, you could order the wrong parts for your car. Clearly, the year, model and commission number of the car are important factors in identifying precisely what spares you need, but be aware that at some earlier date, availability or expediency may have changed the basis on which you should be ordering spare parts.

CHASSIS CHECKS

Ironically, the later IRS chassis requires you make more checks as to its soundness than the earlier ladder chassis. You should have made these checks before purchase, of course, but details are easily missed, so I suggest you recheck the main weak spots of the chassis. Start at the front with the four lower wishbone mountings (Pic 1-1). These can be seen by looking down through the inner wings. These pivots are only attached to the frame bracket by ⅜in studs, while the stresses fed into

1-1. The lower wishbone mounting points are clear to see and you should check all four. This is the front left one.

the rear brackets were only distributed throughout the chassis via one gusset welded to the top of the frame. Both these details have subsequently proved inadequate, particularly the rear bracket (Pic 1-2), and we will cover the required improvements in chapter 2. TR6s built after November 1972 already have the chassis improvements incorporated in the original build, though it goes without saying that every aspect of even their front suspension deserves your very close attention.

There are three vulnerable areas at the rear of the car. Firstly, the four

1-2. The most vulnerable lower wishbone mounting points are the back pair. Here we see the rear left one. This one has already been strengthened.

1-3. The differential mounting pins are also easier to see with the body off and, in this case, the chassis turned upside-down. My pins were more cracked than I'd realised before I dropped the diff, but it's worth taking a close look with the diff in place anyway.

differential mounting pins (1-3), tend to crack away from their respective chassis mounting points and need to be strengthened as a matter of routine (1-4). We explored the problem, the reasons and the solutions in the relevant

1-4. This is what you want to see ...

1-5. ... while this is what I hope you don't find. This cracked bracket is part way through boxing-in and re-welding.

1-6. This is where the trailing-arms attach to the chassis.

restoration guide and will outline the necessary improvements here in chapter 2. In the meantime, let me just tell you that dropping the differential to check the pins is well worth your while. The remedy, should you find cracking (1-5), involves overhead welding, so you may prefer to have the whole thing checked and repaired by a TR specialist!

Be absolutely certain that the two chassis 'legs', which are angled at about 45 degrees and carry the trailing arms (1-6), are absolutely solid and free of serious corrosion and patches. Tap them vigorously with a hammer, and bear in mind that your life could depend upon their integrity. The central cruciform pressings (1-7), into which both these chassis members go also needs to be free of bulges, corrosion and patches,

1-7. There are two central pressings that strengthen the joint where the 'legs' feed stresses into the rest of the chassis. The top one is hard to inspect properly with the body on, but you must be sure that they are not bulging or showing any signs of corrosion on the inside or on the outside.

1-8. Ideally you'll want no damage whatsoever – though that might be a bit optimistic in a 30-year old car. You need to be sure that repairs have been carried out properly and that there is no trace of cracking down the side of a previous weld.

for again the integrity of the car and the safety of its occupants depends upon this highly stressed component being up to the job.

The final thing to check is the main bridge (1-8). This transfers the whole weight of the back end of the car onto the rear springs.

ENGINE CHECKS

Although fitted later in the TR manufacturing programme, there are rather more checks that you will need to make if you have recently acquired a car fitted with the larger of Triumph's engines. You need to drain the engine oil, take off the sump and examine its contents. The specifics to look out for are a plug from the front of the rocker shaft (1-9), and any half thrust bearings

1-9. If you find a loose plug in the sump, the chances are that it came from here. However, an alert previous owner may have noticed its absence and replaced it to maximise the lubrication of the front rockers. If it is missing, you should replace it as soon as possible!

(1-10) that may just happen to be lying about. If there is nothing unusual, you still haven't wasted your time for there is bound to be some oil sludge that is best cleaned out, and you also have the opportunity to check the crankshaft thrust shims.

There can be few TR enthusiasts who are unaware of the dreaded crankshaft end float problems of the six-cylinder engine. You will, hopefully, have checked the crankshaft end float before buying the car, of course, but even so, this is the time to repeat the exercise with, at the very least, the objective of bringing the end float back to minimum tolerance. With the sump off the car, you also have the opportunity to fit one of the improvement options discussed in detail 12 to ensure the end float stays there! With the sump off, the least you should do is to ensure the two half thrust shims are still in place and fit new standard

1-11. It's only this main cap that needs to be removed from 'Number-3' main bearing.

thrust shims of the appropriate thickness to reduce your crankshaft end float.

Many engines will have gone beyond worn thrust bearings, however, in that they were allowed to wear to such an extent that the thrust shims turned inside the bearing housing, and then dropped out. If you do find one or two half thrust bearings in your sump it's quite likely that the crankshaft will have moved so far forward that it will have damaged not only itself but also the block. Sometimes the damage is minimal and the situation can be recovered, but if significant damage has occurred you'll need to think about a replacement or rebuilt engine. We will not go into engine rebuilds here, because we will be duplicating a significant part of 'How to Restore TR250/5/6', but if you do find something amiss when you drop the sump do remember that the crank end float problem is always best discovered early.

Because many readers will be affected by excessive crank float, I will devote a little space to the process of checking and changing the thrust shims while you have the sump off. With a pair of standard thickness thrust shims to hand, undo the rear of the two central main bearing caps, i.e. main bearing number 3 (1-11). Feed the two shims round the crank until they drop out, and replace them with the new standard shims. You don't have to, but it may be prudent to lightly re-affix the main

bearing cap to ensure the new shims stay in place for a few minutes. Next, push the crank backward, via the front pulley, and either measure the distance between the front pulley and the timing cover (arrowed in photograph 1-12) with a vernier, or, using a DTI on the front pulley (see photograph 1-13), zero the dial. Press the clutch to move the crank forward and re-measure the gap (if you're using a DTI, read off the end float). Buy and fit the appropriate thickness shims to correct any excessive end float.

1-12. It's easier with a DTI (dial testing indicator) shown in the next picture, but this is the space available, and the gap between the timing cover and the rear of the crank pulley (arrowed) is where you can measure the float in the crankshaft when checking for and monitoring thrust bearing wear.

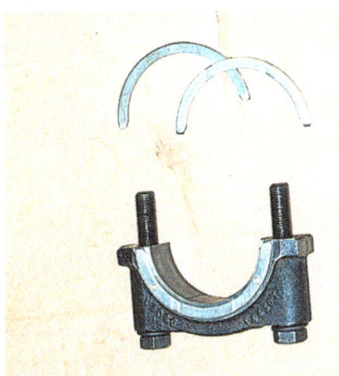

1-10. I hope you don't find any of these half thrust bearings. If you do, though, then a much more detailed check and urgent repairs need to be carried out before you use the car again.

1-13. Engine checks are so much easier when it is out of the car. It's a good idea to get a DTI on the front pulley to check the fore and aft movement of the crankshaft. Buy or borrow one with a magnetic stand to secure it.

If you have to fit a pair of shims that aren't identical in thickness, the thicker of the two is usually fitted to the rear of the crank. Although white metal thrust shims are still available, you should only use lead indium parts (made by AE/Glacier), to ensure maximum longevity. Always fit the soft (grooved) bearing faces of the thrust shims to the crankshaft, and the plain steel backs of the shims (usually marked with the maker's name and thickness) to the block. Torque up the main bearing cap when finally replacing it.

I'd like to return to something I mentioned earlier, *i.e.*, the small slightly tapered plug you may have found in the sump. This will almost certainly be part number 137811 that will have worked loose from the end of the rocker shaft and fallen into the sump. It rarely does any *immediate* damage since it usually drops down an oil drain hole and sits in the sump. The consequences, however, start immediately. If it's absence remains unnoticed the oil pressure in the rocker shaft drops, the lubrication to the rockers (particularly the front ones) is reduced, and rocker wear increases. Eventually you will get rust and squeaking noises in the front rocker arms and accelerated wear in all of them. So, if you find the plug in the sump the first step is to replace it in the front of the rocker shaft. If it has been missing for some time, though, you may be well advised to fit a new shaft/rocker assembly first! Because if its importance, you would be advised to ensure it is still in place every time you service your car!

1-14. This is the original oil filter. They tend to accelerate engine wear on start-up, so you should replace it with the vertical 'spin-on'type as soon as possible.

The next part of the engine to require your attention is the oil filter arrangement. The original six-cylinder oil filter mounts horizontally onto the side of the engine block, as shown in photograph 1-14. While access is superb with the body off, it's very difficult to get at with the body in place, making it tempting to skip replacing the filter as often as is necessary. However, the main reason for this paragraph is to stress that the original design is poor in that it allows oil to escape the filter every time the engine stops. This means that each time the engine is started the main bearings suffer a few seconds of oil starvation. The remedy is easy and should be a routine improvement for every newly acquired six-cylinder TR: fit the vertical canister oil filter that mounts on a Mocal cast housing shown in photograph 1-15. Not only is the filter much easier to get to and change, but it also stops the oil from draining out of the filter once the engine stops, reducing the time delay for oil to reach the engine's working parts each time you start up.

If you fit a vertical filter mounting (usually referred to as a 'spin-on' filter mounting), an oil cooler becomes a further option. Although not absolutely essential for the average road-going car, an oil cooler does become important for fast road cars, and is essential for ultra fast and competitive cars.

COMPETITION

The type and extent of the modifications you are contemplating will, obviously, depend on the use to which the car will be put. Some readers, for example, will just want to take advantage of modern developments and/or technology to improve their car's performance and reliability, or lessen its servicing and repair needs. I have covered these improvements comprehensively in the book. However, because of the recent boom in circuit/track days, there will inevitably be those who have more competition oriented modifications in mind. Although you won't find all the answers you need within these pages, it has been my intention to give you enough information to help you appreciate what's involved, and where to get the additional details you will need.

If you do have competition aspirations, find out what is required of the car before you start any changes. The preparation will undoubtedly be expensive, but it will be more so if you carry out a series of modifications and subsequently find out that some aren't permitted by the respective body(s) governing your choice of motorsport. The *MSA Competitors' Yearbook*, published annually by the Motor Sports Association, provides information on all sorts of regulations, much of which will be relevant to TR owners. It will also help you locate safety equipment, specialised services and performance equipment, for example. Additional information will be found in the regulations applicable to the motorsport of your choice. A great many components on the car will be regulated according to the 'class' you propose to compete in (tyre-width, for example), and you'd be wise to refer to the regulations before making your purchases.

1-15. A vertical 'spin-on' filter.

Chapter 2
Chassis strengthening & roll cages

If you intend to build a competition/ultra fast road car, you will almost certainly have to lift the body from its chassis (even though both may be perfectly sound), to fit brackets for the roll cage and strengthen/improve the chassis. Since this is a task you only want to carry out once, some careful planning is required with regard to what you ultimately want of the car.

CHASSIS STRENGTHENING

The IRS cars were never off-road rallied, because the chassis was considered too flexible, so there is no chassis strengthening kit in a competitive context. However, there are some very important improvements that all IRS owners need to consider, even if you have no intention of competing, for the following areas proved to have been marginally designed in the first place. Triumph improved the situation with the final run of IRS cars, the CR and CF commission numbers, although owners of even these cars need to be aware of the following weaknesses, and alert to the possibility of chassis cracks. The areas to be particularly aware of are:
• The front suspension mounting points. All lower wishbone attachment brackets need to be checked for cracks and accident damage, and all but those

on CF and CR chassis will require additional gussets. The front wishbone brackets are stiffened by only a few millimetres of weld to the steering rack crossmember, and it is a 90% certainty that this small weld has cracked. You can, of course, re-weld the joint, but

you are better to add the new plate or gusset shown in drawing D2-1 and weld it so that it securely joins to and stiffens the rack's crossmember and the front lower wishbone attachment bracket. Photographs 2-1 and 2-2 demonstrate why the extra plate is required. Secondly,

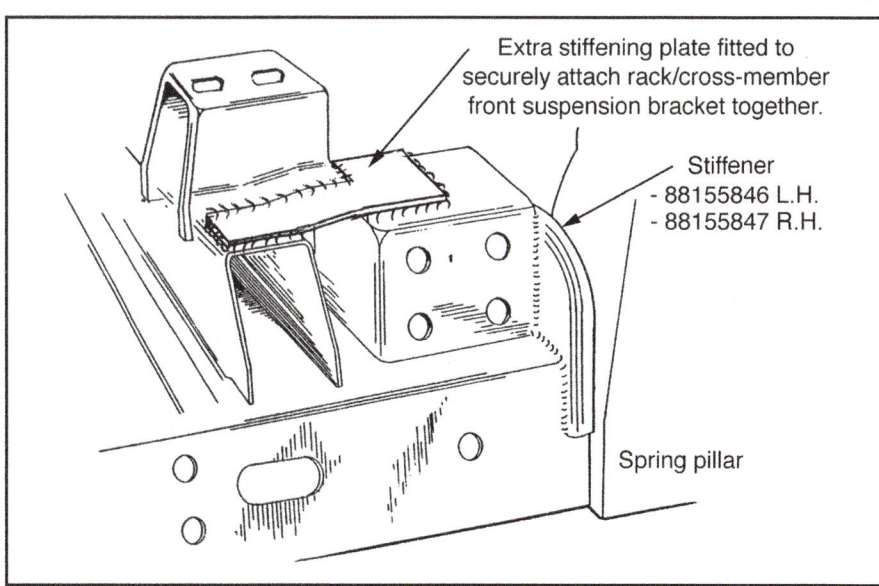

D2-1. Strengthening the front lower left side pivot bracket. (Courtesy TRaction - the magazine of the UK TR Register).

2-1. If your car has been properly restored you shouldn't need to further strengthen the area but, with the body off the chassis, this is the time to check and reinforce the vulnerable spot on all IRS cars.

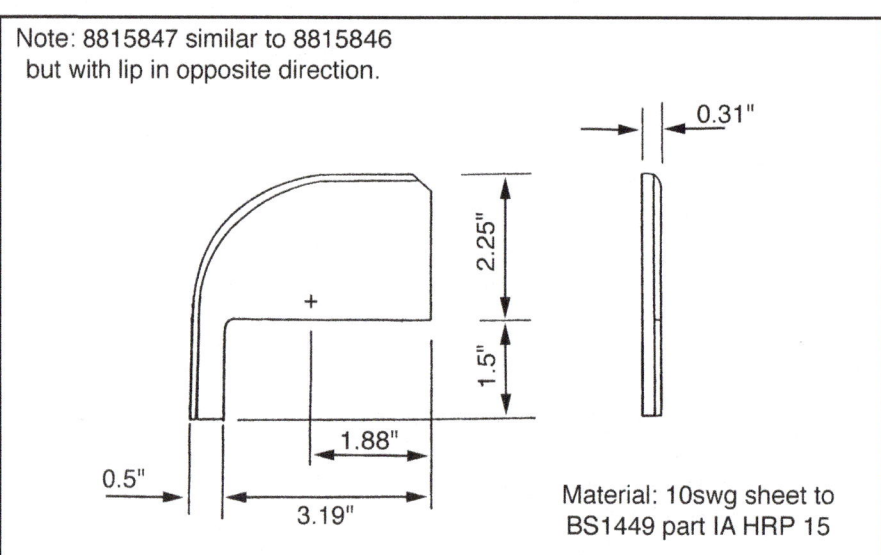

Note: 8815847 similar to 8815846 but with lip in opposite direction.

0.31"

2.25"

1.5"

1.88"

0.5"

3.19"

Material: 10swg sheet to BS1449 part IA HRP 15

D2-2. Dimensional details of the front suspension stiffeners. (Courtesy TRaction - the magazine of the UK TR Register).

2-2. The additional plate required here is shown in diagram D2-1.

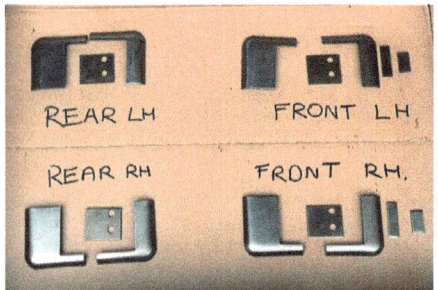

2-3. All the gussets in this strengthening kit are pressed with an edge radius to further increase their strength, but I particularly wanted to draw your attention to the four square 'washers' – each with two mounting holes. Every IRS car should have the square washer as extra support behind the existing chassis bracket, as well as two mounting studs to attach the wishbones to the chassis.

the lower mountings also require the additional pressed gussets shown in drawing D2-2. Finally, cars with only one mounting stud should be fitted with another one, and also a square strengthening washer inside each chassis bracket. (pic 2-3)

• The differential mounting points. Today most cars will have some sort of repair to the differential mounting pins – if not

2-4. You have bought a car for upgrading not restoring, so this sort of diff mounting pin problem should not be in evidence. The picture is useful, however, since it shows what can happen to the mounting pins of a standard road car. Think about the extra stress your up-rated engine and rally or competition endeavours is going to bring to this clearly vulnerable spot!

to all four of them, then at least to the right front one shown in picture 2-4. This pin takes most of the load transmitted through the differential and is the most likely to have cracked away from the spring bridge. The repair kits shown in photo 2-5 are available from all the premier TR specialists. While a good repair can be achieved by a first-class welder from under the chassis with the body *in situ*, the sort of improvement essential to fast road, ultra fast road and competitive cars requires that a plate be pre-welded to the head of each pin. We can see the effect in picture 2-6 before the assembly is then welded to the top of the spring/diff bridge. This should prevent a reoccurrence of the cracking

2-5. This is a 'body-off' diff pin repair kit. A 'body-on' kit is also available, with smaller pin strengthening plates. However, if you're going into competition, you don't want to be welding anything less than the very strongest up-grades ...

shown in photograph 2-4. To carry out this operation properly it's best if the body is completely separated from the chassis. While this repair effectively provides double strength mounting points for the differential, you'll also need to create four complete 'turrets' by boxing in the lower brackets, as we saw in chapter 1.

For ultra fast road and competition cars you'll need to take strengthening the diff mounting one step further by upgrading the diff mounting pins. The standard pins reduce in diameter at the bottom, where the thread is cut. The uprated pins have a larger threaded section and a more consistent diameter down their full length.

• The spring bridge. Even in pristine condition, the bridge that carries the front of the differential and the road springs is of marginal strength. Any ultra fast road or competitive cars should have the complete bridge replaced by a heavier gauge steel one, specially designed for competitive use. (Pic 2-6) At around £80, it has to be worthwhile. It will add a little to the weight of your chassis, of course, but the chassis must be up to its intended use. Consider making this improvement while you're doing the differential mounting-pins.

2-7. The diff bridge is made from an open-bottomed channel, the strength of which borders on marginal for standard and fast road cars. The extra stress of an ultra fast road, rally or track car makes it important that you close the bottom in by 'boxing' the channel. You would add further to the strength of your modification if you welded a shallow folded channel (rather than a flat boxing plate) across this crossmember, as indicated by the arrow. The lips of your additional channel add considerably to its strength while adding very little extra weight.

2-6. ... like this. Note that all four pins have had the extra plates welded to the pin before the pin/plate assembly is welded to the spring and diff carrier crossmembers. I think this is a new chassis, at least the spring crossmember looks new and clearly made from the slightly heavier gauge material appropriate for competition.

• The rear (shock-absorber mounting) bridge, identified by picture 2-7, carries more stress than is generally appreciated. Upgrading the rear dampers will be covered later in the book, but the key issue here is that since even the upgraded dampers are chassis mounted, the stresses are still transmitted through

this bridge. Therefore, whatever rear shock absorbers you plan to use, it's important that some strengthening takes place here.

• The chassis legs used for attaching the rear suspension/trailing arms can be seen in picture 2-8. These need to be checked for integrity, and repaired as necessary (much easier with the body removed from the chassis). There are no specific improvements to make, but those you have must be in a faultless condition, and be replaced if there is any doubt as to their integrity. It's worth pointing out here that there are some subtleties to this area of the chassis you should be aware of. It's hard to see the true extent of the corrosion within the enclosed 'capsule' where the box section (that carries the trailing arms) is attached to the chassis main rails. It is, therefore, essential that you grind off both top and bottom stiffening plates – thus opening up the intersection of the chassis members. The inside of the box section is actually more complex than it looks, in that it has an internal stiffener/spacer to prevent the front and rear faces of the box section closing together when you 'pull-up' the bolts that carry the trailing arms. This spacer has an important secondary role in that

2-8. We talked at length about these vulnerable attachment points in the 'Restoring ...' book and I have already mentioned them here in Chapter 1. However, they are so susceptible to corrosion and stress, even in a standard tune car, that I cannot pass them by when we are looking at a potential competition car with its body off! Do make sure that your arms and top and bottom pressings are absolutely sound and impeccably welded to the chassis.

it uniformly spreads the stress from the mounting brackets out from the mounting bolts.

There are two types of trailing arm box section available, and both have the matrix welded in place. One is designed for those who have elected not to remove their diamond shaped pressed stiffeners. However, for more performance-orientated cars, you should consider the fully assembled and welded chassis sections, together with replacement T-shirt pressings. All the participating specialists can provide strengthening kits for these vulnerable and safety critical areas, and all owners need to regard such improvements as mandatory.

• It is easier to get at the gearbox rear mountings when the body is off its chassis. This is the time to think about the rear mountings that are required by the gearbox you are planning to use. Picture 2-9 gives more information. The gearbox options open to you will be discussed in chapter 6 but, once you've decided what is right for your car, you need to adjust the mounting. More often than not, this will necessitate altering/welding different brackets onto the chassis. In the majority of cases this is best accomplished by fitting the gearbox to the engine (without the flywheel/clutch, and even the crankshaft, if appropriate), and offering the assembly to the chassis. Even if you wish to change the overdrive arrangements (*i.e.* add an overdrive or remove an existing one) of your existing gearbox, the chassis mountings will require change. Even a change from 'A' to 'J' type overdrive will necessitate a change of mounting.

• The separation of body from the chassis also provides an opportunity to carry out some prudent front suspension turret checks. Hopefully your chassis will have been properly restored at some earlier date and I would hope the following are no more than routine checks. These were explored in detail in the *How to Restore* books but, in summary, you should check the vulnerable parts:

• The solidarity of the rear-angled turret support brace, particularly at the bottom (pic 2-10).
• The the shallow bell-shaped pressing that accepts the top of the front coil springs (pics 2-11 and 2-12). You will note 3 fairly short lengths of weld positioned roughly at 90 degrees around the pressing. These often crack, so you would be well advised to continuously weld right around the periphery of the bell/turret junction.

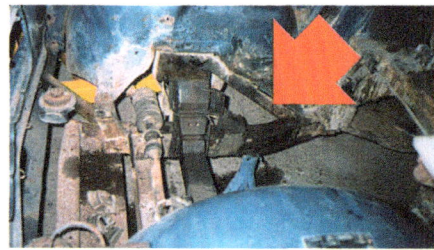

2-10. Check the bottom two inches (50mm) for corrosion (arrowed). However, since corrosion is unlikely in any car being prepared for competition, check the whole brace for previous accident damage. A replacement brace is easily welded in place, but a damaged one might signal you need to check the front turrets too.

• The bolted crossmember that joins the two front turrets (pic 2-13). This can be damaged by a side impact, in which case wrinkling will be evident.
• Check the gearbox mountings for cracks (2-14).

2-12. ... where the dome merges with the flat plate, and also where the plate meets other chassis members.

2-13. The cranked front crossmember can become wrinkled during a side impact, and signals that the front suspension turrets are best checked before you replace the body.

2-9. The chassis mountings are different on the 'A' and 'J' Triumph gearboxes, so what might seem a simple change from an early four-synchro box to a late one will necessitate an alteration to this platform. The situation won't necessarily get more difficult if you're upgrading to non-Triumph gearboxes.

2-11. Any stress cracks are difficult to see unless the chassis has been sand-blasted. However, if these areas have not been fully welded, do so ...

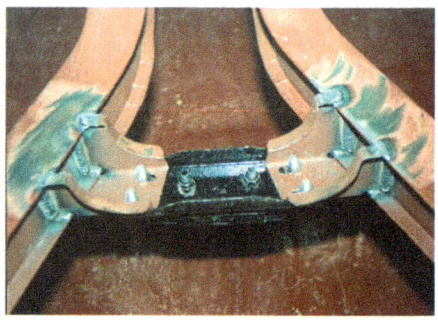

2-14. Bearing in mind that all the gearboxes are mounted to the chassis via flexible rubber mountings, I don't understand why the chassis brackets are prone to cracking. They are, of course, and they need to be checked, re-welded, and, I suggest, strengthened with a few nice gussets across the new welds.

SAFETY STRUCTURES

Anyone contemplating a competition orientated car needs to focus upon the type, design and manufacture of the safety or roll cage early in the planning stage. There are two reasons for this: firstly, the mounting points for the roll cage need to be securely welded to the chassis; and, secondly, the body needs to be assembled around the safety cage/chassis structure. Motor sport is regulated in the UK by the MSA, (Motor Sports Association). It issues its regulating information annually in the *Competitors' Yearbook,* universally known as 'the blue book'. The relevant sections within the book are J (racing), K (rallying) and Q (safety), with the acceptable bar and cage designs sketched within section Q.

The requirements differ according to the type of competition, and you need to study the relevant regulations carefully. For example, if I understand the regulations correctly, you can race a 1991cc TR with minimal protection (just a rollover bar, shown in drawing Q1), but you need a full cage, as per drawings Q5 or 6, for the same car to go stage rallying! I hear that the stage rally requirement was upgraded a few years ago when it was realised that some of the 'Historics' were going faster than some of the modern cars. This was probably a very wise move, and one that historic race cars will possibly follow in due course.

All material must be high quality cold-drawn seamless carbon tube with a minimum yield strength of 350N/mm. You have a choice of minimum tube sizes – 45mm outside diameter x 2.5 mm wall thickness or 50 x 2.0. The steel must also have good elongation properties and weldability. The tubing must be bent cold and the centreline bend radius must be at least three times that of the tube diameter. Further, if the tubing is ovalised during the bending, the ratio of minor to major diameters must be 0.9 or greater. The welding also needs to be of the very highest quality and in truth only a full-penetration gas shielded weld will be satisfactory and must be applied so as no loss of material strength or ductility occurs. All of which points to safety cage manufacture being a job for the professionals.

Rear roll bars

The basic roll bar (Pic 2-15), defined by drawing Q1 in the blue book, consists of a hoop with a rear support. It bolts

2-15. Roll bars must meet defined specifications for motorsport.

to the back of the floor and onto the inner rear wings. This adds absolutely nothing to the rigidity of the car. Rally specification bars have no diagonal braces while race specification bars (2-16) are made from the same material but have welded or removable diagonal braces. Most bars come in a choice of two widths. In both cases the rear hoop main legs extend to the floor and bolt to the chassis. The narrower bars fit between the wheelarches to allow the hood to be erected, while the wider option fits on the wheelarches and gives more protection to the driver, but doesn't allow the hood to be raised. The back stays for the wider arrangement mount to the top of the wheelarch, minimising cockpit intrusion, but I have to wonder how protective this would be in the event of a real shunt. I cannot help but think that the roll bar would deform if the car was rolled, and the windscreen would certainly collapse.

Racetorations has improved on this basic roll bar by offering a 'Q1 drawing'

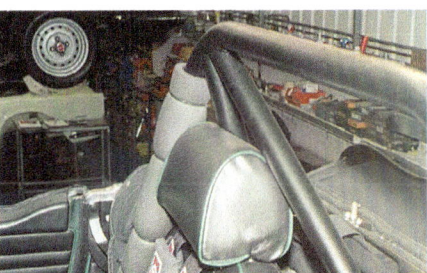

2-16. Installing a roll cage is certainly prudent for fast road cars, pretty well obligatory for ultra fast road cars, and mandatory for all competitive machines. This is an example of a road going roll bar which will allow the hood to be erected. This roll bar is narrower at the top than a full race one would be to allow for this eventuality. Nevertheless, note the substantial triangulation tubing to provide genuine protection.

style bar, supplemented by a second roll bar that fits in the front footwell and follows the contour of the scuttle. This certainly provides some extra rigidity and, if welded it to the scuttle, would further improve rigidity. I gather it makes a dramatic difference to a TR4, where scuttle shake is a serious problem.

Roll cages

A full roll cage, built according to drawing Q5 of the MSA book, offers the only real improvement to protection and stiffening. Although the ladder chassis is strong enough for most fast road applications, a competition car will require a roll cage. Most roll cages are designed to substantially stiffen the whole structure of the TRs, and to protect the driver. Mounting points are on the floor at the front and rear of the doors and the inner wings can be seen at pic 2-17. The big disadvantage, though, is that the scuttle has to have holes cut beside the windscreen pillars for the front legs. This does little for the cars appearance! The official mounting details are specified in section Q of the

2-17. Racetoration's ultra fast road going cages enjoy the benefit of a bolted/removable side-bar, shown here. This facility makes for much easier access when not in 'track day' mode!

MSA book but, in order to help what is a difficult installation, Safety Devices puts small strong feet on the floor of the car to fix the cage to.

A full roll cage, such as we see in photographs 2-18 and 2-19, transforms the car's rigidity beyond belief, making it almost as rigid as a saloon car. The handling under competition conditions is vastly improved, and this must have been a big step forward in development of the TR for stage rallying. Logically it must also benefit those thinking of ultra fast road cars.

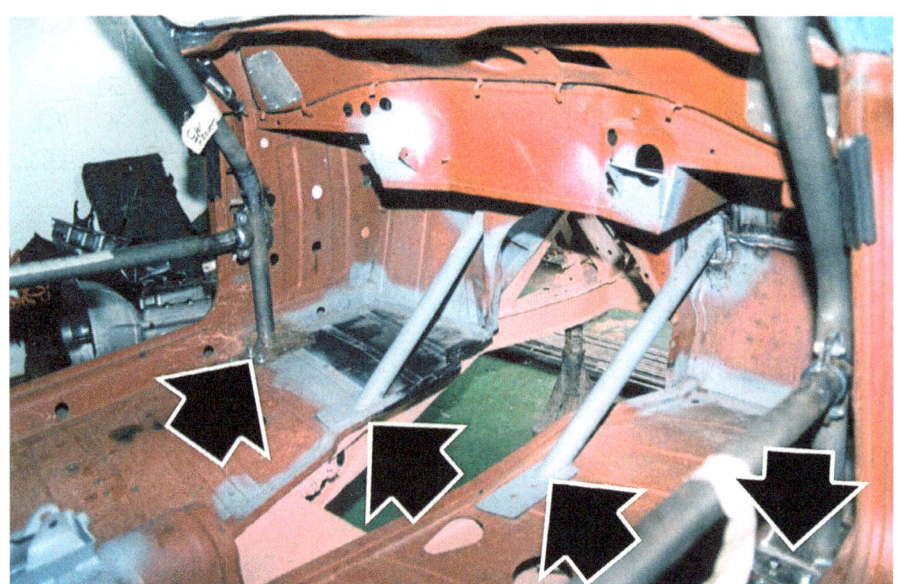

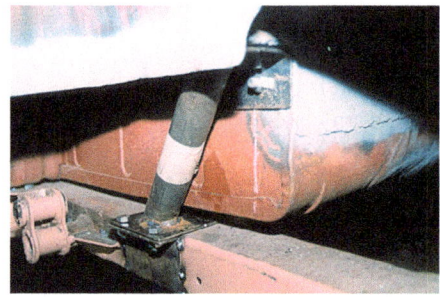

2-20. ... and where they cannot bolt through the floor straight onto a chassis member, a solid chassis mounting has been created and a brace constructed to meet the plate I have arrowed in picture 2-19.

2-18 and 2-19. The full extent of the work, not to mention the skill, required to install a full roll cage to this car is evident from these pictures. You will note that Revington has taken the four mounting feet we see in 2-18 down onto what is, in fact, solid chassis members immediately beneath the floor pans ...

The cage mounting feet are shown in picture 2-20.

Competition cages, when the regulations permit, fit over most of the length of the chassis, strengthening from the top/rear of the front-suspension turrets, through the front bulkhead/ firewall to the tail of the chassis. Historic regulations, however, prohibit anything quite this substantial, and you must settle for a cage with just six mounting points and a limited number of diagonals. In a road car the design tends to be just a rear cage running from behind the driver to the tail of the chassis.

Door bars

These are not shown in the 'blue-books' drawings Q5 and Q6, but they are required for competition. Most designs fit them low at the front (almost at floor level), slanting upwards to the rear/top of the door. They offer minimal impedance to entry and exit, therefore, and provide a good leg support. They do, however, restrict the size of seat that can be fitted.

Some cages allow for these to be unbolted but, whether you use these or the welded type, they should be specifically designed so as not to impede your getting in and out of the car. All other things being equal, you're probably better with the reduced weight, simplicity, fewer protrusions and increased strength of the welded sidebars! Removable members are permitted but the assembled joints must comply with approved designs. The removable members must not be part of the main roll bars, for example, and all fastenings must be of adequate size and material specification.

Quality standards

Most would-be competitors will probably buy a proven, ready made, professional roll cage. After all, life and death hang upon it being up to the job. It would be unwise to attempt to try to develop one yourself. Furthermore, all UK cages should be manufactured to 'MSA Certification' standards, and you really must get that quality assurance before parting with your cash. Of course you could find someone who can supply a very professional looking but uncertified product. Most such cage builders are not conversant with the latest developments and subtleties, however, and are best avoided.

Generally, your cage will be a compromise between cost, weight and complexity. A very comprehensive cage that is light in weight may be relatively costly, particularly if made from the best material. Consequently, it's worth

2-21. Trevor Gilks' TR3A after a horrendous somersault. His life was probably saved by his Safety Devices roll cage.

I am indebted to Safety Devices and our TR specialists for several of the excellent shots that accompany this summary.

Surrey backlight and roll protection

There is one specialised roll bar that deserves our attention since it combines the attraction of a 'Surrey' top with a roll bar. To clarify what I mean by a Surey top; this is a fixed rear window with a removable, usually vinyl, central roof or top. Many owners also refer to the arrangement where a fixed rear window is topped by a hard top as a Surrey. In MG circles this would be called a 'Targa' hardtop – but its name hardly matters so long as we all know what I am talking about. To get to the point, Revington TR has developed an ingenious new Surrey rear window that incorporates a hidden rollover bar for the Michelotti TRs. The fibreglass window frame incorporates an integral rollover bar, with the two back stays we see in 2-22, to provide added safety and strength. The bar fits right up inside the fibreglass frame and affords maximum rollover protection, along with better rear visibility. I would have preferred for the two rear stays to be attached to something more substantial than the top of the rear wheelarches but the main legs of the main hoop do extend to the floor/chassis. However, the arrangement is clever in that the same fibreglass rear window frame can incorporate a comprehensive roll cage, which is very protective.

finding a specialist who can achieve that balance rather than choosing one who can build a lightweight but basic cage that offers little protection in the event of a hefty 'moment'. The MSA Yearbook lists four manufacturers. Not surprisingly, all the participating TR specialists supply roll bars and roll cages.

The best roll bars and cages are, in fact, only as effective as the mounting of the cage to the structure of the car, *i.e.* the chassis. The protection that is offered by a rear roll bar does increase to some degree when supplemented by a front mounted one. However, to my mind, the full benefit is not realised until diagonal fore and aft crossbraces are added and the triangulation of the whole structure takes place – at which point the attachment becomes a roll or safety cage of immense value.

A properly constructed roll cage is not only a very effective safety device (see picture 2-21), it also provides very worthwhile stiffening to the TR chassis of any TR, particularly an IRS! From this point of view, the roll cage is actually a performance-enhancing safety device!

Even with a first class, professionally stressed, fully developed and beautifully made product to hand, the chassis mounting points are all important. Substantial plates, well gusseted and welded to the side of the chassis rails are an essential foundation for these safety critical additions. Again, the MSA Yearbook incorporates several

pages of requirements with regard to the design of the mounting point, the material thickness, and fastenings.

Padding is also covered in section Q and, whatever material you choose, it must be fire retardant. Moulded polyurethane will be most competitors' choice, although high impact Confor foam can be used too. Water pipe insulation is popular as a consequence of it being 10% of the cost! Some protection is essential as roll cages are hard and you'll hit them on every worthwhile bump!

2-22. Although behind a Neil Revington rear screen for what, I guess, will eventually be a Surrey top, this is actually a substantial Safety Devices 'Rally Bar'.

Chapter 3

Handling, diff, driveshafts & suspension

Assuming the front of the car is undamaged (*i.e.* it hasn't been knocked out of alignment), and given a solid chassis (which is not always as solid as the owner thinks), the original/standard IRS TRs are basically very nice cars to drive. They have an excellent reputation for their road-holding and steering, and we should not lose sight of the fact that these cars had little wrong with them when everything is in tip-top condition. That said, the rear suspension and driveshafts of an IRS car offer improvers something of a challenge. We will get to the differential later in the chapter but there are parts of the rear suspension that definitely need to be addressed. Your challenge is to find the solutions that best suit your proposed performance and wallet. In that context, perhaps I should start by summarising the weaknesses within the standard set-up that you will need to address with a seriousness that parallels your performance aspirations.

The trailing-arm mounting bushes compress allowing the trailing-arms to move about.
The driveshafts lock-up under high torque and generate the infamous 'twitch'.
The hubs' stub-axle breaks allowing that wheel to escape.

The universal joints seize.
The hub mounting studs pull out of the trailing arms.
The trailing arms can crack.
The rear end of the car squats under acceleration.

This chapter is divided, in order of importance, into the following sections:

• Rear handling improvements
• Front handling and steering
• Rear drive durability

REAR HANDLING IMPROVEMENTS
IRS trailing arm improvements

After 25 to 30 years, probably the most important things to upgrade are the bushes in the rear trailing arms. Picture 3-1 gives a good view of the pair in question. In standard form they do move around a lot and require improving in the mildest of fast road cars. So, for all standard and fast road cars it's essential to upgrade the rear bushes. Fitting polyurethane bushes to the four swivel points at the front of the trailing arms will radically improve road-holding, particularly if telescopic rear shock absorbers are fitted at the same time. The polyurethane bushes are much harder than the original

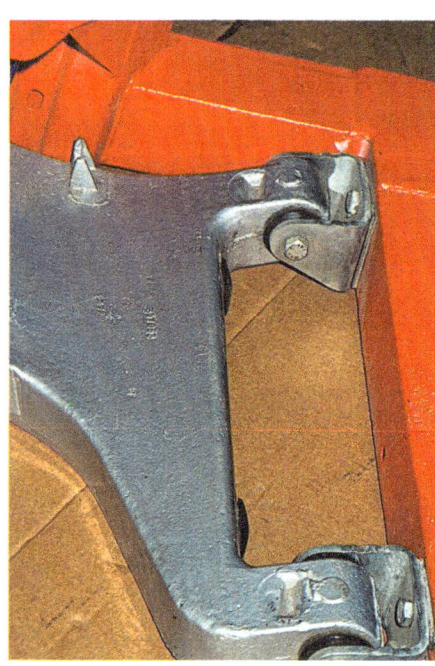

3-1. An excellent view of the rear suspension trailing arm, it's mounting brackets and the all-important chassis mounting member. Note that both mounting brackets have identification notches on the top edges. The trailing arm bushes are polyurethane.

rubber bushes and will transmit some additional road-noise, but the improved road holding makes this a very small price to pay.

Polyurethane bushes come in a range of hardness (shore), and medium-hard ones will improve the whole drivability of the car and should be a routine change for every standard and fast road car. As the bushes get harder their difficulty of fitting increases, as does the road noise transmitted. Superflex seems to have got the balance between ease of fitting, hardness, handling and road noise about right for most standard and fast road cars. Although Nylatron bushes are harder still, and transmit too much road noise for many tastes, they should be considered for some ultra fast road cars. Even aided by pre-warming the bush in hot (but not boiling) water, and using liberal doses of washing-up liquid, all polyurethane replacements will be difficult to fit. The aid sketched in drawing D3-1 will hold the bush square to the trailing arm while you use your vice to squeeze the bush into its housing.

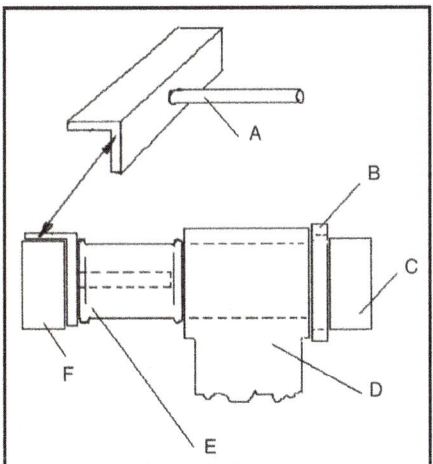

D3-1. Guiding a new trailing-arm bush into position. A. Suitable bolt welded square to angle iron base. B. Spacer (short piece of pipe). C. Vice/vise jaw. D. Trailing-arm. E. Polyurethane bush. F. Vice/vise jaw.

For the top ultra fast road, rally and competition IRS cars there is a further and equally important improvement available solely from Restorations: modifying the trailing arms to accept the roller bearings we can see in photograph 3-2. The power available from engines in the very fast/competition end of the

3-2. The IRS trailing arm roller bearings as they would fit into this arm once the original bushes have been removed.

spectrum is such that even the hardest of polyurethane bushes can distort. Consequently, the car's handling becomes unpredictable as the geometry of the rear suspension changes under high power/torque – just when you don't want it! Restorations has solved the problem by machining the trailing arms to accept two pairs of roller bearings per side. Since these cannot 'give', the geometry of the suspension stays as designed and the car's handling doesn't vary with power variations/applications.

A further minor advantage with the roller bearings is that the modified trailing arm is easier to move through its full arc. The modification work is confined to the trailing arms themselves, and doesn't

3-3. A close-up of Racetorations' unique rear trailing arm roller bearings. Note the twin stainless steel side covers and the central grease nipple that requires a shot from the grease gun every six months or so.

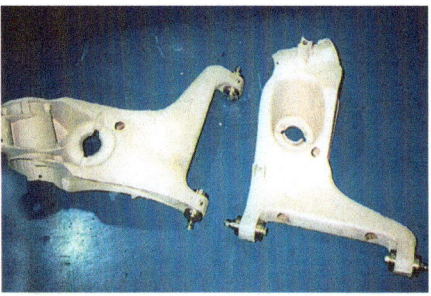

3-4. The IRS roller bearings in place ready to drop into the car. The grease nipples are just visible in the left-hand arm.

affect the car in any way. Each arm is line-bored slightly, faced and drilled for grease-nipples (picture 3-3). Each pair of roller bearings is then assembled on its own mini-spindle and fitted to the trailing arm, as seen in picture 3-4, to allow the passage of the standard mounting bolts. Dirt seals are fitted on the external faces. Although this improvement isn't cheap, at £205 per side, it offers excellent value for money for those with really powerful IRS cars.

With the bushes replaced the next thing to do is get the car onto a modern four wheel alignment device. This will provide toe-in and camber measurements for all four wheels simultaneously. The correct setup (as per the manual) is (front and rear), 0 to $\frac{1}{16}$ inch toe-in.

While you have the trailing arms off the car, check for cracks in the rear trailing arms caused by repeated stress and age. They most frequently go in the two places highlighted in photograph 3-5.

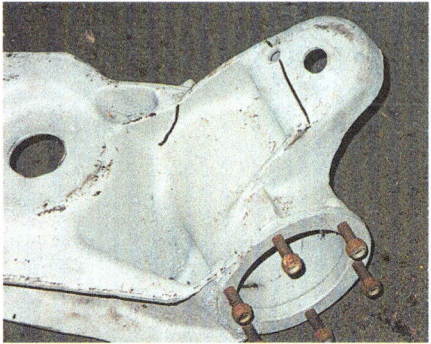

3-5. The IRS trailing arm with the two most common crack points highlighted. Don't confine your inspection to the areas shown, but be sure to inspect and even crack-test both arms where shown.

3-6. Racetorations' fabricated alloy rear mounting bracket for an IRS telescopic shock absorber conversion. Note that virtually all the stresses are carried by the original chassis shock mounting point. The top two bolts bolted through to the body are little more than a vertical steady and are not strictly speaking essential.

3-7. The next step is to fit the shock absorber of your choice.

3-8. This is the TR Bitz mounting bracket and telescopic shock conversion seen from a slightly different viewpoint. This shot emphasises that the stresses are all contained within the chassis – where they should be.

3-9. Another excellent telescopic shock absorber conversion arrangement. This is the CTM design, a company perhaps more widely known for it's work repairing and/or building new TR chassis. These conversions are usually supplied with Koni shock absorbers.

Telescopic rear shock absorbers

Telescopic shock absorbers are an essential modification at the rear of all the IRS TRs – even for the most basic of standard and modest of fast road cars. A pair will transform the handling for the better and they should be placed equal-first on your list of priorities. We can see two examples of the conversion to telescopic shock absorbers in pictures 3-6 and 3-7, and two more in 3-8

and 3-9. All will have a very beneficial effect on the car's handling.

Most specialists believe that dampers work more efficiently when attached to the back of the trailing arm. Revington TR offers an alternative, centrally located position (pic 3-10), which probably works just as well provided the mountings and dampers have been designed and selected correctly. Although I like Revington's coil-over damper design, there is something more attractive about an installation where the damper has to work less hard – making the rear mounted setup perhaps marginally preferable.

Opinions differ as to the value, but some ultra fast cars may benefit from a further upgrade, i.e. fitting even higher rated telescopic units. 'Professional' (or Pro) Spax (identified by the knurled adjustment knobs) have a different internal design to 'normal' shock absorbers and have a differential rebound strength. This makes them much more stable, something that becomes more noticeable the faster the car is driven.

Regardless of the make and class of the upgraded telescopic unit, all are only as good as their attachment to the car allows. You must never fit brackets that feed stresses into the body. These fatigue the body at their attachment point and constantly try to lift the body off the chassis. Brackets that feed all the stresses into the chassis are the route to follow and there are several very effective steel designs on the market. Alternatively, Restorations' design uses an alloy casting which weighs 50% less than its fabricated steel competitors. It doesn't feed any stresses through the body and I'm told that its longevity in high mileage cars has never been a problem. It has also been pointed out to me that the angle at which the telescopic damper is fixed to the bracket is critical and that many of the fabrications do

3-10 Revington's unique coil over shocks design ...

not address this important issue. Look carefully at what you are offered, and check that all components will be suited to your individual requirements.

Rear anti-roll/anti-sway bars

IRS cars are significantly stabilised by anti-roll/sway bars, and these are, therefore, recommended for both the front and the rear. In fact, fitting a rear anti-roll bar will change the characteristics of the car considerably. Road holding will be improved as the rear anti-roll/sway bar limits body roll, the car will corner flatter and more weight will be transferred to the outside rear wheel, promoting oversteer. Furthermore, with modern, and particularly with wider tyres, the car will have better grip, at least on a dry surface.

All our contributors offer rear anti-roll/sway bars. Revington's is unique in that it is top mounted (and thus has no ground-clearance problems). As can be seen in picture 3-11, it exerts its control from the rear of the trailing arms. Racetorations' rear bars are made from 0.625in diameter steel mounted beneath the chassis with tough polypropylene brackets (see picture 3-12). The bar is connected to each trailing arm below the spring pad via a very short link (pic 3-13).

Consequently, none of the flattening forces generated within the bar are lost in its mountings or linkage. In extreme situations, however, there is a possibility that the mountings could foul a curb or other obstacle, so Restorations supply small steel 'skids' to protect them.

If you want to try a rear anti-roll/sway bar yourself, some thoughts as to how you might secure the bar to each rear trailing-arm casting will be found at diagram D3-2.

Weigh up the anti-roll bar end bushes and bar-mountings you intend to use. Conventional rubber bushes will usually be satisfactory for fast road use. However, for ultra fast road cars a harder (polyurethane) mounting bush and/or firmer (even solid) end fittings on the bar will be required. These transmit more of the bar's stabilising effect but do add to road-noise. Competitive cars will need even more roll resistance – usually achieved by a thicker bar and solid fittings!

If you are not fitting anti-roll/sway bars simultaneously, always fit the front first. Fitting a front anti-roll/sway bar, stiffer road springs and better rear dampers may make a rear anti-roll/sway bar unnecessary, so try the car first – in

both wet and dry conditions. If the car understeers on sharper bends you'll need to fit a rear anti-roll/sway bar.

3-13. ... the metal skid/pivot protector is fitted, thus hiding from our view the very neat polypropylene pivots which are bolted directly to the underside of the chassis for maximum effectiveness.

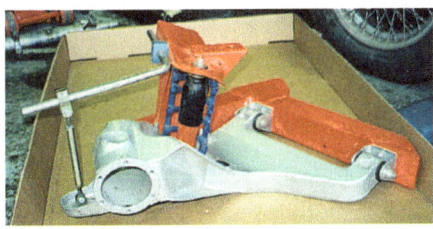

3-11. ... leaves the rear damper mounting point free to fit an anti-roll bar.

3-12. From the side we get a good view of the Racetorations IRS anti-roll/sway bar and its coupling to the underside of the coil spring pan in each trailing arm. The chassis mounting looks vulnerable until ...

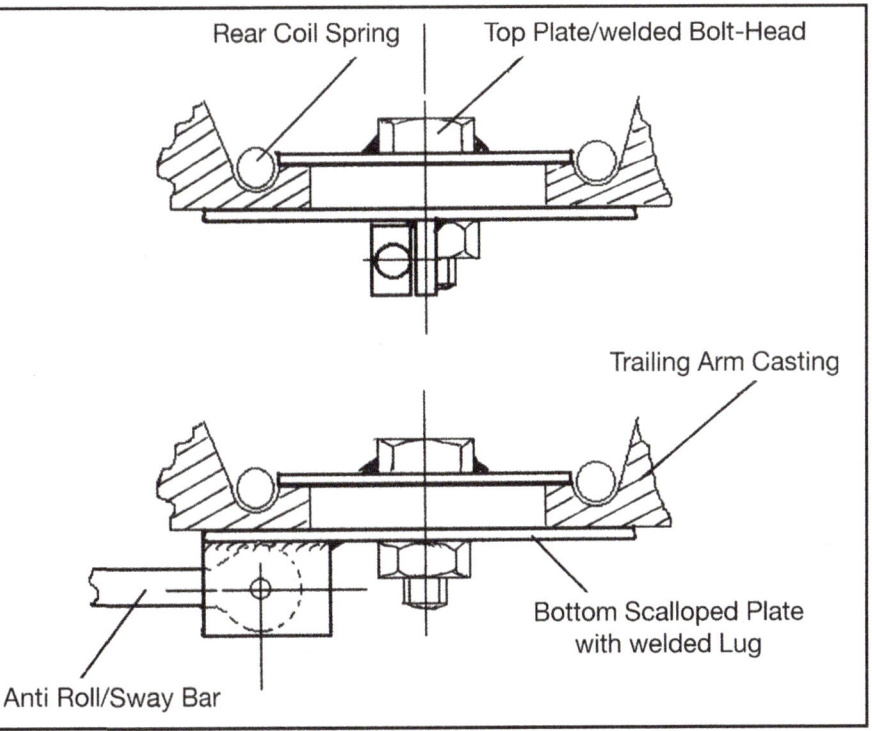

D3-2. IRS rear anti roll/sway-bar fixing.

Rear spring height/ratings

It's generally thought that Triumph fitted the early cars with a rear road spring rating that was a little too soft. These days restorers usually fit TR6 springs, of about 350lb rating, although many owners go for an up-rated spring of 390lb. The latter will chatter the teeth a bit, so try a car first!

The lower the car the less body-roll there'll be when cornering, so it's part of most suspension improvement packages to fit slightly lowering road springs. The camber angles will go negative if/when you fit shorter springs, so you need to make any planned spring changes before setting up the camber.

Clearly you won't want the car to go along 'nose-up', so lowered rear springs must be accompanied by the equivalent lowered front springs.

FRONT HANDLING AND STEERING

The IRS TRs are a joy to drive and there is nothing basically wrong with the front end detail – except its fragility. We covered the remedial work in Chapter 2, so it doesn't bear repeating here except to mention
that much of that work is important from a safety point of view and must be your first priority.

Front wishbone assembly

Almost every reader of this type of book appreciates the benefits to road holding, particularly when cornering, of a lower ride height. Technically, this is because the height of the centre of gravity is reduced as the suspension is lowered, and the car's roll is reduced for the same centripetal cornering force! All the TRs are easy to lower by at least 15mm at the front – by assembling the front wishbones seen in photograph 3-14 upside-down. This, particularly when coupled to many of the modifications we will be discussing, will have a major benefit in terms of reducing body roll when cornering.

There are two ways to approach rebuilding a car's suspension system. An integrated suspension package has everything you need and is designed to just bolt on. The 'kit' includes harmonically balanced front and rear springs, front and rear anti-roll bars together with the relevant mounting brackets and polyurethane bushes, front and rear suspension bushes, full car set in polyurethane and Avo adjustable front telescopic shock absorbers with telescopics for the rear. An exchange steering arm improves the ackermann angle and makes the car 'turn-in' better.

The second approach involves phased upgrades, and Revington has broken all its suspension kits into three constituent parts to enable phased purchase and adoption. Should you wish to follow this route it's important that you fit each phase in order for maximum effect and safety:

- **Phase 1.** Front suspension and steering upgrade, if applicable.
- **Phase 2.** Rear suspension.
- **Phase 3.** Anti-roll bars.

Front suspension bushes

Because all of our experts differs in terms of their priorities and component details, it's important to buy everything for your suspension from one specialist. One specialist, for example, holds the opinion that the standard front suspension bushes on a fast road car are not a priority upgrade, though all rubber bushes are available in a variety of polyurethane grades. If your standard bushes are worn out and have to be replaced, the middle hardness, such as Polybush Touring, Superflex or Superpro, are very good options for fast road cars (picture 3-15). For the majority of fast road cars it's not worth stripping down a good front suspension setup just to fit polyurethane replacements. Racetorations' view, on the other hand, is that all fast road cars will see an immediate benefit from fitting polyurethane bushes to the top and bottom, inner and outer wishbone pivots.

All agree that in addition to the longevity benefits associated with harder bushes, the suspension geometry is retained even when greater than designed-for cornering forces are applied. You are advised to further upgrade the suspension bushes of all competition cars to even harder ones made from nylon with a stainless steel insert. One note of warning – expect to find any residual problems, due to an earlier accident, for example, when

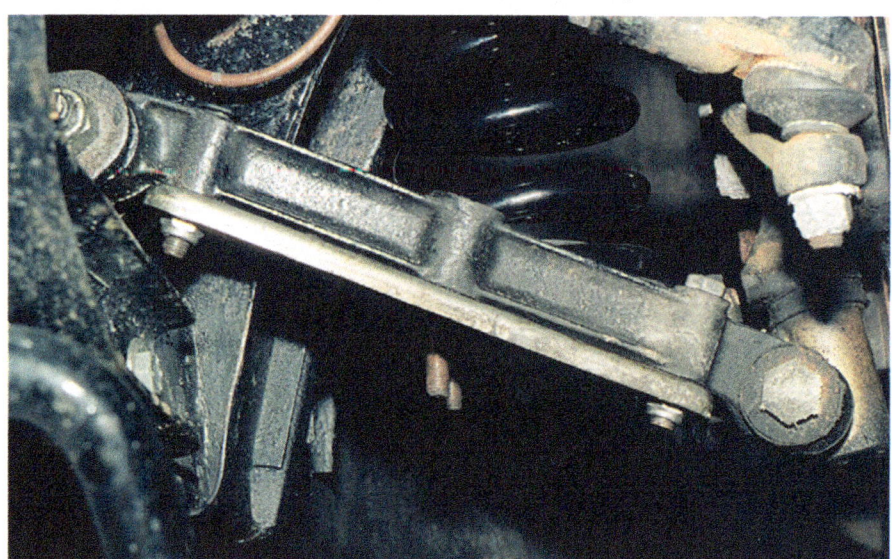

3-14. This picture lets you see the offset nature of the TR lower wishbone and how you can lower the car if you fit them upside down!

3-15. Original bushes within the front and rear suspension were made from rubber – some with metal supporting sleeves, and some without any support. Modern replacements come in a variety of makes, hardnesses and colours, but all are available in polyurethane and are an important upgrade to every TR.

you fit harder suspension bushes. The more precise, less pliable and harder bushes will highlight any slight variations from standard in the car or components that the flexibility of rubber may have previously masked.

Front shocks

It's a good idea, but not essential, for most readers to change the standard front telescopic shocks to adjustable Spax or similar telescopic dampers. The opportunity to fine-tune the suspension using adjustable shocks becomes more and more valuable as the performance of the car increases. These telescopic dampers employ two types of bottom fixing bracket. Cars up to and including the TR4 use the type of bottom bracket seen in photograph 3-16 to attach them to the spring pan, while TR4As (and later cars), use a slightly different bracket since they attach to the lower wishbone not to the spring pan.

3-16. This is the bottom mounting arrangement for an adjustable front telescopic shock absorber. The Spax dampers use a convenient screwdriver adjusting method, arrowed here for identification.

3-17. The TR6 front anti-roll/sway bar can be fitted to earlier cars ...

3-18. ... provided you take the bolted front skid/sump protector/roll-bar mounting too! The effectiveness of the roll/sway bar would be improved if the rubber mounting bushes were replaced by harder polyurethane bushes.

Some of our experts feel that ultra fast road cars will find the latest development from Spax highly beneficial, though others are not convinced. Called 'Pro Spax', these double-adjustable (bump and rebound), telescopic dampers are offered on the basis that they increase the stability of a heavy high speed car by some margin. There is strong opinion, though, that they are probably too complicated even for the TR racing cars, so there the advice is to go for single-adjustable (bump only), Spax, Avo or Koni dampers.

Front anti-roll/sway bars

A front anti-roll/sway bar is regarded as essential for even the most modest fast road car. The bar size, mounting detail and end fittings vary from application to application and from supplier to supplier, but a 0.875in diameter bar with polypropylene mounting bushes is very popular, and some extra detail will be seen in photographs 3-17 to 3-20.

For competition, where regulations allow, rose-joints/spherical bearings on the end of the roll bar ensure that maximum roll-bar rigidity is transmitted to the suspension. The polyurethane bushes used on most road cars are quieter than the rose-joints, which tend to rattle a bit!

Caster angles

TR suspension geometry had changed significantly by the introduction of the TR4, with major advancements in caster angle in particular. Introducing caster angles makes the steering slightly heavier but increases the self-centring characteristics and can make the car generally more pleasant to drive. Watch out for a difference in self-centring characteristics from one lock to the other. This either signals a different caster angle (probably different bottom trunnions) on one side, or that a front turret has been accidentally 'adjusted' during the life of the car.

3-19. A nice shot of this front anti-roll/sway bar on a TR250. Note the very neat polypropylene mounting bushes that transmit all the available anti-roll action to the chassis. These are identical to the rear anti-roll/sway bar we saw in picture 3-12. Note that this number plate is offset towards the camera and that its cross support provides a very convenient place to fit rally plates and the like. From experience, I can assure you that this nice touch (by Racetorations) is very helpful in practice.

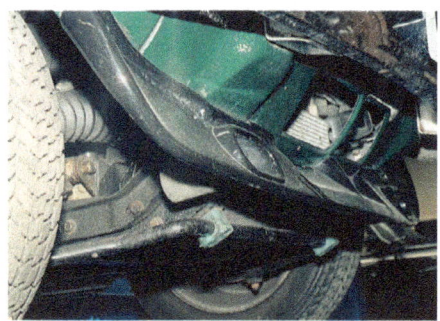

3-20. This shot shows the front anti-roll/sway bar mountings with 'solid' polyurethane bushes, but is also an excellent shot of Racetorations' front air spoiler with its brake cooling ducts. Did you spot the oil cooler?

Negative camber

Modern radial tyres perform at their best with a straight up, or slightly negative, camber angle. This is true for virtually all enhanced TR's, but particularly any form of competition on radial tyres. 1 to 1.5 degrees of negative camber will make the most use of your tyre's grip.

The IRS cars also offer the opportunity to fine tune the camber by shimming-out the lower wishbones – although I would proceed with care and achieve the major part of the negative camber you seek by reducing the length of the top wishbone. We see the effects of negative camber in picture 3-21.

Suspension checking and adjustment is possible at home with a piece of string and a spirit-level. However you do need to know what you are doing and frankly the task is so much quicker and easier with the right equipment that you are almost always better to subcontract the work to professionals.

3-21. Mark Treadwell's '6 has negative camber of approx. 1.5 degrees, as shown in this picture. With the slight body-roll that occurs when cornering, this negative camber presents the tyre to the road in a most advantageous manner.

REAR DRIVE DURABILITY
Differential mountings

We have already addressed the essential 'boxing' of the differential mounting pins in an earlier chapter, but even with this achieved, improved methods of locating the differential are essential for all IRS cars. For standard and fast road specification cars, Racetorations has an excellent improvement, shown in picture 3-22. The usual/standard method of holding the rear pair of metalastic rubber-bonded differential mountings on the IRS cars is by a large plain washer. The people at Racetorations felt that this left too much of the mounting unsupported and can now supply or fit dished-shaped 'Diff Cups' to provide additional support to the rear pair of mountings. These allow you to retain the flexibility and sound-deadening qualities of the rubber-bonded bushes whilst reducing the likelihood of the bonded metal sleeve separating from the rubber mount.

Polyurethane bushes are now available for ultra fast and race cars, see picture 3-23, and these are a major aid in mounting the differential. The original type of front rubber cones inevitably get contaminated by oil and grease, which eventually attacks the rubber and allows the diff some movement on its mountings. This then allows the diff to snatch at the mounting pillars as the power/torque comes on and off, hastening the fracture of the already marginal weld with the front/main diff bridge. Polyurethane bushes are impervious to oil and grease,

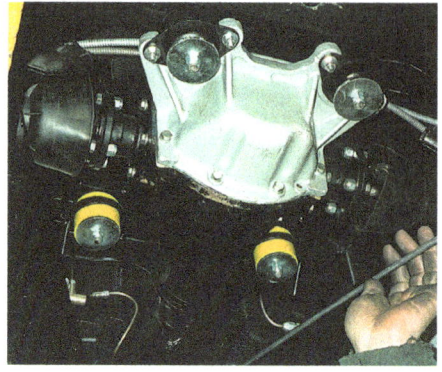

3-23. These polyurethane bushes certainly restrict the differential but they transmit more noise, vibration and stresses to the diff mounting pins. Consequently, the polyurethane bushes should not be used without your first strengthening the diff mounting pins.

though they are harder and will transmit more noise and vibration than the original rubber cones at the front and the metalastic bonded rubber bushes at the back.

If you plan to fit polyurethane bushes, it's essential that you not only fully box the diff pins but that you also reinforce the top of all four pins across both diff bridges. This necessitates at least partially lifting the body from the car. For the fastest of IRS cars, of course, numerous body-off type chassis reinforcing operations are a necessity in any event, as we discussed in Chapter 2.

3-22. An example of Racetorations' differential cover on an IRS car. Of equal interest, however, is the improved rear mounting support washers. These are specially machined cups to provide extra support to the rear rubber bonded mountings that, without this extra support, have a tendency to separate from the internal steel tube allowing the differential more freedom than it was designed to enjoy!

While you are reinforcing the chassis, particularly if your car is to provide very high performance, take the opportunity to fit special uprated plain diameter differencial mounting pins and be sure to substantially reinforce their top ends with a 6in long plate that is almost the width of diff bridge. Pre-weld each pin to the plate we saw in pictures 2-5 and 2-6 before welding the plate to the top of the diff bridge.

Rear hubs

It's highly likely that the six studs in the rear trailing arms (picture 3-24) will need to be replaced because of corrosion and wear and tear. This operation frequently brings about a stripped or worn thread in the alloy of the trailing arm – itself the consequence of the original Triumph design using too fine a thread in the alloy casting. The replacement thread is more often than not re-formed using helicoil stainless steel spiral inserts, with 5/16in UNC threads. The original thread into the casting is UNF, but coarse threads are best into a soft material like aluminium, and any studs that have to be changed are best replaced by UNC threads. However, 'Timeserts' are actually superior to helicoils because they offer a

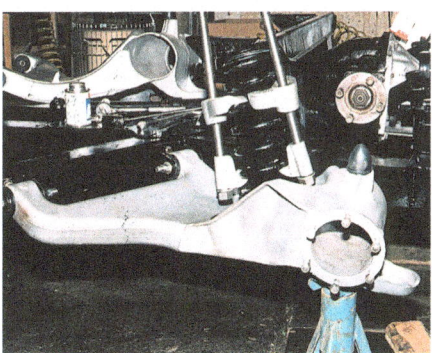

3-24. The six mounting studs on the end of the trailing arm are vulnerable.

completely new thread to the aluminium trailing arm casting.

Driveshaft details/the 'twitch'

Most readers will already be familiar with the reasons for the IRS TR rear-end twitch. For those who are not, it's worth outlining the reasons behind this alarming trait. If the lubrication within the driveshaft's sliding splines, shown in photo 3-25, dries out, or if dirt finds its way passed a (split) gaiter, or if the splines are worn, the torque from the

engine can in effect prevent the splines from sliding as suspension movements dictate. The lower the gear, the more vigorous the throttle use, or the higher the power/torque of your engine, the more noticeable the problem. When the driveshaft's splines lock, the rear suspension movement (which would normally cause the driveshafts to slide and change their overall length), is either prevented completely or at the very least is severely restricted.

In due course, a sufficiently large bump in the road or a reduction in torque when you lift-off, 'unsticks' the splines and the rear suspension takes up its unrestricted position, causing the rear of the car to twitch quite suddenly, unexpectedly and very noticeably!

Owners of standard IRS TRs, along with those with fast road cars, may feel it unnecessary to spend vast sums on altering the basic design and can certainly help the situation considerably by liberally greasing the splines with moly grease – frequently! Interestingly, both left and right driveshafts carry the same part number (RKC454), and can be interchanged in order to apply the drive on the other, hopefully unworn, side of each spline.

Still at the relatively low-cost end

3-25. These male splines wear, become dry (particularly if the protective rubber gaiter splits), and stick in their mating female counterparts. Liberal, frequent applications of molybdenum grease are important. Had you noticed that one spline is wider than the rest and that they only fit together in one orientation?

of the improvement options, for those not intending to purchase completely new driveshafts but needing to improve their universal joints, note that there are two qualities of universal joints on the market. Whatever your car and whatever universal joint was originally fitted, the driveshaft universal joints should always be of the highest quality you can buy, and always have a grease nipple. GKN are the universal joints of choice because of the quality and size of the needle rollers used, but you may need to go to an 'AE' (Turner and Newell) distributor to get them. All your universal joints' grease nipples should get the attention of your grease gun every 3000 miles or so.

The standard original driveshafts are satisfactory for cars up to the original 150bhp. Regardless of the application you plan for your improved TR, however, as soon as you uprate the engine beyond this level of power you need to seriously consider the capability of the rear driveshafts and the associated hubs. There are several hi-tech solutions to the twitch issue, all of which focus on the common theme of reducing the friction within the sliding splines of the rear driveshafts. All the solutions I've examined so far have another common feature – they're expensive! Up until quite recently Revington has been ingeniously using a linear bearing arrangement (picture 3-26), that required re-engineering and fitting ex-Datsun rear axle shafts and rear axle universal joints. Although these proved ideal, they were expensive to manufacture in small quantities and so Revington has come up with a much more cost-effective design capable of handling nearly the same horsepower without locking-up. The basis of the latest design is the use of a large section spline with a modern Teflon coating. This provides a smooth silent drive without the need for volumes of special machining. Incidentally, the larger section splined shaft is the same

3-26. Revington's sliding linear bearing driveshaft. Datsun 180B shafts had to be machined to fit the TR hubs/u/j forming an effective but a bespoke/custom job and, therefore, expensive.

as Revington use for the upgraded propshafts. These driveshafts come complete with both (heavy-duty) universal joints (£175 per shaft including universal joints), and one is available for Stags and Saloons too. Racetorations has a very much stronger solution, shown in picture 3-27 and in more detail in 3-28. It has been well proven in competition conditions.

Several attempts have actually been made to improve the rear driveshafts – though not all were successful, so you need to choose with care. Fairly recently, however, GKN Driveline (makers of the original driveshafts), has successfully employed modern technology and now use a bonded resin, 'Rilsan Fluidglide', coating on the splines. This is claimed to eliminate the IRS twitch by ensuring the splines no longer stick, even under load. Furthermore, the coating is reputed to be long lasting, enhanced by grease nipples to lubricate the splines. The new driveshafts cost circa £200-300 and come with new universal joints. They are available from all our specialists as brand new replacements, and Racetorations has successfully proven them in competition, which bodes well for their future. Note that you do need to plan

3-30. An Achilles heel of the IRS cars, particularly these days, is the rear hubs. This is Racetorations' 'Cosworth' hub.

3-27. A view of the Cosworth hub and improved driveshaft fully assembled. Note the grease nipple for the sliding spline.

3-28. A set of Racetorations' dramatically improved IRS rear hubs and driveshafts. The universal joints are larger than standard, but the Cosworth hubs offer much stronger, safer and more reliable power handling.

your driveshaft upgrade simultaneously with your rear hubs, as we will now see.

The failure of many TR universal joints is certainly caused by normal wear and tear. However, an uncomfortable number fail after renewal. To me this suggests the experience required to assemble a universal joint well is perhaps greater than may be appreciated, at least with the component tolerances that are available these days. When the universal joints were first assembled not only were the assemblers doing it all day and every day, but they also had the benefit of selective component assembly. If one circlip was not a satisfactory fit, for example, or provide the correct

3-29. Cracked for some time, by the look of the fracture, but this is the consequence of the threaded end of the rear hub shearing off – taking the retaining nut, washer, studded driving flange, brake drum and the all-important wheel with it.

pre-loads or balance the joint, they could choose a thinner or thicker one as their experience suggested appropriate. The emphasis on improved universal joints is doubly welcome since the number of repairs will hopefully diminish as the years pass and the frequency of more robust universal joints increases.

Rear hubs

It's not uncommon to lose a rear wheel due to rear hub failure, something I have experienced myself as photograph 3-29 shows. As the age of the cars increases, the rear hubs generally, and the stub axles in particular, are giving increasing problems, and stronger hubs are growing in popularity for even mildly tuned cars. Uprated hubs are actually regarded as essential for ultra fast road and competition cars. Racetorations offer a 'bullet-proof' steel rear hub that is based upon a Ford Cosworth product. In fact, Racetorations still refers to this hub as a 'Cosworth' hub. It can be seen in picture 3-30, and should be considered by all IRS owners, and with increasing urgency as the power available from uprated engines increases. It fits in the standard trailing arm casting but does need a different driveshaft end, though most IRS owners would normally replace the whole driveshaft with an uprated version.

This rear hub was originally designed by Cosworth to take Cosworth levels of horsepower and is far more substantial and reliable than the original

TR units, which, I can assure you, do break! This new hub, which uses 30% thicker, and correspondingly stronger material, and a different bearing arrangement, is highly recommended in spite of its £200 per side price tag.

Trailing arm mounting brackets

In the interests of safety, you are strongly advised to buy new trailing arm brackets. Note: there were different combinations of brackets for different models. Initially, bracket 141399 (identified by 1 notch), was fitted as the inside mounting, and 141398 (2 notches), was fitted on the outside. At commission numbers CP52867/CC61570, bracket 1555502 (3 notches), was fitted to the inside, and 141399 (1 notch), was fitted on the outside. These brackets can be put in upside down, which will destroy the rear suspension geometry, so note that all notches are positioned upwards as we saw in the first photograph of this chapter. Note: at the same time as the brackets were changed, a change took place to the trailing arm castings, and the angles were varied from earlier castings. You must ensure that your rear brackets are compatible with the castings!

Camber

The standard rear camber is minus 1 to plus 0.5 degrees. Adjustment is via the notched brackets but it really needs to be adjusted at a garage with four-wheel-alignment equipment and expertise. However, before you go off to the garage, do double-check that the brackets are all correctly positioned (notches at the top), and that you have the correct notches in the correct position for your trailing arms. Do not adjust front and rear camber simultaneously or you will lose track of what change has brought about what handling characteristic. That is not too important if you like what you've got, but if you want to undo an unsatisfactory trait then it is as well to know what brought it about!

Each trailing arm bracket has its hole drilled in a slightly different position, and this fact can be used to adjust the rear camber angle. You will increase negative camber by raising the position of the outer bracket hole by fitting a different notched bracket. The brackets differed only in the relative heights of the pivot bolt holes. The 1 notch bracket had the highest pivot, the 3 notch was about 8mm lower, and the 2 notch bracket was

about midway between the others. The other relevant factor is that the trailing arm casting changed part way through the TR6 production run. If your camber is inconsistent, it's not only possible that an incorrect bracket has been fitted to your car, but that one or both of the trailing arms has been fitted without its compatible notched brackets. It is a relatively easily situation to correct, but if your camber is incorrect, particularly on one rear wheel, it's highly likely that the problem lies somewhere in the trailing arms/brackets.

Aim for zero or slightly negative camber because modern tyres work best when presented to the road vertically. Even with a rear anti-roll bar, you are bound to get some body roll when cornering, hence the desirability of a touch of negative camber. Make all adjustments with some load on the car – *i.e.* at least a full tank of fuel.

Differential

The differential doesn't regularly present a problem to improvers once fixed to the chassis properly, and will normally accommodate significant increases in horsepower. We looked into sources for replacement differentials in the volume on restoring TRs, and those same sources apply if you plan to improve your car by changing rear axle ratios too. TR4As, 250s and TR6s (US carb), used a standard rear axle ratio of 3.7:1. This ratio is also available from the Stag and/or 2500 Auto Saloon. TR5s and TR6s (PI), used a standard rear axle ratio of 3.45:1 and these could be sourced from a 2500 Manual Saloon and/or a 2500PI Manual Saloon. So long as you retained the gears in their pairs, the crown wheels and pinions can be interchanged, providing the opportunity to raise or lower the rear axle ratio for far less than the cost of a new set of gears.

At this point it is relevant to mention the opportunity to improve the cooling and distribution of the oil within the differential. All IRS cars should consider using Racetorations' special aluminium rear covers. shown in picture 3-31. These differ from standard in two ways: external fins improve the cooling, while an additional internal cast web/oil-thrower keeps the crown wheel fed with oil. Although these changes will benefit the car, they become progressively more important as the power carried by the diff increases, so they're definitely important for very fast

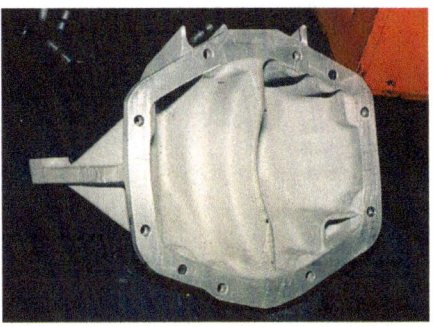

3-31. The Racetorations cast aluminium differential cover has fins on the outside to aid cooling, but this internal web is perhaps even more important since it ensures the crown wheel is kept well oiled.

road cars. Race or rally competitive cars will also find these improvements almost essential, but the additional cost of the even lighter magnesium variant will be very attractive for the fastest of very fast road and race cars. It's worth just mentioning that while no TR had external cooling fins, some of the later cars were fitted with rear diff covers that had an internal oil-thrower web.

Limited slip differentials

Two types are available in the UK for any Girling-axled TR: Quaife and Salisbury. The former is a totally gear-driven modern torque-sensing LSD, and is the cheaper option at about £550. It will only maintain an equal drive output if both rear wheels are on the road. It's certainly better than no LSD at all and would be an asset when, say, starting a race – when both rear wheels are firmly planted on the road. Its cost will make it the choice for most ultra fast road cars.

However, all race, rally and competitive cars, where it's probable that one rear wheel will lift at some stage of the competition, will find the true limited slip capability of the Salisbury £800 design a necessity. The Salisbury unit is a clutch design, where the pressure is applied by bellville (flattened cupped) washers. In UK historic competitions I believe that anything that was homologated before 1965 is allowable, but with this in mind this original LSD design is probably the one required by those following originality constraints.

US TR'ers have their own LSD versions available and won't, I trust, need to resort to the other end of the cost scale – a Detroit Locker (welding the diff up!).

Chapter 4

Hubs, wheels & tyres

Modern wheels and tyres can have a dramatic effect on any TR. I believe it's true to say that the biggest single improvement you can make to your Triumph's handling can be achieved by using modern tyres. This benefit can be extended further by increasing the width of tyre in contact with the road, achieved by increasing the wheel size, while simultaneously decreasing the tyre's aspect ratio. The selection of the most suitable wheels has, like other TR improvements, become more complicated as the performance of the cars and the variety of options increase. Furthermore, we have become more particular about the aesthetics of our cars (modern and classics), and, therefore, of the wheels, which are obviously one of the most visible aspects of a car. Consequently, although relatively few TRs left the factory with them fitted, wire wheels have become the wheels of choice for a very high percentage of today's TR owners. This chapter will explore some of the details of converting a steel-wheeled car to wires, as well as ensuring we fit the wire wheel splined adapters, shown in photographs 4-1 and 4-2, safely. If wires are already fitted to your car, the strength and size of the wheel, and therefore the size of the tyre, can usually be improved upon.

Most owners anxious to improve the performance of their cars will stay with bolted wheels, albeit selecting an alloy alternative. Some may even want to convert their existing wires to bolted hubs in the interests of lighter weight,

4-1. One reason for wire wheeled conversions is the ease with which most hubs can be changed with total authenticity from bolt-on wheel studs to the splined wire wheel adaptor shown here on the right of a sidescreened car. This adaptor was used on all front hubs and on the Girling-braked rear axles. The arrow highlights the importance of cutting down the excessive length of the original bolted wheel studs to be flush with the ends of the special double-chamfered nuts used for splined hub retention.

wider rims and increased diameter. All owners must be comfortable with the aesthetics of their wheels, but the selection must also be made with gear ratios, tyre size, bodywork, brakes and unsprung weight very much in mind. Where to start? Stopping seems fairly

4-2. The wire wheel adaptor in close-up. Note the tapered self-centring recesses for the retaining nuts, which should have also have a taper on the outside to provide the essential for the wire-wheel itself.

important so we will begin by discussing the effect that increasing the size of your car's front calipers has on wheel size.

WHEEL SIZES
Wheel diameters

From a practical point of view, two details affect any decision you may make on wheel sizes: the size of the front discs/rotors, and the tyre size you plan to use. We will explore the latter in more detail later in this chapter. Basically, the faster the car the larger capacity brakes one needs and the larger the disc required. Many historic competition cars will not be allowed an increase in wheel diameter (and many fast road car owners will not want to). This is not a problem, however, since some powerful brakes can be fitted within the TR's 15in diameter. Nevertheless, some ultra fast road and unrestricted competition cars may find it necessary to increase the wheel diameter in order to accommodate adequately powerful brakes. As photographs 4-3 and 4-4 illustrate, the diameter of the brake disc/rotor has a very big influence on the effectiveness of the brakes. 16in diameter wheels, for example, allow an increase in disc/rotor diameter to 295mm – to very beneficial braking effect.

Rim widths

As we explored wheel diameters we used inches to measure the diameter of any car's road wheel – and I guess most readers are familiar with this measure. Some may not however be so familiar with the "J" rim width measurement … which is in fact no more than the width of the wheel's rim, also in inches but very important to those considering improving the car by the use of wider wheels and/ or tyres. So a 15x5J wheel will be 15in in diameter with a rim width of 5in. However if you have in mind fitting wider tyres to the car it is imperative that the tyres are fitted to rims of adequate width. Consequently if your car is currently fitted with 5J rims it is almost certain that

4-3. These are 295mm diameter brake discs/rotors – which are too big to fit within a 15in wheel. As a matter of interest, once you get to this size of brake disc/rotor you will find that it's actually a two-piece construction, perfectly illustrated here with 12 high-tensile fastenings securing the inner aluminium 'bell' to the cast iron ventilated disc/rotor. You will need 16in diameter wheels to fit over brakes of this size …

4-4. …, off, in this case, a rather special MR2 Turbo. Should stop rather well!

you will need to replace the wheels with some 5.5J rims if you want to upgrade the tyre section. Most wheel diameters and patterns are available in a variety of rim widths and photograph 4-5 shows one of the wider ones!

4-5. Most readers will recognise the Minilite spoke pattern, that sits very well on most TRs. This is a 15in diameter wheel with a 7J rim, which will fit only a very select few TRs. Nice to know its available if you get sucked into super-charging your car!

Standard wheel rim sizes are as follows. TR5's and TR250's were fitted with 5J rims. The early TR6's used 5.5J rims, which were upgraded to 6J's about the middle of TR6 production. I outline this progression to underline the opportunity you have to increase rim widths to provide a better foundation for a wider cross section of tyre. Within reason the wider the tyre the better the cornering and indeed the braking capabilities of the car. Although we have not yet discussed the detail of tyre cross-sections it may help you select the correct rim width if I list some popular tyre sections and outline what I think are the extremes of rim width you should contemplate. Do take advice from your tyre retailer before buying new wheels but their recommended rim widths will probably fall within the bands shown in the accompanying table, regardless of wheel diameter.

Road wheel offsets

You cannot assume that your selected wheel size will automatically provide adequate clearance for an upgraded front brake caliper, so the 'offset' of your intended wheel is a further consideration. Minilite alloy wheels, which we will look at in more detail shortly, allow for plenty of caliper/wheel clearance. I would strongly recommend, though, that you borrow a friend's example or buy a wheel

Tyre Size	Absolute Minimum	Ideal Rim Width	Do not Exceed
175x70	5in	5in	6in
185x70	5in	5.5in	6in
195x65	5.5in	6in	7in
205x65	5.5in	6in	7.5in

Table of rim widths.

on a sale or return basis and try them on your preferred front brake setup before settling upon a certain design, and certainly before having tyres fitted to them.

ROAD WHEEL OPTIONS
Steel/disc wheels
In the context of needing to increase the rim width of your wheels and to do so in the most cost-effective manner, the TR6 steel wheel offers many the opportunity to increase rim widths at modest cost. All TR6 wheels are 15in, and the early cars had the 5½J (5.5in) rims seen in picture 4-6-1, while the later examples had the 6J rims seen in picture 4-6-2. These will take 195 and 205 tyres respectively. TR6 steel wheels are not available new, but there is usually a selection of used ones at most TR specialists, including TR Bitz.

4-6-1. The 5.5J rimmed TR6 wheel will provide a useful and inexpensive opportunity for many earlier cars to put a slightly larger footprint on the road ...

4-6-2. ... while later TR6s had a 6J rim, and should give great second service after shot-blasting and re-stoving. It's worth mounting up any wheels you plan to buy and spinning them to check for trueness before you buy, and certainly before you get them re-furbished.

Don't overlook the fact that many have already had a hard life and need to be inspected carefully for damage. Those that pass muster should be mounted on a hub and spun to ensure they run true, and then, and only then, shot-blasted and re-stove-enamelled. There is a very wide selection of alloy wheels available, of course, in a variety of sizes, rim widths and patterns, and most owners opt for this solution.

Alloys
Those looking for seriously fast, ultra fast or competitive cars will mostly opt for alloys. They are lighter, available in a variety of rim widths and diameters, and have a seemingly unrestricted range of centre patterns. Pictures 4-7, 4-8 and 4-9 show some of the options readily available. However, in spite of the options, the car's aesthetics need to be considered for you need to retain some compatibility between the wheels and the car.

Genuine Minilites are available with knock-on or bolt-on fittings in 5.5J rim widths. Revington favours and recommends Compomotive which makes a very nice and light Minilite-style aluminium alloy wheel. You can get a not dissimilar style from KN, but these are heavier and offer no advantages. The third alloy alternative from Revington is Superlite. These are a nice range of Minilite-style wheels in both aluminium and magnesium, the latter in 6J rim width is very light and attractive. Special

4-7. A magnesium Minilite on Neil Revington's TR4 rally car. I think these look good on pretty much any TR.

4-8. There are lots of options in terms of wheel pattern, and an 'open' one like this Revolution alloy keeps the brake discs cool for better braking. You can see the brake disc through the spokes in the wheel. Sharp eyes may note the drilled cooling holes in the disc and that these are 195x60 ratio tyres.

wheel nuts are required to bolt Minilites to their hubs.

Knock-on fittings refer to the spinners that secure, usually wire, wheels to their adapters. However, you can buy alloys with the same spined adapter fitting as a wire wheel. These certainly look very professional, although I must say it would also seem to make fitting a set of alloys unnecessarily expensive. Picture 4-10 shows an example. There could be some logic in centre locking alloys if you had a set of chrome wires that you wanted to keep solely for special occasions, shows, *etc.,*

4-9. There are also the 'Wolfrace' wheels, seen here on Neil Revington's TR6. Most non-competitive cars will have wheel centres fitted.

keeping the alloys for everyday motoring. That route would also add significantly to the cost of your car's footwear, though, bearing in mind you need a second set of tyres too!

You could be forgiven for thinking that the only things that matter about the central part of an alloy wheel are its bolt pattern and whether it appeals to your eye. In fact, the effect of wheel design and consequential airflow might have a major impact on the car's braking characteristics. Wire wheels and alloy wheel designs that use a thin spoke design both allow high volumes of air to pass through them. This provides a significant cooling effect on the disc, and to a lesser extent on the caliper, which should not be underestimated.

This can be illustrated by an example. A car fitted with 5.5x15 72-spoke wheels exhibited a dead response time from the brakes in very wet weather until the water had been cleared from the discs. However, when a set of 6x15 alloy Minilite wheels were fitted, the brakes responded immediately, even in the heaviest downpour. In dry conditions, on the other hand, the brakes became only marginally adequate, and brake fade was very easily induced. Obviously the Minilite wheels weren't allowing as much air to the brake discs as the wires and weren't cooling the brakes adequately. The solution in this case was to fit a pair of air ducts, made from 2 or 3in diameter flexible air hose, to cool the discs.

Wire wheels

Few owners seeking ultra fast road or competitive performance will opt for

4-10. Knock-on Minilites look good and allow you to fit wire wheels for those special show days, but the combination makes for expensive footware!

wires. They are, however, very popular with owners of standard and fast road cars. In fact, because so many cars with steel wheels are being converted to accept wires, we'll need to look in detail at the required hub conversions here. The first point to make here is that the greater the number of spokes in a wire wheel the stronger it will be. So the greater the number of spokes the more suited that wheel will be for an uprated car; a fact you'll need to remember whether you already have wire wheels or plan to convert to them for the first time.

Even the TR5's and TR250's ideally need to strengthen the wire-wheels they propose and widen the rim width too. These owners can fit the early TR6 wheels with 5.5J rims, but the later TR6's used 6J rims, which might be even better.

Wire wheel hub conversions

Generally speaking it will be the owners of standard or fast road cars that will be interested in the aesthetic improvements brought about by wire wheels. Fortunately, all the TRs covered in this book are extremely easy to convert from one type of wheel/hub to the owner's alternative preference. Most owners will buy the kit of hubs and spinners we see at picture 4-11, but there are several important safety related points to watch for when it comes to fitting the kit, particularly when converting a disc wheeled car to wires.

Firstly, the mating faces of both the adapter and the hub must be perfectly clean so that you achieve 100% metal to metal contact over the mating faces. Paint, dirt or other materials trapped between the faces will most likely result in the adapters working loose.

Secondly, the adapters are handed and **must**, therefore, be fitted to the appropriate side of the car (when viewed from the rear and looking forward in the direction of travel). Luckily they are all marked 'left' and 'right'. The knock-on spinners will undo if fitted to the incorrect side of the car!

Thirdly, the front and the back of each adapter nut, part number 110366, is tapered. You therefore need eight nuts per axle to fasten the adapters to the hubs. I believe this is to ensure the back face of the wire wheel can travel its full length up each spline without interference with the edges of the nut.

Next, there is a potential interference problem with the hub's studs. The hubs in a factory-fitted wire

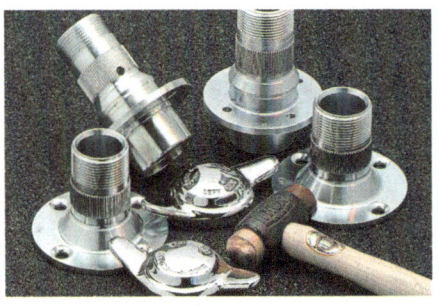

4-11. When converting from bolted to wire wheel fittings, the most economical route is to buy a kit – this being a typical example. Note the designation 'left' on the spinner located in the centre of the picture, and that in order to get the correct adapter on the correct side of the car you are as well to screw all four spinners onto their respective hubs. Then place the left side hub/spinners on the left side of the car – looking forwards from the rear of the car.

wheel installation had shorter studs than those used for disc wheels. You can, of course, change all eight studs per axle to the shorter ones made for wire wheels (part number 110365). However, the vast majority of disc to wire wheel conversions are achieved by cutting the overly long disc wheel studs down – if only because the front studs cannot be changed without removing the hub/brake disc which necessitates removing the brake caliper first! The rear studs can be changed without so much difficulty, but it's still easier to shorten the existing studs *in situ*. If this is your preferred route, it's probably best done after the adapter has been fastened in place and the double tapered nuts properly torqued up. If you the cut the protruding length of stud off close to the end of each nut, as arrowed in photograph 4-1, you should completely obviate all stud interference problems that would otherwise prevent the wire wheel sitting back up the full length of its spline.

As a final check pop a little easily seen grease on the end of each stud (black moly-grease or copper-slip, for example). After fitting and removing each wire wheel in turn (including tightening-up the spinner), check the rear of each wheel for a telltale grease mark. You should find nothing, of course, but any sign of grease on the wheel should be investigated and resolved, for your wheel will be prevented from both going back far enough and running true.

While I don't feel it's best

4-12. Proprietary wheel spacers come in quite a variety of thicknesses, as we see here. The majority of these examples are intended to be used between a bolted wheel and its hubs. Care needs to be exercised, and the wheel studs correspondingly increased in length. However, in the context of spacing a wire wheel adapter away from its hub, to obviate cutting over length studs down, a 6mm thick spacer will do.

4-13. This special adapter spacer from Neil Revington is 6.35mm thick and, when fitted between the adapter and hub, will leave your long studs the correct length for wire wheels. Furthermore these adapters have the correct size clearance holes on the correct PCD for a TR hub.

engineering practice, I should make you aware that some (very successful) conversions use a spacer between the hub and the splined adapter. Though this increases the track by 6 or 7mm per side, depending upon the thickness of the spacer, it's actually done to allow a wire wheel conversion without having to cut the stud length down and/or to overcome any inside wheel to body interference that can come about as the result of using very wide section tyres. Moss markets a spacer kit (TT6902), as do our TR specialists, while I have run a 3500cc MGB with spacers for many years. You can see examples in photograph 4-12, although personally I feel you are best to avoid spacing the adapters if you possibly can. Revington offers the ring spacer you see in photograph 4-13, which it thinks is exactly the correct thickness (6.35mm) to take up the excess bolt on stud length.

TYRE SECTIONS AND PROFILES

There are three things all owners can do to take advantage of modern tyre technology:
• Fit radial constructed tyres.
• Increase the width of the tyre in contact with the road.
• Select the make and compound applicable to your intended use.

The first suggestion almost speaks for itself and indeed very few owners keen to improve the performance of

their cars will still be running on crossply tyres.

Increasing the contact area of your tyre usually means increasing the tyre profile. An important qualification, however, is that you should **never** fit too large a profile tyre on too narrow a rim width. When the rim width is inappropriately narrow (or wide), the tyre's tread pattern is unable to take up it's intended contact with the road while the tyre wall can be rolled off the wheel. Your tyre retailer will advise you but, for example, a 185x70 profile tyre **must** not be fitted to anything less that a 5J rim width, with 5.5J being ideal. We'll discuss rim widths very shortly, but let's resolve the tyre profile issue first! The profile is governed by the aspect ratio of the tyre. All tyres have an aspect ratio of at least 80%, which is to say the wall height is only 80% of the declared tread width. If you have a 165 radial tyre on your TR (with no additional aspect ratio figure shown), then you may assume the tyre's wall height is 0.8x165 or 132mm (5.2in). If your tyre is marked (on the wall), as say, 185/70 (or 185x70), you will gather that this tyre has a 70% aspect ratio, and its wall height will be 129.5mm (5.1in). While the overall suggestion here is that you increase the tyre contact with the road by fitting wider tyres with a lower profile, you do need to exercise some care since the steering sensitivity usually increases as the profile reduces.

It may help you to know how to calculate the overall diameter of any tyre size you are contemplating. Not only is this relevant to the gear ratios on your car but you may find it helpful to estimate what the change in accuracy

of your speedometer would be were you to change your tyre size or profile. The overall diameter of a tyre is the wheel diameter + twice the tyre wall height (where the tyre wall height is measured in mm and calculated by multiplying the tyre width by its aspect ratio). As an example let's calculate the overall diameter of a 15in wheel fitted with a 165 tyre:

15in + (2 x 165 x 0.8mm)
or 15in + (2 x 132mm)
or 15in + 10.3in
or 25.3in diameter

I've mentioned 185 x 70 profile tyres several times so perhaps it would be helpful to calculate the comparative diameter of such a tyre on a 15in wheel:

15in + (2 x 185 x 0.7mm)
or 15in + (2 x 129.5mm)
or 15in + 10.2in
or 25.2in diameter

A 205 x 60 x 16in tyre provides surprisingly little variation in overall diameter, as I hope the following proves:

16in + (2 x 205 x 0.6)
or 16in + 246mm
or 16 +9.7in
or 25.7in diameter

It does, of course, add an encouraging extra width to the tyre's footprint on the road for some of our really quick cars!

One potential consequence of a tyre size change is an inaccurate speedometer. We have to assume your speedometer was reasonably accurate before any tyre changes, but it would be helpful to have some idea as to the probable consequences of a tyre change so you can drive accordingly. Let's now assume you have been using 165 profile tyres but are considering an alternative wheel/tyre combination of, say, 185 x 70 x 15. Looking at the above results, it's clearly safe to assume there will be no material difference in speedometer reading. However, what if you were tempted by the increased contact area offered by a set of 205 wide tyres but didn't really want to buy a new set of wheels. Let's, therefore, work the detail through for a set of 205 x 55 x 15 tyres, with an overall diameter of 23.9in. There would now be speedometer inaccuracies to consider. Let's try to quantify them, to see if they are material.

The current diameter of 165 tyres is 25.3
New (205 x 55) diameter = 23.9
Difference is – 1.4in
Percentage change
is $\frac{1.4 \times 100}{25.3} = 5.5\%$

So, your speedometer would read optimistically (because the tyre diameter has reduced), by 5.5%. It would show *circa* 60mph when you were, in fact, travelling at about 56.7mph. You hardly need for me to point out that, when your new tyre diameter is larger than the old tyre, you will be travelling faster than your speedometer suggests. This change will also adjust the gearing of the car by a similar amount (5.5%). This might suit some ultra fast car/rally drivers, but it'll do nothing for the owner with long cruise/minimal fuel usage aspirations.

There is one potential drawback to choosing a wide tyre with a very low aspect ratio (like the 55 we have just been discussing). The steering can become a little over-sensitive, requiring constant corrections, even, on occasions, when cruising in a straight line. However, you can get better brakes into a 16in wheel. Only you can choose!

TYRES
Size limitations
195/65s fit on TR250/5/6s with no problems, provided you stick to the 6J rim width.

Speed ratings
Before you plump for a particular tyre be aware that most countries impose a legal road speed limit by rating the tyres your car must comply with to satisfy both the law and, in the UK, insurance regulations, nevermind your own safety considerations. Here is an abridged list of the speed rating letter code for the UK, and the respective vehicle's maximum speed capability. I understand the US rating letters and speed limitations are not dissimilar. You must ensure the rating on your tyres is comfortably adequate for the maximum speed capability of your car, whether you intend to use that speed capability or not.

R	*105mph*
S	113mph
T	118mph
U	125mph
H	130mph
VR	over 130mph

V	150mph
ZR	over 150mph

Caring for your tyres
Because tyres are expensive, and are safety-critical components, it's in your best interests to look after them carefully. Most of will tend to store our tyres (when necessary), by laying them horizontally, one on top of the other. This isn't actually good for the tyre, and it's no accident that every tyre fitting company you visit will store its stock vertically. Furthermore, keep all tyres away from sunlight and don't store them in a high temperature location. They do 'like' being stored in darkness though.

All tyres, but particularly competition tyres, need to be fitted with the bead seated perfectly onto the rim of the wheel. You need to be particularly careful when fitting tyres to rims with rim corrosion, particularly on a competition car. The corrosion usually prevents the tyre making an airtight seal with the rim.

Check and adjust your tyre pressures when they're cold. You can dramatically shorten the life of even the best tyres by inflating them incorrectly. Tyre pressure is a very unpredictable and individual variable, as some of the professional racing applications prove. Cars can come into the pits for a change of tyres in order to get an extra pound of pressure in, say, the rears, which is then enough to change the handling characteristics of the car! The optimum tyre pressure will vary from circuit to circuit with the road surface conditions.

Never over- or under-inflate as this may cause severe damage to tyres and/or rims, particularly when accelerating, braking or cornering. Under-inflation causes excessive heat, reduces load carrying capacity and increases tread wear resulting in loss of performance. Over-inflation results in irregular wear rates, rapid wear in the centre of the tyre and light steering characteristics.

Tyre technology
The later TRs will generally use a lower profiled tyre, such as Yokohama 032, so I asked Yokohama for details of the applicable tyres currently available in the UK. I am indebted to Yokohama for the following summary:

• Fast road options – A539 road tyre. Sizes used are 195/60-15 H-rated or 205/60-15 V-rated.

• Ultra fast road tyre sizes are generally the same as fast road options. Yokohama does a high performance road tyre called the AVS Sport but these aren't available in the required sizes, so the A539 V-rated tyre is the next most suitable.

Your choice of rally tyres depends entirely upon the surface, but Yokohama tells me you would probably use A035 gravel tyres, available in sizes 185/65 x 15 or 195/65 x 15. Compounds available are soft or super soft, selection depending on the length of the stages. If tarmac rallying you could use 210/580-15, but 210/625-16 is more suitable. Variables such as air/road temperature and length of stage would dictate what compound to use.

Track competition – 205/60-15 is used for track racing. It is only available in soft compound.

Yokohama also points out that:
• Availability of the above in the US can only be determined via Yokohama in the US.
• All the tyre sizes are subject to rules and regulations of the event.
• Sizes are controlled in track competition, and the TR Register/TSSC race championship competitors are to use Yokohama tyres only.
• Racing tyres should be mounted with the tyre specification code positioned to ensure the direction of rotation is correct.

Neil Revington recommends Colway tyres. These are a re-treaded tyre which still carries a slight stigma but their extensive use in rally and track competition should dispel any slight worries you may have. Many may not even realise that they are re-treads! Contrary to popular belief, the 185/70 profile road tyre is easily available via Revington, as are a number of alternatives from 155 full profile to 205/60s ... no problem says Neil.

The 185/70 profile is also available in Colway's 'Emjo' series. Designed for historic rallying, they are best suited for dry gravel and tarmac stages. I can also tell you that Colway also supplies a 185/65 'Plus Four' low profile 'Forest' tyre, which has improved traction, is puncture resistant and has reinforced walls. The next grade up is the 'Rally Plus', available in 165, 185/55 and 195/60 profiles.

Chapter 5
Brakes

WHAT'S IMPORTANT

Before we get into the details of upgrading your TR's brakes, let's look at a few general brake-related issues first, since there may be some confusion surrounding what's an important brake improvement and what's not. 70% of any car's braking effect comes from the car's front brakes and 30% from the rear. Because the front brakes are so important, therefore, I am devoting most of this chapter to them. Furthermore, I don't believe all owners see clearly enough that it is the diameter of the front brake disc that has the greatest effect on the efficiency of a car's brakes. We'll certainly look at the other factors in a moment, but rest assured, you should always fit brake discs of the maximum diameter that your road wheels will allow. Triumph, as it was then, initially fitted 11in (280mm), and then 10¹³⁄₁₆in (275mm) discs as standard for the TRs we are exploring. The former is the largest disc that can be fitted inside a 15in road wheel. Anything smaller than the maximum and you lose out in two ways. Not only is the mechanical advantage (i.e. the distance from the centre of the pad to the centre of the hub) reduced, but you also run the risk of the pad having to be reduced in width. This is due to there being insufficient space between the

wheel hub and the outside edge of the brake disc to maximise the pad size.

There is a good case for increasing your wheel size purely to enable you to run larger diameter front discs. 295mm becomes practical with 16in wheels, demonstrated by photograph 5-1. This is something you should consider if you're planning an ultra fast road or competitive car. Fast road cars need not take this step, though, for we can improve the TR's brakes while staying with the original 15in wheels.

Disc diameter is so important, and is the subject of so many misunderstandings, that I think a simple calculation is required here to illustrate the difference disc diameters can make. We'll assume you have a choice

5-1. Four-pot calipers on 295mm ventilated and cross-drilled discs/rotors will stop most motors, even the very quick ones!

of 240mm diameter discs or 295mm diameter discs, and that in both cases the width of the brake pads is identical at 50mm. This will result in the average effective radius of the former pads being approximately 95mm, but the latter would be about 122mm giving an improvement in braking for the same pedal pressure of about 30%. The smaller diameter discs can be compensated for, in part, by employing larger calipers (more in a minute), which will lead to better slow speed brakes but which will be prone to fading at high speeds. Not at all desirable! No, the larger the disc the greater the mechanical advantage, the greater the mass to absorb the heat, the greater the surface area of the disc (better cooling), and the higher the surface speed of disc to pad contact area (better braking effect). So, as the saying goes, size does matter!

There is one further issue you should be aware of. The effective radius of the centre of the pads can be increased by using long, relatively narrow pads, mounted near the periphery of the disc. This actually increases the effective braking radius, when compared to, say, a square shaped pad, even if both pads have identical areas. A long, narrow shaped pad normally requires a four-pot caliper design, though, shown in picture 5-2.

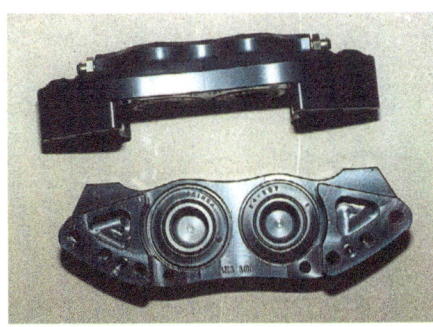

5-2. 'Four-pot' calipers refers to the total number of pistons per caliper. Here we get a view of one half of Hi-Spec Motorsport's 'Billet' caliper and can see two pistons and their dirt seals. The dirt seals are very important in fast road and ultra fast road cars. The two pistons we can see are of the same diameter, but most caliper manufacturers make 'differential' calipers where the sizes of these pistons vary.

CALIPER CAPACITY

The second most important consideration for upgrading your TR's front brakes must be the squeezing ability of the calipers – and the surface area of the piston(s) is an effective comparison in this respect. In a few minutes we will explore a shortlist of brake options open to improvers but I would just like to take a moment to examine an example to illustrate this point. The original TRs all had two-pot calipers (i.e. they have 2 pistons), each of 54mm diameter. The combined surface area is therefore 2 (pistons) x π (Pi) x 27mm x 27 mm (radius squared), or about 4580sq.mm. An alternative caliper with four 1.5in (38mm) diameter pistons will have a total piston surface area of about 4550sq.mm, and offer about the same capacity to squeeze pad to disc. Consequently, there should be very little difference in pedal travel when switching from a TR caliper to any four-pot with 38mm pistons.

Another potential scenario is a four-pot caliper with 41mm diameter pistons (there are several available), and this offers 15% extra squeezing capacity over the original TR calipers. However, there would be proportionally more pedal travel which many may find unacceptable. So, if we're trying to improve the stopping power of our TR we need to strike a balance between some extra squeezing capacity and pedal travel. I think I can offer you just the thing a little later in the chapter.

PAD AREA AND FRICTION MATERIAL

Since pad area plays a part in the effectiveness of the caliper, the extra pad area of four-pot calipers will improve the brakes roughly proportionally to the increase in pad area. The effectiveness of the friction material will have a huge effect on the brakes, and this is where brake technology has advanced in leaps and bounds in recent years. Standard TR pads are 78 x 68mm (5304sq.mm), and EBC Ford 291 pads were identical to the small-pinned TR pads. They fit the earlier calipers/pins, of course, if drilled out!

I don't have information on the pad areas of all the pads referred to in this chapter but here are two important comparisons:

• Wilwood Dynalite 2 are 100 x 65 (6500sq.mm)
• Hi Spec are 98 x 60 (5880sq.mm)

EBC Kevlar brake pads

Although Kevlar is very expensive, it's an excellent binding fibre. Non-metallic, with low abrasive qualities, it is cleaner and less abrasive on discs/rotors. The materials used in normal brake pads carbonise at the temperatures generated during daily braking, and carbon dust is generated as a matter of routine (to be found around the wheel rims every time you clean the car). Kevlar pads don't surface carbonise until 550-600 C, well above the temperature generated by normal daily braking. This is particularly beneficial to alloy road wheels.

The friction factor of conventional pads varys from 0.25 up to 0.35. EBC tells me that its 'Greenstuff' pads have a 0.46 friction coeffecient and, therefore, expect most users to notice an immediate improvement in 'bite' as a result of the improved frictional effect. I regard friction levels as a useful indicator but no guarantee of brake bite, but EBC says that Greenstuff is one of the most grabbing compounds on the market today. Furthermore, EBC claims its Greenstuff pads exhibit zero brake squeal.

Kevlar pads are more resistant to fading than conventional materials. All pads contain some organic materials, particularly resins, that bind the pad's constituent materials together. As these overheat, the resins revert to gas and cause the pads to 'aquaplane' on a gas film, resulting in brake fade. Kevlar pads may initially fade once or twice before

settling down, but more conventional pads are likely to suffer from continual dynamic fade throughout their lives.

Grooves, slots or cross-holes in discs/rotors break down the surface gas film when the pads overheat. They also keep pad surfaces clean, and they scrape away burnt carbon deposits on the pad surface. They are, therefore, highly recommended.

One further point, Greenstuff is effective from cold and needs no warm up time.

Selecting the right compound is particularly important when it comes to brake pads. Many owners use EBC Greenstuff in their fast road and ultra fast road cars, and leave them in place for track days. That is perfectly in order says EBC, but you should always take a spare set of pads, perhaps even some EBC Redstuff, in case you need to upgrade at the track for longer life, and don't forget to check your pads before you drive home. Red grade can be used on the normal roads, but is less responsive than Green until warm. With a friction level of around 0.32, Redstuff will feel more like standard original brakes. Yellow is the top Kevlar grade, usually reserved for track use, and costs about £30 per set.

Hawk brake pads

Hawk Performance Inc. uses ferro carbon materials in its pads which have been developed and manufactured for the racing community. Hawk says that all ferro carbon materials are non-fade, have been evaluated up to 1600 degrees F, and offer lower wear rates and higher friction values than all other competitive materials on the market today.

Hawk products are used in numerous serious racing applications including NASCAR, CART, Formula 2000 and 3000, and truck racing, so it clearly has excellent experience to draw upon. Hawk makes a wide range of compounds, from which I have selected just four relevant ones to evaluate in a little more detail, although you should take your retailer's expert advice before using any on your car.

'HP' compound is designed for fast and ultra fast road use, and provides high friction, hot or cold. Hawk says it offers long disc/rotor/pad life, yet generates extremely low dust and is virtually noise free. 'HP Plus' compound is for ultra fast road and competitive use, and Hawk tells me that it can be used on the race track and then driven home safely – provided you have checked that adequate pad thickness remains! Hawk advises that the compound generates extremely high friction and is resistant to 'elevated' temperatures, but you should expect increased disc/rotor/pad wear, noise and dust. Hawk declares it suitable for club racing events. 'K' compounds provide a medium friction, low cost pad that operates virtually from cold. It's intended for light duty road/racing applications. 'Blue 9012' is a medium to high torque brake compound providing low pad and disc/rotor wear in ultra fast road, rally and circuit use. Cost is about £60 per set. It is specifically recommended by Hawk for low to mid temperature effectiveness.

DISC/ROTOR MASS
The final general factor to consider is the mass of the brake discs/rotors themselves. The mass of the disc will affect its ability to soak up the heat generated by braking. If even a standard car, for example, was forced to effect emergency braking from high speed, the standard 12mm thick discs would heat up very quickly, possibly to the point that a layer of gas and brake dust interposes itself between pad and disc, and the brakes would fade. Thicker discs/rotors would absorb more heat and delay the onset of brake fade. 22mm thick ventilated discs offer a higher mass, are better able to soak up heat, and are, therefore, much more effective in today's fast moving traffic conditions. We can see a comparison with a 12mm disc in picture 5-3.

Ventilated discs/rotors, as their name suggests, are manufactured with internal ventilation to further increase their ability to handle and dissipate the heat resulting from pad-disc friction. Cross-drilled holes can further add to

5-3. On the right is a ventilated disc/rotor which is 22mm thick. The standard non-ventilated rotor on the left is 12mm thick and has been cross-drilled to aid water, gas and dust dissipation. Nevertheless, it won't have the thermal mass of the thicker unit.

5-4. Now also cross-drilled, the ventilated rotor on my TR's hub.

the disc's effectiveness by improving cooling, removing dust and gas when the discs get (really) hot, and they also speed the clearance of water in wet conditions. Although ventilations offer an additional benefit in many applications, they don't increase disc/rotor mass, so they only delay the onset of brake fade to a very slight degree. We can see a ventilated and cross-drilled disc in picture 5-4.

We need to be careful, however, not to overdo the disc/rotor size for, as with most things, there is a conflict of interests; increased disc size increases un-sprung weight which adversely effects road holding!

FRONT BRAKE IMPROVEMENTS
Standard performance TRs
For those looking for only a slight increase in cooling, better brake dust removal and improved grab, cross-drilled variants of the standard 12mm disc/rotor, together with better pads (possibly Kevlar) should suffice. Although this is regarded as an 'entry level' improvement, I must tell you that I have tried it and feel that it did not bring about the increase in stopping power that I thought necessary for my fairly standard TR6.

However, these components are available from all the TR specialists and the upgrade will probably cost circa £150.

Standard and fast road TRs
As already discussed, the greatest benefits in any brake upgrade come from an increase in brake disc diameter and/or piston area. Do not, therefore, expect wonders with this upgrade, for neither the disc diameter nor the size of caliper piston is increased. In fact, your original TR calipers are retained, albeit in modified form. That said, the increased grab of Kevlar pads and the greater mass and cooling effect offered by a pair of 22mm thick ventilated discs should not be underestimated. The pads should improve the brakes, and the discs/rotors should delay any fade brought about by heavy or repeated braking.

The upgrade is available in two forms. The basic kit supplies two 9mm thick spacers for fitting to your existing TR calipers, which are so widened to fit over the pair of 275mm ($10^{13}/_{16}$in) diameter, 22mm wide ventilated discs included in the kit. The kit will include Greenstuff Kevlar pads, pins, pad clips and wheel spacers and will cost £150 from Hi-Spec Motorsport. You will appreciate the cost of this kit is more or less the same as buying a new pair of cross-drilled original specification (12mm thick) discs, but much better value for money in that you get the 22mm ventilated discs. The new discs also come cross-drilled for absolute maximum cooling, brake dust and water clearance, and you can see a progression of pictures of this upgrade in 5-5-1 to 5-5-4.

The final components you will find within this kit will be a pair of laser-cut 3mm thick wheel spacers. These should be fitted between wheel and hub if you are using standard steel wheels. Those with conventional wire wheels shouldn't need to use spacers, although it would be wise to spin the wheels carefully after assembly. The wheel spacer is probably not necessary for Minilite wheels either, but if there is the slightest interference between the wheel and the caliper, fit the spacers provided.

You should reuse your existing caliper mounting bolts and the short hydraulic pipes that couple into the calipers. Consequently the change from imperial to metric calipers (the latter used stepped bolts) that took place towards the end of 1972 should be irrelevant.

You could also try Hawk pads from your stockist, but these will certainly cost you more and, at the fast road level of performance at least, are probably unnecessary.

5-5-1. Not easy to see in this shot, but this is a late (i.e. metric), standard TR6 caliper as removed from the car ...

5-5-2. ... split and awaiting re-assembly with two 9mm thick spacers per caliper. Note that one pair of spacers has a cross-transfer hole and seal recess for the brake fluid to operate as normal on both sides of the caliper.

A second version of this kit is available from Hi-Spec and is basically the same but includes caliper reconditioning and fitting the widening spacers to your (split) calipers. This option is helpful if you are uncertain about the history or performance of your calipers or are nervous about fitting the widening spacers to your calipers yourself. The additional cost for this extra service will be in the order of £100 for the pair.

5-5-3. Using longer bolts to re-assemble both halves of the caliper, with the spacers sandwiched between ...

5-5-4. ... we can now see that the widened caliper comfortably straddles the 275mm diameter 22mm wide disc/rotor, and awaits the relocation of the standard sized pads. Longer pins are obviously required to hold the pads in place, but these are supplied with Hi-Spec's kit.

Ultra fast road and competitive brakes

Perhaps it's not surprising, given the importance of brakes, but the choice of brake improving modifications for the highest performing cars is very wide indeed. I will begin my reviews with a kit from Hi-Spec Motorsport that I believe offer the best brakes for the money.

I fitted a set of Hi-Spec's 'Billet' differential piston calipers and 280mm (11 1/4in) diameter 22mm thick ventilated discs. These EBC 347 discs have the same offset as TR discs, thus minimising the modifications. The kit costs circa £450 (+VAT and carriage), but the aluminium four-pot calipers and EBC Greenstuff Kevlar pads provide far superior stopping performance at all speeds. The calipers come fully sealed against grit and water, an important consideration for road-going cars, which not all the alternatives enjoy. I wanted to retain my 15in diameter wheels, and the 280mm discs/rotors are the absolute maximum that will fit in the space available. The increased disc diameter, coupled with the additional pad area, significantly increases the capacity of the brakes, while the 80% thicker discs provide increased disc mass to delay the onset of fade. The normal/initial pedal effort is significantly reduced and there is a very satisfactory progressive feel about the pedal, with 'lots more' brakes available if you need them. Very comforting! The heavier discs increase the unsprung weight of the car, of course, but this is offset by the extraordinary lightness of the Hi-Spec calipers, which have been machined from solid billet for maximum strength and rigidity. The kit includes a pair of bespoke machined mounting brackets, the discs are cross-drilled, and a pipe adapter will be included for each side of the car.

Bearing in mind that the standard TR calipers have a piston area of 2 x 54mm or 4580sq.mm, some additional information about Hi-Spec's range calipers is appropriate. They make two-, four- and six-pot calipers which makes it possible to obtain the most suitable caliper for each application. However, it is the four-pot calipers that are most relevant to the vast majority of TR applications, and these are available in three versions:

• Four pistons each of 1.5in (38mm) diameter giving 4550sq.mm piston area
• Four pistons each of 1.625in (41mm) diameter giving 5335sq.mm piston area

As I mentioned, I selected the third option, a differential piston caliper of two 1.5in (38mm) pistons, plus two 1.625in (41mm) pistons giving a 4940sq.mm piston area. These four-pot calipers offer the potential for using bigger brake pads which, of course, further increases the stopping power of the brakes.

The specially machined aluminium caliper mounting brackets, which bolt straight to the TR's caliper mounting plate, can be seen in the photographic sequence 5-6-1 to 5-6-6. No wheel

5-6-1. Moving to the more powerful Hi-Spec front brake upgrade, the kit is designed around a pair of 280mm, 22mm thick discs/rotors ...

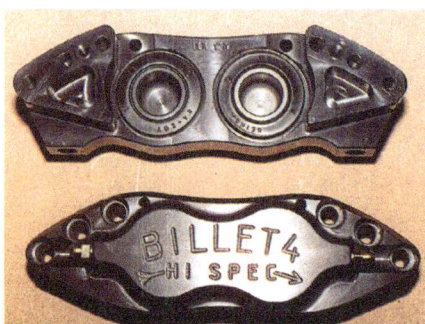

5-6-2. ... and four-pot calipers machined from aluminium billet.

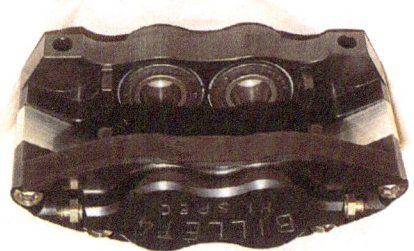

5-6-3. The calipers are universal, in that they can be spaced to suit whatever disc is deemed best suited for each application. Here we see one caliper assembled with spacers.

spacers are required, nor is there any need to worry about pad retaining pins, for the new aluminium calipers completely replace the original calipers, pads and pins. If your car is pre-1973 you will need to retain and reuse your plain ⁹⁄₁₆in caliper mounting bolts. If yours are the CR/CF 16mm shouldered variety you'll need to buy four new caliper mounting bolts (part number BTB610), since Hi-Spec's caliper mounting brackets come machined to accept the

5-6-4. A special mounting bracket is also supplied to bolt to the standard TR caliper mounting lugs and offers a face-plate ...

5-6-5. ... on which the caliper itself is securely fastened by the pair of cap heads seen here.

5-6-6. The pads and pins are supplied with the kit and the completed assembly looks very business-like.

most common caliper mounting bolt (BTB610), with a ⁹⁄₁₆in diameter plain shank.

A (flexible) pipe adapter is included with the kit for each side of the car to couple the new caliper to the original flexible brake hose. I must add that if you have not already fitted stainless braided front hoses, this would be the moment to make that upgrade too.

Don't forget to bleed your brakes when you have completed the change over!

Other options

You may wonder what alternatives are available:
• AP Racing (picture 5-7) makes absolutely wonderful calipers, that cannot be bettered for strength, rigidity and power (but they will set you back about £230 each, plus discs, mounting brackets and pads). It could cost in the order of £1000 to upgrade a TR via this route, and I explored it no further on the basis that this was out of the question for the vast majority of readers. However, if you want the best, Racetorations has experience and will be pleased to talk to you.
• Most auto enthusiasts will have heard of the American-made Wilwood aluminium calipers. Although bottom of the range, the 'Dynalite 2' is only

5-7. Automotive Products' racing division provides the four-pot calliper, and Racetorations the ventilated cross-drilled disc/rotor and the special lightweight aluminium hub for this competitive machine. The alloy hub reduces the weight by about 50%, which is doubly beneficial since this is unsprung weight.

marginally cheaper than Hi Spec's four-pots but offers inferior rigidity and, in my view, are not such good value for money. Pictures 5-8-1 to 5-8-4 show these being installed. If you would like to see a larger (and more expensive) Wilwood, take a look at picture 5-9.

• Your third alternative is to use

5-8-1. Wilwood has long supplied aluminium billet calipers to enthusiasts to upgrade the brakes of high performance cars. The 'Dynalite' is the bottom-end of its offerings, and is multi-shimmed to space out the caliper halves to suit the disc/rotor in question.

Revington bespoke four-pot calipers, shown in picture 5-10. These bolt straight onto the TR mounting points without the need for intermediate or adapter brackets. However, be aware that Revington's design uses standard TR 12mm thick non-ventilated discs. The calipers themselves are cast aluminium for minimum unsprung weight. The four 38mm pistons provide virtually the same total surface area as a pair of standard TR pistons (54mm, 2⅛in diameter), so, while they don't offer any additional piston surface area, they won't alter the standard pedal travel. The RTR 3301 costs roughly £650, while the RTR3301DD caliper and disc kit is *circa* £700 including VAT. The DD suffix indicates that the discs in that kit are cross-drilled to maximise dust and gas dissipation.

• You can call on your local salvage yard and explore the possibilities of using other four-pot calipers. I use ex-Princess four-pot calipers on my MGs, but these are now pretty much unavailable. I tried using ex-Volvo 240 four-pots on the TR. Unfortunately, although the mounting

5-8-2. The caliper uses a bridge pipe to carry brake fluid to the outer half of each caliper. You can see the pipe looping under the bottom of the caliper in this shot. Note the mounting bracket.

5-8-3. This is, of course, the outer half ...

holes were close they would not fit the TR without machining which, being a safety-critical component, I wasn't prepared to consider. Once you've found some calipers with the correct mounting holes, reduce your shortlist by choosing calipers that come off a car with ventilated discs (thereby ensuring that you do not need to split and widen the calipers). Look particularly closely at Toyota cars and light commercial vehicles, for John Lye in the USA has discovered that the four-pot calipers from a 1979 to 1983 Toyota petrol-fuelled four-wheel-drive pickup bolt straight onto the TR mounting lugs, see pictures

5-8-4. ... while this end-on shot shows the ventilated disc (included in the Wilwood kits), the home for the pads and the pin method of pad retention.

5-9. The larger, and frankly better, Wilwood Superlite SLII caliper is designed to need few spacers for most applications. It still requires a bridge pipe though.

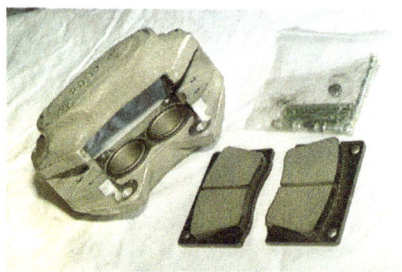

5-10. Revington's bespoke/custom four-pots certainly offer an improved pad area, four-pot pistons, the largest practical disc and direct mounting to the TR hub. However, they still use the original (i.e. unventilated), 12mm thick discs, which, to my mind, is an opportunity missed.

5-11-1 to 5-11-4 and note the bigger pad areas. John reports a significant improvement in braking as the result of using the calipers even though he retained the standard/stock discs/rotors. To my mind the upgrade would be even more effective were these calipers spaced and ventilated discs fitted.

Front brake squeal

Because of the many hours of development work that goes into ensuring the harmonics of the components all comply with each other and do not generate unpleasant noises, modern brakes rarely squeal. However, when we modify brakes, although our work maybe perfectly safe and very effective, we can generate some unpleasant harmonics that reveal themselves as brake squeal. Picture 5-12 shows one effective remedy.

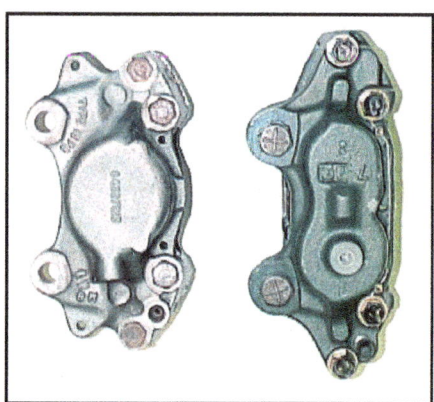

5-11-1. Dan Masters sent me these comparisons of the two-pot TR caliper (left), and a four-pot Toyota caliper with the same mounting hole centres.

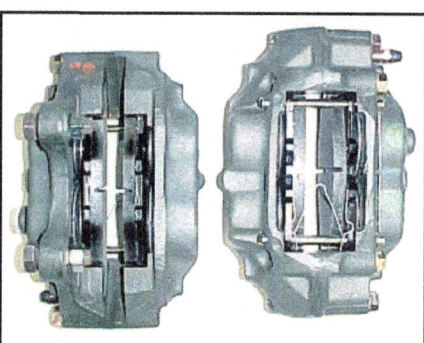

5-11-2. You can guess from this front/rear shot of the Toyota caliper that it uses the same disc/rotor thickness as the TR. I can confirm that the cut out in the calipers is ⅝in for a ½in thick disc.

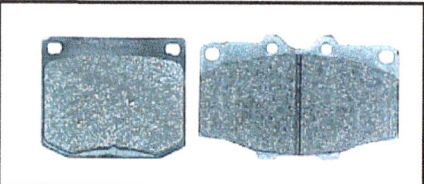

5-11-3. The Toyota's (right) pad areas look to be in the order of 40% greater than the TR's, seen on the left.

5-11-4. The Toyota uses the late/metric/stepped TR securing bolts I referred to in How to Restore Triumph TR 5/250 & 6.

BRAKE LINES

'Copper' brake pipe kits are available for all TRs from your favourite specialist and are definitely recommended. In fact the material is not strictly speaking copper, it is cupro-nickel but it has the same corrosion-resistant characteristics as copper. You don't need to worry about flaring tools because the pipes come ready-flared. They come coiled for ease of shipping, so you will need to straighten them. Put one end in the vice, with suitable wrapping/protection,

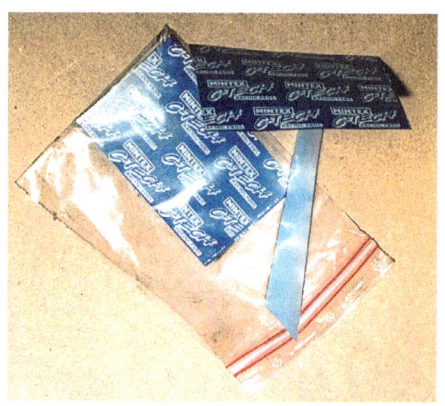

5-12. Brake squeal can usually be resolved by sticking a pad to the rear plate of each brake pad. These are Mintex, but most brake component manufacturers supply the black 'tar-like' pad.

hold a rag round the pipe adjacent to the vice and, starting with a 45 degree **bend** behind your rag/point of straightening, pull hard down the full length of the pipe. If you don't introduce a bend, but merely try to pull the pipe straight, you will not achieve a truly straight pipe. There are then, of course, various radiused bends to position correctly if the pipes are to be both safe (i.e. not kinked), and to look their best. Putting the radius in is best done using one of the large varieties of pliers available from most auto-factors available in 45- and 90-degrees. Photographs 5-13-1 to 5-13-3 will give you some additional help with the installation.

You won't need me to remind you that flexible hoses are a safety critical part of your car, and that the stainless steel braided flexible hoses are better than the original hoses. Firstly, they are more resistant to abrasion. Secondly, they are also more resistant to the inevitable very slight expansion that takes place when you brake, and will give your brakes a more solid feel. This is particularly important on the IRS cars where there are four flexible hoses within the system (rather than the three on earlier TRs).

The finest quality stainless braided hose available is AQP racing hose. This is compatible with petroleum and synthetic lubricant, hydrocarbon fuels and liquid engine coolants, and can operate at higher temperatures for longer periods. Light and flexible, it's easy to work with and its stainless steel cover will ensure long lasting durability.

5-13-1. 'Copper' brake lines are almost corrosion free and easier to bend. They're available from any of the TR specialists.

5-13-2. There is both safety and pride of workmanship at stake when it comes to installing brake lines. This is a very neat installation where the lines have the nice even rounded bends you would be wise to copy.

5-13-3. Brake lines are bound to be a fraction too long. This raises anther safety detail, for you may find it necessary to 'lose' a couple of inches of pipe from time to time. Do so carefully, using this excellent example if it helps.

The construction consists of AQP elastomer tube, partial stainless steel wire inner braid, and a full stainless steel outer braid with a maximum operating pressure of 1000psi.

BRAKE SERVOS

Contrary to popular belief, brake servos do not actually improve the 'effectiveness' of the brakes. They do reduce the required pedal pressures, though, and make the brakes feel more like those in a modern car. Brake servos were fitted as standard to these cars and took the form of a close-coupled dual circuit unit fitted immediately in font of the pedal box. If the brakes on these cars are felt to be inadequate and the servo is working (see *How to Restore Triumph TR5/250 & 6*), then you'll need to look at improving the front calipers, or adding a second servo.

An extra servo

TR250/5/6 owners can adopt this change whether they have totally standard front brakes or have tried any of the upgrades but still find the brakes fall short of expectations. **Note:** This modification does not actually improve the stopping power of the car's brakes and will not delay the onset of brake fade. In fact, it may actually accelerate the onset of brake fade under heavy braking. Fitting a second brake servo, however, will reduce the pedal pressure required to stop the car.

Note: This modification can only be applied to cars where the twin braking system is split front/back.

Before you contemplate this modification you need to be quite sure your existing servo is working properly and that the rest of the braking system is in good order and not the underlying cause of your dissatisfaction.

The method of checking that your existing servo is working, and also some basic checks on your front and rear brakes, was explained in *How to Restore Triumph TR5/250 & 6*. The improvement involves fitting an additional single line remote servo in the engine bay on the passenger-side bulkhead/firewall to further assist the front calipers (see photographs 5-14-1 and 5-14-2).

The TR250/5/6 all have dual line systems and an existing dual-line servo close-coupled to the master cylinder as standard. I suggest you leave all that in place but remove the hydraulic brake pipe that goes from the rear (nearest the servo) master cylinder port (which feeds the front brakes), to the distribution point on the left side chassis rail. A Lockheed Type 6 remote servo adds a 1.9 multiplier to the pedal pressures and, at about £140, is rather cheaper than

all the Girling single line remote servos I've seen advertised. Whatever your choice, take care to mount the air-valve between 4 o'clock and 8 o'clock to simplify bleeding the hydraulics. With the new servo in place replace or modify the original pipe and couple that to the side 'inlet' coupling of the new servo.

Note that with RHD cars you can shorten the original pipe and apply

5-14-1. This is a second servo fitted into the front brake line on a TR5. It adds 1.9 times pressure to the front brakes.

5-14-2. This is a Lockheed Type 6 unit fitted after consultation with Lockheed. It has reduced this car's pedal pressure dramatically, but hasn't actually improved the effectiveness of the brakes. Note that the air valve points (correctly) downwards, and that by mounting the unit on the passenger side bulkhead/firewall, the owner has also achieved the correct upward angle for the body of the servo.

an end fitting that is compatible with the brake servo you have selected, remembering that Lockheed components use a different thread to Girling brake parts. With LHD cars you will certainly need to fit a new longer pipe from the original servo to the side inlet port of the new servo.

All cars will require two additional pipes to be made up and fitted to the car. Firstly, a hydraulic line will be required between the end of the servo and the distribution block on the left side chassis rail, while, secondly, a vacuum pipe will need to coupled from the new servo to the inlet manifold. **Don't forget to bleed the brakes!** With this work complete, you have, in effect, fitted in series a second servo to the front brakes of your car where at least 70% of the braking effect comes from.

As picture 5-14-3 shows, it's possible to alter the front to rear balance and allow for its adjustment from time to time as changing conditions require. In this Racetorations example, the normal close-coupled master cylinder is replaced by two separate master cylinders actuated by a balance-bar.

5-14-3. A standard TR5/6 servo fitted with a balance bar and twin front/rear master cylinders in place of the usual integral dual master cylinder. A close look at the balance bar will reveal that it is offset to give additional braking pressure, probably in favour of the rear brakes (the front brakes having been beefed-up by upgraded calipers).

This gives you the advantage of a servo with any combination (within reason) of front/rear balance.

REAR BRAKES

Although largely satisfactory for standard and fast road cars, the characteristics of the rear brakes can be improved for ultra fast and competitive cars. Like the front brakes discussed earlier in this chapter, changing the frictional grab of the lining material is the most easily achieved and, therefore, most popular route. It's not quite so easy to change the size of the rear drums as it is to change discs at the front, but several cooling aids are available. Furthermore, you can vary the internal diameter of the rear wheel slave cylinder to suit your needs.

Once one's car gets to ultra fast road standard, the original rear lining materials need to be reconsidered, and Mintex M20 is the usual choice. Many competition cars are still very happy with M20 linings.

Drums

Datsun 240Z 'Alfin' rear brake drums are available for thoise TR's where SOME rear brake overheating is occuring. The cooling fins are fairly small, though. They do look a bit like the original Alfin rear drums but, for fast road cars that are being worked hard enough to warrant help, the fins may help cool the rear drums a little. Racetorations can supply its own not dissimilar alloy drums (seen in picture 5-15) that will fit any TR with 9in diameter rear brakes.

Ultra fast road cars, where the brakes are being used hard enough to generate real heat, may be better with the large finned aluminium casting available from Racetorations (picture 5-16-1). It fits over the existing brake drum and offers many more fins (and thus cooling area) for your money.

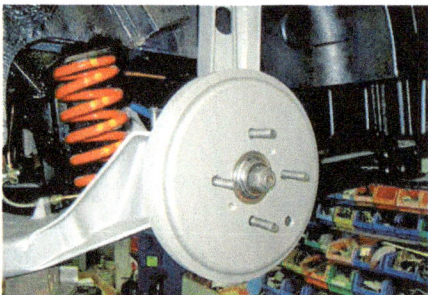

5-15. A light-wight alloy drum with steel braking inserts.

5-16-1. Racetorations' deep finned aluminium cooling addition to the rear drums fits over the existing drums. A magnesium version is also available for competitive cars. Can you spot the four small brass retaining bolt holes?

5-16-2. Racetorations' aluminium cooling addition to the rear brake drum in situ, with a 'mini-fin' drum posed in front of the hub for comparison purposes.

You can see the comparison in picture 5-16-2. Any owners planning for race, rally and competition events will certainly be interested in better cooling the rear brakes but, since they will want to keep additional weight to the very minimum, they'll usually choose Racetorations' magnesium variant.

If you are racing and the drums are still getting hot, duct some cool air over them.

Slave cylinder variations

Designed for, and perfectly satisfactory in, standard and fast road use, the rear wheel cylinders may need 'tuning' for ultra fast and competition cars. If you feel you want more aggressive rear brakes then you will need to reduce the size of the slave cylinders. 0.625in would be the smaller size used by most to upgrade their rears, but if your rear brakes are locking and you want to ease their application, try the 0.75in diameter cylinders.

IRS handbrakes

The handbrake on the early TRs was mounted on the side of the prop shaft tunnel and enjoyed an excellent mechanical advantage (leverage). From the TR4A to TR6, though, the handbrake was moved to the top of the prop shaft tunnel, its length was reduced, and it was required to operate two cables instead of one. All this resulted in reduced mechanical efficiency and a 'poor' handbrake. Before you contemplate the compensatory modification that forms the main part of this suggestion, you really would be wise to ensure that none of the contributory problems outlined in *How to Restore Triumph TR5/250 & 6* apply to your car.

If everything is in tip-top condition, consider extending the handbrake levers on the rear back plates, as illustrated by pictures 5-17-1 to 5-17-3. Drawing D5 shows how this completely reversible modification can be done, increasing

the mechanical advantage of your handbrake by over 40%. The drawing shows an extension from 70 to 100mm. If this is still not to your satisfaction you can, within reason, further extend the length of the removable extension pieces, although you need to bear in mind that as you increase the mechanical advantage the distance your handbrake lever has to move to apply the handbrake increases. I think you will find the drawn extension is quite sufficient providing the rest of your handbrake is in good order.

SILICONE BRAKE FLUID

Many people recommend the use of silicon brake fluids, including some of the experts who contributed to this book. I spoke to Lockheed many years ago and was told that silicone fluid held any water in it as globules. On the other hand, although Dot 4 or 5 glycol hydraulic fluids certainly attract water, they retain it dispersed in suspension. Lockheed felt, therefore, that brakes using silicone fluid were much more likely to loose their effectiveness if those water droplets boiled.

My own experience, in relation to MGBs, indicates that silicone fluid would seem to be the common factor in a spate of sticking servo units. I didn't talk to Lockheed on this occasion but the

5-17-3. The resultant assembly looks like this and reverts to standard in a few minutes since no cable adjustments nor alterations to the lever(s) are required.

MGOC did and apparently established that the silicone fluid has less lubricating properties than glycol based fluid and that there probably was a correlation. There is no doubt that silicone fluid is much kinder on the paintwork of its host car, but it's equally true to say that the manufacturers of many of the braking components we use do not recommend its use.

5-17-1. The standard TR250/5/6 handbrake lever arrangement will surprise few readers, but the mechanical advantage can be increased by extending the lever ...

5-17-2. ... with a pair of these fabricated extension arms.

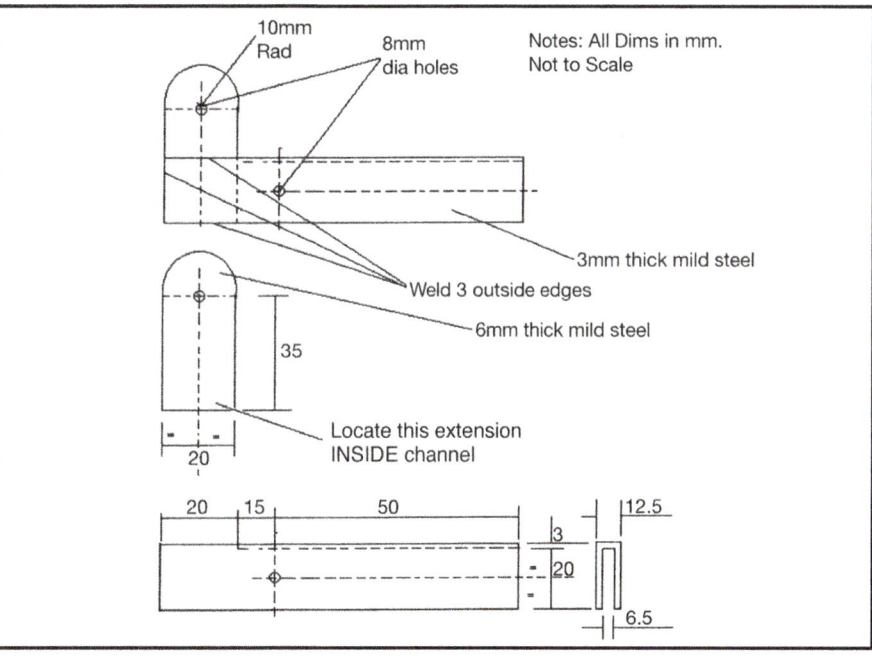

D5. Extension pieces for IRS handbrake.

Chapter 6
Gearbox, clutch & overdrive

CLUTCH
Summary

The primary reason for the six-cylinder car's unenviable reputation for a fragile clutch is that the cars were originally fitted with a 0.75in bore master cylinder. Although this worked fine, it was probably just on the safe side of marginal. Triumph then fitted a 0.7in bore master cylinder from mid -1970. Although this lightened the feel of the pedal, it removed what little safety margin there was from the slave cylinder's travel. So, improvement number one for all six-cylinder cars is fitting a 0.75in bore clutch master cylinder as a matter of course, regardless of your performance aspirations. Even with this improvement in place, the standard clutch system components remain vulnerable to wear, so these need to be in tip-top condition, as was explained in some detail in *How to Restore Triumph TR250, 5 and 6*.

The pressure and friction plates for standard and fast road cars are satisfactory provided your first choice is the OE Laycock (picture 6-1), and you restrict your alternatives to Borg and Beck 'blue spot', or the AP/Lockheed unit. Ultra fast road and competitive cars will need to rethink the power handling capability of these parts, and the release

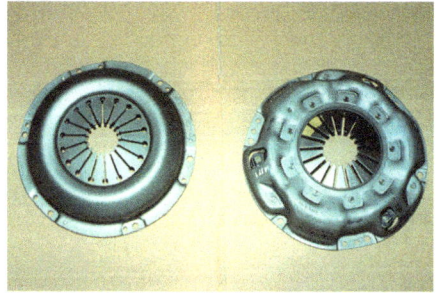

6-1. The preferred six-cylinder clutches are a small but select band. There is no doubt that the OE pressure plate supplied by Laycock, shown here on the left, is favourite. On the right side of this shot is your second choice, the Borg and Beck unit.

mechanism, and we will look at this detail very shortly.

I do recommend you investigate all of the solutions available from TR specialists, and select just one supplier from which to buy all the related parts in one delivery. If you mix and match components from different specialists, you're both transfering the responsibility for the assembly onto yourself, and increasing the possibility that the resultant assembly may not work so well or for as long as you might expect.

Clutch pressure plates

All our specialists offer the uprated friction and pressure plates that are essential to handle the power developed by ultra fast and competitive six-cylinder engines. Revington offers an uprated clutch plate which, I am assured, will not noticeably increase the pedal pressure but will provide extra drive for those ultra fast uprated engines. Similarly, Tilton

6-2-1. For fast and ultra fast road applications this Tilton single plate 'Rally' unit should stand up to more than average punishment. As we can see, it fits on a standard diameter flywheel and can use any TR method of disengagement, from standard to co-axial. They fit all TRs from '2 to '6.

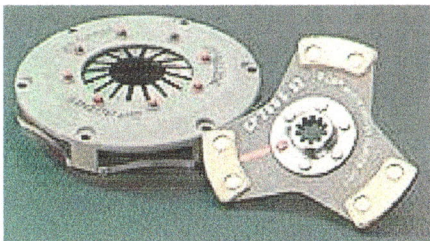

6-2-2. The small contact area of AP's rally and competition 'paddle' clutches necessitates high contact pressures that in turn make the pedal pressure very heavy for road-going applications. Some versions are available with four paddles as well as the three paddles seen here.

(US) does a single plate set, shown in picture 6-2-1, that is more robust than the usual replacement contenders, while those with competitive engine power and torque need to think either in terms of Tilton's sintered 'race' set, or AP's offering shown in picture 6-2-2.

Paddle clutches have a relatively small frictional area and need much higher spring pressures to provide the friction. This makes the plates very hard to open so pedal pressures are very high. Consequently, they are really only suited to competitive cars that are trailered to and from the race or rally venue.

Most specialists take the view that the six-cylinder engine's clutch has a deserved reputation for being shortlived and unreliable, and recommends changing even the standard six-cylinder cars' clutch to that shown in picture 6-3.

Competitive alternatives include two clutches with vigorous action and high noise-transmission, making them suited to competitive use only. In most cases a 7.25in diameter single plate

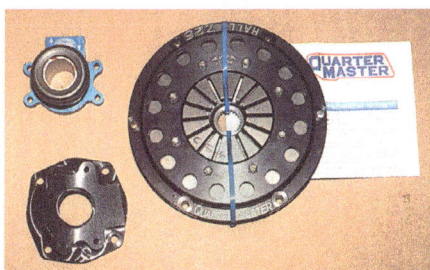

6-3. Quatermaster's single plate clutch set with a coaxial hydraulic release cylinder/bearing top (left), and the spacer/mounting plate used to mount the cylinder to the front of all TR gearboxes.

Tilton clutch will resolve most client's needs – although for the most powerful six-cylinder cars a 7.25in twin plate unit is recommended.

Both single and twin plate clutches are best actuated by a coaxial hydraulic release cylinder mounted on the rear face of the bell-housing and working over the gearbox's standard first-motion shaft. We will discuss these in a bit more detail shortly.

Clutch release bearing carrier
It is worth pointing out that the TR2 used a rotating phosphor-bronze clutch release carrier which never proved at all troublesome. Once Triumph introduced the non-rotating, pinned type carrier, however, some minor clutch troubles started to occur. Not all were so minor or so infrequent once the six-cylinder cars went into production! Consequently, Revington recommends the rotating phosphor-bronze carrier seen in picture 6-4, for the whole range of TR clutches. It more or less mimics the original carrier design except for the fact that the pin that prevents the original design from rotating is omitted. Revington's carrier will, by design, rotate to obviate the wear-groves that occur with Triumph's later designs and materials.

6-4 All six-cylinder TRs are fitted with a pinned steel thrust bearing carrier. This is Revington's phosphor bronze un-pinned (and therefore rotating) improvement.

Clutch release bearings
Neil Revington was telling me that he noticed that the longevity of the four-cylinder car's clutch release bearing was far superior to the later six-cylinder car's bearing. He attributes this to the fact that the four-cylinder clutch design incorporates a return spring that pulls the release bearing away from the clutch when not in use. The later design did not have this facility, leaving the bearing

in contact with the spinning clutch. Consequently, Revington now offers an especially designed and purpose-made external six-cylinder clutch release mechanism. It incorporates an adjustable slave push-rod and a return spring. Triumph's original design was clearly intended to remove one item (adjust the clutch), from the service requirements, which is understandable. With Revington's mechanism in place you'll infinitely extend the life of the clutch thrust bearing, albeit at the minor expense of an annual push-rod check/adjustment. The Revington design allows the retention of the original Lockheed slave cylinder.

There is an alternative adjustable clutch slave cylinder for the owners of six-cylinder cars to consider – basically re-introducing the predecessor to the Lockheed self-adjuster! The kit includes a new Girling slave cylinder and adjustable slave push rod, which Moss thinks (and I agree), is likely to prove more reliable and increase clutch longevity. There is no gain without pain, however, for, like the Revington kit, you need to adjust the Moss slave rod every 12000 miles – every couple of years for most of us! The Moss part number for the Girling cylinder is 516788, but don't forget, you'll need a pipe adapter as well as the push rod and fork. The latter are supplied with the Moss kit seen in photograph 6-5.

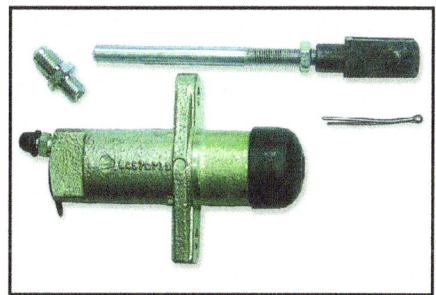

6-5. It may seem like a retrograde step to introduce a clutch slave cylinder that requires adjusting when the car is fitted as standard with a self adjusting one! Moss, however, thinks this is in fact a step in the right direction, and I think so too, particularly if you also fit a return spring. The spring pulls the clutch thrust bearing off the clutch fingers when not in use. I use a couple of carburettor return springs and find it not only makes the clutch run quieter but should ensure the longevity of clutch fingers and thrust bearing.

6-6 The cross shaft runs in a sintered bronze plain bearing pressed into each side of the bellhousing. The bearings need to be increased in length at the first opportunity to ensure that wear does not detract from the full operation of the clutch mechanism. This same picture shows the extra pin, or in this case 5mm bolt, that provides additional essential strength to the fork/shaft mounting.

Cross shaft bushes

The two phosphor bronze bushes that press into the gearbox bell-housing and carry the cross shaft are too small for longevity. The integrity of these bearings is important for full clutch-release action, regardless of which type of clutch your car is fitted with. So, whether they seem worn or not, if you still intend to use the cross shaft/fork method of disengaging your clutch, replace the two bushes with the full-width, upgraded ones, or with two pairs of the original bushes. The original part number is 137651 but, ideally, you want full casting-width ones. Check that the cross shaft isn't worn when you remove it to replace the bushes. Picture 6-6 shows the location of the bushes in question.

Strengthening the clutch fork

Picture 6-6 also illustrates this next point very well indeed. In *How to Restore Triumph TR 5/250 & 6* we mentioned that the six-cylinder TRs are prone to breaking the tapered pin that screws into the fork and locks it onto its cross shaft. There is a heavy duty pin available but it's still not the complete answer, so the following minimum improvement is recommended for all cars. Strengthen the clutch fork's attachment to the cross shaft. I have tack-welded my Stag's fork to its cross shaft (long story as to why), but this is not a good option for you to consider because you will have to destroy the cross shaft to get it out!

Once the tapered pin has secured the two parts together, the TR trade prefers to drill a 3 or 4mm diameter hole through fork and shaft and to drive a 'roll-pin' through the two parts, **in addition** to the standard tapered pin. I've drilled a 5mm diameter hole through my TR6's fork/shaft assembly and secured them using a 5mm nyloc nut and bolt – additionally retained with stainless steel locking wire (*a la* aircraft industry).

Modern release methods

We spent several pages in the restoration books on the clutch, its release mechanism and some solutions related to the original design. The whole system, however, is still marginal, particularly in the six-cylinder cars, and any improvements are, therefore, well worth your very serious consideration next time you have the 'box off the engine'. The modern alternative to the whole Triumph gearbox clutch release mechanism is an annular hydraulic cylinder. Four different makes are available in the USA, at least one of which is regularly imported into the UK.

These types of release mechanism dispense with the external clutch hydraulic slave cylinder, cross shaft, bearing and carrier, not to mention the dreaded fork, and thus simplify the whole clutch release mechanism by providing an internal expanding cylinder around the first-motion shaft. The new annular slave cylinder consists of an aluminium housing which is bolted to the front of the gearbox, fitting over the snout. Inside this housing is a hollow sleeve with the clutch release bearing

6-7-1. Racetorations always use stainless braided hoses in their hydraulic throw-out bearing installations. Note the route & "bulkhead" connections used to exit the bellhousing, that the top hose is use to bleed the cylinder and ...

mounted on its forward face. The inner sleeve and housing have oil seals at both ends. Hydraulic oil enters through a port between the oil seals and forces the inner sleeve forward, moving the release bearing forward and operating the clutch. Not only is this system simpler and more reliable than the original, but it also provides for extremely quick gear changes. You will need to run two hydraulic lines into the bellhousing, but that is easily accomplished through the, now redundant, cross shaft holes. One pipe actuates the cylinder from the clutch master cylinder, while the second line is the bleed from the annular cylinder and is sealed once the clutch hydraulics have been bled.

You could also consider the Tilton 'throw-out' cylinder which is widely available in the US.

Also officially called an annular release bearing, Revington and Racetorations regularly import a range suitable for the six-cylinder engines and whichever clutch cover you select. You will see a typical high quality Racetorations installation in pictures 6-7-1 and 6-7-2. These kits (which cost about £265), include a special adapter plate that bolts to the rear of the bell-housing and can be seen in pictures 6-8-1 and 6-8-2.

US readers should speak directly to Tilton Engineering, McLeod Industries

6-7-2. ... the bleed hose is routed to a convenient external bleed nipple. Bearing in mind the vulnerability of the original cross-shaft fork-pin & the stress imposed by many 6-cylinder clutch-covers, this modern clutch actuation mechanism offers improved reliability and is much more efficient than the long chain of components used in the standard clutch operating mechanism. Furthermore the gearbox comes out & goes back into the car far easier when the end lever is missing!

or Weber Performance Products to get more information on their respective products.

GEARBOX IMPROVEMENTS
Gear ratios

The majority of gearboxes in use today are the 4-synchromesh units which were produced from the very early

6-8-1. These are also coaxial clutch release cylinders – Tilton (USA), imported by Revington TR. Two types are available, one for the early spring and one for the later diaphragm clutch.

6-8-2. We can see the unit assembled to the bellhousing and piped up. The top (looped) pipe will be the bleed pipe that will be sealed by the normal bleed nipple external to the bellhousing.

1960s through to the end of the Saloon, Dolomite, Stag and TR6 models in the late 1970s. They come in two different formats, the A and the J, each with its own overdrive option. With the aid of photographs 6-9-1 and 6-9-2 you should be able to differentiate one from the other. Both are basically good gearboxes and, because they were used in a wide range of models, there are a variety of ratios available to the (professional) rebuilder, obviating the need for expensive special close-ratio gears if you don't want them. I will recommend some strengthening modifications for the ultra fast and competitive cars later, but first we'll look at gear ratios, for there are common misconceptions.

As well as the circumference of the rear wheels, there are three components which affect the full range of gear ratios within a motor car. It's not just the gearbox ratios that need your attention, indeed they may be the least important of the details that affect the overall gearing of your car. While driving in top (4th gear), it is the rear axle ratio (and overdrive if fitted and engaged) that reduces the engine's revolutions to an rpm that the rear wheels can cope with. The gearbox itself is a direct 1:1 drive, so the gearbox only comes into the ratio equation when an indirect gear is engaged. Therefore the gearbox has, in a way, the least effect on the overall gear ratio of the car.

Since the rear axle ratio is employed all the time the car is moving (obviously), it should, therefore, be our first consideration, although it can't be viewed in isolation. Rear axle ratios of 3.45, 3.7, 4.1, 4.3 and 4.55:1 are

6-9-1. You will get few clearer views of an 'A' overdrive. Note the vertical actuating solenoid on the left of the unit and slightly angled (downward) speedo drive right centre.

6-9-2. The tail end of a 'J' type overdrive with – not shown- a 'J' type gearbox. Note that the flat rear mounting 'pad' just forward of the drive flange signals this is a TR overdrive unit, while the rectangular 'sump' at the bottom of the picture, together with the position of the solenoid, declares this to be a 'J' model overdrive unit. Mind you, Laycock de Normanville kindly removed any doubt by fixing an identification plate that says 'J' type overdrive!

available. The first two are by far the most popular for standard and fast road cars, the 3.45 ratio offering a good balance between fuel economy and acceleration. For ultra fast road cars the 3.7 ratio (fitted to all US six-cylinder cars), would be the ratio of choice since it offers better acceleration than the 'taller' 3.45. The fuel economy of cars with a 3.7 ratio does suffer, though. Turning now to the overdrive – not every reader will appreciate that there are three overdrive ratios available for the overdrive. The standard ratio incorporated into all A type, factory-fitted overdrive units offered a 22.5% engine rpm reduction for any given road speed. This improved to 25% with the introduction of the J units. However, if you're having your overdrive rebuilt, it's possible to have it effect a 25% or 28% reduction, reducing engine rpm correspondingly. Indeed, ultra fast road cars can get the best acceleration and cruising fuel economy by fitting a relatively low (say 3.7), rear axle ratio and a 28% overdrive ratio. I can confirm the pleasure that this combination offers. It's all in the gear ratios!

For cars competing in sprint and hill-climbing competitions, a 4.1 rear axle ratio and LSD is the way to go. By using the 4.3 and 4.55 ratios, TRs in different stages of tune can be adapted to give their best performance on a wide range of race tracks.

Change the indirect gear ratios in your gearbox with caution for, as unexciting as it may be for some readers, the factory knew a thing or two about the gear ratios it elected to use. The term 'close-ratio gearbox' sounds very 'expert' but, for all road cars, even the ultra fast ones, I'd say it's generally a mistake and a waste of money to modify the indirect gears. If you have any of the early cars and want to fit a taller first gear with slightly closer differences between the rest of the gears, then fit a post 1972 (J type), gearbox and, if required, the related overdrive unit. This actually achieves two improvements: the ratios are slightly 'taller', as already mentioned, and the gearboxes and their overdrive units are much more rugged and far more reliable.

Potential competitors may still be wondering whether special close-ratio gearboxes are not still a good idea. Perhaps I should add the *caveat* that it depends upon the type of competition start you expect, which may be a matter of geography! I feel that a special close-ratio box is of very questionable benefit when a standing-start competition is involved. If you need to start from a standstill, as is usually the case in UK competitions, you won't be able to get the revs up quickly enough to take advantage of the camshaft, and will find yourself losing ground off the start-line if your ratios are too high. In fact, in this circumstance you may want to fit a shorter-ratio first gear, such as that available from Racetorations, which improves your speed off the start line.

The rolling starts that, I believe, are often employed in Europe and the USA, on the other hand, do allow you to benefit from a taller first gear.

Strengthening modifications

Darryl Uprichard of Racetorations explained the reasons for strengthening the gearbox. Although they improved in parallel with engine development, and the J type gearbox was undoubtedly the best built, they never really kept pace with engine development. Consequently, once you start to tune the car and/or put the gearbox to above average stress, you start to reveal its weaknesses. However, improvements in gearbox strength and reliability can be achieved by upgrading several of the internal components simultaneously with a gearbox overhaul.

Although I give some DIY rebuilding advice later in the chapter, I believe that there are too many pitfalls involved in rebuilding and upgrading your gearbox at home. Instead, I would redirect all those without gearbox rebuilding experience towards our professional specialists. Although all of our specialists can supply rebuilt standard gearboxes, I'd suggest there is no point in having a standard box rebuilt professionally. You should use the specialist's expertise to the full and have the box upgraded. Here are some of the improvements to discuss with your preferred specialists.

Fitting an uprated laygear is a necessity for every gearbox rebuild. One uprated version of the TR laygear set (from Moss), takes its cue from the stronger Stag variant. It comes with three needle bearings, two at the rear of the laygear to double the load capacity of that end. The kit, which can be seen in photograph 6-10-1, fits otherwise standard gearboxes and includes bearings, circlips and thrust washers.

Racetorations, however, has found that the higher power that its engines generate may necessitate four (instead of the original two) roller bearings within the laygear cluster. It also recommends twin roller thrust bearings in place of the TRs original phosphor-bronze thrust rings. You can get the flavour of Racetorations' improvements from photographs 6-10-2 and 6-10-3. These strengthening modifications become even more relevant and important for ultra fast road, rally and competition cars, mandatory, in fact, but first let's explore the layshaft upon which the layshaft bearings run.

How to Restore TR5/250 & 6 details how to check for a disintegrating layshaft and the important remedial action that is required. It bears repetition, however, that the quality of layshaft on which the

6-10-1. Moss's laygear set comprises of the laygear we see here manufactured to accept 3 (standard 'boxes use 2) needle-roller bearings.

layshaft bearings run is vital. Basically, a new layshaft will be required by every gearbox rebuild, and any layshaft stands more chance of longevity if the loads it has to carry are spread over a wider bearing surface. However, there is little

6-10-2. Gearbox improvements are essential for any fast road, very fast road or competitive car. We looked at the roller thrust bearing improvement earlier. This picture shows the typical damage to a layshaft and the solution, which is to fit a second set of roller bearings at both ends of the laygear. You can just see the second inner set here – thereby doubling the contact area between laygear and layshaft.

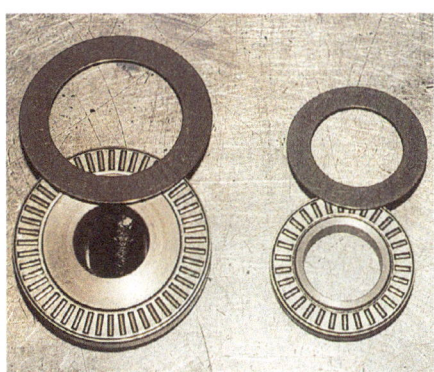

6-10-3 Triumph Stag gearboxes were upgraded from the TR units in two ways. One was to improve the laygear thrust washers by an improved thrust bearing. The original Stag thrust bearings are no longer available so Racetorations has designed a common improvement for both Stag and any TR gearboxes.

value in upgrading the number of needle bearings within the laygears if the shaft on which they bear/run is going to disintegrate.

The quality of aftermarket layshafts is such that they all need to be tested before fitting. Check yours out by either banging the old layshaft against the new one, to see whether the new one bruises, or use a file on the new shaft to see if the case hardening is good. Neither test will mark a good shaft. However if your new shaft is rendered useless by bruising or scratching, consider that it's better to find that out prior to assembly than in a few months' time when swarf from a disintegrating shaft ruins the bearings in the box and in the overdrive. You can rely on the professional specialists to ensure that the layshafts they fit are of the highest quality.

If you are in two minds about the expense of an external rebuild and upgrade, bear in mind that the Stag variant of the TR gearbox was judged to require the additional roller bearing within the laygears, and the improved thrust washers at each end. The Stag only produced 150bhp, roughly the same as an early PI TR6, but the its torque was a little higher and the car was considerably heavier than a TR. Nevertheless, in all Triumph gearboxes the static/plain layshaft is under constant pressure, being forced away from the main shaft by the power transmitted through the intermediate gears. Furthermore, the helix angles cut on the gears is also

trying to force the laygear forward, out of the front of the 'box in drive, and back through the rear of the 'box in over-run. All these forces are increased, of course, the more power you put through the engine and the more vigorous you are with that power. So, an uprated engine, particularly those intended for ultra fast road or a competitive applications, are likely to find even a rebuilt standard gearbox wanting, and the strengthening modifications discussed here essential.

Some TR owners building a fast road car may well find a good or rebuilt Stag 'box adequate to their needs if the engine power is *circa* 160bhp. The first motion shaft is different, though, as you can see in picture 6-11, and it will need to be changed to the shorter TR shaft during the rebuild. As already discussed, the layshaft bearing in the highly stressed Stag application had a tendency to drop out, and Triumph introduced the dual bearings at this high stress point.

Another Triumph/Stag improvement is not normally fitted to a standard TR gearbox overhaul, though it is available as an optional extra for those intending fierce starts in a competitive environment. This involves fitting roller thrust lay-gear bearings, and is an essential upgrade for all competitive cars.

Revington and Racetorations automatically include a modified second-gear bush where/when appropriate in all their gearbox overhauls. These have been developed based upon the last J type 'top hat' bearings and, while they may not be suitable for all early 4-synchro gearboxes, they are a very valuable upgrade where they can be fitted. In spite of their extensive use. Revington/Racetorations also point out that the boxes with brass top-hat bushes had a weakness with the second-gear bush. Indeed, it's quite common for the

rim of the top hat to fall off! Triumph corrected this upon the introduction of the last variant TR6 'box about 1972/3 (at the same time as the J-type overdrive), and Revington/Racetorations will also fit the strengthened part to any 4-synchro box they rebuild.

Close ratio straight-cut dog gears

The extra noise emitted by these straight-cut gears makes them suited only to competitive cars. However, for the race track, a straight-cut close-ratio dog-box is understandably popular. The straight-cut gears you see in picture 6-12 may be noisier, but they are significantly stronger than the helical gears used in gearboxes produced for all popular road-going cars. They reduce power loss too. Furthermore, straight-cut gears allow for easier gear changing. Not easier in the sense of 'silky-smooth', for you still need to be positive when engaging a these gears, but easier in the sense that use of the clutch is no longer mandatory. Although using the clutch still reduces transmission loads, if the driver gets the gear change timing slightly wrong, or only gets the clutch part-way to the floor, or forgets in the heat of competition, or is just too busy fighting the next car off his door-handles, then the straight-cut 'box will change without difficulty, fuss or damage. Perhaps we should all have one! These gears fit all 4-synchro gearboxes. Most competitors choosing this route will fit the full set, costing about £1750, but there is an option to fit only the first gear ratio if you wish.

6-11. As we can see here, although the splines are the same, the Stag's first motion shaft is an inch or two longer than its TR cousin.

6-12. Not only are straight-cut gear sets very easy to use on the race track, they are also easier to fit into the gearbox than the standard gear sets.

Improving gear selection

Ultra fast road and race cars benefit from a modified gear selector/top cover to the gearbox which roughly halves the gear change 'gate' travel. Called 'quick shift covers', there is a slight increase in the force required to select a gear since the change involves reducing the mechanical advantage of the gear-changing mechanism. These are available from all our contributors and you can see a picture of an original selector extension in picture 6-13.

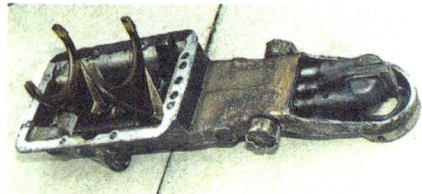

6-13. The top extension cover on a TR gearbox may house more than you were expecting – including the selectors. By reducing the mechanical advantage of the gear lever you reduce the distance it has to travel to move a selector rod and thus engage a gear.

DIY REBUILDS

I have reservations about encouraging TR enthusiasts to rebuild gearboxes at home, since I believe there is more to the task than many appreciate. Used on the Dolomite range, the Stag, all the various 2000 and 2500 Saloons, and the TRs from TR4 through to the J box variant used in the TR6, experience counts for a great deal where the interchangeability of parts is concerned. The length of the respective first motion shafts and the first gear ratios, for example, are different from one variant to the next. Inexperienced rebuilders in particular are best to avoid swapping parts from two or more 4-synchro boxes for a number of reasons.

Firstly, only a trained eye will be able to detect the degree of wear that is acceptable in a synchromesh hub. Furthermore, the synchro hubs differed during the course of the (long) production run. Earlier boxes were fitted with 'asymmetrical' gears, while the later 'boxes used 'symmetrical' gears. The terms apply to the type of synchro hubs fitted to each gearbox, but there were other component changes too, so these colloquial/generic terms cover a range of components, some of which are not interchangeable.

As I explained earlier, the basic 4-synchro gearbox was used in a variety of Triumph cars,. This fact can be the downfall of some inexperienced gearbox rebuilders because Triumph introduced some absolutely minute changes for some models. Consequently, gears from apparently identical gearboxes can be fitted during a home rebuild only for the owner to find the rebuilt 'box jumps out of gear, for example, for no apparent reason. There was also a major change to all input shaft and mating counter-shaft gears' helix angles around June 1973. In order to reduce gearbox noise, the helix angles were changed from 35 to 40 degrees. This change makes it impossible to **fully** assemble a gearbox with such widely different helix angles. It's possible to **partly** assemble such a 'box, but once the mismatch becomes obvious you need to start again. So, when procuring new or used parts, you must first ensure you know what the helix angle is on your gearbox, and that the replacement parts are compatible. This is one of those particularly important spares items that I was referring to in the first chapter when stressing that you need to buy spares that are compatible with what you have, not with what the car was originally fitted with. Many, indeed probably most, gearboxes have already been rebuilt, a good number with components different to those originally fitted.

Components from different gearboxes should not be mixed by the inexperienced DIY re-builder. Although experienced professionals mix parts, even they can be surprised by the fact that the same mix in one 'box will produce a satisfactory result while, in the very next 'box, the same mix proves quite unsatisfactory. Perhaps as a consequence of this unpredictability, the home restorer could already have a mixture of symmetrical and asymmetrical components in his gearbox without ever knowing it, and it may be working reasonably well. The mere act of stripping such a 'box and re-assembling it has been known to generate all sorts of undesirable characteristics. Get it wrong, and you could end up with a gearbox that:
• jumps out of gear, particularly on over-run
• pops out of gear at the slightest touch
• on the gearlever
• presents you with a very hard/stiff difficult gear change

Most owners initial reaction to these problems would be to alter the spring pressures within the top cover in an effort to hold it in gear or ease the gear change as the case may be. This may have a partial/slight beneficial effect in the short-term, but this is not the solution and the problems are more than likely to return.

Nevertheless, Triumph's use of the basic 'box is impressive, and bodes well for the availability of many parts for many years.

Oil retention

The Triumph gearbox has a breather hole to allow the excess air (resulting from heat expansion), to escape. A professionally rebuilt gearbox will have had this detail attended to, but many home-restored gearboxes, and even a number of factory rebuilt boxes were refitted to their respective cars without the breather's blanking plug being removed. Some plugs were broken off, leaving the base *in situ*, preventing the air within the gearbox from escaping. Consequently, the oil is pressurised into escaping from every nook and cranny it can find. So, if your gearbox has an above-average preponderance to leak oil, check that the breather hole is free. Where and how large is this tiny but important hole? The 1/16in hole is located right at the front of the gear change extension.

OVERDRIVES

There are different objectives and preferences regarding overdrive units. For example, few race, sprint or hill-climb cars would want to carry the extra weight of an overdrive unit, although many rally enthusiasts will want the close-ratio benefits that the standard 22.5% reduction an overdrive can provide. The A type overdrive can have overdrive ratio applied to 2nd, 3rd and 4th gears, effectively giving a 7-speed close-ratio gearbox. Where an overdrive is fitted, owners of fast road, and possibly some ultra fast road cars, will be interested to hear that the 28% reduction ratio is available on both A and J types and will help motorway/freeway/autobahn cruising.

The last of Triumph's J type gearboxes are generally regarded as the best. The Js were certainly easier to maintain and, consequently, are a little more reliable. Nevertheless, rally enthusiasts may still want an earlier overdrive unit on their car since these 'bang-in' without any delay. This is because the A units run at full pressure all the time and thus engage quicker than the J type, which only pressurise when 'in', and so take a moment to build up to 'engaged' pressure.

Overdrive improvements

The modern materials used to form the cone clutches within the overdrive unit have improved so that the coefficient of friction today is perhaps three times what it was when the TR's overdrives were first made. This means that the increase in force required to lock the competitive overdrive's conical clutch is much reduced, with the consequence that the increase in hydraulic pressure once required to engage overdrive in competitive cars is no longer necessary. Competitive cars may still find the early overdrives (as fitted to TR2/3/3A/4), which used a big piston case an advantage because of their very fast engagement. However, road-going cars may find the later smaller accumulator overdrive units preferable because of the softer overdrive engagement.

The uni-directional clutch transmits all of the power during those, albeit brief, moments when the overdrive is neither 'in' nor 'out'. The original A and J-type uni-directional clutch was 'non-floating', in that the rollers rode-up the ramps independently within the clutch. Were one roller to get a bit ahead or behind the majority, the whole power load became focused in that one place. Later uni-directional clutches became known as 'floating' clutches, and find their own position so that all the rollers take an equal load, increasing capacity and reliability. If you're having an overdrive unit rebuilt, ask that a floating uni-directional clutch be fitted.

Adding an overdrive

Moss supplies an overdrive conversion kit which avoids a great deal of hassle, as well as negating uncertainty about the quality of the donor unit. You'll still need to fix a rear gearbox mounting, though, and you may want to take the opportunity to fit a new gearbox cover. You won't, however, need to find a donor gearbox/overdrive unit.

Most donor units will not be of TR origin. Mine were both from Saloon cars, which is fine in principal, although some gearbox contents are incompatible with others (see symmetrical and asymmetrical above). The speedo drive can also be a problem. Most overdrives provide a 22.5% reduction ratio, but some offer a 28% reduction (ex-Standard Vanguard, for example), which I have already explained is preferable for high speed cruising. If you're contemplating a prospective gearbox/overdrive purchase and want to know what reduction the unit has before you buy, the answer usually lies at the front of the serial number, which will begin 22/ ..., 25/ or 28/ ... It is perfectly feasible to buy a 22.5% donor overdrive and have it rebuilt and upgraded to 25% or 28%, though it will cost more.

The most cost-effective way to add overdrive to your car is to fit a complete ex-Triumph Saloon or Dolomite gearbox and overdrive unit (usually available for about circa £150). You will be able to make some comparisons with the help of picture 6-14. The later J type gearbox is generally more robust and has slightly taller gears, and the J overdrive has several features that make it more reliable than the earlier model. Consequently, you score a double improvement if you fit the later gearbox/overdrive to your car. Will it fit? Certainly, though you'll need to use a Saloon clutch friction plate since, for some extraordinary reason, the splines on the TR's first motion shaft are different from those of the Saloon. You'll also need a TR speedo cable appropriate to your new J type gearbox.

You should check and replace any worn parts within the bellhousing, strengthen the clutch fork's attachment to the cross shaft and fit a new sintered spigot bush in the flywheel before the marriage is contemplated. You would also be prudent to test (electrically), the overdrive inhibitor and reverse light switches before the 'box goes in the car. If you want to keep some degree of originality, you can use an ex-Saloon A type gearbox and overdrive – although this generates difficulties in view of the location of the speedo drive, as we saw in *How to Restore Triumph TR 5/250 & 6*.

You may find the rear mounting of the Saloon's box incompatible to your TR gearbox mounting arrangement. You can see the difference in picture 6-15. Moss and Racetorations make a converter bracket kit, part-number 211361X, for a shade over £50.

I strongly recommend that you keep your original gearbox in storage (after you drain the oil). A future owner may not regard originality in quite the same way as you do, and may only be willing to buy the car if the original gearbox is available as part of, or additional to, the deal. The stored 'box need not take up too much room if you grease the first-motion shaft, lay a couple of blocks of wood in a corner of the garage and

6-14 Three comparative gearboxes, all with overdrives fitted. On the far side of the photograph we have the correct TR2 to early '6 'A' type gearbox and overdrive. The central gearbox is a 'J' type correct for later TR6s. Note its extra support for the gearchange casing. On the right (nearest the camera), the vertical mounting tells us this is a Saloon gearbox, confirmed by the fact that the speedo drive exits the 'box high in the casing and horizontally. The TR speedo drive will be low down and angled at about 30 degrees to miss the tunnel cover, and can be seen in both other units.

stand the original box upright on the wood.

Note. Always get a used donor overdrive unit stripped and cleaned before fitting it to your original box – see the notes about layshaft swarf gathering in the overdrive unit and then re-contaminating a rebuilt gearbox in the appropriate restoration book.

There are other changes that you will need to be aware of when trying to fit a non-TR gearbox/overdrive into your TR. Non-TR A type overdrives will almost certainly need their accumulator springs, solenoid mounting brackets and rear mounting bracket changing for TR compatible components. Non-TR J types will probably require a TR pressure relief valve.

If you have an A type overdrive already and want to use it for rallying, it's possible to uprate it so that the overdrive comes in instantly. You would be ill advised to carry out this modification for fast road cars, though, but ultra fast road and rally cars will find it beneficial. The modification requires that the accumulator piston be increased to its maximum size. In fact, genuine A type overdrives from TR2 to TR4 already have

6-15 For comparison, here are two 'A' type gearboxes with overdrives – identified at a glance by the large brass sump nuts. The one on the left is a variant from a Saloon (2000 and/or 2500), or a Mark 1 Stag, as revealed by the horizontally-mounted solenoid and vertical mounting studs. Were this gearbox from a TR, the solenoid would be mounted vertically, as per the right side unit. You will have noted the flat rear platform for the rubber Metalastic mounting pad on the right side unit, identifying this as being of TR origin. Note the solenoid lever and through-shaft and how vunerable it is.

the larger pistons fitted as standard. However, an overdrive from a non-TR source or from a TR4A will have the smaller pistons fitted, and these operate the overdrive in a much softer manner. In fact, the engagement can be so vigorous with the 2 inch pistons that it's **essential** that the differential mounting pins are boxed and increased in diameter – as described in chapter 3. I also strongly recommend you reduce shock loads throughout the transmission and the diff mounting pins by closeting the transmission.

Provided you buy an ex-Saloon, Stag or Dolomite gearbox/overdrive unit that is compatible with your own non-overdrive box, experts can fit the overdrive and tailshaft of your new unit to your original 'box. The rear mounting will still need a non-standard mounting, and some suitable mounting plates welded to the chassis. This work is best tackled if/ when the body is off the chassis. In the case of the A overdrive, you will still have a non-original speedo-drive location. Your speedometer is almost certain to need recalibrating since TRs used 15 inch wheels and the other donors used 14 inch wheels. Recalibration of the speedo is best left until the car is on the road and all modifications completed. The technique and source is explained in *How to Restore Triumph TR 5/250 & 6*.

If you're using a non-TR gearbox/ overdrive you'll have to consider the rear drive flange. These are available new, or you may find a used one at a spares day. However, you can have the one you get with the non-TR 'box altered. The alteration will involve taking a slight skim from the non-TR flange's recess, and then turning the flange through 45 degrees and re-drilling the bolt holes on a slightly bigger PCD.

Take great care if tempted to buy a standalone overdrive unit without its tailshaft. You may save some cash if you subsequently follow the Moss overdrive upgrade detailed in the next section, but only if the overdrive unit you bought separately is compatible with your gearbox. The tailshaft from a non overdrive 'box is longer than its overdrive equivalent and will cost a great deal of cash to convert. In fact, you may be better buying a new main (overdrive compatible) shaft – although you need to be aware that this part alone will probably cost more that the second-hand overdrive unit you have just bought!

Moss overdrive additions

A typical 4-synchromesh non-overdrive TR4-6 gearbox will usually need to be rebuilt, and almost every professional supplier will want to ensure your satisfaction by rebuilding your gearbox using a new main shaft and supplying and fitting a suitable overdrive unit. The cost for this is around £1150 for an A 'box and £850 for a J type. These figures assume there is nothing completely un-serviceable within your gearbox (like a broken case, for example), and that you have no donor overdrive unit available. You can reduce the cost by sourcing your own overdrive unit either as part of a complete gearbox/overdrive assembly or by buying a complete overdrive unit. These actions will save you about £175 for an A overdrive, and £100 for a J.

The full kit from Moss will include bezels, switches and wiring. It's expensive upgrade, but many regard it as very worthwhile. However, there's still the option of a five speed gearbox conversion which is lighter than a gearbox with overdrive and, therefore, definitely worth thinking about.

Closeting the transmission

I am sure the purists will scoff but when not in an urgent hurry I feel it helps reduce the shock loads on my transmission (and IRS diff-mounting pins in particular), if I part-dip the clutch briefly when engaging or disengaging overdrive.

Uprated overdrive controllers

While pure circuit race cars are unlikely to have 35lbs of overdrive unit fitted to the car, the control of the overdrive can be modernised to advantage when fitted to fast road and ultra fast cars. I have found this controller very enjoyable and helpful. Basically it automatically takes overdrive out whenever the gearlever passes through the neutral gate. Some may not enjoy the fact that whenever you change gear (say from overdrive 3rd to top, or overdrive top to 3rd), it will always automatically cut out the overdrive. However, the idea is that this device gives you the option of a six or seven speed close ratio gearbox (depending upon the model), as follows:

A type 'boxes:	1	1st gear
	2	2nd gear
	3	overdrive 2nd gear
	4	3rd gear
	5	overdrive 3rd gear

| 6 | top/4th gear |
| 7 | overdrive top |

J type 'boxes:
1	1st gear
2	2nd gear
3	3rd gear
4	overdrive 3rd gear
5	top/4th gear
6	overdrive top

Obviously, you don't have to engage overdrive coming up the box until you wish to do so, and you still have the manual four speed gearbox ratios with 5th gear (*i.e.* overdrive 4th), if that's your preference.

The second advantage this logic control unit offers over a conventional overdrive (in or out) switch is that you cannot inadvertently leave the switch engaged (in) when employing 1st or 2nd gear. The standard inhibitor switch still prevents the overdrive from actually engaging when you're thrashing around 1st and 2nd gears. However, if you have accidentally left the conventional overdrive switch engaged (and I will bet we all have), and change into 3rd, you will find yourself actually in overdrive 3rd gear with the conventional switch. Most cars find this too large an increment for best performance.

Two variants of the overdrive controller are available: Racetoration's

'WAC3' solid-state overdrive control package provides for a gear lever-mounted control button. If you wish to engage overdrive you merely have to press the button. If you're in overdrive and wish to come out without changing gear this can be accomplished just as easily – just press the button on the gear change knob. An 'overdrive engaged' warning light can easily be installed, and I've found this helpful from time to time.

Revington's offering is very similar except that the control switch is mounted on the steering cowl. It requires a downward flick regardless of whether you're engaging or disengaging the overdrive. Revington offers a dimmer facility on the warning light, either when you buy the kit or as a retrospective fitting. Switching on the main lights automatically dims the 'overdrive in' warning light. This is a very good idea, as ours is a bit bright at night and I would suggest this as a useful addition.

Diagram D6 demonstrates that installation is not difficult.

FIVE SPEED GEARBOX UPGRADES

Since we've thrown all 'originality' constraints out of the window, owners of standard, fast road and ultra fast road cars, particularly those currently without overdrive, may want to take a different

route to adding a gear ratio appropriate for motorway/freeway/autobahn cruising. There is much to be said for fitting a modern five speed gearbox: it's lighter, often more robust, and is probably no more expensive than rebuilding/upgrading/fitting overdrive to your original unit.

The most straightforward solution is to buy a five speed conversion kit from Moss or Autogear Transmissions. Based on the Ford Sierra five speed gearbox, it costs £950 plus VAT and includes a co-axial clutch release mechanism similar to those we spoke about earlier in this chapter. This eliminates the shortcomings of the TR clutch, and should make the overall installation trouble free. The standard conversion uses a fully rebuilt Sierra gearbox, which will certainly cope with up to about 200bhp. A close ratio version based upon the 4x4 is also available, it costs about £75 extra, and should cope with anything the TR engines can push out. Picture 6-16 will give you some idea of what this product looks like, while the ratios available in the two Ford Sierra boxes warrant a little additional space:

Standard ratios: 1st – 3.65, 2nd – 1.97, 3rd – 1.37, 4th – 1.0, 5th – 0.82
Close ratios: – 3.36, 1.81, 1.26, 1.0, 0.825

You should not need to alter the flywheel unless you are taking the opportunity to lighten it. You can also re-use the old diaphragm clutch cover, if it's serviceable. However, I would not recommend risking a used cover unless it was no more than a few weeks old!

6-16-1. A Sierra 5-speed gearbox kit. The propshaft & drive flange are made especially for the conversion & included in the kit. The other main components are: spigot bush, clutch set, bellhousing, speedo cable, rear cross member & mountings along with a modified gearlever.

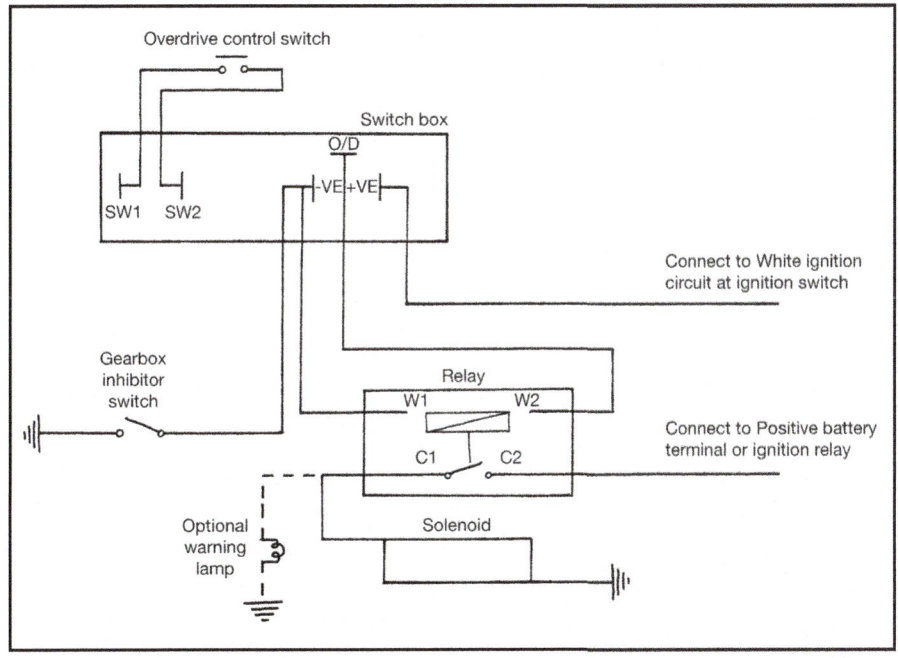

D6. Outline of wiring required for overdrive logic controller.

6-16-2. The Sierra gearbox conversion in situ.

The only remaining extra would be to get your speedo re-calibrated.

The standard Sierra gearbox is an alloy bellhousing with an iron main gear casing. In this form the gearbox weighs around 80lbs (35kg), which is in between a non-overdrive gearbox and an overdrive variety. If you want to reduce the weight still further, Moss can provide the main gearbox built into an alloy casing but, at a further £325, these are prohibitively expensive for all but the most serious competitors!

The Japanese solution

The Toyota Supra gearbox has an alloy case and weighs only 77lbs – about 50lbs lighter than a TR gearbox with overdrive. Like most modern five speed boxes, it has very well spaced ratios, and it is very robust. So, basically, this is a five speed conversion with all pluses. It is available from TR Bitz and includes a special bellhousing, a new steel engine back plate, a clutch plate, a speedo cable and a crankshaft pilot bush. You will get the picture (!) if you study 6-17.

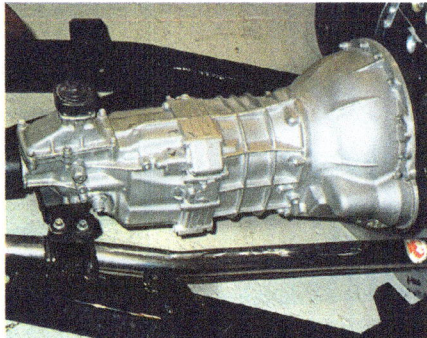

6-17. Note the superb bespoke/custom bellhousing that marries this Japanese five speed gearbox to a TR Bitz six-cylinder engine and IRS chassis.

There is no reason why you cannot also consider the Toyota Celica 'box. These are slightly less desirable since they have a steel casting and weigh 90lbs (or 45kg), but still offer a weight saving over the original TR 'box and overdrive.

Other options

Dellow Automotive in Australia and Conversion Components in New Zealand (full addresses in Appendix I), specialise in supplying gearbox conversion kits. They don't say they can marry any engine to any gearbox, but the range of kits they offer is impressive. Their kits include the all-important bellhousing, and, where necessary, a new engine back plate and numerous smaller components. Dellow tells me that its bellhousings now omit the Triumph cross-shaft but use a conventional fork on a pivot actuated by the original Triumph slave cylinder mounted on the outside of the bellhousing. Their 'Toyota five speed into Triumph' kit comprises a bellhousing, pivot ball, pilot bush, clutch fork and clip, clutch plate, thrust race and carrier, speedo cable and angle drive and tailshaft yoke. That will cost about 900 Australian dollars, and shipping will cost a further 175 to 300 Australian dollars, depending upon the speed you require the kit and your location.

Logistics necessitate you finding your own gearbox, of course, so let's take a look at a few options you may care to give thought to. The Sierra's Ford Type 9 gearbox we discussed earlier was produced from 1982 to 1987 and will be available from most UK breakers yards. Not only will you be looking for a 1.8i or 2.0i car, but one where the bellhousing unbolts from the gearbox casing. You'll not go far wrong if the Ford part-number reads 8797 7003 AA, but double-check that the first motion shaft extends only 175mm from the front of the box, not, as in the case of the 2.3i gearboxes, 210mm. Since the 'box will most likely have been liberated from a well used car, it's prudent to check all the gears before paying for it.

The original five speed Rover LM77 box as fitted to the SD1 and TR7 is getting hard to find, or at least good ones are getting hard to find. However, how about a brand-new successor – the latest R380 version? These are available new and are fitted with synchromesh on all 6 gears, i.e. reverse gear and all five forward gears. These are

6-18. Found behind numerous Rover cars in the 70s and 80s, including late TR7s and all TR8s, this five speed LM77 gearbox/transmission will carry all the power that a six-cylinder motor can put out, provided it's in good shape. The problem is that they are getting old and tired and you might be better off with the almost indistinguishable more modern version – the R380.

available without a bellhousing from RPI Engineering in the UK and its agents in the USA for circa £1000. (pic 6-18)

Two Borg Warner gearboxes deserve a few lines. The T5, shown in 6-19-1 and 6-19-2, is strong, compact, light, smooth-changing, and, while it can be found occasionally in the UK, is readily available in the US. In fact, this is likely to be the first choice of most US improvers! Ford began using the T5 in 1986, and GM followed in 1988, but

6-19-1. You will recognise the faithful Triumph 'box/tranny on the right. The T5, on the left, is quite a bit bigger, particularly across the bellhousing, which means the width of each footwell will need to be reduced to get the stronger gearbox into the car.

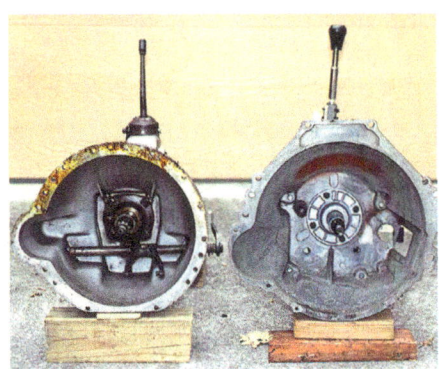

6-19-2. The view from the engine shows the bigger bellhousing. Clearly, you're forced to rethink the clutch actuation method since there is no cross shaft or fork – thank goodness! A coaxial hydraulic clutch release/throw-out cylinder is the solution.

it's the Ford units that will be of most interest. The GM gearbox is built with an 18 degree twist to one side which, while this doesn't affect the assembly onto the bellhousing, means the rear gearbox mounting bracket must accommodate the twist and installers must accept the gear lever will exit the tunnel at an 18 degree angle. The Ford T5 also has a tilt, but only 2-3 degrees. The rear mount is also tilted to compensate so a 'flat' mount is all that's required. In fact, a standard, if inverted, TR6 rear transmission mount will do the job. As far as the T5 gear ratios are concerned, the first four gears in all of these 'boxes are identical, but fifth gear's ratio can vary between .73:1 to .63:1 overdrive gear. For very high speed cruising the .63:1 gears seems favourite with a 3.7:1 rear axle ratio, but might be a little too high if you are also planning to use a higher axle ratio. DandD Fabrications makes adapters for the T5 and may have a TR6 one suited to the spigot/pilot bearing/trans input shaft.

The other Borg Warner option is a development of the T5. The T56 is, and its obvious once you know, a six speed variant of the excellent T5. Sixth gear ratio is 0.5, or half engine speed, so this option is only for those enjoying a top of the power range engine, such as a 3500/5000cc 8-cylinder generating huge torque. Be prepared for this to be an expensive choice and difficult to fit into the space available! The compensation

6-19-3-1. The T56 viewed in isolation is difficult to scale but I would guess it to be about the same length but around 20% wider and deeper that the T5. The T5 will intrude into the driver's footwell, as you will see in Chapter 15, so fitting a T56, while not without many advantages, does need some careful thought and pre-planning.

6-19-3-2. Check out its size before you jump in. The (much) smaller comparison is a T5.

... a six speed TR! Has to be worth a pint at the pub just to tell the story of how you got it in the car since it is, as photo 6-19-3 shows, a bulky piece of kit.

PROPSHAFTS
Upgraded propshafts
As the power/torque produced by the engine increases it follows that the standard universal joints fixed to the propeller shaft become more susceptible to wear and/or breakage. Most retailers, including Revington and Racetorations, offer propshafts with uprated universal joints available as an outright purchase or on an exchange basis. All owners with uprated engines are as well to contemplate stronger universal joints but those owning IRS cars should consider that a universal joint bearing failure will necessitate dropping the diff to get at the problem. Consequently, the time

to consider this improvement is when the gearbox or diff are out for other reasons. There is the added benefit of an improved quality of balance with these uprated propshafts. This is an advantage to all TR drivers but particularly those where the diff is securely strapped to the chassis (all IRS cars), and/or those expecting high propshaft rpm on the race track or German autobahn.

Revington and Racetorations have also been aware of the need to upgrade the TR where wear occurs on the splines of the propshaft. Consequently, both have developed a new propshaft with a much larger, and, therefore, stronger spline. Furthermore, the spline is coated in PTFE which not only reduces the sliding friction but reduces any take-up knocking noises. The job is followed through properly with heavy-duty greasable universal joints. For those with competitive aspirations you can get evenlarger universal joints as an optional extra.

Kevlar safety strop
This is a small but potentially very important safety aid for race cars that bolts to the floor either side of the front end of the propshaft tunnel. Although breakage of the front universal joints and/or propshafts is rare, if it does happen there is no way you can stop the propshaft flaying about without stopping the car – and that usually takes a moment. This tough piece of modern material constrains the propshaft from inflicting the worst excesses of personal injury (see picture 6-20). These are only available through Racetorations.

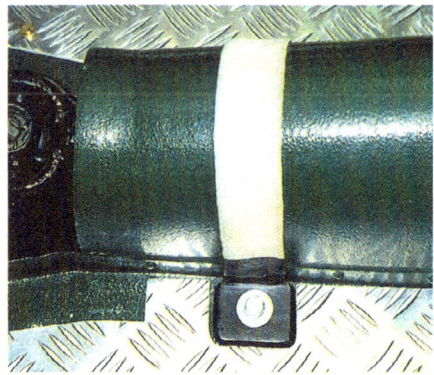

6-20. No, don't get in a strop – it's only there for your good!

Chapter 7

Ignition system

LOW-TENSION SYSTEM
How it works

The best induction system in the world is useless if you cannot ignite the charge. An effective and reliable ignition system is, therefore, important, and you need to consider carefully what you need from it. While there are plenty of upgrades

7-1-1. From this shot it's not easy to appreciate that this is indeed a Lucas 'Sports/Gold' coil. It pushes out a fatter spark, but at the expense of the life expectancy of the contact breaker points.

available, some are expensive and could be wasted on your car.

First, let's look at what the original contact breaker system has to do to provide you with your sparks. This system is one of the main causes of breakdown and under-performance, which is not entirely surprising when you think how long the concept has been around. It is required to produce a nice fat spark, the bigger the better, consistently, in hot or cold, rich or lean conditions. Bear in mind that at 3000rpm the make/break of the points has to occur 100 times per second in a four-cylinder engine, and 150 times per second in a six-cylinder engine. Each opening and closing of the points generates an additional small, low tension spark, which, in isolation, is of no consequence. However, over, say 100 hours (6000 miles at 60mph) and at, say, just 100 times per second, it's understandable that these sparks will burn our contact breaker points and wear will take place.

Most of us fit 'Sports' coils – the Lucas version can be seen at 7-1-1 – to improve our sparks and help starting and road-going performance, but additional secondary voltage from the coil necessitates more primary current through the coil and across the points.

The higher the current across the points the shorter the life of the points. However, in addition to 'burning', contact breaker points also 'bounce', particularly at high revs – or at least the 'heel' that follows the distributor's cam does – causing misfiring and lost performance.

Consequently, there's a lot to be said for at least replacing the points and condenser with a retro-fitted breakerless system, and there are numerous alternatives to consider.

RETRO-FITTED BREAKERLESS SYSTEMS

The reliability and fatter spark generated by breakerless systems makes them very attractive for all engines. Breakerless ignition triggers eliminate points burning and the periodic maintenance that goes with points, but also make the condenser redundant. Then there is the bounce issue. The more cylinders an engine has the more lobes (bumps) there are on the distributor's cam. The more lobes there are the more difficult it is to control the points and, in particular, stop them from bouncing at medium to high revs. Furthermore, after at least twenty-five years use, most bearings in the body of the distributor are worn resulting in some side-play in the shaft, generating further inaccuracies in timing.

There are two types of breakerless ignition triggers – magnetic and optical. The optical systems render shaft play inconsequential and thus rejuvenate all but the most worn distributors.

Both systems use an amplifier (a typical example can be seen in 7-1-2) to turn a minuscule initial pulse into something that is sufficiently powerful to switch the coil on and off in the same way as the contact breaker does. Sometimes, the amplifier is external to the distributor, sometimes actually internal to the initial sensing module.

7-1-2. Some systems manage without an external amplifier, but this is a typical external one.

Magnetically-activated systems have six, tubular, equi-spaced magnets fitted inside a circular disc. The disc is fitted over the cam that once opened the points. A sensing module fitted to the distributor's baseplate produces a tiny electrical pulse every time a magnet passes. The distance between the magnet and the sensor being crucial – a distributor with a worn shaft is not ideal for this upgrade. Optical systems use a chopper-disc, again mounted over the same cam, which have slots to 'chop' an infra red beam passing between a light emitting diode and a silicon

7-1-3. This is a chopper disc (note the cut-out slots) for an optical system.

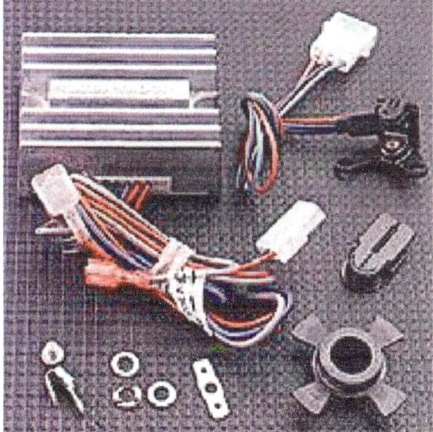

7-1-4. Lumenition makes the optically- and magnetically-triggered breakerless systems we see here.

7-1-5. Petronix/Aldon's 'Ignitor' system is commendably compact, fitting within the distributor body/cap without the need for external amplifiers.

phototransistor. Photograph 7-1-3 shows a typical 'chopper' disc. In this system it's the transistor mounted on the baseplate that generates the initial electrical pulse.

Breakerless systems are evolving

with amazing rapidity. Two systems are available from Lumenition, one can be seen in photograph 7-1-4, while Petronix/Aldon's 'Ignitor' system can be seen in 7-1-5. The Ignitor system looks a little like a mini-cassette and, like all these systems, it is very easy to fit. It's magnetically-activated, and completely replaces the points and condenser arrangement.

With the ignition system virtually bounce, burn, and, therefore, maintenance-free and generating a healthy trigger, it's time to consider whether that trigger is being initiated at the best moment for your engine – *i.e.* do you have the optimum ignition 'curve' for your engine and fuel?

OPTIMISING THE TIMING
Ignoring for the moment the effect of vacuum advances, the faster an engine revolves, the further advanced (*i.e.* before top dead centre) the spark needs be delivered to fire the cylinder's charge for maximum effectiveness. Altering the time 'curve' is really a job for experts, to be carried out on a rolling-road, but you may be interested in the process, and in what will have been evaluated by those experts when the arrive at a revised curve.

There has to be a starting point – *i.e.* the static advance or number of degrees btdc that number 1 cylinder fires, and this forms the bottom of the ignition curve. There also has to be an upper limit at which point the spark advances no further. This is the rpm at which the ignition is as far advanced as Triumph felt prudent, and is known as the 'all-in' or fully advanced point. Thus, the static/start and the all-in points define the ignition curve.

In spite of its name, the ignition 'curve' is a straight line, because that was the only way that the technology of the day (a pair of spinning weights restrained by springs) could alter the point at which the spark was delivered. Technology has moved on, of course, and today computers can provide a true ignition curve, as we'll see later in this chapter. However, sticking with 1960s technology for the moment, the static advance btdc, the mass of the centrifugal weights, the tension of the springs, and the post that stops further advance within the distributor can all adjust the position and slope of the ignition curve. Why would you want to change the curve? Well, the type of fuel, and the state of engine tune would be the main reasons behind any such revision.

The fuel you'll be using today is quite different from that available when the car was first built, the tuning manuals were written, and Triumph designed its timing, static, and all-in points. Furthermore, you've probably also modified your engine, carburation and exhaust system – all of which will make the original timing settings redundant! A well-modified engine should burn fuel more efficiently than a standard engine, and, consequently, will need an earlier advance curve. However, the camshaft, compression ratio, carburation and intended use (*i.e.* Sunday drive to the pub, occasional track-day, or straight competitive car) all affect the choice of curve.

Most standard ignition advance arrangements are not aggressive enough for today's fuel, particularly with modified engines, and usually miss the opportunity to optimise the power and torque of the engine. Clearly, you can damage your engine by being too aggressive with the advance curve, but that doesn't mean you have to be overly conservative.

In order to appreciate the changes that can be brought about, let's explore in outline a revised ignition curve and see what it might look like. The reference books will tell you 'your' engine should fire 4 or 6 or 9 degrees btdc depending upon which book you're reading and the engine in question. This is the starting or static point and will be illustrated in D7-1 as the bottom/left end of the line. You can easily adjust that point, gradually advancing the timing one degree at a time for as long as the idle revolutions per minute are increasing and the engine is running sweetly. When you go past the optimum static/idle point the engine will start to sound harsh and the rpm will reduce slightly. If you had a stroboscopic timing light, you'll probably find you've set the static advance several degrees in advance of that recommended by most manuals!

The all-in end of the ignition advance curve is defined as when your maximum mechanical advance (*i.e.* that provided by the expanding weights) is fully applied. Rarely did manufacturers of 1960/70s cars set the distributor to achieve all-in advance before about 3400/3500rpm. You'll see this point shown in D7-1 as the top/right point of

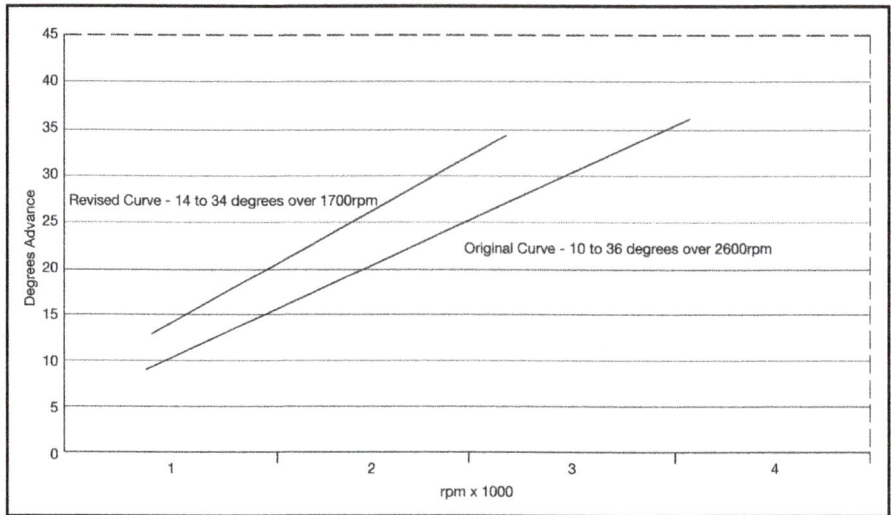

D7. Typical examples of original and revised advanced curves.

the initial curve. Today, most cars' all-in advance should be achieved by the time the engine reaches 3000rpm. For some engines the all-in point should be reached at even lower rpm.

Advancing the all-in point is achieved by fitting a pair of weaker springs to control your distributor's centrifugal weights. Weaker springs allow the distributor's weights to swing out earlier – which moves the top of the shaft earlier, and introduces the advance curve earlier.

You might find that your engine starts to pink/detonate as the rpm builds beyond the all-in rpm, which suggests your total advance is too great – *i.e.* you're advancing the ignition by, say,

7-1-6. Hopefully you will be able to see two weld spots (arrowed), that basically lock the mechanical advance mechanism to allow the electronic advance curve to have full control of this car.

26-degrees at the all-in point when (as an example) 20-degrees would be sufficient. How would you know the all-in point of any distributor? Well, it will be stamped on the weights as, say, 10-degrees, or perhaps 13-degrees. Note that the distributor's advance is half that which the crankshaft 'sees', so the weights in these examples provide respectively 20 and 26 degrees all-in.

If a distributor is over-advancing, and this is most prevalent in high compression engines (say 10:1), you'll still wish to advance it earlier using softer springs, but to also restrict the amount of total mechanical advance. This is achieved by building up the pillars, shown in picture 7-1-6. The pillars act as a stop to prevent the balance weights swinging-out further than their 10-degrees (or 13 or whatever) of allotted advance. Most tuners looking to restrict the degrees of advance will put a blob of hard MIG weld on each weight to restrict the swing.

Over advanced all-in ignition can also be the consequence of the increases you have brought about, coupled with the advance that the vacuum diaphragm attached to the side of most distributors brings about. Many competition cars dispense with the vacuum advance because it plays little or no part in enhancing performance. It is operated by vacuum and thus is virtually inoperable during acceleration because there is very little manifold vacuum available to move the diaphragm. However, on cruise, when

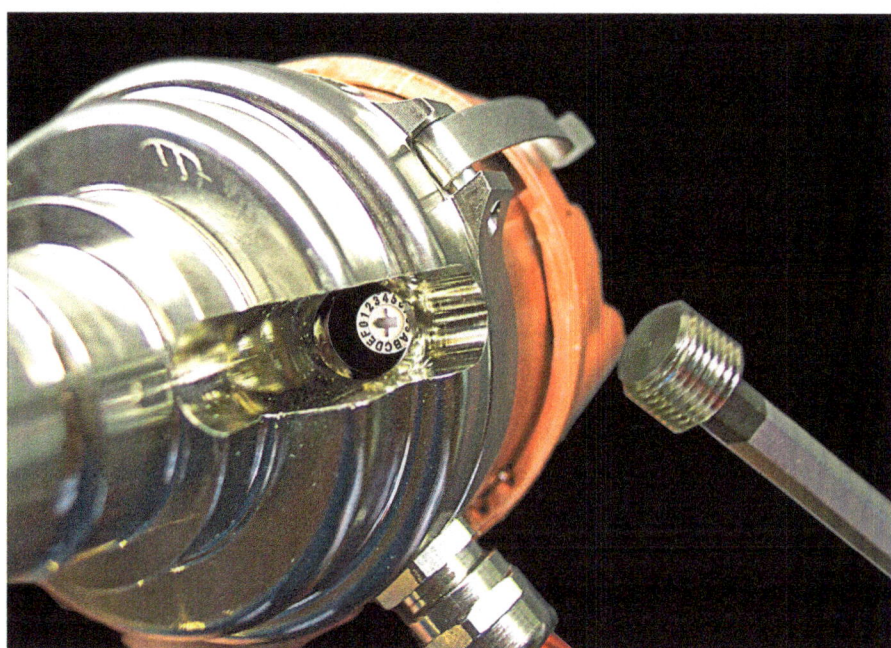

7-1-7. 123-Ignition's rotary switch-controlled ignition selection is, to my knowledge, unique, and brings modern digital control and tuning options to our classics.

manifold vacuum levels do increase, the diaphragm can advance the timing by a further 10 or 15 degrees, depending upon the diaphragm fitted to the distributor. This generates little by way of performance benefits, but perhaps an extra 2 to 4mpg in fuel economy. Thus, it's possible that any performance distributor you purchase will have the fixings for the vacuum diaphragm blanked off, and those familiar with the European petrol injected six-cylinder engines will already have a distributor without a diaphragm.

Although unlikely, your performance expert may feel that your distributor is not providing sufficient total advance. In this event he will take a sliver off the face of each balance weight to allow it to move that bit further, thus increasing the total advance. The summary of these changes in the ignition curve of a distributor can be viewed at D7-1, which shows the changes that a professionally prepared performance distributor will provide:
• The static advance changing from say 10 to 14 degrees btdc which moves the curve upward by 4 degrees.
• Fitting weaker springs to allow a faster rate of advance demonstrated by a sharper inclination to the line.
• Adding weld to limit the movement of

the advance weights thus curtailing the revised curve by 2 degrees.

You will perhaps now appreciate why I said that altering a distributor's advance curve is a job for experts with rolling roads, or the purchase of a professionally-modified distributor, which we will explore next.

PERFORMANCE DISTRIBUTORS
Most Triumph retailers will have performance enhancing distributors to offer. A new or refurbished distributor will obviously have had new bushes fitted to the body, thus eliminating any 'play' in the central shaft, and opening-up the option of a magnetic trigger. There are two performance dizzy purchase routes you can follow. The refurbished/ upgraded original (sometimes referred to as 'factory rebuilt'), which usually necessitates your old dizzy in part-exchange, or, these days, you can buy completely new distributors, available thanks to the capabilities of modern CNC machines that turn the parts from aluminium billets.

I would expect the former to be the cheaper solution and perfectly adequate provided you purchase from a recognised TR specialist, and enquire about the details of the ignition curve. Don't be afraid to ask what changes

have been made to the distributor and what benefits you can expect in terms of performance, bhp, torque or fuel increments. Some distributors will not be suited to your intended use by virtue of the advance curve's static and all-in positions, and you'll need to check that. You also need to establish that a breakerless ignition trigger is pre-fitted, find out its make and type, and whether it is included in the price. Then there are new distributors, each with its own pros and cons.

You can buy several brand new Lucas model 22D6 and 43/45D6 distributors for later cars, depending upon the engine in question. As with a refurbished unit you would need to ensure the ignition curve suits your needs and that it takes account of modern fuel and tuning. As you'll see in the next section on high tension components, some enthusiasts have experienced unreliability with current Lucas caps and rotor arms that would, I presume, be identical to the components used in these new assemblies.

However, whatever the static and all-in points, the ignition curve of these products will still be early 20th-century, straight-line ignition technology. Although the static and all-in points are adjustable, it's a long-winded and, without a rolling-road, very hit-and-miss adjustment. Thus, I like idea of changing the ignition curve at the turn of a switch and having the flexibility of a 123-Ignition distributor (see photo 7-1-7). With 16 curves to choose from, this seems like a step towards computer-controlled ignition, but these new distributors do have a disadvantage for TR owners – there's no mechanical drive for the original tachometer. You can get over this problem by fitting an electronic drive within your original tacho, so this does not preclude from the advantages of 123-Ignition's product.

The 123\GB-6-R-V model ('GB' for UK-made cars), see picture 7-1-8, replaces most 6-cylinder Lucas-distributors where the shaft is turning in a counter/anti-clockwise direction. They are an important step away from the straight-line advance curve, and incorporate a fully digitally mapped electronic system in the body of the distributor. A standard Bosch rotor arm and cap ease replacement anywhere in the world with high quality high-tension components (more in a few lines). These distributors have one mechanical

7-1-8. No special or ancillary amplifiers, coils or triggers are required with a 123-Ignition distributor. Note the Bosch cap – a step forward in reliability terms, perhaps?

connection to the engine via the original distributor drive that provides the essential engine-speed information. Electrically, you still need to connect the coil, but interestingly the manufacturer says that the microprocessor's ability to alter the dwell-angle reduces the risk of coil overheating (at low speed) and maximises the spark at higher revolutions. So, they're simple to fit and have already gained wide acclaim for their simplicity, efficiency, smooth and maintenance-free -operation.

The digital advance curve has 16 options – not necessarily all applicable to your engine, but available with the turn of an adjuster screw – and the unit can come with or without a vacuum connector/advance. This vacuum unit is also good news because it uses an electronic pressure transducer to read the manifold depression and feed the information to the internal microprocessor. They provide the advantages of mapped systems with the convenience of the original distributor. They also offer spark balancing, automatic power-cut after 1 second, and gear-shifting retard.

HIGH-TENSION COMPONENTS
If you want the best performance from your car it's very important to use top-grade high-tension ignition components. The distributor cap, plugs, high-tension leads and coil are all equally and vitally important to both the short-term good performance of the car and its ongoing reliability.

Distributor caps/arms
Reactions and experiences are mixed in so far as distributor caps and rotor arms are concerned. Most users have had no problems with any make of cap, while others are convinced there is trouble around the corner if you use anything other than a supposedly genuine Lucas replacement cap. I have always paid the extra and used Lucas branded cap and rotor arms and have never had a problem. However, as the conclusion of Triumph production recedes further into history, 'original' parts no longer remain 'original'. Thus, often what is on the box may does not mean that the contents are identical to what was originally fitted to the cars.

In recent years new rotor arms have proved a case in point. When hot they have been shown to lose their insulating factors and route the spark to earth/ground, thus causing a sudden (and in fact very difficult to identify) breakdown. Replacement with a spare (cold) rotor arm brings about an immediate restart, and this has happened sufficiently often for it to be subsequently established that the manufacturer had indeed changed the moulding ingredients so that some arms broke down at a specific temperature. Although now remedied, this example confirms that the label on the box may not be totally reliable, particularly as our cars get older and fewer on the ground. Perhaps, this is a further reason to consider ignition systems that utilise current high-tension components, such as the 123-Ignition.

Sparkplugs
The sparkplugs and ignition leads can also have a deceptively good or debilitating effect on the car's performance, and both warrant our close attention. We mostly take these for granted but the standard sparkplug design can affect the issue via their 'temperature', and some readers may not appreciate that sparkplug design has been improved via multi-earth electrodes and/or the constituent materials. Let's spend a few moments brushing-up on one or two of the subtleties of the traditional single electrode sparkplug, since quite large sections of this book address engine modifications and there is little point in improving the engine and then fitting the wrong plugs! In fact, such a step may not only nullify your best efforts but also actually result in expensive damage.

There are numerous modifications that will not affect the sparkplug selected. If you have or plan no more than a change of air-filter, inlet manifold, exhaust manifold/header, silencer/muffler, or distributor, then it's unlikely you will need to consider a change of sparkplug from that specified as original equipment. However, if you increase your engine's compression ratio, change the cylinder head configuration, introduce a gas-flowed head, or change the pistons, then a change of sparkplug may be helpful. Modifications that increase the compression ratio are likely to generate more power. With more power comes more heat, which may necessitate the sparkplug removing more heat than was the case in the engine's original configuration. Thus, it is usual to fit a 'colder' plug as an engine's level of tune is increased. We'll need to check symptoms, but, following an increase in the compression ratio, you might be well advised not only to fit colder plugs but also to adjust the plug gaps to take account of the denser mixture that results.

So, symptoms might signal that a change to a colder plug should be considered? Pre-ignition is the simple answer, for this MIGHT be the consequence of the sparkplug tip getting too hot and acting as a hot/pre-ignition source. Assuming you have raised your compression ratio, that there are no other causes of your pre-ignition, and that you're not experiencing plug fouling, then a plug that conducts more heat away from the tip is worth trying, and the next 'colder' plug should reduce tip temperatures by 75/80C. In any event, it's better to run with a plug that is too cold than one that is too hot. The worst that can happen with a cold plug is that your plugs will foul-up. On the other hand, a plug that is too hot will result in pre-ignition, which can cause serious engine damage, so study your plugs closely for signs of silver or black specs, melting, or breakage at the tip, any of which signal pre-ignition problems.

If you're experiencing plug fouling problems following engine modifications, check the plugs closely for the above symptoms, and don't be too quick to fit a hotter plug. A hotter plug will conduct less heat away from the tip, will, therefore, run at a higher temperature, and thus burn off more of these deposits. You need to first assure yourself there are no alternative problems requiring your attention before hotter plugs are fitted, particularly if you have already raised the combustion temperatures by increasing your compression ratio. Naturally, the type of deposit/fouling can vary, and needs to be reviewed. Heavy, dry, black deposits can suggest an overly rich mixture and potential carburation problems, retarded timing, or simply too wide a plug gap. Wet, black, oily deposits can indicate a leaking head gasket or piston ring/valve-stem problems. The latter may not necessarily be serious if you've just rebuilt the engine, for some gentle running/breaking in (with the correct oil) may improve the situation. There are lots of alternatives to consider before you resort to a hotter plug. Incidentally, it's very difficult to thoroughly clean the insulator within a fouled sparkplug, so the plug is unlikely to be fully recoverable and is best replaced.

I mentioned the sparkplug gap in the last paragraph, and that detail also warrants further discussion in circumstances of engine upgrades. First, bear in mind that a sparkplug is made for many applications and, consequently, the gap set at the factory during manufacture may well be a very popular gap, but may, in fact, not be correct for even your standard engine never mind your up-rated one. So, start with the OE recommended gap, remembering that insufficient gap can cause pre-ignition while too wide a gap can generate misfires, loss of power, poor economy, as well as the problems mentioned in the previous paragraph. If you've raised the compression from OE spec, you could reduce the gap by about 0.002/0.003in or, if you've fitted a high powered ignition system, you can open the gap by about the same amount. In other words, if you have both raised your compression and fitted a high-powered ignition system you should stick to the recommended OE gap setting! If in doubt, always use a slightly wider gap in preference to a slightly smaller one, thereby reducing the risk of pre-ignition.

A final detail for those switching to EFI, ignition or engine management systems – *i.e.* systems controlled by an on-board computer – particularly if you experience erratic idling, misfire at high rpm, engine run-on, or abnormal combustion. Stray voltages from your ignition system may confuse your electronics and the fitting of 'Resistor' sparkplugs can improve that situation.

As their name suggests these have a resistor built into the core that is also used to reduce radio interference and will make little or no difference to your engine's performance.

And you took your sparkplug for granted! Now all you will be worrying about is how to select hotter or colder plugs. I wish I could report a standard system for plug grading, but, since there is no uniformity from manufacturer to manufacturer, we will have to note two contrasting examples and leave you to establish the specifics for your preferred brand. The concept is simple, one group of manufacturers use a higher number to denote a colder plug. The justifiably popular NGK brand uses this system and, as an example, the BP6 plugs are the next colder plug to the BP5. On the other hand, Bosch uses a lower number to denote a colder plug!

Like many technically-orientated features in our lives, the humble sparkplug develops at an amazing pace. Not so very long ago we saw the expanded use of the multiple-earth electrode plug, seen at photograph 7-2-1. Platinum plugs arrived on the scene not, it seems to me, so very long ago with a service life of 60,000 miles (in some applications the service interval stretched to 90,000 miles) but already these are superseded by Iridium plugs with 120,000 mile life. That's not to say that you can fit a set to your TR and forget them for the likely life of the car, because their principle use will be for modern engines. Nevertheless, they are certainly worth exploring and, when coupled with modern, maintenance-free ignition systems, taking advantage of. However, like any chain, the overall strength is only as good as the weakest link, so we now need to look at the ignition leads.

7-2-1. The improvement made to even the common sparkplug is evident here, with the newer four earth version on the right.

THE PLUG LEADS

Like the sparkplug, the plug lead has changed dramatically in the last few years. The silicone-based lead has completely taken over from the now obsolete copper and carbon-cored leads, but for any form of ultra fast or competitive use an induction wound core is recommended. There are several manufacturers, each producing several grades of lead. For conventional coil ignition systems 7mm high-tension leads are probably satisfactory, although the 8mm size is better still. For those with some of the more sophisticated ignition systems, you are advised to use 8mm leads, while 8.5mm leads are probably best for ultra fast road and competitive applications. You will appreciate that the larger the lead the greater its insulation which will reduce the chances of cross-firing between leads, although the initial outlay will likely be several times what you could 'get away with'.

NGK Blue semi-transparent leads are very highly regarded. Magnecor is another of the manufacturers who make ignition cables suited to any system that has been upgraded. In fact, TRs with the standard ignition systems may benefit from the superior 7mm and 8mm cables/leads. These leads are specifically designed and constructed to conduct the maximum output generated by the ignition system to the sparkplugs, and to provide suppression for radio frequency and electro-magnetic interference. The 7 and 8mm cables incorporate a ferro-magnetic core for radio suppression, and a 2mm, chrome-nickel, 120 turns per inch winding designed to provide magnetic suppression, as well as a capacitive reserve to help ignition coils regenerate at high engine revolutions. Insulation is via an EPDM insulator with fibreglass re-enforcement, all covered by a high strength, high temperature resistant silicone rubber jacket. The 7mm cable jacket is designed to withstand 400°F (190°C), and the 8mm cable jacket some 450°F (210°C).

Manufacturers claim that when used on older, worn engines, or engines operating in extreme (cold or hot) ambient temperatures, easier starting and improved running under load will be noted. Further, the 8mm leads will resolve many of these problems usually exacerbated by the installation of many high-energy aftermarket ignition systems. They suggest that some engine modifications subject the standard ignition leads to extra heat that can destroy non-silicone insulated cables.

Like the sparkplugs before, there is much more to many auto components that are so easily given little or no thought. However, we're not finished yet – at least we're not finished with the very top end of ignition lead technology, for there are 8.5 and even 10mm leads available for the competitors. Magnecor's KV85 Competition (8.5mm) and R-100 Racing (10mm) Ignition Cables are designed for racing applications and/or where ignition cables are required with a heat resistance in excess 450ºF (210ºC).

All Magnecor components, including cable, speciality terminals, boots and crimping tools are available separately should you want to make your own ignition leads.

CHARGING THE IGNITION COIL
Saturating the coil

As mentioned earlier, reliable high performance at elevated revolutions can be a problem because the coil needs about 15 milliseconds to reach its peak magnetic saturation. Consequently, the coil has insufficient time to reach full saturation above 1500rpm for the TR5/250/6 engines, which explains the multi-coil ignition systems used in more recent high performance cars.

The standard ignition coil is quite suitable for standard cars enjoying no more than spirited road use, although you would be wise to at least upgrade to a Lucas 'Gold', Bosch 'Red', Bosch 'Blue' or Aldon 'Flame Thrower' coil for fast road use. Of these, the Bosch Blue is probably the most potent, generating some 47,000 volts and, consequently, necessitating a breakerless ignition trigger. However, the coil's recharge constraints remain a weakness, at least for the ultra fast road and competitive cars, even with all the above high-tension improvements in place.

In fact, some competitive cars are barely above tick-over/idle before the coil finds itself with insufficient time to fully re-energise itself above 1500rpm. Today we have improvement opportunities, if not for the ignition coil itself at least in the way its magnetic field is regenerated for each spark. Called a capacitive discharge system, this achieves its objective by incorporating capacitors within a (new) ignition module. These capacitors are charged to about 350 volts, which is, of course, much higher than the car's

7-3-1. Phil Vella took this great shot of a Jacobs 'Ultra-Coil' for me. It forms part of an MSD kit and can only be used in conjunction with its ...

original 12 volts. The high voltage is discharged across the coil's primary circuit thereby dramatically shortening the coil's regeneration time.

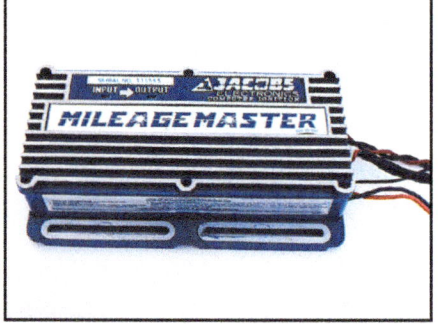

7-3-2. ...multi-spark discharge 'black box'.

There is an further method of ensuring the cylinder's fuel mixture charge fires. A conventional ignition system fires the plug once per cycle, and, consequently, the engine occasionally 'misses', particularly common on high-compression engines turning at high rpm. This is not (usually) due to the ignition system failing to present some sort of spark to the plug, but rather that the spark was insufficiently strong or sustained to ignite the cylinder charge. Higher voltages sparking across a bigger gap would certainly help minimise the loss of efficiency, but an even higher voltage sparking across a bigger gap several times is more likely to ignite the

7-3-3. Dick Taylor kindly contrived this shot to illustrate not only the model 60BTM MSD unit, but also, just to the left (normally) remote ignition adjustment control.

charge, every bit of it, every time! Hence the value of capacitive and multiple discharge systems and why we are examining them now.

Jacobs makes such a system (called Energy Pak Computer Ignition) and can provide the essential compatible coil. The system is a combination of capacitive discharge and multi-spark ignition. This automatically fires multiple sparks per cylinder spanning 20° of the crankshaft rotation up to about 3000rpm. Above 3000rpm there is insufficient time to fire each plug more than once. The primary Jacobs components are shown in photos 7-3-1 and 7-3-2.

Alternatively, the Automatic Controls Corporation in the USA makes a multiple spark discharge (MSD) unit. The primary capacitive discharge voltage of the MSD system is 470 volts – nearly 40 times the TR's original 12! The MSD6A is probably the kit best suited for most engines under discussion unless you also want a rev limiter, in which case ask for the MSD6T. You may find one refinement interesting, fun, and indeed useful. The MSD system allows you to adjust the ignition timing by +/- up to 7 degrees ... from the drivers seat! Photograph and caption 7-3-3 may also prove interesting.

Crane Performance offers its Fireball HI-6 multiple spark capacitive discharge electronic ignition. This has a built-in, programmable rev-limiter, and can be run with either Crane's PS91 coil for road use, or the PS92 for competitive applications.

A final thought provoking point – as the induction system increases in capability, and the effectiveness of coil, plugs and plug leads improve, the limitations of the rotor arm and distributor cap become more exposed. We touched on this point earlier in the chapter, but with the improvements discussed in place the cap and arm are the weakest links in the high-tension distribution system. In fact, you could generate faults within your arm and cap that have otherwise given years of excellent service, purely because the rest of the system is stressing them more than ever. As a consequence, modern high-output ignition systems do not distribute the spark via a distributor but have the direct coil to plug connections seen in many engine management and/or ignition systems. We'll look at engine management in Chapter 10, but let's spend a little time talking modern ignition management.

COMPUTER IGNITION MANAGEMENT

Although we've examined how to get a bigger, more consistent spark across an ever-widening sparkplug gap, and studied changing the ignition timing, the distributor continues to be the hub of both high and low tension ignition management, in spite of all its weaknesses and timing

7-4-1. Up-to-the-minute engine management with ignition curves and spark distribution provided by computer. The absence of a conventional coil and distributor confirm that control is exercised from ...

7-4-2. ... the footwell. The ECU you see mounted at the top of the passenger footwell is, in this case, an Omex CPU unit. The perforated relay mounting is hinged at the top of the picture so that it too will eventually clip up to the top of the footwell out of harm's way.

compromises. Although undoubtedly better than originally supplied with the TR, the ignition system retains the original concept of a straight-line ignition advance curve that is controlled by mechanical weights, springs and vacuum. Subsequent engine development has shown that the optimum point at which the spark needs to be delivered varies, and certainly doesn't follow the simple line that centrifugal force, with or with vacuum control, generates. At some points in the rpm range the ignition needs to be slightly retarded, while an increase in rpm of only perhaps 500rpm necessitates an amazing amount of ignition advance.

The whole situation changes when you overlay the effects of engine load – none of which can ever be adequately handled by a distributor-controlled ignition system. This job is routinely carried out by electronics in modern cars, but is now available for all TRs via retrofitted engine management systems.

There are two aspects to engine management: fuel management, usually called electronic fuel injection (also known as efi and discussed in Chapter 10); and ignition management.

Electronic ignition management can 'read' the engine's various parameters via rpm, throttle position and coolant temperature sensors, and has the computing power to convert its ignition 'map' into the optimum ignition point given the sensor readings at any one millisecond. The correct ignition map is generated and optimised through experimentation with a laptop computer which loads the system's computer, or ECU (electronic control unit), with the necessary data. If you subsequently note a flat spot or some other detail you would like to change, the stored data for the ignition or, if you also have efi, the fuel map(s) can be tweaked using a laptop computer. Some electronic management systems even allow you to alter the appropriate map while the engine is running.

You can install full engine management in two stages, but if that's your plan you need to initially install an

ECU with adequate computing power for the subsequent upgrade. However, many enthusiasts are happy to use conventional but efficient carburation for fuel induction, and to control just the

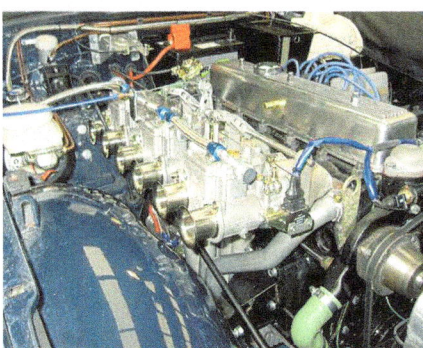

7-4-3 A trio of Weber 40DCOEs provides the induction, and some 200+bhp, for this six-cylinder engine which interfaces with an Omex mapped ignition ECU via ...

7-4-4 ... the throttle potentiometer (arrow 1), and the temperature sensor (arrow 2). The crank sensor is out of shot, but is attached to the timing cover. The 6-into-1 stainless steel exhaust system is very interesting, too, as the metallic-ceramic coating dramatically reduces radiated heat and thus under-bonnet temperatures. It also removes the potential fire hazard of oil impregnated bandage wrapping, and is much more durable.

ignition 'half' of their engine by computer – and indeed this approach has much to commend it. You can see such an example in pictures 7-4-1 and 7-4-2.

The key to this ever-changing technology is the availability of programmable ECUs. While you'll find more information on programmable ECUs in Chapter 10, here we will confine our review to looking at computer ignition management via Omex ECUs in an effort to give you the flavour of what's possible. As Darryl Uprichard of Racetorations explained, Omex's 100 series provides for mapped distributorless ignition for four-cylinder engines, and the 150 series units for distributor control of up to eight-cylinders. Larger ECU computing power is available from this company, and numerous other programmable ECUs if required. However, enthusiasts looking for serious power and performance need look no further than the example shown in 7-4-3 and 7-4-4. Engine control via Omex ignition-only ECUs has two very significant advantages over some competitive ECUs – the cost can roughly be reduced by 50 per cent, and the system can be self-tuned with a security code incorporated to ensure only authorised adjustments are possible.

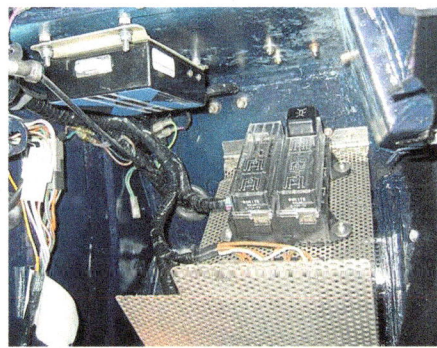

7-4-5 The business end of the Omex ignition management installation with the ECU and extensive fuse board neatly hung/hinged from the passenger footwell 'roof'. The engine position is via a crankshaft pulley sensor, while throttle and temperature information is collected via the sensors we saw in the previous picture.

Chapter 8

Camshaft

The camshaft is at the heart of the engine. Certainly, an engine will only perform as well as the weakest link in the combustion process allows; hence air-cleaners, carburettors, combustion chambers, compression ratios, exhaust arrangements, ignition systems, *etc.*, all contribute to the performance of the engine. The size and shape of the valves are also factors, but very little affects the engine as much as the camshaft. A camshaft can bring out the very best (or the worst), from the other performance factors.

Changing the camshaft is a very popular pastime, but its job is often misunderstood, and many cam changes can result in little or no improvement in the engine's performance. The two absolute basics with regard to camshafts are that the **lift** of the camshaft usually determines the power of the engine, whilst the **duration** determines the characteristics of the engine. In this chapter we will look at these two factors in more detail, of course, and also one or two subsidiary matters to help you select a suitable cam.

PRIMARY TASKS

The cam performs two vital tasks, which is why it's so critical to the engine's effectiveness. Not only does it carry out the obvious valve opening task, it also holds the valves open for a specific duration, thereby controlling the air/fuel mixture entering and exiting each cylinder. It is the shape of the cam lobes which affects the duration, and the only 'adjustment' you can make is to machine the cam to alter the point at which the opening sequence starts. Although this is important, this adjustment can't compensate for the wrong cam. You can, of course, 'retard' or 'advance' the cam from its designed relationship with the crankshaft (referred to as the 'installation figure at tdc'), but, frankly, you're better concentrating on installing the cam in its intended position and using vernier gears to get it correct! More on this subject later.

Despite the wealth of advice available on the subject of camshaft upgrades, many people get it wrong. The main problems stem from not being clear as what you want from the camshaft, not communicating this clearly to the 'experts', and finally not fully appreciating the differences between camshafts, fast road versus rally, for example. Many even order a new camshaft from a catalogue without clearly understanding all the facts. Although done with the best of intentions, the usual tendency is to over-specify the camshaft grind, which could have unexpected and often disappointing consequences. I will return to camshaft sourcing a little later.

All engines rely on moving air swiftly and efficiently through the combustion cycle, and the more efficiently the air moves the greater the engine's potential. The general understanding is that the camshaft opens the valves at the requisite moment in the combustion cycle and that the various designs differ by virtue of the amount of valve-lift offered. When choosing a camshaft, most assume that the greater the lift, the 'hotter' the cam, and the greater the effectiveness of the airflow. True, the greater the distance the valves open, the more air/fuel mixture can enter and exit the engine and the greater the torque. However, besides valve-lift, we also need to consider duration (the time the valve is open, measured in degrees of crankshaft rotation), which determines the 'rpm potential' of the engine and its power band. For any given engine the longer the duration the higher up the rpm range the power band will take place. The cubic capacity of the engine must also be taken into account, as must a host of other factors which I will outline in the following paragraphs.

The first factors to explore are the problems that too much valve lift can generate. The maximum amount of valve lift that our engine can accept is controlled by the clearance between the valve and the piston, and the distance the valve spring can compress before the coils touch, or 'bind'. Merely fitting a high-lift cam in an existing engine without checking these factors can end in (expensive) tears. It may be that recessed pistons are required, and it's highly likely that a more open coil within the spring will be required. Recessed pistons then raise the question as to whether the compression ratio of the engine will reduce because you are unable to compress the cylinder's charge. Furthermore, if you increase the coil spring's clearance, will the resultant spring have adequate longevity to close the valve, without bounce, for millions of cycles? To increase the lift during any given time span, the valve must be lifted faster. The inertia of a standard valve train already stresses the camshaft, cam followers, *etc.*, and these stresses increase dramatically as you increase the rate of acceleration of the valve lift. Not only does longevity of the whole valve train become a real worry, but there is also a danger that the cam follower will lose contact with the cam, stay suspended for a split second and then crash back down onto the cam as the spring attempts to regain control. In short, you have introduced valve-bounce!

Generally speaking valve lift has a beneficial effect on engine power/torque, though it exerts less influence on the engine's characteristics. The greater distance the valve is lifted the greater the gas flow (just as you would expect), giving an increase in power across the rev range. It has no effect on the 'position' of the power band. High lift cams can also help reduce exhaust emissions, provided the cam's duration does not introduce large periods of overlap. At one time cams were given only modest lifts, and gasses were helped through the engine by long periods of duration. This inevitably gave extensive periods of overlap (when both valves were open simultaneously), and increased exhaust emissions. More recent cam designs employ higher lifts with reduced duration, thus keeping exhaust emission levels low. This trend requires improved manufacturing techniques, at least for non-competitive cars where the owner will expect the cam and its followers to have a reasonable life expectancy.

DURATION AND POWER BANDS

The very highest specification cams (like those used in GP racing cars), generate quite a narrow power band. However, most of the cams that serve the TR world generate a power band that is about 3000rpm 'wide'. Let's not complicate the issue just yet but stick to deciding where we want our 3000rpm wide band? A very traffic-friendly, drivable car will have a low power band, 1000 to 4000rpm, for example. However, the power will tail off, initially slowly but with increasing rapidity once 4000rpm is exceeded. A cam with a middling band will offer its power from 2000 to 5000rpm, while high-band cams will not 'come onto' the cam until about 3500rpm, but will still be producing power at 6500rpm. Even the middle-band would be difficult to drive in traffic, while the high-band cam would be undrivable in traffic. So, selecting a power band that suits you is not quite so straightforward, since it's not possible to go from 1000 to 6500rpm and you'll have to find a compromise at least with the level of technology we are playing with. If you want lots of power right at the top of your rev range it will have to be at the expense of your bottom end power and tractability. Modern technology, of course, has found an answer in the variable valve timing used in Honda VTEC and Rover VVC K series engines, for example. These start with short duration valve openings at low rpm and increase the duration as the rpm increases.

Not only must your intended use be borne in mind but so too must the weight of the car. The same engine in the same state of tune in a heavy car will require a slightly different cam profile compared to the same engine fitted in a light car. Generally speaking, heavier cars need a lower power band (shorter duration), cam than light cars. However, the car's intended use then comes into the equation and confuses the issue! Those with heavier cars who are seeking good cruising speed and efficiency, and who are also prepared to compromise a little initial acceleration, may choose a mid-band cam with its increased duration and rpm!

More often than not, the higher the compression-ratio the greater power the engine will develop. Almost every reader will appreciate that, and know that CR is the consequence of squeezing the cylinder's charge into a small space, sometimes a very small space, in the combustion chamber. Few may realise that the camshaft's duration affects the issue, since cylinder pressure increases with compression ratio but decreases as the camshaft's duration increases. Therefore, an excessive duration cam can actually reduce cylinder pressures and performance! Consequently, if you plan a long duration camshaft, then the compression ratio may need to be correspondingly increased. However, this usually only applies to small to medium capacity engines since larger engines can take, and indeed benefit from longer duration cams without the need to increase the compression ratio. It makes sense if you think about it – the larger the engine's capacity the more air it needs to move, so a camshaft with

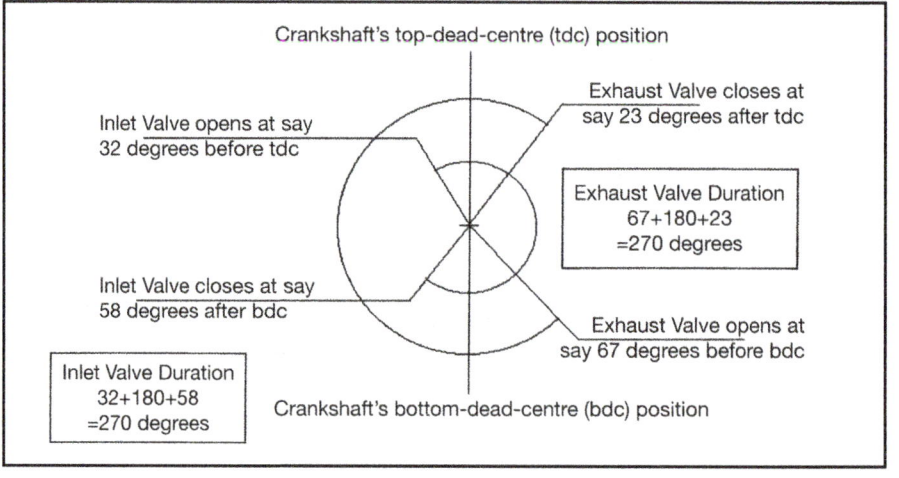

D8. TR camshaft duration diagram.

good lift and long duration helps the engine's efficiency. I guess it's a matter of percentage of air within the engine, but the larger the engine the less likely you are to have to increase the CR to compensate for a long-duration cam.

Drawing D8 shows how camshaft durations are built up. This diagram is of a four-stroke engine, of course, so you are looking at two revolutions of the crankshaft. Both valves are closed during the compression and combustion stroke, although it seems that both valves are open simultaneously for part of the cycle, which in fact they are – it's called overlap and we'll look at it shortly. The uninitiated might expect the exhaust valve would open at bdc after the power stoke and remain open until tdc of the exhaust stroke. They might also expect the inlet valve would open when the piston is at tdc after the exhaust stroke and would remain open until the piston reached bdc after the induction stroke. However, the movement of gases does not happen instantaneously, so valve timing has to be such that the inertia of the gases is both taken into account and, in fact, helped a little. So, keeping the inlet valve open beyond bdc has been found to allow more mixture into the cylinder in spite of the piston starting to rise at the beginning of its compression stroke. Trials have also proved that more exhaust gasses are expelled if the exhaust valve is left open past the piston's tdc, even though the piston is starting its induction stroke.

It makes sense once you picture the respective gases as a collective 'lump' moving under its inertia towards, say, the exhaust valve, with the new charge, as another lump, following on behind. The trick is to know when to close the exhaust valve. Once you have this 'inertia', or momentum, concept in your mind, it's not difficult to appreciate that the faster the engine runs the greater the inertia of the entering and exiting gases and the more the duration/timing of the cam has to take account of the gas flow. In fact, the combined momentum of the exiting exhaust gases (which helps to pull in the incoming charge), and the incoming mixture (which helps to push out the exhaust gases), is

called 'scavenging', and is accepted as a significant benefit of an effective cam design.

However, cams with long overlaps definitely have their place in very high performance engines and, as a rule of thumb, you can assume that the longer the overlap, the less tractable the cam is at low rpm and the better its performance at high rpm. To calculate overlaps you need the inlet opening and closing points (given as 32-58 degrees), and the exhaust figures (67-23). To calculate overlap, add the first inlet figure to the last exhaust figure, in this case, 32 + 23 or 55 degrees of overlap, which is a comfortably tractable cam. By the time you get to about 80 or 90 degrees of overlap you can expect power to be at the very top end of the rpm band and the car to a pure race car!

'COMING ON THE CAM'

As we discussed earlier, high performance cams are intractable when driven at any rpm that is lower than their intended effective power band. This performance is often referred to as being 'off cam'. The engine will not only feel as if it is ineffective, unwilling and 'lumpy', but it will sound unhappy too. Such engines usually backfire within the exhaust system (unburnt fuel igniting), and can also spit back within the induction system. They generally sound 'out of tune'.

The sound changes dramatically when engine rpm gets into the bottom end of the cam's power band, and the engine is said to be 'coming on cam'. At this point the exhaust gases reach a speed and gain sufficient inertia where they stop trying to exit via the inlet valves (called reversion), and start scavenging the cylinders. The engine sounds and feels totally different, for it's now operating as its design intended. Mapped ignition systems and/or efi (see chapter 12), can considerably improve the engine tractability at low rpm, since injection doesn't rely on induction gas speed to drag fuel from a carburettor's venturi.

Although other factors affect when an engine comes on cam (like gas flowing the exhaust system and the

induction system) my personal rule of thumb for 'on cam' rpm bands for each of the potential camshaft durations is as follows:

270	1000 and 5500 rpm
280	2000 and 6000 rpm
290	3000 and 6500 rpm
300	3500 and 7000 rpm
310	4000 and 7500 rpm

HARDENING THE CAMSHAFT

Nitriding is often mentioned in motoring circles and most readers will appreciate that it is a method of hardening the surface of the iron and steel components used in engines, gearboxes and rear axles. Nitriding is also often referred to as case hardening. Nitriding is a gas treatment which should leave a 0.010in deep skin of hardened material over the surface of the component. The process is as follows: the component is placed in a sealed oven, the temperature is raised slowly to about 500 degrees C in an atmosphere of ammonia gas, the ammonia reacts with the surface of the component to form a thin but hard case of ferrous nitride.

All cams must be nitrided to withstand the wear they are put through by the cam followers. Remember, these are forced down upon the cam's lobes by some pretty tough valve springs. Most improvers will also have their reground crankshafts nitrided too, since the regrinding of the crank's bearing surfaces will have removed any original case hardening.

SOURCING A CAMSHAFT

Aftermarket camshafts are big business, and many successful installations are supplied each year. However, you should now be aware of the problems involved in buying a camshaft in isolation, and/or from a supplier inexperienced in the subtleties of 25 to 50 year old TRs. I strongly suggest, therefore, that you buy your cam from one of the TR specialists listed in Appendix 1, and, where relevant, at the same time as you buy any other related tuning parts, such as cylinder heads, valves, valve-springs, rockers, cam followers, *etc*.

Chapter 9

Carburettor induction

CARBURETTOR DESIGN PRINCIPLES

When it comes to fuel injection, or electronic fuel injection, one very important matter is within your control – the spray of fuel from the injectors. The emulsification of the fuel within the cylinder is so important to the subsequent combustion that everyone will appreciate the importance of checking/cleaning/refurbishing the injectors to provide a uniform spray of fuel, ideally conical. Millions of small droplets uniformly distributed within the airflow make for better combustion, and this is one (of several), reasons why injected fuel is usually more effective than most carburettor induction systems. Apart from changing jets or needles, there is little you can do to improve the fuel emulsification of any carburettor; it's all down to the design of the carburettor, and that's beyond your control. Needless to say, emulsification is one of the vital details that the carburettor designers pay a great deal of attention to.

You may not realise that there are several places where a carburettor can inject fuel into the incoming air stream. Perhaps like me, you've never even given any thought as to whether fuel injected at the edge of the air steam was the same, better or less effective that

a centrally injected fuel spray. By now you will have guessed that the location of the fuel spray does indeed affect the emulsification of the fuel/air mixture and, to cut to the chase, the more central the fuel is injected the better the emulsification is likely to be. Consequently, although SU, and probably Stromberg, will have spent hours trying to get the same superb emulsion as Weber and Dellorto, they have not succeeded, which is why a DCOE Weber usually provides that little bit more top end performance than either SUs or Strombergs. There are several reasons for this, but the primary one is

9-1. The auxiliary venturi in this 40mm choke Weber injects the fuel as centrally as possible for maximum engine effeciency.

9-2. While the design is slightly different for the 45mm version (which surprised me), the principle of central injection of fuel is retained.

that Weber and Dellorto carburettors spray fuel into the centre of the airflow, making for greater uniformity of fuel/air emulsification. You can see the principle in photographs 9-1 and 9-2. The design of SU/Stromberg carburettors requires the fuel to enter on the edge of the air flow, which doesn't permit the same degree of uniformity of emulsification. Furthermore, the SU/Stromberg 'bridge' also causes an irretrievable loss in top end performance. You can check out my point by studying photographs 9-3 and 9-4.

That said, the SU and the Stromberg are very good carburettors, especially so given their cost. Both can be made to run very well indeed, of course, and twin SUs on six-cylinder engines are generally quite underrated.

9-3. The fuel enters the incoming air stream at the point arrowed, right on the (bottom) edge of the air flow. The design of the carburettor makes a change impossible.

9-4. It's less obvious with the piston right up (picture 9-3), that the bridge inevitably acts as a restriction, but you can see the constriction as the piston descends. Did you spot the anti-run on valve in the throttle disc at the back of this and the preceding picture?

I believe that most enthusiasts should look at getting what they already have right before moving on to more exotic setups, and I hope this chapter will help them do just that. I'm sure few would believe that the mid-range acceleration from both SU and Weber carburettors can be identical, which bears thinking about considering the respective costs of each and the fact that most of us are more interested in acceleration than top speed. However, the uniformity of the Weber's spray pattern will always give the '*Doppio Corpo Orizzontale*' model E the superior top end performance, which will attract those readers who are happy to pay any money to get the absolute maximum from their competitive cars. Incidentally, the Italian nomenclature means double body horizontal type 'E'.

Before we get down to examining ways to optimise each type of carburettor, let's spend a few lines considering the implications of a little bit of history, for which I am indebted to Des Hammill, in order to quantify the difference between SU and Weber carburation. In 1952, when Jaguar was preparing to race its XK-engined cars at Le Mans, the engine was initially fitted with triple 2 inch SUs. However, Jack Emerson decided that he should test the, then new, DCO3 45mm Weber carburettors to see if the engine went better with them. The three Webers increased the maximum bhp by some 8-9%, allowing Jaguar's test engine to provide a further 20bhp than had been possible with the SU carburettors. SU was informed of the results, and Peter Knight of SU went to view Jaguar's engine running with the Webers. Harry Spears refitted the triple 2 inch SUs on the very same engine and it was re-tested, while Peter Knight re-tuned the SUs in an effort to redress the balance. With the SU's pistons all fully lifted and the air/fuel mixture ratio checked as being correct, the 20bhp discrepancy remained and the comparisons were accepted as valid. Sidedraught Webers were universally adopted by Jaguar for use on all XK racing engines from that point on. The Weber's one choke per cylinder clearly improved the carburettor's efficiency while, as mentioned earlier, introducing the fuel into the middle of the air-stream via the auxiliary venturi, along with the absence of a 'bridge', combined to achieve the better results at the top end of the engine's rpm.

The first thing to appreciate is that these tests were not a failure on the part of SU carburettors but more a demonstration as to the absolute brilliance of Weber's masterpiece of carburettor engineering. If maximum bhp is what you want, sidedraught Webers (or Dellortos), are needed to release the last 5% to 10% of top end power. So why are we wasting our time exploring the SUs? There are several very good reasons, actually, starting with the fact that the majority of TR owners don't need the last few percent of power from the very top end of their engine. Secondly, most would prefer not to spend sizeable sums of money on carburation equipment, largely because it's unnecessary since, far from being outclassed, the majority of engines run extremely well with the SUs. Thirdly, tuning and jetting sidedraught carburettors needs to be consigned to a rolling road. Whilst this is fine for the competitors, I'd guess the majority of readers would like to setup their own carburettors. This is quite practical with SUs. Finally, the original equipment twin SUs give a good balance of efficiency, and deliver good miles to the gallon. Mpg is something Webers and Dellortos are not noted for.

So, the faithful SU does have a lot to offer and, if we could give it a bit more of a sporty image, might even become the carburettor of choice for the majority of readers. Although, in the interests of simplicity, I plan to purely compare the most popular of each type – *i.e.* SU and Weber, the comments for each are usually just as applicable to Strombergs and Dellortos.

SU CARBURETTORS
Related components

Whatever your performance aspirations it's important that the effectiveness of your induction system is not compromised by restrictive air filtration (which we will explore a little later), or an inefficient inlet manifold. The last of the six-cylinder inlet manifolds were, not surprisingly, the best of those fitted by the factory, and you should use the one that is appropriate to your engine. They were illustrated in the relevant restoration book and it's important that you use the most effective, i.e. 'swept', manifold available. Pictures 9-5, 9-6 and 9-7 should act as a reminder. Owners of US six-cylinder TRs may find that the most effective swept inlet manifold will not fit

9-5. The early six-cylinder engines used the 'log' shaped inlet manifold which is unlikely to provide smooth unrestricted airflow for the mixture.

9-6. It's hardly surprising that the last of the six-cylinder inlet manifolds was the most effective ...

9-7. The fuel injected six-cylinder engines enjoyed a similar 'straight-through' inlet manifold arrangement to that employed by Weber carburettors – which perhaps contributed to the higher power outputs of the PI model TR's.

the inlet ports of their cylinder head and also that they need to acquire and fit a UK spec/ported head in order to allow the use of this manifold.

The car's performance is quite likely to be a major disappointment unless you have previously raised the compression ratio to *circa* 9.5:1, fitted a decent camshaft that allows the cylinders to scour and recharge completely, **and** fitted a good extractor exhaust manifold, such as we see in picture 9-7!

SU carbs – the best choice?

Two makes of carburettors were fitted as standard equipment on Triumph's 2498cc six-cylinder engine. All were used in 'twin' format, with HS6 type SUs and 175 Strombergs being pressed into service at various times. We explored what TR used what carburettor, how to identify each, what were the preferred inlet manifolds, how to set-up and how to repair the carburettors in *How to Restore Triumph TR 5/250 & 6*, so I don't propose to repeat those topics here, although I would like to reiterate that Strombergs were more effective than most owners appreciated, though SUs were easier to adjust and, therefore, probably the carburettor of choice for the majority of owners. That point remains valid for, although SUs don't currently have a 'performance carburettor' image, compared to sidedraught Webers or Dellortos, for example, there is much that can be done to improve them, and they are incredibly adjustable, as I will show.

The SU carburettor works on the principle that the greater the engine vacuum the higher the carburettor pistons lift. This in turn withdraws the tapered fuel control needle from its 'jet', allowing more fuel to be drawn into the incoming airstream. If the speed of piston lift is slow, the injection of extra fuel will be slow and the car's acceleration will be correspondingly unexciting. Conversely, if the piston shoots up into the top chamber instantly, the injection of extra fuel will be correspondingly increased and the car's acceleration proportionally improved. We will look at how the piston's speed of response can be improved in a moment, but for now just consider how important the shape of the needle is to the increase in fuel available to the engine. A very gently tapered needle allows only a little extra fuel into the engine even with the piston fully raised. Conversely, a sharply but evenly tapered needle will introduce lots of extra fuel but only when the piston has risen far enough to present the thinnest part of the needle to the jet. Consider, however, the potential increase in performance a concave shape, in place of the current (almost) straight line taper, would bring, especially with a fast piston. It'll do nothing for fuel economy, of course, which is why SU didn't adopt the idea, but it will improve acceleration.

Most enthusiasts with fast road and ultra fast road cars are looking for acceleration rather than top speed.

SUs are capable of delivering the acceleration, albeit at the cost of fuel economy. SUs do allow you great deal of control, though. For example, you can drive to a track day on a standard pair of SUs, change the piston/needle assemblies in the paddock, enjoy your spirited track event, revert to your 'road' pistons/needles and drive home quite normally. You can also adopt this concept when you need to attend an emissions check. We'll return to this arrangement a little later in the chapter.

If you don't envisage track day driving, but are, nevertheless, looking for excellent acceleration, part of the answer lies with the rear axle gearing, which is discussed elsewhere in the book. However, the setup you choose for your SUs needs to be a compromise between acceleration and fuel economy.

I strongly recommend Des Hammill's *How To Build and Power Tune SU Carburettors* (also from Veloce Publishing). I will *precis* the principles of tuning SU carbs in the next section, with Des's kind agreement and help. However, I recommend all road going applications should stay with a pair of 1.75in SU carburettors and buy a copy of Des's book. Those relatively few owners preparing their car for racing should buy a set of sidedraught Webers or Dellortos and drop straight down to the Weber section later in this chapter. You'll need the optimum top end power these technologically superior units offer, as well as a new inlet manifold, a correctly designed linkage, and a complete tune up, all of which won't be cheap.

Setting standard SUs

For those who have decided to read on, there are several basic details to check and correct as necessary if you're to get the best from your SU carburettors.

The first is to ensure the carburettors are not leaking air or have any mechanical defects. Since we explored finding and correcting these elsewhere, I don't propose to duplicate that detail here. The next important detail is to make sure that the carburettors are set up exactly as the manufacturer recommended. To do this the SU carburettors have to be totally serviceable, as does the entire throttle linkage. If the two butterflies aren't opening simultaneously, and/or aren't opening fully when the accelerator/gas pedal is fully depressed, optimum performance is not possible. The linkage

9-8. A Gunson 'Carbalancer'. Once you get to this level of sophistication, it's a real necessity.

is really the downfall of twin SUs when the carburettors have been well used, but it can and must be fixed. New linkages are available from Burlen Fuel Systems.

Focus next on ensuring that the right needles and piston springs are fitted to the carburettors, that the dashpots have oil in them and that they actually retain the oil. I outlined the procedure involved in synchronising a pair of carburettors in my restoration book, where I suggested a piece of hose to help you listen to and correct the respective air flows. At the level of tuning we are concerned with here, however, the equality of air flow required necessitates a much more accurate method, and a direct reading gauge is required. The cheapest is the Gunson 'Carbalancer'. You can see the unit in action in picture 9-8, and the ease of using one of these excellent meters means that no serious tuning enthusiast can afford to be without one.

All SUs fitted to Triumph TRs use red or yellow piston springs, with the red springs being the more common. The red piston springs are the lighter in weight and offer less resistance to piston lift, so they provide slightly better engine acceleration. The needles need to be the correct ones not only for the engine, but also its tune and for the carburettor's return/damper springs. However, different companies have different

opinions regarding which spring/needle combination work best, and if you were to call three different suppliers seeking their recommendation I would be surprised if they agreed on which needles/springs you should be using!

It's my recommendation that a standard engine with standard air cleaners should have the standard needles fitted to it in the first instance. These have been selected by SU to give the best possible power (with economy) for that engine. However, you should be prepared to carry out some acceleration and fuel economy testing to establish which needles and springs are going to work best on your engine. The red springs will allow the pistons to rise faster, which will increase acceleration but decrease economy, while the yellow springs will slow the rate your pistons can rise, and thus improve fuel economy at the expense of acceleration.

The standard SU needles will be correct for the standard Triumph engines on the basis of a balance between reasonable power and acceleration with fuel economy. However, rarely, if ever, did the factory or the SU engineers take maximum acceleration into account since the resultant fuel penalty would have been unacceptable to the average TR owner. So, with your car running as the factory intended, how do we improve the acceleration?

Improving acceleration
Any deviation from the standard recommended needles and piston springs in an effort to improve acceleration is going to result in fewer miles to the gallon. A faster lifting piston and/or a richer needle means more fuel is going into the engine. There is no way around this. If an increase in fuel usage is unacceptable to you, stay with the standard recommended SU setup.

However, for those with modified engines who would prefer an increase in acceleration (and possibly some additional top end speed), to the highest mpg, try experimenting using a second set of pistons/needles and springs. By keeping your 'standard' piston/needle/spring combination unaltered you will always have a reference point to fall back to if you go wrong or find the consequences of your experiment unacceptable. For each change, in the absence of a rolling road in your garage, run a series of acceleration tests over 0 to 30, 0 to 50, 0 to 70 and 40 to 70mph for each change. Record the times **and** the specific parameters of each test. It's so easy to find yourself wondering at a later date was, for example, test 5 with or without oil in the dampers? Here are a few things to try:

• Change the springs to red. At full length these provide a four gramme rating against piston raise. Progressively shorten them to reduce resistance to piston rise. You can get as far as a two gramme rating, but make the change gradually and in conjunction with the changes to the needles themselves outlined below.
• Spin each (spare) needle in a drill and, using fine emery cloth on an area about mid-way along, increase the 'necking' of each needle along the lines shown in diagram D9.

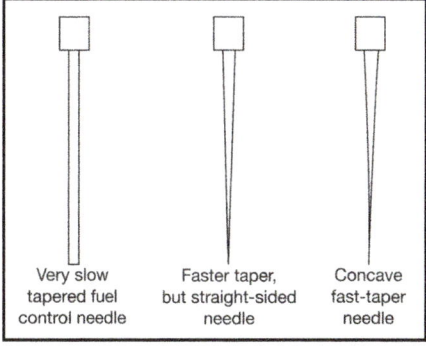

D9. SU needle shapes.

| Very slow tapered fuel control needle | Faster taper, but straight-sided needle | Concave fast-taper needle |

• Contrary to general belief, the effect of fitting intake trumpets to the intake side of SU carbs is hard to detect when on test – it's even possible that they are marginally detrimental to the carburettor's performance. The advice here is do not fit them! However, there is some slight benefit to be gained from filing a radius to the mouth of the body. Try that and note the effect.

• It's important that cool air is delivered to the carburettors. Not only must it be as cool as possible, and filtered, but it should not be forced into the carb. The 'cool' stipulation will surprise no one and this is usually achieved by fitting a couple of 2in, or perhaps one 3in, diameter flexible tubes from the front of the car (say from behind the radiator grille). Allow the cool air to discharge adjacent to the carburettors' air-filters but don't try to 'close-couple' the ducts to the carburettors. Carburettors need to

9-9. The cool air duct for the induction system is well in evidence and very important, but I have to tell you that I took this shot principally to illustrate the superb fibreglass Racetorations radiator air duct. It funnels the maximum amount of air from the front of the car to the radiator for maximum cooling effect, and looks good too. Far better than the standard fibreboard one I have on my car and *much* more effective than no duct at all.

suck tranquil air in, not have it forced in supercharging style! Photograph 9-9 will show what I mean.

• The air filter is important – and the open box Jaguar XJ6 style is an idea pattern to copy, although there are alternatives available. A pair if K&Ns are also acceptable and you can see a picture of a suitable pair in picture 9-10.

9-10. These are K&N KN56-1400 pancake air filters in front of the SUs with a heat shield behind the carburettors. This heat shield would be even more effective where it to have self-adhesive heat-reflective foil on the rear face.

Using SUs competitively

A pair of 1.75in SUs provides plenty of capacity for the 2.5 litre six-cylinder engine. The uniformity of emulsification from SU carburettors can probably be improved though, by fitting three 1½in SUs to the six-cylinder engine. This is something those who race on particularly tight budgets may wish to experiment with. This approach should bring about some improvement in air/fuel distribution and performance, but I wouldn't bother doing it unless you can lay hands on a suitable inlet manifold. To the best of my knowledge there isn't one available, and the cost of making an efficient bespoke/custom manifold puts the suggestion out of court.

Instead, particularly for occasional track days, you can change the dashpot/cover/needle assemblies on both SUs at the trackside quite quickly to transform the car's track performance. This allows for a sedate economical drive to and from the track day on your standard road-going twin SU set-up. Upon arrival at the meeting you switch top-end assemblies on both carburettors to pre-prepared and tested 'race' assemblies. These will be fitted with enlarged/concave shaped needles, no oil in the

dampers and with the return-damper spring omitted. This will increase the acceleration and mid-range performance to that of a Weber, knock a complete hole in your mpg economy, and put you to within a few percent points of a Weber's top end performance – perhaps only 5 or 8% less. All that for £5 to £10 and some rolling road set-up times.

Swapping Strombergs for SUs

Many TR owners view the Zenith-Stromberg as inferior to the equivalent SU. Strombergs were never as easy for the home enthusiast to adjust and tune, possibly by design, for they were fundamentally pre-set at the factory. However, they need to seen in the context of providing equal power as the SU with fewer emissions, at least for engines in standard tune. Furthermore, TR250/6 owners who have switched to SUs from the original Zenith-Stromberg (without further engine modifications), have found it impossible to detect a difference in their car's performance.

On upgraded six-cylinder engines, however, the 175 Stromberg carbs are likely to be disappointing, particularly if they're still fitted with the emission control equipment. The gas flow that is required by an upgraded 2500/2700cc engine-producing, say, 150-180bhp is probably beyond the Strombergs since they have a shorter piston movement than the 1.75in SU. However, before you make the change to SUs, particularly if you are experiencing difficulty finding a pair if suitable carbs, try some experiments with the needles/springs/top assemblies from an old pair of Strombergs. The method

9-11. The anti-run on valves introduced in the early 1970s may have helped run on tendancies, but did nothing for the air flow through the carburettor. They can and should be removed, and new discs fitted to the throttle spindles. If you suffer from run on take a look at the index in *How to Restore Triumph TR5/250 & 6.*

and reasoning outlined above for SUs will hold good for the Strombergs and you have very little to lose.

For those keen to get straight to the easier-to-adjust SUs, find a pair of ex-Saloon/Sedan HS6s with the identity tag BDU (2500TC or 2500S, post 1974). These cars will also yield the best inlet manifold for the 'sixes' fitted with an UK inlet ported head, as depicted in photograph 9-6. Wherever you live, you're best avoiding SUs with waxstats (on the bottom), since the consequential heat on the 'stat can incorrectly adjust the SU! Also, you should avoid carburettors with the anti-run-on valves incorporated in the throttle butterflies, shown in picture 9-11.

Whatever your SU, it's a good idea to fit a heat shield between your carburettors and the heat generated by the engine and its exhaust manifold. You may have noted an example in photo 9-10. They are particularly helpful when unleaded fuel is used since this boils at a much lower temperature than leaded fuel.

For those living in hilly or mountainous regions, SUs have one further advantage: they automatically correct the mixture level with changes in elevation and thinning air.

Enlarging the choke size

It's important not to over-provide choke or carburettors bore size. It is tempting to think your standard 2500cc engine will go better with 2in SUs. This is unlikely to be the case for it is absolutely essential to generate sufficient vacuum within the carb to draw fuel into the carburettor's venturi. If you over-provide choke size, your engine may not generate enough air speed to draw fuel evenly, at least at low rpm. So in general, standard or fast road 2500cc six-pots may not move sufficient air volume to generate low-down torque from (twin) 2in (50mm) chokes, although a highly tuned 2500 engine might be worth a try. A 2700cc six-cylinder engine is the most likely entry point for 2in SUs – but do not dispose of your 1.75in too quickly!

For the majority of readers who are interested in improving their standard, fast-road or ultra fast road TR, the tunability and versatility of the SU is very hard to beat. If you're thinking about a competitive car where absolute performance is your only interest, then, of course, the Weber is your route. It's interesting, and indeed relevant,

to note that, in general, the higher an engine's tune the more effective a Weber becomes at coaxing even more power out.

WEBER CARBURETTORS
It's not just the carbs

I opened up the section on SU carburettors by stressing that there were other related components that, like links in a chain, were at least as important as the carburettor. With the Weber carburettor these related components are even more important if the full top end performance of the engine is to be realised. I've stressed the cost of the Weber carburettor setup, of course, but you need to regard their installation in the context that if you're buying the most advanced and potentially powerful carburettors, you'll nullify their potential if just one of the other parts is not up to scratch. The cam, exhaust, ignition, gas-flowing/valves/compression ratio of the cylinder head, the pistons, con-rods, crankshaft, air-supply and air-filters all need to be equally matched and of the highest calibre. These topics are all dealt with elsewhere in this offering but the matter is of such importance if you are going for the ultimate in engine output that I feel it's essential to set the scene here.

The inlet manifold is one of these very important links in the performance chain. Moss sells a manifold assembly in three separate sections, whilst a TWM single casting manifold is available from the US. The linkages are rose jointed and included, the casting is of excellent quality and, at around £200, this kit appears the better value for money (picture 9-12).

You're advised to fit air filters/'socks' to each choke's ram pipe. These foam

9-13. A very nice Weber installation included to highlight the inlet trumpets – which come in various lengths and can effect the rpm band for maximum torque. Note the fuel pressure regulator nicely located on top of the driver's footwell (very bottom left of picture).

9-14. These intake trumpets have been covered by a one-piece 'sock' foam air-filter by ITG. Pipercross make similar such filters & both suppliers off one or two-piece socks.

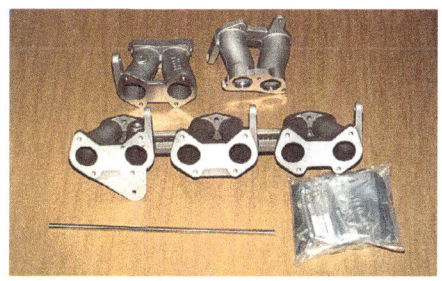

9-12. The six-cylinder's single piece manifold is in the foreground, while the pair of individual manifolds for the four-cylinder engine is at the back. The bag of fittings makes up the rest of your manifold kit.

type air filters will cost about £50 in total, but allow the ram pipes (fit long ram pipes), to remain in place, thus smoothing the airflow into each choke and maximising the carb's performance. They can change the torque characteristics of your induction single handedly. You can see the naked ram pipes in picture 9-13, and a suitably socked pair in picture 9-14. K&N air filters (picture 9-15), are another consideration but, since they apply to several induction systems, we'll look at them in a little more detail later in the chapter.

Ideally you should also fit an airbox to deliver cool air from the front of the car. An example can be seen in picture 9-16. Where there is room you should consider the relevant ram pipe the first priority and, if you can't get a complete

9-15. I can tell you with complete confidence that these are K&Ns. I personally prefer the K&N filters but the enforced absence of the trumpets may be too high a price to pay. Only the rolling road results will tell you what is best for your car.

A fully gas-flowed and ported cylinder head is essential. Inserts for unleaded fuel do not improve performance, but you should take the opportunity to 'unlead' the head too. You need to have the combustion chambers balanced and the compression ratio set for at least 9.5:1.

Bearing in mind that, since we're at the competition end of the tuning and the rpm spectrums, expect forged con-rods, steel crankshafts, camshaft bearings and stronger cam followers to require consideration/budgeting.

An extractor exhaust manifold and enlarged bore exhaust system are mandatory and the costs also need to be borne in mind.

Kit costs

As I have said earlier, the vast majority of road-going cars will be well served by other means of induction. Some ultra fast road cars may opt for three 40DCOE Webers while triple 45DCOEs for competition cars will provide for better performance right at the top of the rev-range. As a rule-of-thumb, therefore, I suggest that unless you expect to be consistently using your engine at and above 5000rpm, you're almost certainly wasting your money on Weber carburettors.

The induction kit seen in picture

airbox into the space available with the ram pipes in place, duct cold air as per photograph 9-17.

No point in having all this wonderful carburation capability if the camshaft is not hot enough to allow the engine to scavenge properly. Expect duration of *circa* 285/290, with lift in the order of 0.39 to 0.40in.

The fuel supply volume and pressure is very important (and not cheap), but since this topic is shared with other induction systems it will be discussed later in the chapter. Speaking of fuel, however, Webers have a reputation for supplying a rich mixture at low revs, which can make for difficult starting particularly when hot. There's not much you can do about the rich mixture,

in that this is where the power comes from, but you can minimise starting difficulties by ensuring your ignition system is upgraded to deliver a much larger spark than that presented by the standard system. The ignition curve and timing needs to be correct, of course, and 11 degrees static btdc and 31 degree total (*i.e.* a 10 degree distributor advance), will be the order of the day.

9-16. An air box for a four-cylinder car. Note the cold air duct exiting picture right and the crankcase breather and flame trap roughly in the centre of the picture. You'll need a very similar arrangement for your six-cylinder engine.

9-17. The fresh/cool air duct to the carburettors shown here is a very worthwhile suggestion if you want to get the maximum efficiency from any induction system. Here we do not have an airbox in place, but as a second-best arrangement are ducting air to the vacinity of the Webers.

9-18 costs in the region of £1500-1750, including links, filters and air boxes. For this sort of sum you can get a fully reconditioned PI system setup on your car (which is very hard to beat), or go a long way towards a Webcon or Lumenition efi kit.

Rolling roads

The carbs must be jetted adequately 'out of the box' to allow you to get to a rolling road for fine tuning. Unless you do an all-inclusive deal (which I would advise), there will be the additional costs to budget for. You must get assurances from your potential supplier that he will 'coarse' jet each carb for your application, and I would only buy my set from a supplier who will include an hour or two on a rolling road once the car is running. However, if the engine is new, and therefore 'tight', a second, rather shorter rolling road check will be necessary once the engine is run-in, and you'll probably have to pay for that.

The chokes and emulsion tubes should be correct and unlikely to need revision, but there may be some small adjustments to make to air correction and/or main jets. Consequently, a fine tuning session on the rolling road is essential, and this will be true each time you fit or change a bolt-on tuning 'goody'. You'll need to consider, therefore, whether it's best to make all your tuning changes at the same time. You should also buy as much of your improvement kit (*i.e.* cam, exhaust, *etc.*, as well as the carbs), from a single supplier, and ideally take your car to that same supplier's rolling road. If you live a long way from your supplier this may be impractical – but if it is practical then you'll probably be

able to negotiate a package deal so that your rolling road session is part of your improvement kit deal.

Naturally all the suppliers I spoke to are ready, willing and able to fit the parts to the car if that's your preference, but you'll get as much advice as you need over the telephone if you decide to fit the parts yourself.

Choke sizes

The DCOE Weber carbs we are interested in come in two choke or venturi sizes and you need to select the one most suited to your expected use. The smaller 40mm choke provides for higher airflow through the chokes and thus earlier/low speed torque. It's the better choice for most road going applications. The larger 45mm choke size obviously allows for a slower airflow through the carb and will give more power at the higher engine revolutions. This is the preferred choice for competition applications.

Jet sizes

Since, if you follow my suggested route, you are only going to go to the expense of Webers if you are competing in race or sprints, it follows that there is no point in buying the 40DCOEs and that you will be jetting your 45DCOEs for maximum performance and power. These are the sort of jets you can expect to fit, but do not go looking at the resultant fuel consumption figures, you will only upset yourself:

Main venturi for six-cylinder engines	33mm
Auxiliary venturi	4.5
Main jet	125

Emulsion jet	F16
Air jet	185
Idler jet	50F9
Pump	40

You will get much more detailed information from Des Hammill's book, *How to Build and Power Tune Weber and Dellorto DCOE, DCO/SP & DHLA Carburettors*.

Webers versus PI

Firstly, there is little difference in performance, certainly in any road going application, between Weber carburettor cars and those fitted with a well tuned Lucas PI system. However, Webers can easily be jetted to suit any cam and/or engine condition, and that certainly is not so with an injection system. On the assumption that the engine and PI system are in good condition and correctly tuned, the PI system is better at delivering the correct fuel/air ratio over a wide range of engine speeds. It is, however, susceptible to engine and PI system wear. Overall I think the PI system and triple Weber carburettors on a six-cylinder engine are evenly balanced.

There are a couple of important differences, though, starting with the fact that PI is a very specialised topic and you can't take the car to just any tuning shop and expect experienced servicing, tuning or spares. Webers are much better understood by a wider selection of tuning shops and many will even stock most of the parts required. Webers score again with their accelerator pump, an advantage that neither PI, Stromberg or SU carburettors enjoy. Consequently, when you put your foot down with a Weber carburettor you automatically inject fuel into the cylinders, which provides for a surge in acceleration. The competitors all inject fuel by vacuum, which, while very effective when set up correctly, will lag an accelerator pump most of the time.

Weber versus SU

In a racing environment, as we have already evaluated, the Webers are best at providing top-end power. We have also mentioned that SUs can be made to go **much** better than most enthusiasts realise. I read some comparisons that one owner made between **standard** SUs and triple 40DCOE Webers on his six-cylinder engine which I thought were interesting and relevant. He said

9-18. The Weber setup ready to bolt to a race car. These are 45DCOEs allowing maximum top-end fuelling. Note the three individual heat shields and the intake trumpets.

that with the standard (*i.e.* unmodified), SU he was peaking at 119bhp at the rear wheels. With the same engine and related components, of course, but using 3x40 choked Webers, the maximum power increased to 131bhp. What I found particularly interesting were the improvements up the rev range, which he listed as 3-5% in the 2500-4000 rpm range, 10% at 5000rpm and 12% at 5500. However, I believe that up to about the 4500-4750rpm (a range that few fast road cars exceed with any frequency), I think the SUs could have been made to go just as well, for rather less expenditure!

RELATED INDUCTION DETAILS
Fuel pumps
Regardless of which carburettor you use, I would advise the use of a solid state electric. I would suggest a Facet Red Top for six-cylinder cars up to ultra fast road, but you may need to take advice and run two pumps for competitive use. Available from Demon Tweeks, these are an essential contributor to this performance package, particularly if you are expecting to 'press-on' occasionally. They are best mounted close to and just below the bottom of the fuel tank. I've used a Red Top with a Weber AFB carb for many years without any problems but if you experience carburettor flooding as the result of higher fuel-line pressures I suggest you try fitting an adjustable fuel pressure regulator close to the carburettors to overcome the problem. **Picture 9-19** shows a fuel pressure regulator in this context.

Fuel hoses
Braided fuel hoses are available from many suppliers, and these are recommended for added security against chaffing. You can buy a variety of hoses from our specialist contributors with and without a fuel cut-off tap. This is usually a very good idea, providing additional safety when working on the fuel system or laying the car up.

If you are ever tempted to reuse a length of flexible fuel hose – don't, at least without checking on its compatibility with unleaded fuels. What seems like a perfectly sound flexible fuel hose from the outside may have been eaten away from the inside by the unleaded fuel you are now using, or are about to use.

Also bear in mind that flexible fuel hoses, even if they are compatible with unleaded fuels, come in varying grades,

and that for any flexible hose running inside the cockpit or boot you need the appropriate grade that will not permeate fuel vapours. A third grade of fuel line is available (and **must** be used) for competition use.

K&N FILTERS
Wherever possible, buy your air filters at the same time as you buy your carburettors. Try to ensure that your preferred supplier handles a range of filters, K&N, Pipercross and JR, for example, so that his advice is not coloured by what's available in his stores.

It's surprisingly difficult to find sufficient space for adequate air filters within the engine bay of a six-cylinder car. ITG does a good range of filters that will fit. However, we need to look at numerous other solutions as the chapter progresses.

Your air filter is very important indeed in two ways: keeping harmful dirt out of your engine; but doing so with the very minimum of restriction to air flow. The contribution your air filter makes to the smooth and efficient

9-19. We saw a fuel pressure regulator (not to be confused with an efi component of the same name), from some distance a few pictures back. This is the beast in close-up.

airflow to the carburettors should not be underestimated. However, because I feel the majority of readers will be using applications that suit K&N filters (*e.g.* SU, Strombergs or Petrol Injection), I intend to focus this section on K&Ns, and you may be surprised at the variety of shapes, sizes and types that are available.

Why a low resistance air filter?
The simple answer to this question is, of course, improving engine efficiency. Some may look for the improved efficiency to show up as better mpg.

Generally, depending upon your vehicle, driving habits, load on the engine (towing, for example), existing air system restriction, and other factors, low resistance air filters will usually improve fuel economy. However, efficiency changes are usually best measured by rolling-road power curves rather than a subjective and very imprecise measurement like mpg which depends on traffic density, weather and driving style. Typical dyno results show an increase of 2 to 4% bhp purely by fitting a low resistance air filter. You may think that because the engine is running more efficiently you will, if anything, be able to lean the mixture. The opposite is required, in fact, and you should (back to the rolling road or at least a gas analyser), richen the mixture screw(s) slightly because the engine is now flowing more air and needs more fuel to maintain the ideal fuel/air ratio.

Not surprisingly, different makes of filter use different methods of construction. To the best of my understanding synthetic fibre, foam or paper filters don't have the very small fibres that the cotton used by K&N does. One of the additional advantages of the K&N method of construction allows the filter to be re-used after washing. While you should check the filter annually you will probably find it unnecessary to actually wash it more frequently than every 30,000-50,000 miles, depending on driving conditions. The filters come pre-oiled, but will need re-oiling after every wash. Full fitting, washing and oiling instructions are supplied with every K&N, and in my view it's worth sticking to K&N cleaning and oiling materials.

The filter media is made from layers of white cotton gauze and can be damaged if you're not careful. You can brush it with a **soft** brush, but nothing too stiff or hard. The cleaner is a non-detergent degreaser which will not harm the filter, while most solvents will attack and/or harden the rubber seals. A mild detergent might be a possibility but thoroughly rinsing detergents out of a filter is rather like getting soap out of a sponge – it takes ages. K&N oil is blended to provide a very efficient tack barrier and has a red dye added to show how much is being applied. If the filter looks pinkish-red, it is oiled. Never use one un-oiled as it would lose much of its filtering ability. Alternatives like mineral oil will soften and destroy the rubber sealing edges of the filter.

Chapter 10

Electronic fuel-injection & engine management

Engine management, in simple terms, consists of two electronically-interlocked systems, the computer-controlled ignition discussed in Chapter 7 and, using the same computer or ECU, a electronically-controlled fuel injection system. It's time to explore the other half of engine management, electronic fuel injection, and look at some methods of integration in the six-cylinder TRs.

EFI – AN OVERVIEW

TR engines, like any internal combustion engine, can be supplied with fuel by electronic injection. Would-be converters have two basic alternative routes to their goal, but perhaps even before we start exploring these it might

be helpful to take a general overview of how electronic fuel injection works, starting with its advantages and disadvantages:

• efi is 'greener', probably with less harmful emissions than carburettors, and some systems ultimately offer the ability to use a three-way catalytic converter to be 'fully' green.
• More fuel-effective, offering more power for any given fuel consumption: which isn't quite the same as saying it offers lower fuel consumption!
• efi has some ability to self-adjust to modifications and is ideal in its ability to cope with all road going conditions. Proper mapping provides the correct

mixture for any given set of conditions improving power, torque and drivability.
• It's the way engine management will go in the future, with, in my opinion, increasing rapidity, and it may be prudent to anticipate the trend, particularly if you envisage owning your TR for many years and perhaps one day having to submit it to rigorous exhaust emission tests.
• It's considerably more complex and will almost certainly be more expensive than conventional induction systems.

As owners of many six-cylinder PI cars will already appreciate, efi is quite different to any carburettor fuel supply arrangement, and it's essential we explore efi fuel flow principals, perhaps in conjunction with my schematic outline diagram D10-1. The fuel flow starts with the fuel tank, but even an efi fuel tank is different to its carburettor counterpart. An efi tank needs to have a vortex generating swirl pot in the initial feed pipe (to ensure the fuel has no air bubbles in it), and also has a fuel return pipe to handle the large volumes of fuel returned to the tank as a matter of routine. Many readers will already see some parallels with Triumph's Petrol Injection, and, although there will be differences in detail, the basic similarities will continue.

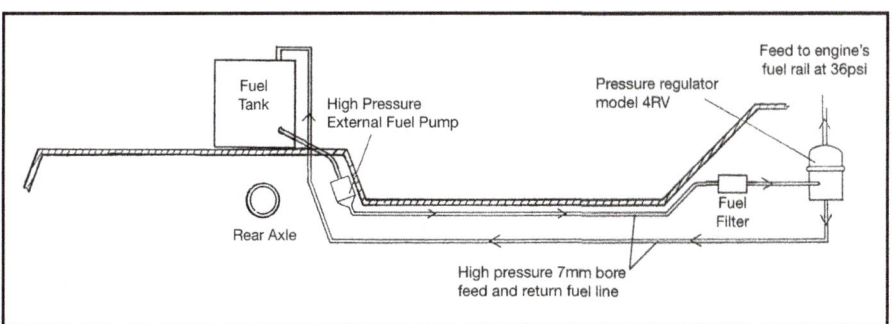

D10-1. Schematic outline of efi fuel-flow.

The pump and pipework

The efi's fuel pump is quite different to the fuel pump required for carburettor induction, but not all that different to a PI fuel pump. Many may be surprised to hear that most efi fuel pumps 'only' generate about 60psi, roughly 40% less than the Triumph PI system pump. Since lots of cars use efi systems, suitable secondhand pumps are readily available from a variety of makes and models. In fact, almost any externally pumped efi car can provide a pump. The exceptions are those cars with their fuel pump integral within the fuel tank. A model 4FP fuel pump is ideal and, unlike the PI system's original Lucas pump, the efi pump must be mounted in line with the bottom of your fuel tank. Photographs 10-1-1 and 10-1-2 show some fuel pump locations, all of which should be fed from the fuel tank's swirl pot with an 11mm bore (12mm o/d) pipe.

10-1-1. Although this is my MGB, this shot does demonstrate the need for the efi fuel pump to be mounted low in the car's structure.

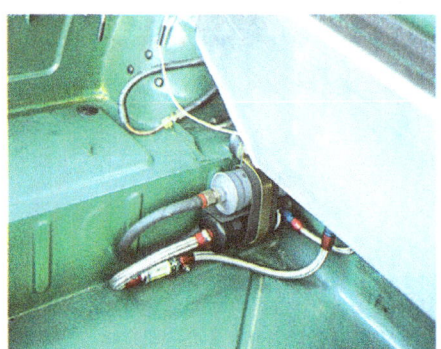

10-1-2. This is the conventional Bosch fuel pump location for a TR, but with an efi system up front you need a different fuel pump generating about half the psi required by the original PI system. The efi pumps are readily available at most breakers' yards.

These pumps distribute fuel via five rotating metal rollers. They supply at high pressure and in considerable volume but, conversely, do not draw fuel well and, if strained, can make a considerable noise. If the pump is noisy it's either mounted above the bottom of your fuel tank, is worn, or has restrictions before or after the pump. If your pump is still noisy, having resolved these problems, wire in a resistor from another efi system to reduce the pump's running voltage, which usually reduces pump noise.

You'll need to pipe the pressure side of the pump via a 6 or 7mm i/d pipe to a fuel filter (Lucas part number 6FU or Unipart number GFE7096), located under the car or in the engine compartment. If space is limited try one of the much smaller **injection** filters used on many Vauxhalls. These employ identical push on ends to the 6FU and carry AC Delco part number GF516 or Motoquip's part no. VFF 154. The 6FU series filter should be changed at least every 48,000 miles, or four years, whilst the smaller ones are rated at two years or 24,000 miles. With all the debris that can be picked up from older and dirty petrol station tanks

I would, in fact, recommend halving both those service intervals and suggest you consider fitting two fuel filters, one before and one after the pump.

Fuel can now be pumped at about 60psi through the fuel pipes to the fuel rails which complete a circuit of the engine's cylinder head. As the fuel rail runs around the engine the (electronically controlled), injectors are 'T'd off' at the appropriate locations opposite each of the six cylinders. We can see this inphotograph 10-1-3. At the tail end of the fuel rail, **after** the injectors, comes the fuel pressure regulator. This is vacuum controlled but on average regulates the fuel in the fuel rail to about 36psi. The system works by pumping large volumes of fuel, so the (considerable), excess released by the pressure regulator is returned from the engine compartment to the fuel tank via a second 'return' fuel pipe.

The injectors

There are efi systems where there is one main injector. However, all those we are looking at use one injector per cylinder and are, therefore, called multi-point

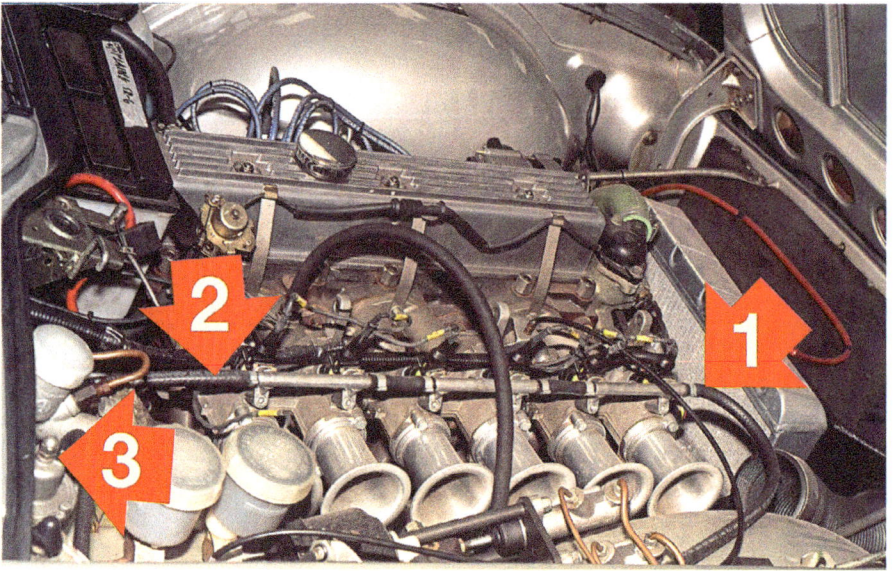

10-1-3. The fuel rail on an efi system runs in a loop starting from where the feed pipe enters the engine bay from the rear mounted fuel pump. It usually goes through a fuel filter at this point and from there to the front of the engine and rearwards (arrows 1 and 2), presenting a 'tee' to each fuel injector. It then runs to its pressure control valve (sometimes called a fuel pressure regulator), shown, in this case, by arrow 3. This a slightly special FPR that is referred to as a 'rising rate' (x1.7 fuel pressure), regulator. The torque enhancing air intake trumpets improve the flow in efi cars too. Did you spot air tube to allow cool air to the system, the twin brake master cylinder reservoirs and the aluminium water radiator?

injection systems. Each open on a command from an electronic control unit (ECU) that is basically a small computer. Most people assume that the injectors are phased to open with each cylinder's inlet valve. Usually this is not so, the injectors open simultaneously on the vast majority of efi systems.

The ECU is programmed, or 'mapped', to hold the injectors open for the right period of time to suit the engine's circumstances. The engine's circumstances vary, of course, and data regarding throttle opening position, air flow, engine rpm, engine coolant temperature and exhaust oxygen (in the case of a catalyst car), all affect the ECU's 'decisions' and injector opening time. Additionally, the amount of inlet manifold vacuum controls the fuel pressure regulator via a diaphragm/vacuum pipe arrangement, very similar to the advance/retard mechanism within a distributor, and thus the pressure of the fuel in the fuel rails.

The final preliminary I would like to explore before getting down to specifics is that there are three types of efi triggering systems. The earliest system used the distributor to not only inform the ECU of the position of the engine as well as its speed, but also to distribute the high tension electrics to generate a spark. Later efi systems (1980s, for example), no longer use the distributor to tell the ECU where the engine is (and its rpm). Sensors on the crankshaft do that job more accurately but the distributor is retained in its original guise, however, to break the primary ignition circuit and distribute the sparks. The 1990s saw the efi system triggered by the crankshaft sensors – but now the distributor's ignition role had been superseded too by engine management systems that control the sparks. You'll see the relevance of this evolution as the chapter progresses.

MEASURING THE AIRFLOW

The fuel needs to be mixed precisely with the incoming air, and there are three ways of measuring the fuel requirements for a given rpm: 1) Measure the flow of air to the throttle-body(s), and the position of the throttle butterfly(s). This is the 'air-flow' or 'air-mass' systems used on many production engines. 2) Measure the pressure in the inlet manifold. The manifold absolute pressure (MAP) system used by some production engines where a multi-cylinder inlet

plenum can be incorporated into the design and used to supply the ECU with pulse-free information. 3) Measure the position of the throttle using a throttle positioning system sensor. This TPS method is used by the vast majority of competition engines. Today's ECUs can use any of these inputs, or a combination of them, to work out the engine's fuelling requirement, and, most importantly, they are easily reprogrammable. We will look at programmable ECUs in more detail shortly, but first we'll explore each of these general fuelling options in a little more detail.

Most enthusiasts have heard of air flow metering (AFM) and/or air mass (also called 'hot-wire') metering, and some will even have an air-flow measuring system on their 'daily drivers'. Photographs 10-1-4 and 10-1-5 will provide confirmation of these forms of metering. The air-flow/mass meter systems used in many other production cars have the advantage of being independent of production tolerances/wear in the engine and of being generally

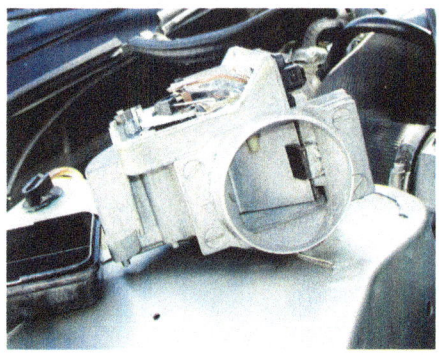

10-1-4. The air-flow or 'flapper' method of measuring air flow volume.

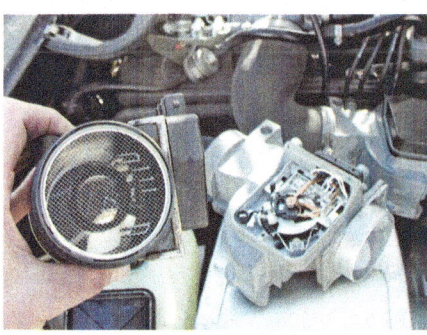

10-1-5. The long-term reliability of the LH air mass meter seen on the left is better than the L-Jet's flapper meter, since there are no moving parts to wear.

foolproof. A throttle position sensor is still fitted, but is mainly used to give the ECU basic data on rate of opening and roughly where the throttle is – *i.e.* open or shut. However, high performance engines find the air-flow and, to a lesser extent, the air-mass meters intrusive, particularly so when the throttle-body has individual intakes requiring a complex single intake passage through, of necessity, one air meter. The system requires an inlet plenum for the straight six-cylinder engines, see pictures 10-1-6 and 10-1-7, but there are alternatives.

In fact, the same limitation applies to manifold absolute pressure (MAP) control. These systems are also known as speed density systems, and can perhaps best be described as working in reverse to engine vacuum. A high MAP reading equals low vacuum and thus high engine load. Light load produces low MAP readings or high vacuum. The MAP sensor seen at 10-1-8 requires only a vacuum hose to the intake plenum, but pulsing and variation in individual intake pressures restricts its use to a common plenum (*i.e.* one single inlet) air-feed system, as would be the case in a TR250/5/6.

A throttle positioning system can be accurately set, via a sensor like that shown in picture 10-1-9, to fit the particular engine's fuel mapping. The advantage of such systems is that you don't need to closely control or monitor the air entering the system. On the other hand, any degradation brought about by spindle-wear or for any other reason will be immediately reflected in engine performance. This is not an issue with typical performance engines, and probably not with most readers' cars,

10-1-6. The TR5/6 plenum can be modified with an adaptor ring to provide the essential airtight connection with ...

10-1-7. ... the (left to right) air-filter, air-flow-meter, and flexible connecting hose in question.

10-1-8. A close-up of the MAP sensor as mounted on the side of the plenum. MAP systems are much less sensitive to vacuum leaks, which are the scourge of MAF-controlled EFI, but merely generate increased idle in a MAP system.

10-1-9. Albeit on a DCOE carburetor, this throttle position sensor and its electrical connection to the (out of shot) ECU are plain the see.

but is not ideal in family saloons doing high mileages. TPS is, therefore, today's route to efi or engine management for (four- and) six-cylinder TRs, and we'd better look at some of the constituent components and systems.

TPS INLET MANIFOLDS AND THROTTLE-BODIES

The 'straight' engines we're focused upon have aftermarket inlet manifolds primarily supplied for Weber DCOE conversions. The manifolds we saw in chapter 9 may be included in any complete kit of efi/engine manifold parts you purchase, but they are available individually from most TR specialists. They might be supplied as a trio of castings, intended, of course, for fitting three DCOEs, or the single casting shown in picture 10-1-10.

The manifolds are simple castings devoid of any temperature sensors (which are usually found in most 'production' manifolds) and the location of sensors may exercise your mind until you look back to picture 7-4-4 for clues. These manifolds provide the link

between the engine and the all-important throttle-body that not only provides a platform for mounting the injectors, but a throttle butterfly for each cylinder.

In theory you have a choice of butterfly, barrel, or slide throttle controls in the throttle-body, each of which requires its own specially-designed throttle-body. However, for the vast majority of readers with the level of power, technology and rpm associated with our classic engines, butterflies offer the most progressive throttle control and optimum power. The practicalities of installation and availability are also factors. Consequently, we'll only be exploring butterfly controlled throttle-bodies in this chapter, but even so, there is more to selecting a throttle-body than you might imagine.

The technology related to just butterfly throttle-bodies is complex, so you're best to use an experienced supplier and, ideally, a proven kit for your engine. However, with thanks to Jenvey Dynamics for guidance and photographs, I would mention that there are three major initial factors (in addition to a host of consequential details) to consider: which type of butterfly body; the related mounting arrangement (inlet manifold); and the throttle-body bore size. In many ways these factors are interlocked, but, for clarity, we'll consider them one by one.

For all practical purposes there are two types of throttle-body. Twin-body units, similar to a Weber DCOE carburettor design are almost certainly the

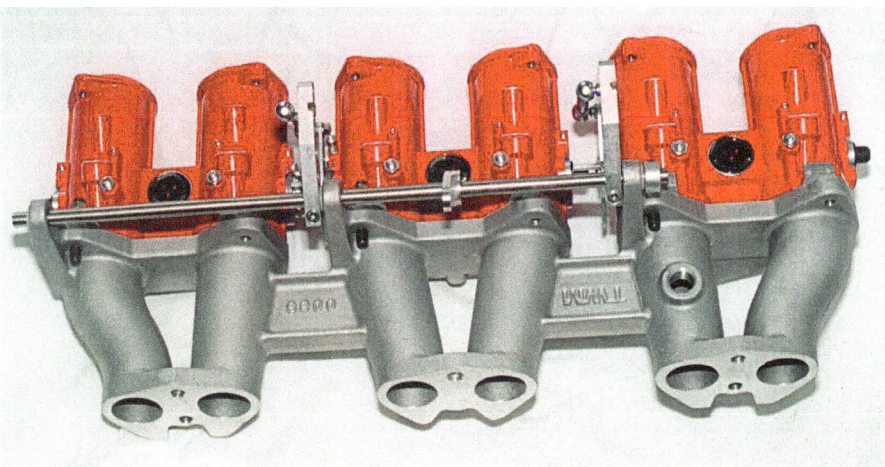

10-1-10. Such inlet manifolds are usually cast and machined with Weber DCOE carburation in mind, but provide the marriage with three DCOE-sized twin throttle-bodies here.

10-1-11 Jenvey's standard/stock single throttle-body.

10-1-12 An alternative single throttle-body.

10-1-13 Very short bodies have no space for injectors, but this 91mm long twin throttle-body with a DCOE pattern flange has injector mountings, while ...

most frequently used throttle-body in our environment. However, single-body units are technically likely to offer more power, but double the mounting and linkage complexities. Both types are available in a variety of body lengths, as you can see from photos 10-1-11 and 10-1-12.

Professionals tend to start by selecting a suitable inlet manifold and the relevant number of twin-bodied throttle-bodies, and, as stated earlier, most of the engines we're exploring have a cast 'DCOE' inlet manifold available, and that's usually the basis of the engine/throttle-body marriage. Two lengths can be seen in photos 10-1-13 and 10-1-14.

When it comes to throttle-body bore-size, there has to be an initial impulse to fit the largest bore you can. However, throttle-body bore size is governed by your choice of inlet manifold bore and, rather like a carburettor, too large a throttle-body bore lowers the flow resistance and the speed of air-flow. Naturally, a smaller diameter will speed the airflow but also improve throttle-response/control and atomisation of the mixture – so expert advise is invaluable on this one detail alone! Regardless of bore diameter, you should fit the straightest manifold that space, circumstances, and availability allows, not forgetting to make allowances for the essential inlet ram pipes upstream of each throttle-body. Ram pipes are a technology in themselves, but the effect of length will be along similar lines to those mentioned on page78.

The other vital contribution the throttle-body makes is to provide a mounting for the injectors. Picture 10-1-15 shows not only the injectors

but a very neat fuel-rail too. A multi-point system employs one injector per cylinder, and the size (i.e. flow capacity) of the injectors is a consideration as is the angle and the position/location of the injectors. Usually the best position, particularly for retrofitted performance based installations, is immediately downstream of the butterfly to maximise the atomisation of the mixture via the air-turbulence created by the butterfly.

The injector's seat in the throttle-body is another issue for consideration, in respect to diameter, length and seal. Most of the better-known injector manufacturers seem to have settled on a common 14mm O-ring seal, but injector-lengths can still vary and, in turn, can affect your choice of fuel-rail. Then there's the question of electrical impedance of the injectors – 16ohms is the norm these days, but they must be matched to the ECU's requirements, and might be best purchased simultaneously with the ECU to avoid any miss-matches.

Take a look at Jenvey's website for

10-1-14 ... this alternative is 118mm long with injector mountings.

10-1-15. Although this pair of twin throttle-bodies are mounted on a Honda compatible inlet manifold, I thought the picture showed the injector, ram pipes and fuel rail so well as to merit inclusion.

additional detail on throttle-bodies and note (later in the chapter) the frequency with which its throttle-bodies are incorporated into the pre-assembled efi and/or engine management kits that are available.

PROGRAMMABLE ECUS

The heart of any computer-managed system is the ECU – often located well out of sight but, nevertheless, the driving-force behind any ignition, efi or engine management system. Although not the main focus for TRs, you may be interested to hear that they can be retro-fitted as a replacement ECU for an existing efi system if you wish to modernize and ease the tweaking of the system – provided the injectors in particular are compatible with the ECU's output. One example is Superchips' fully-mapped ignition conversions for existing efi systems. These use the Lumenition Optronic distributor trigger and are well proven. The conversion requires the distributor baseplate be tack-welded so no movement is possible, after which the Lumenition trigger is simply connected to a solid extension of the camshaft and, therefore, engine rotation. A remote ECU is reprogrammed by Superchips but is easily altered by use of a dedicated hand-held programmer that can be hired or bought separately. These systems are 'only' 2 dimensional, but the mapping is still far better than any mechanical system can ever achieve. Consequently, more torque, a smoother engine, more power, and better fuel efficiency are quite normal improvements.

I'm sure that the majority of readers would wish to employ modern technology to the full, and thus maximize the potential of these, sometimes, very powerful computers, by fitting new fuel and ignition systems. However, while you certainly need to be thinking ahead to what you may eventually wish to fit to the car, there's no point in fitting computing capacity beyond your eventual needs. Naturally, you'll need to very careful to ensure that the ECU you're contemplating is compatible with the numerous other components you'll need. To my mind there's also much to be said for installing, proving, and getting experience of one half of the full engine management duo before developing the other half of the management system. I also think you'll minimize your complications if you buy as many components from one supplier as is possible.

The software is as important as the hardware, so you'll need to ask each potential supplier if they can provide a choice of fuel maps for your sort of engine and its state of tune. These are essential starting points, but adjustment will be necessary depending on your car and the use to which you're putting it. This leads me on to the ease of adjustment of the fuel/ignition maps. In most cases you'll need a laptop computer in order to carry out DIY tuning. You also need to ensure that your computer's ports (i.e. Serial, USB, etc.) are compatible with your short-listed suppliers' hardware, and that your operating software will talk to theirs (Windows 95 or better is a frequent stipulation). Some systems, Edelbrock's for example, are tunable but come with their own 'stand-alone' programming unit so you don't need a laptop – a detail that some may find preferable. Some systems, Webcon-Alpha springs to mind, can only be tuned/adjusted by an approved dealer. Some systems, such as those by Omex, can be 'locked' by a password, something I would recommend.

EXAMPLES OF AVAILABLE ECUS
Haltech

The Haltech E6X is the latest Haltech programmable ECU offering 'real-time' programming of fuel injection and ignition on 4-, 6- or 8-cylinders. The E8 ECU is capable of controlling sequential injection on 4-, 5-, 6-, 8- and 10-cylinder applications. With 8 channels capable of controlling injection and ignition duties, the E8 can support most modern engines with multi-coil ignition systems, as well as conventional distributor ignition systems and various auxiliary engine functions.

Holley

Holley is best known for its performance carburettors, but also offers the Commander 950 injection system and pre-assembled kits. These multi-point efi systems are intended to provide all the components and hardware needed, including intake manifold, billet throttle-body, billet fuel rails, injectors, and related miscellaneous parts that have been partially pre-assembled and tested prior to packaging. The heart of any efi system is the programmable ECU, and Holley claims its is easily programmed, and provides the user

with a high level of tuning flexibility. The Holley system allows for real-time tuning of all parameters via Windows-based software, and sounds good, but I think the company is aiming for the Ford and Chevy V8 market mainly.

MoTeC

The M48 is MoTeC's engine management system ECU providing sequential injection and individual cylinder fuel/ignition trims for up to 8-cylinder engines. It uses 3 dimensional fuel and ignition mapping and ignition control to give you the ability to drive your ignition modules and set your spark timing to its absolute best at all points. MoTeC claims that all M48 models have the accurate control necessary to meet legislated emissions requirements, including closed loop narrow band lambda control. It can utilise nearly all original equipment and aftermarket ignition triggers, modules and coils, and can be triggered by either a hall-effect switch, a logic drive, or a magnetic sensor. The M48 reads its sensors 2400 times per second, and the entire control program is recalculated 200 times per second, which demonstrates its power. Furthermore, there is a comprehensive group of computer software tools available for the M48, including: engine setup, tuning diagnostics and utilities; monitoring, data logging and analysis;

utilities for loading new program code and enabling special features.

MegaSquirt

MegaSquirt markets a programmable ECU in kit (i.e. component) form, which is suitable for engines with any number of cylinders up to 16. They are attractive for several reasons: the cost, the established forum, factory on-line support, and technical repair facilities. However, remember this Mega Squirt disadvantage – you need to assemble the ECU yourself, which requires soldering the numerous components to its printed circuit board. Mindful of this issue, MegaSquirt has set out to offer EFI without the user requiring:

• Programming skills – the necessary codes are already pre-loaded, and tuning is a straightforward Windows application.
• PROM burning experience – a serial port connection facilitates fuel tuning parameters as well as software updates.
• Advanced electronic skills – if you can solder and follow directions you should be able to assemble MegaSquirt's kit.
• The latest in laptops – MegaSquirt just stipulates a serial-ported laptop running Windows.

There are four elements to the MegaSquirt control system, and drawing D10-2 may help identify them. There

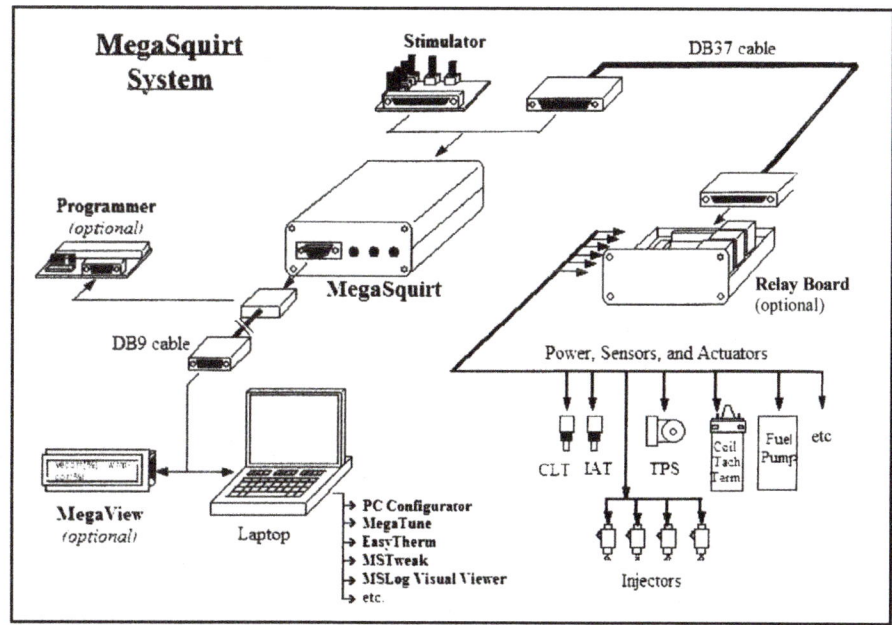

D10-2. The four elements to the MegaSquirt control system).

are two processors to choose from and three PCB options. The faster chip in the 'V3' (latest) PCB will give you the best and most easily installed system. The software consists of an embedded code (also known as firmware to the experts) stored in the ECU and the tuning software which is stored in and operated from your laptop. The tuning software also allows you to monitor the system's operation.

The MegaSquirt systems are in use, as their forum will confirm, with completely new installations on a wide variety of engines. Furthermore, the benefits of full engine management are considerable, if perhaps costly elsewhere, so it's good to know that you could, perhaps, install MegaSquirt's efi controls first, and then, at a later date, explore the other half of full engine management.

Omex

Omex advertises a range of bolt-on, plug-in throttle-body and engine management kits that will, of course, be based upon their most relevant ECU. Omex suggests this to be a simplified way of assembling a full set of engine management parts from one supplier at a fixed cost, with one technical back-up source, which, I must say, sounds very attractive. Furthermore, the company claims that whatever your engine and requirements, they can almost certainly be met, although I'm not sure this sweeping statement applies to Omex TR-related kits bought through its retailers, such a Demon Tweeks, which only lists relatively modern high-volume vehicles.

Omex certainly has a good range of ECUs, from its 100 series upward. As an example, the 600 model has the capacity for full engine management, and Omex claims it to be easy to install and map. The system offers 3D mapping and user adjustable correction tables which are programmable in real time, while the engine is running or when stationary. Suitable for normally-aspirated engines of up to 8-cylinders, the basic controlled parameters include: semi-sequential fuel injection for up to 4-cylinder engines or grouped (i.e. simultaneous) injection for up to 8-cylinder engines. Distributorless ignition is within this ECU's capacity for up to 4-cylinders, and distributor-controlled ignition for up to 8-cylinders. Two cooling fan controls are incorporated, along with a separate

tachometer, shift light, and fuel pump outputs. Mappable coolant temperature compensation/ enrichment for engine warm-up is standard/stock and full technical backup is also available.

The big advantage of the aftermarket systems/kits is that you have some technical backup if you strike installation or subsequent operational difficulties, and we'll look at two further kits in just a moment. Before that, you may be interested to explore some other programmable ECU information sources:

- DTA Race Electronics
  – www.dtafast.co.uk
- EFI Technology – www.efitech.co.uk
  or www.efitechnology.com
- Emerald – www.emeraldm3d.com
- General Engine Management Systems
  – www.gems.co.uk
- MBE Systems
  – www.mbesystems.com
- Racetech Developments
  – www.racetechdev.co.uk

ENGINE MANAGEMENT BY KIT

The smoothness and drivability of the six-cylinder cars fitted with efi has to be experienced to be believed. All the power and urge of the original Lucas system is retained, but the manners

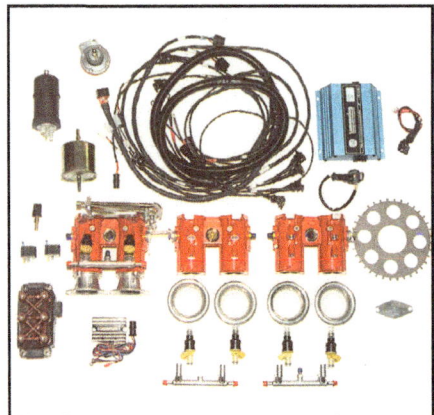

10-2-1. There is a very similar looking kit available for each of the five basic efi systems from Revington, this one happens to be one of the Lumenition ones for efi. Clockwise, I can see the (probably Bosch), fuel pump and filter, a rising rate pressure regulator, the significant wiring harness, the ECU, the crankshaft pulley timing wheel, the inlet manifolds, mini trumpets, injectors, fuel rail sections and the timing sensor and amplifier.

and reliability of the car are totally transformed to modern day standards. Indeed, I'd advise any reader who is about to spend many hundreds of pounds refurbishing the original PI system on their six to drive an efi car before taking the plunge. They'll find that the engine management system gets the timing and fuel ratios correct for every eventuality, and the drivability of the car really is transformed. This is achieved by three-dimensional fuel and ignition mapping, checked and adjusted quite automatically at millisecond intervals by the system's ECU. The frequency of the computer's sensor checks means that there is no time lag, which you can get with a carburettor induction system. You can select from several options, which I will detail later, and buy a kit of parts and the appropriate software. The cost will be in the order of £2500 to £3500 depending upon the kit you choose.

10-2-2. This is a full engine management (i.e. electronic fuel injection as well as ignition generation and timing), set-up on Revington's Lumenition test car while ...

10-2-3. ... this is the equivalent full engine management system using Webcon components.

There are two proprietary competitive systems designed for home installation using the Revington kits shown in photograph 10-2-1. You will get the flavour of each in pictures 10-2-2 and 10-2-3. Both use up-to-the-minute full engine management technology and, perhaps for this reason, the parts are expensive. I also suspect that the components have had to be designed to suit a wide range of applications and that this has done little to trim the costs. Perhaps because of the cost of a full-management system, both are available at various levels of sophistication, as can be seen from pictures 10-2-4 and 10-2-5. The top grades offer precise fuel and ignition control (*i.e.* full engine management), via in-car microprocessors (ECUs), and will bring your TR's engine management right up to date. The second proposal we will address shortly only offers control of the fuel systems. This fuel control can, of course, be supplemented by any of the ignition enhancement systems outlined in Chapter 7, or upgraded with the appropriate manufacturer's sparks package at a later date.

Two companies (Lumenition and Webcon-Alpha), supply programmable

10-2-4. The efi set-up is using Lumenition components. Note that the coil/distributor are still being used to generate and distribute the sparks, although you will also note that the vacuum advance has been removed from the dizzy. Running along the inner wing in the forefront of the picture are the pipes to/from the oil cooler with the (highly recommended), thermostatic control valve highlighted.

10-2-6. We are looking upwards from the floor of this TR at the underside of the passenger's footwell and seeing the ECU. This is certainly where I would recommend you site yours. This looks like a Bosch one to me, possibly transferred from a donor vehicle.

10-2-5. A nice comparative picture to 10-2-4 from almost the same angle, this shows the further stage of engine management. We can see the Webcon efi stuff on the far side, but, nearest the camera you'll note there is no coil or dizzy, just a very clever electronic 'black-box' to generate the sparks.

ECUs along with the requisite kits for throttle body injection, pumps, computers, amplifiers (to upgrade the initial signal to a level that will open your injectors), and sensors for a DIY engine management installation. The respective components are available from Demon Tweeks, Racetorations and, of course, Revington, who kindly supplied the majority of this information and photographs. The heart of the system is, of course, the ECU, which needs to be tucked safely out of harms way. Heat, knocks and water need to be avoided at all costs, and in photograph 10-2-6 we see the ECU tucked above the passenger-side footwell. The electrical wiring associated with either of these proprietary kits is inevitably complex, as picture 10-2-7 demonstrates. If therefore you have difficulty with electrical matters, efi might be something for you to think twice about.

The Webcon parts and systems are distributed by Weber Concessionaires (UK) Ltd., for the parent Weber Company, which, of course, you will correctly associate with performance carburettors. However, it also produces engine management systems for racing and rally cars as well as some very high performance sports cars. The Webcon engine management system is slightly more sophisticated and expensive than the other on review here. It does offer better starting and smoother hot idling, though, due to its additional air valve. The Lumenition engine management system is very slightly less sophisticated and less expensive than the Weber approach – so both manufacturers have something to offer. You can see the kits in pictures 10-2-8 and 10-2-9.

Within each kit you get sensors to provide your ECU with the following environmental information: ambient air temperature and pressure, coolant temperatures, throttle and crank positions, so your system will 'be aware of' every situation and supply the appropriate fuel volumes and optimum ignition timing for all circumstances.

There are lots of opportunities for efi installations to go wrong, and

10-2-7. This is the same car we saw in picture 10-3-2, but seen from another angle giving a closer look at (part of), the electronic spark generating and distribution box. You also get a clue as to the electrical complexity (to many readers), of such installations by the three relays and the thickish wiring harness. However, it will all be well documented and carefully laid out for when you come to install it!

10-2-8. This is a Webcon six-pot, in fact another shot of the TR5 we saw in picture 10-3-2, while ...

10-2-9. ... for comparison, this is Lumenition equipment being installed to a four-cylinder car.

Neil Revington, who has extensive experience with both systems, is in a position to recommend the basic Weber or Lumenition parts you could use. Furthermore, he is able to select and provide an initial ignition curve from his bank of maps and is happy to offer advice or help with installations. I consider this to be invaluable given that we are dealing with cutting edge technology that few of us understand in detail. He will also be happy to advise which of the options available to you are likely to be most suited to your application. Revington uses Lumenition equipment in three variants, while Webcon equipment is offered in two variants as follows:

• The first Lumenition systems on offer uses a sensor in the distributor to report the crankshaft's position, as best one can using an indirect sensing method. This system also retains the distributor to initiate the sparks via a coil and distribute them in the conventional way. This will cost approximately £2850 for a TR6.

• The second Lumenition system senses the crankshaft position via the crankshaft itself. This is more accurate and, therefore, more desirable in our quest for spot-on engine management. The distributor is retained to distribute the sparks. Cost for a TR6 is *circa* £2950.

• The third and most sophisticated Lumenition system on offer is full engine management, with crank sensed triggering of both fuel and ignition systems. The ignition is provided by a six-pack coil with three amplifiers to generate and direct the sparks. Cost for the TR6 is about £3150.

• The initial Webcon system uses crank sensing but retains the distributor to generate and distribute the sparks. It is directly comparable the second option above. Cost is about £3250 for our TR6.

• The full engine management Webcon system also uses a crank sensing trigger and efi augmented by a distributorless ignition system. Cost will work out at about £3450 for a TR6.

Conclusions

• The standard Webcon throttle body is 40mm, or the same size as a 40DCOE carburettor, while the Lumenition standard body is 45mm in diameter. In both cases, though, alternatives are available. As we discussed in Chapter 9, a trio of DCOE Weber carbs will give good low-down torque with '40s',

whereas the 45mm choke variety is favoured for ultra fast road and competitive cars. Lumenition systems are perfectly tractable enough to be enjoyed on the road.

• All five systems, even those that retain the dizzy, can be introduced in two stages if required.

• The Webcon systems provide a slow running/warm-up air valve (picture 10-2-10), which monitors and adjusts the tick-over/idle speed.

• The Webcon system can only be tuned by a Webcon specialist with the necessary specialised equipment. However, the components are of the highest quality, it's the more sophisticated of the two systems, and provides the more gentle-mannered control.

• The Lumenition system (picture 10-2-11), is cheaper and certainly achieves what it sets out to do, but does so in a slightly less subtle way than Webcon's product.

• The advantage with the Lumenition system lies in the fact that you don't need to go to a specialist to get it tweaked. In fact, you can even buy the software, plug your own laptop into the system and alter the mapping to suit your own circumstances. If you don't like what you've done, you can change the mapping back, or do something different

again. A real 21st century toy with practical applications for the motoring enthusiast!

• Although it's possible for either system to be installed at home, Neil Revington's experience and research means that the important details are available. Therefore, ECU mapping, pipe lengths, bracket designs, crank sensor alignments, tank alterations, *etc*., should be pretty well spot-on for your car. The kits come with instructions showing where everything goes, of course, but perhaps most important of all, there is technical help and advice on the end of the telephone, so you're not really on your own.

10-2-10. Webcon's extra air valve situated adjacent to the clutch master cylinder.

10-2-11. Yet another angle on the Lumenition components. Note the (arrowed), fuel rail, the excellent throttle mechanism and the original style of spark distribution via the dizzy (very top of the picture). From the distributor's presence, this is most likely to be an efi rather than a full management system.

Chapter 11

Original fuel injection system

Today's unleaded fuels boil at least 5 degrees (C) below that of the fuel which the Lucas pumps were designed to handle. Some say it's as much as 7-degrees: whichever is correct, this factor is bound to cause some difficulties. I recall a colleague in the 1970s who had a PI (petrol injection) Triumph saloon which was regularly troubled by overheated, under-performing fuel pumps, so perhaps the pump was 'on the limit' even in those (good old!) days? That said, for a TR, the performance of the original petrol injection system, provided it is in good condition and fitted in conjunction with a TR5 camshaft, is very hard to improve upon. There's also no doubt that the combination of wear and tear and the change in fuel volatility continues to cause some owners heartache, although improvements are possible and solutions to hand. Consequently, we will look first at some improvements to the original 150bhp setup, and some ways to better the performance of the later 125bhp design – but you will be disappointed if you are expecting to read how you might double the power from either of these systems! We will certainly look into the detail of how you can improve the reliability of the petrol injection system and there may be the odd surprise. The main change to a Bosch fuel pump is very

well documented and will come as no surprise to most readers, but some of the additional suggestions included here may help optimise your Bosch pump.

IMPROVING THE ORIGINAL SYSTEM

If you feel your petrol injection system regularly malfunctions, whether it's fitted with the original Lucas pump or a Bosch replacement, the first point to consider is that the PI system works off the engine's vacuum. When the inlet vacuum is depressed the PI system 'thinks' the engine is calling for more fuel. Consequently, the system will 'compensate' for the low vacuum by enriching the mixture regardless of whether that low vacuum is brought about by your opening the throttle or as a consequence of engine wear. For the Lucas PI system to perform well the engine needs to be in very good condition, and a vacuum gauge on the inlet manifold of a CP (150bhp), car should read a shade over 6in Hg (six inches of Mercury), at tickover (850rpm). A CR (125bhp), car should read 7in Hg.

The second area for your attention if you feel your engine is in very good shape but the system is generally under performing, is the Lucas fuel pump shown in picture 11-1. They do tire,

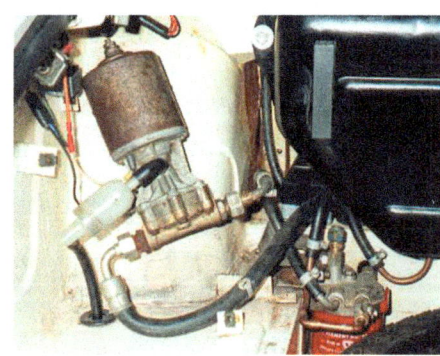

11-1. The original Lucas fuel pumps are progressively being replaced by the Bosch pumps we see later in the chapter. The fuel filter on the pump drain is not a good idea and should not be copied.

as we all do after 30 years' hard work, but you can do something to improve its performance and prolong its life by, firstly, ensuring it's in as good a shape as possible. I think it's worth recapitulating here how the original system was designed to work so that you will more readily appreciate where changes may be helpful.

As we will touch on later, the Lucas pump was intended to deliver about 16 Imperial galls (72 litres) of fuel per hour. Now, clearly you were never going to consume that volume of fuel, perhaps 4 gallons per hour could be expected on the road, which left the majority of fuel to cool the pump and recirculate back into the fuel tank. So, the fuel tank was used as a 'heat sink' and, certainly with a full tank on a cool day, problems would be very rare. However, as the fuel level drops and the ambient temperature rises, the capacity of our fuel tank heat sink decreases and, while problems may still be unlikely, the margin for safety is reduced. If someone now drops the boiling point of our fuel by 14 or 15%, there are real problems in the offing, particularly if the system is also subjected to its least effective conditions: traffic congestion. As the fuel temperature rises the pump's ability to pump fuel decreases, the flow of cooling fuel reduces, the temperature of the fuel in the pump increases further and, before long, vaporisation and a standstill result. All that ignores the high probability that the pump is worn, and incapable of pumping 72lph today, even in ideal conditions!

So, what can we do about the situation, whilst retaining the Lucas pump? Start by recognising that the fuller your fuel tank, the greater your heat sink capacity. Secondly, appreciate that you will never be able to regard the Lucas pump (not necessarily the whole PI system), as 100% reliable with today's volatile fuels. There are several pages of information in *How to Restore Triumph TR5/2505 and 6* to help you, but the electrical supply issues are so important that I'll *precis* them here for emphasis. An inadequately electrically supplied Lucas pump will not pump sufficient fuel to cool itself, so:

• Ensure that the electrical system generally, and the feed wire to the pump in particular, are in excellent order.
• Early cars had an inadequate electrical feed cable to the pump that dropped the voltage available at the pump. Upgrade your feed cable to at least 28 strand x 0.3, and ensure it's supplied from a good source of power*.
• Simultaneously, run a separate earth cable of similar capacity from the engine's earth strap.
• Fit a relay and ensure the secondary feed to the relay is of good capacity. Change and solder any terminations that are not in absolute pristine condition.
• Upgrade the alternator to one that is comfortably capable of generating

11-2. It may seem strange to see a picture of an alternator within a chapter on Petrol Injection, but the electrical power supplied to the PI fuel pump has a significant bearing on the performance of the pump.

at least 10% more than your needs. A 55amp capacity one shown in photograph 11-2, and this would dramatically improve your fuel pumping reliability.
• The fuel pump is the heart of any fuel/petrol injection system. Regardless of which pump you are using, or propose to use, it must be fed will the highest voltage available in your car. Although the problem was later corrected, TR5s and early TR6s were fitted with inadequate fuel pump wires. I went into the detail in the restoration book, but this is a particularly important point for owners of earlier PI cars.

If none of these suggestions improve your system, it's time to take a look at the original pipe work which connects the tank, CAV filter and pressure release valve (PRV). Triumph changed this at about car CP 50000, and it probably did have some effect on reliability. If you have an early car (with the PRV mounted on the chassis), and regard some of the suggestions that follow later in the chapter as too radical, then this might be a minimal change option for you to consider. I must point out, however, that since these changes were introduced by Triumph, the volatility of modern fuels have further changed the whole basis for the Lucas filter/pump system dramatically. Consequently, I mention this 'tweak' with the caveat that I don't believe it will resolve all the PI problems that modern fuels generate on its own. The work involves blanking off the air purge pipe and the PRV return on the filter housing, and fitting later pipes and routings which bring the returned fuel from the metering unit and the PRV to the top of the fuel tank. **Note**. If you are contemplating this change, you can

do absolutely no damage by fitting a larger bore pipe from the tank to the filter/pump, a modification we discuss in a bit more detail later in this chapter.

BRINGING THE 125BHP SYSTEM UP TO 150BHP

Most owners of 125 system cars will primarily be interested in bringing their car's performance up to that of the earlier cars. There are two factors involved in this, the first being the smoothness of both the tickover/idle, and the second, the 'pick-up' of the car when the throttle is opened. We'll touch on both of these later, under the heading of Improved Throttle Linkages, for they apply to both the 125 and 150bhp systems, but this upgrade is particularly important to the 125 system where the original throttle controls are, not to put too fine a point on it, inexact. Consider this: owners spend large sums of money on new, beautifully-balanced fuel delivery metering units but often ignore the fact that the air supply must be correspondingly balanced if the engine is to run to its potential. Consequently, if you have a CR car, before you try upgrading the fuel delivery system, do change the method by which you set-up, balance and adjust the butterflies, and thus the air supply on these post-1973 cars. Prestige Injection offers what I think is a particularly effective solution, shown in picture 11-3, although all the main TR specialists have one available and you will see the Revington one in picture 11-4.

It's possible to improve the 125 car's performance by upgrading the PI system, but to get the full benefit there is more to the change than most initially appreciate. The full change involves an upgrade in camshaft to the original TR5 cam and a change in the metering unit to the 150 version. This is because the

11-3. Prestige Injection's improved throttle linkage makes for more accurate setting of the individual throttle butterflies and, therefore, smoother running ...

11-4. ... as does Neil Revington's equivalent product, fitted above an original exhaust manifold.

camshaft and metering unit work in very close correlation and **must** be matched. It becomes obvious if you recall the importance of the inlet manifold vacuum to the operation of the PI system, and a quick check will confirm that there really is quite a difference in operating vacuum

11-5. This picture would never apply in a real life situation as it is a mixture of two different injection manifolds. I assembled them for this photo to show the differences between the earlier '150' manifolds on the left, and the '125' manifold on the right with its extra balance pipe at the rear (top of the photo).

between the 125 and 150 systems.

You can, of course, also swap the 125 inlet manifolds for the earlier 150 style manifold and, since they are so similar at first sight, I've included picture 11-5 to indicate the differences. However, this is less important than the camshaft/metering unit change detailed above, for modifications to the original 125 manifolds are quite feasible. If you choose not to change the inlet manifolds then I would recommend you install your idle air valve in the front CP position shown in picture 11-6. You can, incidentally, also install a second idle air valve to the rear of the front balance pipe, and I'll cover this later in the chapter!

FURTHER PI IMPROVEMENTS
There follows a series of suggestions for you to consider. Bear in mind that the wear on the gearing of the Lucas fuel pump will be unique to the car to which it is fitted. It may be, therefore, that something that works on your car will not improve another.

Improving the airflow
You can improve the airflow to the inlet manifolds in two ways. The first and easiest step that all cars aspiring to fast road car status should carry out is to dispense with the front canister and paper air filter and fit the K&N air filter seen at 11-7 in its place. K&N part number is KNE87, and you'll find the filter at most K&N stockists and/or listed in Moss's performance catalogue.

For ultra fast road and competitive cars there's a two-stage improvement to consider. Check my findings, but I

11-7. This K&N filter fits the PI system and reduces air-flow restrictions. A different K&N filter would be required if you enlarged the inlet manifold.

think you'll agree that the cross sectional area of the 6 manifold inlets exceeds that of the main tubular inlet manifold by about 40%, so the main manifold is best increased in diameter. It's currently some 3.125in (80mm), in diameter and should be at least 4.25in (110mm), in diameter to provide an unrestricted airflow to the inlet manifolds. In fact, the usual practice is to increase the diameter to around 5in (125mm), and this is achieved by slitting the length of the tube underneath (where it's less obvious), and welding in a strip of 20swg mild steel and a new rear closing disc to the inlet manifold. Choose a diameter that allows a standard K&N conical filter to be fitted straight on the end and, of course, make sure the K&N is fed with cool air straight from the front of the car.

Whichever route you follow, note my K&N cleaning recommendations in Chapter 10.

Relocating the Lucas fuel pump
The Saloon cars which used the Lucas PI system had the Lucas fuel pump mounted on its side. Mounting a pump on its side (see picture 11-8) seems like a good idea because the pump's bearings will be under (a little) less load, and this must help reduce frictional heating within the pump. Furthermore, I would also lower the pump to the bottom of the boot/trunk-well in order to get the greatest head of fuel available (every little helps).

The Saloon cars had a special mounting bracket for the pump, and I would have no hesitation in mounting my pump via one of these brackets, although you may prefer to continue to mount it vertically to get it into the front left corner of the spare wheel well.

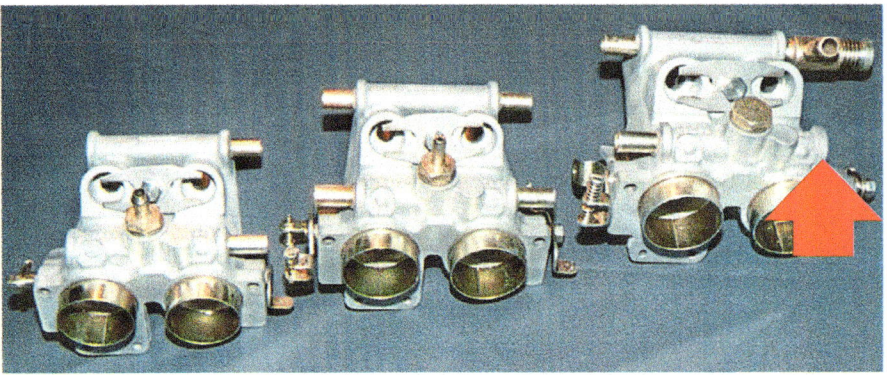

11-6. These are a set of '125' inlet manifolds with the idle air valve shown in its original position (top right of the picture). However, if you relocate it to the front (arrowed), row of balance pipes and blank its original location hole off, you will improve the idle control. Later in the chapter we'll talk about also fitting a second idle air valve!

11-8. The saloon PI fuel pump was mounted horizontally in this bracket/mounting cradle, which may have benefits for your system.

The filter and the Lucas fuel pump

As you will see later in the chapter, I am of the opinion that a fuel filter should not be placed on the suction side of a fuel pump. A light filter, such as an in-line gauze unit, may be in order, provided you remember to clean/replace/service it regularly, and provided it's in a glass tube and is intended only as an indicator of fuel contamination. However, something the size of the original PI filter holds all sorts of potential restrictions, for anything except a Lucas pump that is in very good order. These pumps suck very well indeed, though, and a pre-filter the size of the CAV unit should not be a problem. However, as we said, every little helps so we are as well to ensure the CAV filter is presenting the minimal restriction possible.

Revington TR has carried out some research in order to establish what current replacement elements are suitable for an original CAV filter, and I'm indebted to Neil Revington for providing me with his conclusions. Fundamentally, Revington believes there is only one element/cartridge (which has to be imported), that will provide a satisfactory fuel flow when mounted prior to a Lucas pump, and it's important that you use that cartridge if you want reliable performance from your PI TR. It may be available from some of the other premier TR and PI specialists, but Revington sells it under part number GFE5296CAV. The only other way you can be absolutely sure that you have a suitable cartridge in place is to buy a genuine Lucas/CAV replacement element, part number CAV296 from your nearest Lucas agent!

Relocating the (PRV) regulator

I have no experimental proof, but I am not convinced that the pressure regulator was originally placed in the best location. It would, in my opinion, be best located just before the metering unit, in the engine bay. This adds to the plumbing complications since it significantly lengthens the return pipe but, more importantly, this location reduces the opportunity for pressure drops. I do have experience of efi installations and make this suggestion on the basis that all efi systems have the fuel pressure regulator installed at the last possible moment. In fact, fuel pressure is regulated after the injectors in an efi setup, which, for a PI system, translates to immediately prior to the metering unit.

Lucas pump cooling coils

I also recommend fitting a cooling coil around the Lucas pump motor. These were originally made from round tube but you can get coils made from square tube now, which is better since you get more contact area between the coil and the motor, thus improving heat transference. The heat is dissipated to the fuel that's being returned to the tank by the pressure relief valve. So, as I said earlier in this chapter, you need to be mindful of the fact that you may be cooling the pump but you are only transferring the heat into your heat sink/fuel tank. Consequently, you still need to ensure you keep the heat-absorbing capacity of your tank up by keeping the fuel level high, particularly in hot weather, and especially if you are likely to encounter any slow moving traffic.

Primer fuel pumps

If you couple a primary pump in the fuel line from the tank to the Lucas pump (i.e. **before** the Lucas pump), you not only take some of the load off the Lucas pump but you also reduce the likelihood of the Lucas unit cavitating. The make and/or type of primary fuel pump isn't particularly vital (I've even heard of SU pumps being used successfully, see picture 11-9-1). However, the higher the pressure of the primary pump the less work the Lucas original has to carry out. The SUs generate 3 or 4psi, but I would prefer something that provides about twice that pressure without straining itself. I also think that there is much to be said for modern solid-state electronics, especially after being let down by SU pumps (some new) on several occasions.

11-9-1. If you think of using an SU fuel pump as a primer for the main PI pump, I strongly recommend you fit one with the new electronic triggering mechanism seen here.

Although you can now buy solid-state triggered SU pumps, they offer no increase in pressure, so I suggest a Facet Red Top primary pump that is both solid-state triggered and generates 7 to 8psi. The Facet Red Top also has the slight advantage of an, admittedly small, internal filter. Meanwhile, remember that the primer pump **must** have at least the capacity of your principle pump, in the case of the original Lucas unit's 72 litres per hour, and that an additional fuel pump will only add to the importance of a first class electrical supply, alternator, etc. Picture 11-9-2 shows a Red Top in situ.

11-9-2. A Facet Red Top fuel pump can also be used as a priming pump for the Lucas unit, and its extra pressure makes it the preferred option.

Idle air bleed valves

There were three different methods of supplying and controlling the air needed by the PI system to allow the engine to idle smoothly. The very first TR5s did not incorporate an air-bleed adjusting screw. The air for engine idle was supplied by cracking open the throttle butterflies, just as one would with a carburettor. However, with three pairs of butterflies necessary in a six-cylinder PI system, it proved impossible to set these very early systems up to idle consistently and smoothly. In fact, Lucas/Triumph quickly issued a retrofit kit that incorporated the front bleed valve that we are familiar with these days and the vast majority of cars will long since have been modified. If yours happens to one of the few unmodified ones without an air-bleed valve then fit a valve to the front (currently blanked-off) balance-pipe, or fit a set of early ex-2500 PI Saloon inlet manifolds with the air valve already in place. This will bring your system on a par with the middle and best of the three standard PI arrangements.

The best arrangement was fitted to late TR5s and early TR6s (the CP TR models made up to about November 1972). This had **one** balance pipe between each manifold and can be seen in photograph 11-10. The throttle mechanisms fitted as standard to these cars allowed the butterflies to be set closed at idle, idling air being supplied

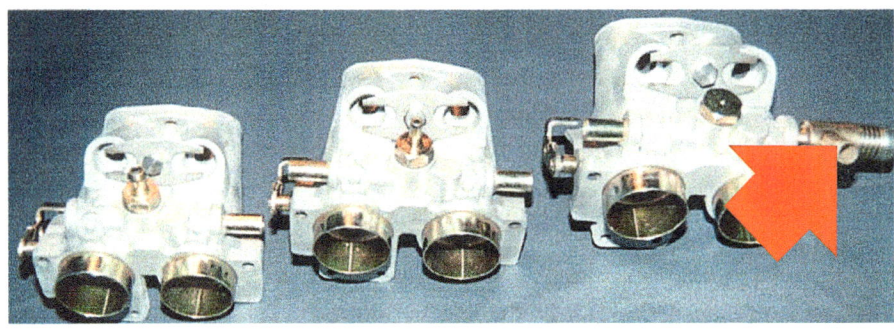

11-11. The idle air valve highlighted here is a very important component for a smooth tickover/idle.

through the air valve situated at the front of the engine (pictures 11-11 and 11-12). Even this 'best' Triumph system can be improved upon.

The third standard system was introduced post-November 1972 for the CR models, but this, too, was difficult to set smoothly. I can best identify the system by telling you that it had **two** balance pipes between each of the three inlet manifolds and is known as the 125bhp system. This third system will be dramatically improved if you reposition the idle air control valve to its earlier CP position, as we saw in picture 11-6. This improves the uniformity of the system's fuel/air mixture at least to the level of the 150bhp CP system. You'll need to remove the manifolds, linkages, *etc.*, unplug the air valve and remove the blanking plug that closes the other balance pipe. Swap the valve and blanking plugs over and shorten the pipe from your repositioned air valve to the air box. This 125 system can be further

improved by blanking off the whole of the front set of balance pipes (*i.e.* the set nearer the cylinder head), **individually** – *i.e.* each pipe end needs closing. The one nearest the driver is already closed, and you'll have just blanked off the very front one when you relocated the air bleed valve, but there are four others that require a blanking plug. A 0.2in thick alloy disc pressed in place will do the job nicely. This is one step more than just repositioning the bleed valve.

Mark Treadwell suggests a third step that applies to both 150 and 125 systems: adding a second air bleed valve at the rear of the air distribution tube. With normal (front) bleed valves, the first four cylinders get virtually all the idle air that's going, and the 5th and 6th cylinders run rich at idle due to the absence of air. If you fit a second air valve and feed the hose to the back of the inlet tube and close the original front valve almost right down, you will get a much improved distribution of idle air and, consequently,

11-10. Ironically these earlier CP or '150' PI manifolds are perceived as the more effective. They can be identified by the single balance linking pipes highlighted here.

11-12. Seen here in its more usual environment, but with its air feed pipe removed for clarity. Note too the overhead throttle linkage that contributes much to setting the PI system up accurately and the free flow tubular exhaust manifold which comes into its own as the revs build-up!

11-13. Even with the idle air valve in its best original (CP) position, back cylinders are starved of air at idle, and tend to run rich. Mark Treadwell carried out what I think is a great improvement by fitting the second idle air valve you see highlighted here.

11-14. You get a better view of the modification in detail in this close-up.

a much smoother idle. You will see what he is suggesting in photographs 11-13 and 11-14.

Improved throttle linkage

Because the tick-over/idle and opening of the three sets of throttles is very difficult and time consuming to synchronise properly, several specialists have designed improved throttle linkages. All are recommended, but you need to decide which one offers the facility that is most important to you, and which offers the best value for money. All those I've looked at run across the top of the throttle bodies on special bushed mounting brackets. Some cross-shafts are made from stainless steel. The three connecting rods attach to each spindle end and the rod's left and right threaded ends allow the length of the

11-15. The installation of a free-flowing exhaust manifold will probably interfere with the original 'underslung' throttle mechanism. By repositioning it above the manifolds, the adjustments are easier and more precise. The same throttle cable can be retained, and the problems with the exhaust manifold eliminated.

11-16. This particular throttle mechanism has a stainless steel cross-shaft running in friction-free nylon bushes. However, it's the precision with which the throttle butterflies can be set via these (arrowed), adjustable links that is the primary reason for fitting this improvement.

rod to be adjusted very easily, quickly and accurately. The increased accuracy of the set-up allows for smoother idle and pick-up, and will eliminate butterfly flutter if the shafts are in reasonably good condition. The original throttle and choke cable are usually retained which, if required, allows for the use of extractor exhaust manifolds and return springs to be fitted to each of the throttle butterfly shafts. Costs are generally in the order of £175 depending upon your selected supplier and specification.

We saw a couple of pictures showing an overview of the type of changes involved but you may appreciate the more detailed information shown in pictures 11-15 and 11-16.

Fuel tanks

Although the original fuel tanks look the same from the outside, the tanks fitted to the later cars (post-CP50000), have the benefit of an internal baffle. This stops the fuel in a half empty tank surging about, particularly when cornering vigorously, and starving the pump for a few seconds. This fuel surge can lead to air locks in the system and can even stop you in the same way as fuel vaporisation with a Lucas pump does. Of course, you could keep the tank more than half full all the time! You could fit a late fuel tank, of course, but these aren't that frequently available and all are old with sediment and/or rust as a further deterrent.

You can improve the situation by fitting a supplementary swirl pot. This has the advantages of increasing your fuel capacity slightly while enabling

you to supply the Bosch pump with a nice large bore fuel pipe (I use 12mm od central heating copper pipe, but there are those that say 15mm is best). Furthermore, you ensure the pump is constantly fed with air free fuel, for that's what the swirl pot does, it spins the air out of the fuel supply. You can buy swirl pots from Demon Tweaks in the UK and Summit in the US, but may have to feed it with a small secondary fuel pump if you can't get its location low enough to allow gravity to do the primary feed job for you. If you've got a really good fuel tank and would prefer not to have a separate swirl pot, you may be able to find a fuel tank repair expert able to wash out your existing tank and fit an internal swirl pot. The pot from an ex-Ford Granada tank is a popular choice, but have him enlarge the outlet pipe before welding the tank back up. **Do not** try it yourself, for you'll most likely send yourself, car, house and family into orbit! Serck-Marston has done some good fuel tank work for me in the UK.

There is, of course, the option of fitting an uprated modern tank to consider. Revington's replacement aluminium tanks are shown in picture 11-17. They reduce the weight of the car slightly but, perhaps more importantly, increase the fuel capacity from approximately 48 litres (tanks varied in capacity), to 54 (TR5/6PI), and to 61 (TR4/4A/250) litres (about 10.5, 11.7 and 13 imperial gallons respectively). This equates to a useful 35 mile/30 minute increase over the original fuel capacity. TR6 tanks have proper swirl pots fitted internally to de-aerate the fuel and keep the supply of fuel constant, even when cornering, but this feature can be fitted to any replacement fuel tank. Furthermore, consider the build-up of rust and rubbish that has occurred over the 30 to 40 years of the tank's earlier life. You can and must fit a fuel filter in

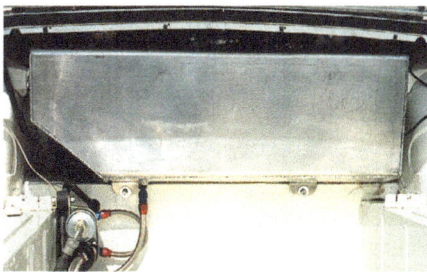

11-17. No rust or fuel flow worries with this slightly increased capacity fuel tank.

your fuel line but, as they say, prevention is better than cured. Normal tank, no swirl, is *circa* £325 from Moss, Revington and, no doubt, many other specialists.

Fuel pipes

Make sure the fuel flow from the tank is unrestricted. It sounds a silly detail, but the standard tank exit fitting is an unintentional restriction reducing the 8mm exit to less than 5mm. Prestige Injection makes an 8.5mm exit that will help fuel flow.

A flexible fuel pipe is a flexible fuel pipe ... isn't it? Well, of course that's true, but were you aware that some rubber/flexible fuel lines are (slightly) porous and allow vapour to escape? These are the normal type you will be sold by your local motor factors and are perfectly satisfactory and safe when used outside/under the car. However, in a TR there are several situations when you may want to run a fuel line inside the car or in the boot/trunk. Many Bosch fuel pumps are mounted in the TR's boot/trunk even in standard or fast road cars. Many competitive cars run the majority of their fuel lines inside the car for safety, and where flexible lines are used these need to be of the more expensive less porous standard or, preferably, of the highest 'competition' standard. Always fit the best when it comes to matters related to brakes and fuel: ptfe inner fuel hose with external stainless steel protective braiding.

These ptfe/braided fuel hoses are also available for addition safety or 'insurance' over the engine and seem a very good idea, although I have heard of them being less reflective of heat and, consequently, instances where they are prone to fuel vaporisation problems. If you have braided hoses from the metering unit to the injectors and are suffering from air locks from time to time, particularly after the car has stood (hot), for half an hour, try insulating the outside of the braid. A length of rubber hose slipped over the outside of the braided hose, an insulating wrap applied to the outside or a length of silica textile fireproof sleeve may not look as elegant but is to be preferred to air lock problems.

THE BOSCH FUEL PUMP

There is no doubt that the best and understandably the most popular solution to many PI problems is to upgrade the fuel pump to a Bosch.

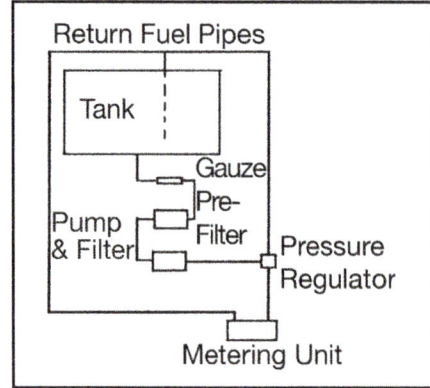

D11. Bosch pump fuel flow diagram.

Piping in the Bosch pump is not difficult, but I have added an outline drawing (D11), to help, but care does need to be exercised with regard to pump selection. Not only must the selected Bosch pump be adequate, in terms of flow and pressure capacity, but so too must its location and filtration (that is, if you are not to be disappointed with the outcome). Furthermore, there seems to be a fair amount of incorrect information circulating, most of which will result in disappointment for all but a (very) fortunate few. Let's start by reminding you of the flow and pressure specification of the original Lucas pump, for clearly any replacement you contemplate must at least equal the original specification and, where you are upgrading the engine in terms of capacity, should ideally increase that capacity. The original Lucas pump (No. 54073012), is rated at (approximately say the specs), 100psi (6.9 bar), with a maximum delivery of 16 gallons per hour (about 72 litres/hour).

Before you go rushing off to the scrap yard, I need to emphasise that the vast majority of efi systems run at a lower pressure (most at about half), than that required by the Triumph PI system, which makes your chances of finding a truly satisfactory pump at a scrap yard virtually nil. 95% of the pumps you find will provide the flow you need but are not going to provide the very high pressure (by today's standards), that the Lucas PI system requires to operate properly. Generally, most cars with a Bosch K or KE jetronic system operate around 5 bar, although I will mention a couple of specific cars later in this piece in order to give you an opportunity to telephone one or two specialised breakers. However,

if you do contemplate a used pump and can find a suitable donor car, I'd strongly recommend you remove the pump yourself and check the part number!

I should also mention that, when fitting any Bosch pump, you must mount it lower than the original Lucas pump. The Bosch pump pressurises the fuel superbly but it cannot suck fuel anywhere near as well as the original Lucas unit, so it must be mounted lower than the Lucas pumps. You should also upgrade the capacity of your alternator and implement the electrical improvements I mentioned right at the beginning of this chapter, preferably simultaneously, but at worst, very shortly after installation of the Bosch unit. The extra amperage required by the Bosch pump will so load the original 16 ACR alternator that you will burnt it out within a few months, so a larger capacity 18 ACR 45amp unit is essential for long term reliability of both alternator and pump.

Bosch's B 261 205 413 pump is the best to use, and, at 210 litres/hour at 10 bar, is the only pump Bosch recommend for use with the Triumph PI system. Its superior specification is clear and is the only pump those of you with enhanced engine performance should contemplate. However, it will be expensive since no retail price is set and you would have to enquire at a Bosch parts supplier for their price and order it.

An Audi motorsport pump (Bosch part number 0 580 254 044) is an option for those with pretty standard engines. It's priced around £185 plus vat, provides 172 litres/hour at 7 bar, and is, therefore, likely to work quite well in the vast majority of TRs. Another pump that should be adequate, if marginal, is the Audi Quattro 2.3 Turbo pump (Bosch part number 0 580 254 929). It offers 142 litres/hour at 6.5 bar and is priced at around £95 plus vat. It is readily available new but is unlikely to be available secondhand.

Most of the TR specialists sell kits that comprise pumps and/or a filter. If the kit has a filter, it's usually close-coupled with the requisite banjo connections. It's worth checking the specification (pressure and flow), of the pump with your potential supplier. Costs of the kits vary, but average about £250 at the time of writing if a filter is included. Malcolm Jones, of Prestige Injection, tells me that his pump was recommended by Robert Bosch GmbH who tell him it should reliably cover 120,000 miles, a shade more than most TRs are likely to need! This kit includes ptfe/stainless hoses, a larger tank fitting, cleanable pre-filter and a downstream efi filter, and all electrical wiring. It's fitted in the boot space as can be seen in photo 11-20.

Bosch pumps have been located in roughly the same position as the original Lucas unit but this is not a good place. Most successful installations site the Bosch pump inside the left front corner of the spare wheel well for the pump needs to be below the bottom of the fuel tank. Pictures 11-18 and 11-19 shows a Revington kit so placed. However, if you were to look at the Bosch pump in its original installation position in the relevant OE applications, you'd find the pump installed under the car (in both a cool airflow and as low as practical). I favour the left-side rear wheelarch if you can't get it on the front of the spare wheel well, perhaps with a stone guard to save it from taking any major knocks (illustrated by picture 11-21). However, any Bosch pump that runs hot enough to make you think it should be moved to outside the boot is either underspecified, has been installed incorrectly, or has some sort of restriction in the pipe work.

We talked about the importance of an adequate fuel flow to the Lucas pump, which moves some 72 litres/hour. Consider how much more important an adequate fuel supply is to a Bosch pump

11-18. The Bosch pump/filter combination does tuck neatly in the front-left corner of the wheel well. The filter is on the top of this duo ...

11-19. .... as you can see from this side view. Note the tap on the feed pipe from the tank and, bottom left, a cleanable pre-pump filter.

moving about twice that volume! You really do need to fit a larger fuel supply pipe to the Bosch pump if you are not going to inhibit its efforts. If your Bosch pump is noisy, chances are your fuel supply pipe is inadequate. I feed my Bosch pump via 12mm central heating copper pipe.

Bosch recommends a small pre-filter be fitted between the tank and pick up side of the pump, with the main filter provided on the outlet side. I noticed a suitable component in Demon Tweeks' catalogue (part number PRO806), but Prestige Injection does one too. The location of the main filter is not critical, and can be anywhere from front to rear of the car, so I suggest the engine bay is best from an access point of view. However, to handle the PI pressure levels the filter would have to have banjo type hose connections. Suitable main filters are much more widely available than the pumps thenselves. Bosch tells me that you could still stick with the original Lucas CAV filter, fitted downstream of the pump. Other options include Bosch part number 0 450 905 145 (fits on the Quattro 2.3 Turbo plus many other cars), or Bosch part number 0 450 905 203 (Mercedes 500 and many more). There are many others you could use, but remember that banjo connections are required. For those contemplating continuing with the original filter I would add the comments that you should both use the correct filter element as highlighted above and change it at the specified service intervals. For those using a 7 bar pump,

11-20. Prestige Injection, like most of the TR Specialists, does a fuel pump kit which includes stainless braided/ptfe lines hoses for safety and a cleanable pre-pump filter. Note the neat close-coupling right in the corner of what would be the wheel well.

I think it suitable to use a filter from a Bosch K or KE Jetronic efi system. It's as well to check, but, although these systems run at 5 bar, the filter should be able to cope with 7 bar without too much of a problem.

11-21. A Bosch fuel pump for a Petrol Injected TR – Racetorations style. The pump is mounted on the outside of the spare wheel well, which keeps it as low as possible, and in the cooler air outside the car. For those concerned about exposing the pump to road debris and water, remember that they are designed to be mounted under the car and that I have run an efi car with a similar Bosch pump mounted under the car for 10 years.

The main filter will probably be sited in the engine bay but picture 10-1-1 tells you more about their pre-pump filter & location.

Chapter 12
Six-cylinder engine

The overall design of the six-cylinder engine is, subjectively, not as good as the four-cylinder engine, and it may be as well that we list the weaknesses and prioritise them so as to understand why a number of improvements need to be explored later in the chapter. It's a very long stroked engine, even by the standards of the day but, nevertheless, it can be made to rev very fast (taking piston speeds way over their recommended figure ... yet it works).

I'll start with a summary of the weaknesses that surface in standard and fast road cars:
• The oil filter arrangement is inadequate (picture 12-1) and a vertical spin-on arrangement is essential.
• The crankshaft's thrust bearing surface area is inadequate allowing crankshaft end float to occur (picture 12-2 identifies them). Furthermore, the method of retaining the half-thrust bearings allows them to fall out completely! Consequently, full upper and lower

thrusts faces are installed. It's a fiddly job and needs careful thought, but Austin Maxi and/or Peugeot thrust faces are often used.
• It has very small diameter cam followers that are marginal when it comes to fast road cars. An easy upgrade, though (picture 12-3).

For competitive use the list of shortcomings and solutions for the six-cylinder engine can be summarised as follows:

12-1. It seems extraordinary that Triumph's test programme failed to realise that this oil filter arrangement allows oil to drain away, delaying oil reaching the bearings upon start-up.

12-2. These are not actually the original inadequate thrust bearings, but the Racetorations upgraded versions.

12-3. As you can see, the cam followers are about the same diameter as your index finger, which makes them vulnerable to wear and sideways movement when a high lift cam or a reground cam with a reduced base circle is employed.

12-4. Not that it makes much difference where it breaks, but the majority of cranks break here, near the rear of the crank where the cumulative stresses of five pistons converge.

• It was not fitted with replaceable camshaft bearings.

• It has a four-bearing crankshaft. However, while nothing can be done to correct this basic inadequacy, it is possible to strengthen the main bearing caps. Not all four need to be strengthened, usually just 2 and 3, the central ones, are changed for steel.

• The crankshaft breaks, usually just in front of the 6th con-rod, as a consequence of high rpm (picture 12-4). A steel crank is available and should be used if more than 6500rpm is expected. A front crank harmonic damper increases the life of the crank in competitive use, but even a steel crank will eventually go (perhaps every 4-5 years). The modified US damper makes for a smoother running engine, so it's applicable to fast-road cars too. However, you'll have to move pulleys and the water pump forward.

• The con-rods are inadequate. Steel con-rods are, therefore, even more applicable in the six because it tends to

12-5. Note the additional flywheel mounting holes in this steel crankshaft.

rev a bit higher, and also because of its increased stroke.

• Going to the ultimate solution to the first two points, you can fit a steel crank that has been designed for Cosworth's smaller sized journals. This results in lighter weight round the big ends and less friction.

• The basic piston design is satisfactory so changes in design are not required, but you need pistons made from forged aluminium if you plan to race your six-cylinder.

• The four crankshaft to flywheel bolts are increased to 8 if you are using a standard six pot crankshaft, but this is increased to 12 fixing bolts if you are to use one of the many steel crankshafts (picture 12-5).

• The stresses on the camshaft are very high indeed, due in part to the size of the lobes, which has been dictated by the minuscule cam followers, (picture 12-6). Furthermore, there are six pairs of valve springs pressing against the cam, adding not only to its loading, but to the load on the camshaft bearings too.

• However the cam runs directly in the block without any cam bearings.

12-6. The cam followers are barely adequate for standard applications, and certainly need upgrading if you contemplate a hot/high lift camshaft and high rpm. This is the larger one described in the main text. Racetorations' followers are ready to fit to a block which has had all 12 follower bores increased in size.

Thus for ultra fast road & competition applications it's mandatory to line bore the block and fit camshaft bearings if you want to prevent the camshaft from walking through the block. The sleeve type bearing from a Triumph Spitfire Mk III engine is the usual choice as the bearings are the same as the six-cylinder engine's camshaft. Two each of part numbers 142647 and 142648 are required. Furthermore, it's important to carry out this improvement before any damage has taken place since it becomes far more difficult to correctly reposition the now hardened and oval bearing recesses. As an interesting aside, the Spitfire engine is the same engine (less a pair of cylinders), as our six-cylinder TR engine, so it's not surprising that the Spitfire's cam bearings are usually fitted. A Land Rover set will also fit and most good auto machine shops can carry out the line boring.

• The costs are proportionally higher due to the six cylinders. A full-race six-cylinder engine will cost £12-13,000.

ESSENTIAL UPGRADES FOR ALL ENGINES
Spin-on oil filter

Repeating myself I know but this is one of the primary improvements **all** owners of six-cylinder TRs need to make. Furthermore, it **must** be fitted so that it points down towards the road. The design is such that it is possible to fit one at any angle, including pointing upwards, but this completely negates the whole objective of the spin-on adapter as it allows the filter to empty of oil when the engine is switched off. As with the original Triumph filter arrangement on the side of the engine, an empty, or part empty spin-on oil filter requires the initial oil flow on start-up be used to fill the filter, thus delaying the supply of oil to the engine. The spin-on filter shown in picture 1-15 fitted **vertically downwards** stays full of oil, so each time the engine is started the oil supply gets to the engine's working parts straightaway.

You need to plan ahead for this improvement, however. This should be is a bolt-on addition once your upgraded engine is back in the car. Sadly, due to the inconsistency in manufacture of the six-cylinder engine block, some welding may be necessary to some blocks and, consequently, it's important that you check one detail before fitting a spin-on filter casting. Cast and machined into the block is a sealing ring recess and, central to that ring you will see a plinth/boss which has been tapped with a coarse thread to accept the mounting bolt for both the original and spin-on casting adapter. Unfortunately, in some blocks the small central plinth/boss can be cast irregularly, or even off-centre, sometimes by as much as ¼in (6mm). This may not be a very frequent problem but it is frequent and important enough to alert you to check for anything that prevents the centre of the spin-on filter base sealing effectively against the block. An off-centre or irregular boss will at least partially reduce the flow of oil through the spin-on filter assembly, nullifying what you thought was an improvement in your engine's protection.

If you're planning to fit a spin-on filter to your running car, check that the tapped hole goes through the centre of the boss leaving a sealing face right around the periphery of the boss. If all is as it should be, buy and fit your spin-on. If not, leave the original filter in place. If you're in the process of reconditioning or upgrading your engine, take an early look at this detail. With the engine out of the car, particular when un-assembled, it's easy enough to increase the size of the boss with weld and face it off so that a nice flat sealing face is re-established around the big tapped mounting hole.

Thrust bearings

Triumph only fitted a half thrust bearing ring to the crankshaft, located in the crankcase rather than in the main bearing cap. This weakness has since become notorious. The danger, as I am sure you've heard, is that the half thrust ring will wear unusually quickly since there is only half a ring to carry the crankshaft's forward thrust loads, including the axial thrust imposed by the clutch. This wear eventually creates enough play or clearance between crankshaft and block, identified in picture 12-7, to allow the half thrust ring to turn, or worse, to fall out of its seating. It ends up in the sump doing absolutely no good whatsoever, whereupon the crankshaft end float, without any effective restraint, increases dramatically. There are two consequences to this: firstly, you lose the clutch resistance as the flywheel moves away from you every time you dip the clutch; and secondly, the crankshaft has nothing but the block to restrain it, so it damages itself and the crankcase. This sounds irreparable, but our contributing

specialists can recover most situations. They machine away the damaged areas of both crank and block, re-assemble the crank to its block with standard thickness half thrusts, and measure the (doubtless hideous), end float. The best remedial action normally involves machining the main bearing cap to take a half thrust washer (as we will learn about in more detail shortly), and then, making two special half phosphor bronze bearings for the rear of the main bearing cap to take up the excessive float. This has the additional long term benefit, which we will discuss in more detail shortly, of providing a full rear thrust bearing face.

Prevention is better than cure, however, and our specialists can help prevent the problem in the first place. Racetorations offers what I think must be the easiest upgrade, and we already saw the solution in picture 12-2. The original thrust bearing design incorporates a tag with, in effect, cutaway areas either side. Racetorations believes its improved replacements virtually double the bearing area available simply by not cutting away material either side of the central tag. The best ideas are often the simple ones.

There are some other excellent solutions available and, if the Racetorations solution is not to your liking, you should certainly incorporate one of the following options even if you are not rebuilding the engine. Revington believes that a second half thrust ring needs to be fitted to the rear/clutch side of the block. Thus, in outline, you need to buy a pair of new standard thrust rings (£3), then remove the sump and the number 3 main bearing cap. Push both front and rear half bearings round so they fall out, and replace them with your

12-7. This is the main bearing cap that holds both half thrust bearings in place.

pair of standard thickness half thrust rings. You will almost certainly need to temporarily replace the main bearing cap for the next operation. Measure the crankshaft end float with a DTI and note the overall fore and aft movement. Remove the bearing cap again along with the standard thrust half thrusts, and send the end float information along with your bearing cap to Revington. They will machine the rear face of the bearing cap to receive a second half thrust ring as shown in picture 1-10.

If no further modifications were included, there is a very strong probability that the bearings would spin as the crankshaft revolves. To guard against this, Revington also drills one of the identical half bearings with two holes each and brass pins it to the rear of the newly machined bearing cap. The other matching half bearing is returned to you together with a third half thrust bearing (not necessarily identical to the other pair), for fitting in **front** of the main bearing cap in the normal way. With the thrusts and bearing cap re-assembled it would be prudent to check that the crankshaft end float indeed falls within tolerances (0.152 to 0.203mm) before you refit the sump. Incidentally, I would order the other things you'll need (at least a new sump gasket, oil and filter), so that everything comes in the same parcel.

Wherever you get your thrust bearing improvement from, it's worthwhile, and reassuring, to check the crankshaft's end float every year for a couple of years after this significant and essential improvement.

FAST ROAD IMPROVEMENTS

The first level of engine tuning mostly involves 'bolt-on' goodies to improve the basic engine's breathing capabilities. If you have a good engine and a 150 PI system, it would be a mistake to assume that much by way of bolt-on equipment will significantly improve the induction. If yours is a 125 system, on the other hand, then it's certainly worth perusing the chapter that focuses on PI systems, for the car will go better with some upgrading to the 125 system.

If you are not actually competing, I think there is merit in exploring other options. There could be much to be said for acquiring or persevering with a PI system or setting up a pair of SUs for fast road use! On the injected engine there has always been a fuel vaporisation problem that will only require more and more consideration as the boiling point of modern fuels decreases. However, we have addressed these issues and the solutions in the preceding chapter, so don't discard the PI option too quickly. SUs have untapped capabilities too, even the much maligned Stromberg can be (dramatically), improved, so read on, and talk to various experts. If you must fit Webers to a fast-road car, 40DCOEs average are the solution, while 45DCOEs are required for track use.

Remember that the overall performance of an engine is the combination of a (long), list of features, not just the induction! Virtually every aspect of the engine's components, the ignition system (the focus of an earlier chapter), the exhaust system, even the efficiency of the air filters plays its part in what can be likened to a 'chain', which we all know is only as strong as its weakest link. For those rebuilding their engines with performance in mind, while there are many other considerations, there is no doubt that there is no substitute for cubic capacity (as the saying goes), so let's start by exploring the opportunities for enlarging the capacity.

Cubic capacity/bore size/pistons
A general rule-of-thumb that applies to all engines states that the only way to really increase torque is via additional cubic capacity. Obviously, the increased capacity also gives the improver the opportunity to gain extra power. Whether it's an increase in torque or horsepower you're interested in, it's clear we need to look at ways of increasing the capacity of your engine. To do this effectively with the Triumph six-cylinder unit, we need to subdivide the increments into three, based upon bore (and thus piston), diameter. If you have ambitions to increase your bore (and piston), size above 78mm, it becomes essential to actually move the centre of cylinders 2, 3, 4 and 5 in order to equi-space them. This is an expensive operation, and puts this category of upgrade out of reach of all fast road and even some ultra fast road cars. Therefore, we'll only look at bore sizes at or over 78mm in the competition class of engine upgrades, discussed later in this chapter.

We are left to explore engines with bores of 74.7mm (*i.e.* standard), up to 78mm diameter here. In fairly modestly tuned engines, it's usually in order to use

cast pistons, but beyond modest tune you really need to switch to forged pistons for longevity and reliability, although I will have one special cast piston to suggest in a few moments. Engines using 74.7 to 75.7mm (*i.e.* standard plus 0.040in), diameter pistons form the first category of upgrade. The cast piston is inherently weak because of the oil ring slot around the crown, which leaves very little metal where the body merges into the crown. Consequently, there is minimal material in this area which is why most cast pistons are prone to crack here and why, to use another 'rule-of-thumb', you are prudent to switch to forged pistons before you reach the factory's largest size of cast piston: 76.2mm (+0.060in). You'll see some interesting comparative pictures at 12-8-1 to 12-8-3, which should help you appreciate some of the subtle but important differences between cast and forged pistons.

The second category of engine, therefore, starts at and includes 76.2mm diameter forged pistons and extends to 78mm diameter forged pistons. Such engines will certainly be built for the faster fast road cars, and possibly some ultra fast road cars. We have already established the necessity to use forged pistons, but the upper limit on bore size

12-8-1. An original style cast piston on the left, a forged replacement by Omega on the right. At first glance the forged one looks shorter than the cast piston. In fact, from gudgeon pin to crown the dimensions are the same in this case, although you can buy short four-cylinder pistons which necessitate longer con-rods! However, that is not the case here.

12-8-2. Same pair of pistons, slightly different view.

12-8-3. The additional strength of the forged (right side), piston becomes obvious from the underside. Note how the side areas are beautifully radiused into the underside of the piston crown. Expensive, but you can see the value for money forged pistons actually offer.

and thus capacity is the actual cylinders themselves. The wall thickness available is one factor but so too is the amount of material between cylinders 1 and 2, 3 and 4, and 5 and 6. As you increase the bore of the cylinders, the material becomes thinner and thinner and, at about 78mm diameter, becomes too thin to ensure an adequate seal with the head gasket.

So what engine capacities have we been talking about? A small table may help:

• 74.7mm diameter (standard) bore size provides 2498cc.
• 75.7mm (+0.40in) is the top limit for cast pistons and provides for 2658cc.
• 77.5mm (+0.112in) generates 2689cc.
• 78mm bores (+0.132in) increase the capacity to 2724 cc.
• 79.5mm pistons are the maximum achievable and gives our competition friends 2830cc.

You may also need to budget for a forged piston on the basis of engine-tune. It's worth emphasising that were you to build a very highly tuned engine that you intended to rev vigorously and frequently, you really would be prudent to fit forged pistons regardless of bore sizes. The standard slotted cast pistons are just not strong enough for elevated horsepower, although you may recall that I mentioned a few lines ago that there was one special cast piston that you could think about for fast and some ultra fast road engines. Originally designed and made for non-Triumph motorsport purposes, but now modified and made available by Racetorations in 76.5 to 77.5mm diameters, it offers the opportunity for some to reduce the cost of engines in these bore sizes. However, these pistons aside, another rule-of-thumb may help for, regardless of bore size, above about 160bhp forged pistons are prudent and above 170bhp they are essential.

At one time the higher coefficient of expansion of forged pistons necessitated larger skirt/bore clearances with a corresponding increase in oil

12-9. The length of the block is particularly vulnerable to torque-twisting once you start boring the cylinder mass away to enlarge the bores. The block's rigidity is not helped by the fact that it's open at both ends with only an alloy bridge at the front and the oil seal housing at the rear to box it! This block-brace kit increases the rigidity of the block

12-10. Comprising three supplementary steel main-bearing caps, a much stronger steel front 'bridge', and a steel oil seal housing the kit dramatically reduces stresses being transferred onto the main bearings and the cam, and possibly even further afield.

consumption, emissions and piston-slap noise. Today, though, many forged pistons have a coefficient of expansion that is less than the original cast pistons. Hyper-eutectic alloys, in particular, with their denser structure, have recently allowed designers to retain the 0.002/0.004in bore/piston clearances normally associated with cast pistons and are well worth specifying.

The selection of the most appropriate pistons and boring the block for a uprated Triumph engine requires considerable experience. Consequently, I think that you are better to consign the work to a specialist,such as Racetorations, in spite of the additional difficulties of transportation, than to ask your local engine reconditioning machinists, however skilled they are with the average automotive engine.

Omega, Acrolite and Cosworth are UK piston manufacturers, and all prefer to make pistons in batches that are basically too large for the practicalities of stocking a selection of sizes. Most specialists have resolved the problem by turning to US forged pistons, such as JE and Wiseco. The latter makes them in batch sizes relevant to the TR improvement market, and its products are available from Racetorations. Both are made from forged hyper-eutectic aluminium, which as we have already agreed is both stronger and lighter than the original cast pistons. Furthermore, their coefficient of expansion is less than the original pistons, thus allowing tighter bore/piston clearances to be used in fast road and ultra fast road engines. Naturally, a racing engine gets much hotter than it would in a fast road car, which requires the piston/bore clearance be increased even when using these superior pistons!

Although the factory recognised the marginal rigidity of the block, inherited from its 1600cc parentage, by adding a strengthening rib along the bottom right-hand-side of the block after the early TR6's, the block still needs all the rigidity help it can get. You exacerbate the vulnerability every time you increase the size of the bores and at +0. 040in a block-brace kit is prudent for fast road engines and mandatory for all race engines and fast road engines bored +0. 060in and above. You can see Racetorations kit at pictures 12-9 and 12-10.

CAMSHAFTS
We dealt with general camshaft matters

at some length in an earlier chapter, but there are some specifics to address and a few points to reiterate. One common mistake is to presume that one change, say fitting a pair of Weber carburettors, will transform the engine entirely on its own. Webers will certainly improve the induction, but their benefit will be very restricted unless a free-flowing exhaust system is also fitted. The existing camshaft also needs to be checked and confirmed as suitable. You'll need a dial gauge (a DTI to many), to establish the lift and a degree wheel to check the timing. These improvements may generate a 10% increase in power, and you could get a similar increment in torque.

Another reminder: the intake (or exhaust), valve open duration of a camshaft is indicated by the time that the respective valves are off their seats, *i.e.* open, but not necessarily fully open. The longer the cam duration the longer the valves are held open, which allows for increased cylinder charging and/ or scavenging at higher rpm, although this is usually at the expense of low rpm smoothness, power and performance.

It is surprisingly difficult to improve the CP six-cylinder engine's performance for fast road cars. The TR5 camshaft and 150bhp petrol injection makes for a hard-to-beat package. This camshaft has an excellent profile and a well-adjusted petrol injection setup is remarkably effective for fast road applications. This makes bolt on goodies difficult to justify, perhaps with the exception of an effective exhaust manifold and system. In fact, some camshaft profiles can upset the system dramatically and the fast roader is almost certainly wise to stay with the TR5 cam profile, or something very like it. The TR5 CP spec is: inlet 33-65 degrees, exhaust 65-35 degrees, lift 0.250in, duration 280 degrees (gives an overlap of 68 degrees).

Owners of the later 125 engines faced with a need to change a worn out camshaft in their fast road car should give the TR5 cam very serious thought, particularly if they plan to improve their petrol injection system to 150 levels. We looked at the PI system changes in Chapter 11, and you'll recall that a camshaft upgrade was a prerequisite. You'll not find that surprising when you look at the specification of the 125 cam: the TR6 CR cam offers: inlet 18-58 degrees, exhaust 58-18 degrees, lift 0.240in, duration 256 degrees and an overlap of 36 degrees. So, for fast roaders with a 125 PI system, upgrade it by all means but stick with it.

All our contributors feel they can offer even better camshaft options when it comes to ultra fast road and competitive cars. This need not result in a completely intractable motor, and each tell me that it has developed a range of excellent camshafts which retain tractability yet give good power increases. Most are produced from reground originals (if the condition of the original cam is good enough). There is no question that the ideal is to have your camshaft profile ground on a new blank, but it's considerably more expensive. Nevertheless, this method retains the original full base circle on each lobe, which is an advantage and worth the extra cost of the new blank if you are going ultra fast or competitive applications.

You do need to be a little careful when buying camshafts, however, for although they sell well, many do not have as great an effect on the engine performance as is sometimes suggested, particularly if bought in isolation. When it comes to competition levels of improvement, however, there is no doubt: a new/reprofiled camshaft is essential.

Needless to say, Racetorations has a range of camshafts which are tractable and powerful. It's interesting and relevant to mention that Darryl's very first attempt to get his (four-cylinder), TR going better was to redesign the profile of the camshaft using the motorcycle technology of the day! Revington also offers a range of cams for the six-cylinder engine as follows:

12-11. This is actually a four-cylinder timing-chain tensioner, but the six-cylinder one, although built into the cover, is very similar in concept. It's clearly incapable of retaining chain tension and, therefore, crank/cam relative positions.

	inlet	exhaust	lift in	duration
Fast road	37-63	73-27	0.290	280
Sprint	37-73	73-37	0.264	290
Rally	42-68	78-32	0.309	290
Race	52-78	88-42	0.339	310

The Revington cams are interesting in that they start with what seems like a fairly long duration (280 degrees). Certainly it seems long were you to compare it to the four-cylinder engine's duration. However, you'll recall that the original pre-1973 TR5 six-cylinder engine enjoyed a long duration cam (280 degrees). Consequently, if we are looking to add extra power to a six-pot, it's necessary to give the fast road cam at least the same duration but look to increased performance from the additional lift. Revington's Sprint cam is 290 degrees, while the Rally cam stays with 290 duration but has a much increased lift. The highest performance cam is designated Race and has a 310 degree duration and 0.339in lift.

TIMING CHAIN TENSIONER

Both four- and six-cylinder TR engines have a weakness in their design when it comes to keeping the timing chain taut. The standard method is a bent piece of spring steel that has no capability to stop the chain from whipping, and consequently allowing the camshaft to vary the relative position of cam to crankshaft. This tends to play havoc with the timing, at least to the accuracy that a racing engine requires! Needless to say, Racetorations offer a ratchet type tensioner for both four- and six-cylinder racing engines. Picture 12-11, while not an authentic six-cylinder tensioner, is sufficient to explain the problem.

VERNIER TIMING SPROCKET

With performance camshafts it's very important to set the camshaft to crankshaft timing to the optimum. Unfortunately, Triumph's design for fitting the original six-cylinder camshaft drive sprocket, shown in picture 12-12-1, was not quite as flexible as the earlier four-cylinder arrangement. To provide the essential fine adjustment for the highest tuned engines seeking absolute optimum performance, 'vernier adjustable cam gears, shown in picture 12-12-2, are available from Revington. Cambridge Motor Sport's offering is shown in picture 12-12-3, while Racetorations also regards this component as important and can also offer a compatible vernier cam gear.

12-12-1. The standard top/cam sprocket is adequate for most fast road applications but leaves a little to be desired if you are squeezing the last ounce of performance from your six-cylinder engine.

12-12-2. A vernier cam sprocket will enable you to set the cam/crank relationship absolutely spot on for your cam's design parameters.

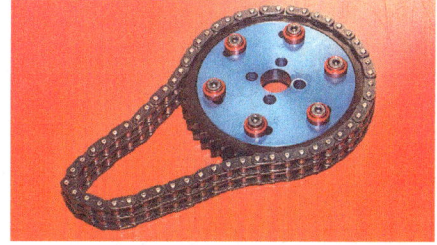

12-12-3. As will Racetoration's own version.

CYLINDER HEAD

After the camshaft, the cylinder head plays the next most important role in dictating engine performance. It will, therefore, need to be gas-flowed, of course, and you would be silly not to take opportunity to have hardened exhaust valve seats fitted to allow the use of lead-free fuel, too. The use that the head will be put to will have a major influence on the modifications and, inevitably, the cost. The degree of gas-flow work that you have carried out will have some influence on performance, for example, but a huge effect on cost! Valve size can also have a significant effect on performance but must be a compromise, as valves that are too big will cause gas flow problems at low and mid rpm. Compression also has an effect on performance and, again, will be a compromise since you must not go too high if you are to avoid pre-detonation.

All our contributors do a range of improved cylinder heads, all of which are gas-flowed, and all are tailored to each individual's needs. 'Road' heads usually incorporate standard valve sizes, but in unleaded compatible materials, so phosphor-bronze guides and stainless steel exhaust valves are fitted as standard to all heads. 'Race/Rally' heads usually incorporate bigger valves.

Neil Revington strongly suggests all head rebuilds be carried out in harmony with each individual's engine specification. This way, he stresses, the correct valve springs are fitted to suit the lift of the camshaft, and coil binding is avoided. He recommends great care when someone tries to sell a standard, say Stage 2, head. The pistons you are using may not be compatible and/or the CR may be wrong for your engine (at best a disappointment, at worst, destructively expensive).

US cylinder heads

All US heads were originally machined to give a much lower compression ratio than those for the UK, so you'll need to have their compression ratio increased. This necessitates machining, of course, but you need to first check on the porting of the US head. Many of the US cars (all the TR250s and the early TR6s), had slightly different cylinder head porting to standard UK heads and, since most tuning equipment is designed for UK heads, you'll need to reject the 'narrow' inlet port US heads. Picture 12-13 shows the alternatives, but even

so the differences between the three pairs of circular inlet ports cast into the side of each head are hard to see. There is a gap between each pair of ports which, if you measure from the inside of one port to the inside of its other half, will be either 9/16in (0.563in, 14mm) or 7/8in (0.875in, 22mm). Select the wider ported heads and machine it to increase your compression ratio.

Prior to machining a low compression wide port head, it's important that an expert checks the head first to ensure it has not already been planed earlier in its life. This check is carried out by closing the sparkplug hole with a bolt, and then measuring the cubic capacity of the combustion chamber with a pipette. This will enable the experts to calculate how much metal to remove to give you the compression ratio you need. Most aim for about 9.5:1 for fast road engines, and the majority of US heads need about 80 thousands of an inch machining from their mating face. Ultra fast and competitive cars may want a higher CR, which will, of course, require additional material be removed. We'll come back to compression ratios later in the chapter.

If you're not sure how to identify a low compression head you can in fact do so with ease even with the head fixed to the block. There's a lug sticking out on the left/distributor side of the engine. This is about 1/8in on a high compression head, but increases to perhaps 1/4in on the thicker low compression units. It's even easier to tell the difference when the head is off the car since you can also

12-13. It's difficult to see even with the cylinder heads alongside each other like this. Nevertheless, the top early US head does have each pair of inlet ports slightly closer together than the UK counterpart. You can identify the UK head by its roll pins (arrowed), which (if left in place), only permit PI inlet manifolds to be fitted.

check to see if the combustion chamber has a lip to it. A high compression head will flow straight from the mating face to the concave of the chamber, whereas a low compression head will have a lip or boundary 'wall' about 1/8in high. In the UK, a late US head that has passed the above checks will also need the hole plugged where the ERG valve will have been removed.

Pushrods

The length of your pushrods will depend upon the camshaft you are to use and the amount you have planed off the cylinder head. When you fit a camshaft that has been ground on a new blank, the base circle of each cam should be as per the original camshaft, and the effect on pushrod length will be minimal. However, if you are fitting a re-grind, the cam base circles will have been reduced as part of the re-grinding operation and this will mean that a longer pushrod will be required to retain the rocker geometry.

Even if you find that the change in length required is minimal, there are still some very good reasons for renewing and upgrading the pushrods. First, there's the clicking noise that worn pushrods can make from each end sphere, which collectively can make an engine very noisy indeed. Inspect both ends of any pushrods you are thinking of re-using. Ensure the fit into the cam followers and the rockers is not sloppy, and that it is the outside edges of the spheres that will carry the loads, leaving the centre of each spherical end with clearance to carry the essential lubrication.

Even if all seems well with your original pushrods, you should still be very careful about re-using them since nearly all pushrods flex when handling the action required by a high-lift/fast-ramping cam. This problem is applicable to all competition and most ultra fast road engines, you'll lose the valve opening speed intended by the camshaft designer if your pushrods flex. Competition engines are best fitted with stronger pushrods, therefore, and Racetorations' chrome-moly pushrods are not only made to your specific individual length but are unlikely to flex even with the strongest valve springs and steepest ramped cam. They also have new spheres to ensure the end fit is perfect.

You need to be particularly alert to the potential consequences of fitting overly long pushrods if your cylinder head is a US one. If you plane the head, fit the original pushrods and then turn the engine over, you risk snapping a rocker arm or two. Furthermore, this can even occur when you refit the same pushrods that came from you own engine (if you have made alterations to the cylinder head, that is). The pushrods are different for each major difference in compression ratio. There were in fact three lengths of pushrods, but the ones of primary interest are the longest (US) rods and the shortest (UK) ones. If you increase your compression ratio by having say a low compression ex-USA head reduced in thickness, you need to replace the pushrods with the UK version.

You will get a clear indication as to whether your pushrods are indeed over length when you fit the rocker gear and try to adjust the tappets. If you seem to virtually run out of thread on the rocker adjusting screw, you probably need the shorter/earlier screw and/or shorter pushrods. You can buy spacers that fit beneath the rocker shaft pillars and thus raise the whole rocker assembly to compensate, but I'm sure you agree that it makes more sense to get the job right and fit the correct pushrods for your head's compression ratio.

Incidentally, if you are unsure whether the pushrods or adjusting screw lengths are correct for your car as you assemble the top end, stop. Don't try turning the engine over or running it for you could, as I said earlier, break a rocker arm or strip a half-in adjusting screw and do more damage. Check with an expert first and fit the correct parts.

Gas flowing

Gas flowing the cylinder head is one of the absolute key contributors to power, and warrants a book in itself. The shape and size of the valves and valve seats, shown in picture 12-14, are crucial, so are best left to the professionals in view of the inter-valve spacing and the specialised equipment required to form the three-angle hardened valve seats used today. However, you can contribute, particularly if you plan a fast road car, by improving the gas flow to and from the valve heads yourself. For ultra fast road and competitive cars this work is probably best left to the experts if you want the very best results, though the work is protracted and expensive. So an outline of gas flowing at home may help some of the everyday cars go that bit better. You will need some cutters and grinding tools, of course, and Peter

12-14. This TR5 head looks about ready to go back on the block after the ports have been gas-flowed. Take advice from the specialists who helped with this book before contemplating enlarging the valves for the clearance (arrowed), is fairly small.

Burgess (address in the Appendix), stocks a range of porting accessories that may make the job that little bit easier.

Inlets first. You need a round template 1.3in (33mm) in diameter. This could be an old valve or a circular piece of wood, for example, which will indicate where to grind excess material from the inlet ports as it is slid through the length of each port. The constant circular shape is important, so take care not to lose the circular shape until you get to the area just in front of each valve. Here the emphasis changes from metal removal to grinding smooth and blending the faces of the casting. Once you are satisfied with the shape of your inlet tract, you need to improve the finish to some degree (though not to the point of a 'mirror' finish since this would take too long and would probably be of little benefit). Use a fine stone followed by emery cloth to get what might be described as a reasonable finish.

The exhaust tracts present a slightly different challenge (they are rectangular). Your first priority should be to ensure each port lines up with its hole in the manifold gasket. Grind the ports until there is indeed a close correlation between exhaust ports and gasket, then smoothly blend that shape back into the exhaust tract. Follow the grinding with the same stone/emery stage until you achieve a reasonable but not necessarily polished finish. Picture 12-15 shows the manifold gasket being used as an intermediary. Once the port holes in the exhaust ports are altered to match the gasket, the gasket should be offered to the exhaust manifold itself and any mis-matches or non-alignments in the edges corrected.

12-15. Clearly a nice 'extractor' tubular exhaust manifold (six to two to one, is my guess), but even the tiniest step between exhaust port and manifold will create undesirable turbulence and resistance.

Compression ratios

The ideal CR will very much depend upon the fuel available to you and the intended use of the car, so the ideal/maximum CR can't be specified here. However, as a rough guide, the majority of UK fast road cars run with a CR of 9.5:1. Carburettor inducted cars using unleaded fuel could experience run-on problems above a 9.5:1 CR. Ultra fast road cars will have a CR somewhere in the region of 10.25:1 perhaps, and competition cars may run anywhere from 11.5 up to 12.25:1.

Whatever you do, be very careful that your pushrod lengths are compatible with the compression ratio (i.e. the height), of your cylinder head. A slightly over-long pushrod will destroy the geometry of the rockers, while grossly over-length pushrods could break rockers as the valve springs, seen in picture 12-16, compress until there is no more space between the coils, at which point something has to give!

12-16. There looks to be plenty of room between the coils of this uncompressed valve spring. However, the space reduces when the spring is compressed to hold the valve shut and reduces still further when the cam forces the valve open.

Should it be necessary, reducing the CR of your six-cylinder head is difficult since it has not proved economically viable to manufacture the variety of thick copper gaskets available for the four-cylinder engines. However, a solution is available as long as as replacement heads are readily available, albeit with low CRs which will require planing. Indeed some ex-US heads will require substantial amounts of material removing if a CR of circa 9.5:1 is to be reached and road performance optimised. A reminder of the US cylinder heads to look out for and avoid is shown in picture 12-17.

You can get a rough idea of your CR without actually removing the cylinder head. Remove the number one sparkplug and get the piston to exactly tdc on its compression stroke. Jack the car up so that the plug's opening is as high as you can safely get it and build a 'dam' of plasticine or blue tack around the lower half of the plug hole. Fill a graduated syringe up to its top graduation with engine oil and inject the oil into the combustion chamber. If you are reasonably quick you should fill the combustion chamber and have oil left in the syringe. It's the amount of oil in the syringe that we are interested in for that will enable you to deduce how much oil was required to fill the combustion chamber. Once you know how much you've injected, remove as much oil as you can from the chamber (the syringe and a short length of windscreen washer tubing should enable you to suck a very high proportion out), and then remove the plasticine dam and clean up inside

12-17. This is a reminder that, while later cylinder heads from ex-US cars were not so afflicted, the initial cars had a slightly narrower gap between the (circular), inlet ports which precludes fitting tuning equipment. Consequently, if you need to find another cylinder head for any six-cylinder car, it's best to pass over any with the narrower inlet ports.

and outside the chamber with a rag. Remove a lead from the coil to ensure none of the cylinders can fire and then spin the engine over for a few seconds before giving the head a final clean-up and then reconnect everything. If your six-cylinder engine is nominally 2498cc, a few seconds with a calculator will tell you that each cylinder's swept volume is 416cc. If you divide that figure by the volume of the combustion chamber (for example, 48cc), you arrive at the CR of, in this example, 8.7:1.

'Unleading' the cylinder head

In my restoration book I advocated not rushing into fitting inserts into your valve seats until other mechanical issues dictate you remove the head. Certainly, if the engine is running well, don't remove the cylinder head just to have it unleaded. In the meantime use an AWA (an anti-wear additive). I've not tried them all, so ask for MIRA (Motor Industry Research Association) reports on all the products you are considering and go for the one that allows the least recession. I've heard good reports about Millers VSP-Plus for road going cars, and very good reports about CVL (Competition Valve Lubricant) in racing engines. Both products are based upon potassium.

Any exchange/uprated cylinder head you buy these days will already be converted for unleaded fuels. If yours hasn't, but is currently off the car for an engine rebuild, now would be a good time to have it done. The process, which is the same for aluminium as for cast iron heads, involves machining a recess for the hard, sintered in fact, insert used for each exhaust valve seat (photograph 12-18). This is definitely not a DIY job but, since it's a topic that will be relevant to every reader at some time, I thought it would be of interest to establish what work and costs were involved.

The machine shop must select the appropriate insert (in terms of bore and outside diameter and grade of sinter), for your head. The size issue is relatively self-explanatory, of course, in that you need a bore that is compatible with the throat size of the particular cylinder head you are about to machine, and an outside diameter that will accommodate the exhaust valve in question. There are hundreds of sizes to choose from and at least three grades of sintered insert. For unleaded petrol/gas it's usual to use a high machinabilty grade consisting of a blend of finely dispersed Tungsten-

carbide, tool-steel and alloys of iron. The makers say this provides machining characteristics comparable to cast-iron yet the insert is extremely hard and suitable for naturally aspirated and turbocharged engines.

The first step in the process is to remove the old valve guides and fit new ones. This is important since virtually every subsequent operation will rely on a mandrel that will be positioned in each valve guide to provide the accuracy of each machining operation. The old valve seat is then machined away with great care, for it's important to ensure the outside diameter of the hole is absolutely correct for the selected insert. In fact, the hole needs to be a prescribed amount less than the insert's outside size, and to ensure this my hosts Bailey and Liddle actually bore the hole twice. The first cut is never quite to size because the cutter warms up and expands. Consequently, they slightly adjust the boring tool after the first holes have been bored and go for a second, much finer, dead-size cut.

Next up is driving the new inserts into their recessed bores. Although already an interference fit, the insert plays its part by expanding into the bored recess and providing a dependable valve seat that will not move, even at the elevated temperatures in a combustion chamber.

12-18. In the foreground the insert has been machined flush with the combustion chamber, while the next insert is being machined to the profile of the exhaust valves provided by this TR owner. You can establish whether your valves seem likely to be up to the vigours of unleaded fuel by a quick magnetic check. If the valve attracts a magnet it will be too soft for use with unleaded fuels and must be replaced with one that contains more stainless/nimonic materials, which will not attract a magnet.

There are still two machining operations to carry out. The first, shown in photograph 12-18, involves the same setup (including the all-important but unseen guide mandrel), and brings the top of the sintered insert down to the level of each combustion chamber. The second requires selecting a cutter that matches the profile of the exhaust valve to be used, and machining out the inside of each insert until the valve sits properly in the head/insert/combustion chamber ... nothing to it really! The final operation is carried out by hand to blend-in, where required, the base of each insert with the its respective exhaust passage.

The cost of fitting new valve guides and unleaded compatible exhaust valve seats to a six-cylinder TR head will vary depending upon how much preparatory work you do yourself. Prices range from about £150 for just fitting inserts to your stripped and pre-cleaned cylinder head, to about £450 for the comprehensive service of fully stripping, fitting inserts, supplying all parts and re-assembling your head ready to bolt to your block.

In addition, you need to ensure that the numerous fuel lines and seals with which the fuel comes into contact during its passage from tank to cylinder are also compatible with unleaded fuel. Unleaded fuels are made from a different chemical mix to leaded fuel and, basically, the original rubber seals and flexible fuel lines are unable to handle the unleaded variety. If all seals and lines are not changed to unleaded-compatible viton or neoprene materials then fuel leaks become very probable. Frankly, the integrity of the fuel lines and seals is far more important than the improvements that almost everyone concentrates on (the valve seat recession), and you'll be advised to install continuous copper lines before switching to unleaded fuels.

ROCKERS
Bushed rockers
I like Revington's approach to improving the standard rockers. Neil advocates boring out the standard, possibly worn rockers, to accept a oilite bush. This is, of course, ideal in that the bush (and possibly the rocker shaft if un-nitrided), is all that subsequently needs replacing when wear eventually occurs. They don't alter the ratio of lift, but it's still imperative that valve springs appropriate to the lift of your particular cam are fitted. Too little clearance within the valve spring will result in coil binding,

with the consequence that pushrods will bend and, in extreme cases, rockers get broken.

Roller rockers
Available from most of our contributors, these alternatives from Cambridge Motor Sport are shown in picture 12-19. They are simple to fit, if slightly expensive at £450. Fitted primarily to reduce valve stem wear, they may reduce friction within the valve gear because of the roller bearings at both pivot and tip. They come with a hardened rocker shaft and two types of steel rocker posts. The standard TR rocker has a 1.5:1 ratio and this can be replicated by a compatible set of roller rockers from Cambridge Motor Sport. The benefit of (both types of), roller rocker is that the wear on the valve guides is much reduced, so the 1.5:1 units have their advantages. However, care needs to be exercised if you're tempted by the increased valve opening offered by a 1.6:1 ratio set. A high lift cam and 1.6 ratio rockers are neither advised nor required for fast road use, although you may use that combination on a competitive car where the valve springs have been chosen with this combination in mind. Consider the potentially dire consequences of 'bound' valve springs brought about by over opened valves.

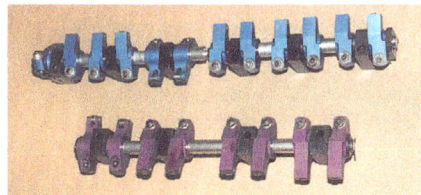

12-19. The four- and six-cylinder roller rockers. The differences are imperceptible at this distance, but I think the top two-piece six-cylinder set are the standard 1.5 ratio rockers, and the set nearest the camera are (four-cylinder, of course), 1.6 ratio.

VALVE GUIDES
Premature wear in the guides is usually the result of the valve gear being at the wrong height for the valve lift that will be generated by your camshaft. Triumph got the height of the valve gear correct in the first place for the cam lifts it was designing into its engines, however, if you fit a camshaft that increases the anticipated valve lift, then it follows that the height of the valve gear will be

12-20. I heard conflicting views on crankshaft dampers and think it best that you make your own mind up after seeking advice from the particular TR engine specialist you have been buying parts from. What is consistent, though, is that some form of damping pulley is required on the front of the crankshaft.

incorrect. You need to get the rocker height halfway within the stroke of the valve if you seek maximum mechanical effect and minimum sideways loads on the valves and the valve guides. If the cam you fit increases the valve's opening from standard by, say 0.125in (3mm), it's likely that the rocker shaft pedestals will need to be reduced in height by 0.063in (1.5mm). You'll also need special valve springs since you will have absorbed the original 3mm clearance and there is a danger of coil binding and excessive strain on pushrods, rocker arms and rocker bearings. Rocker pedestals are available from Revington and our other contributors.

Front crankshaft dampers
The six-cylinder engine has some odd harmonics at high rpm, which can lead to catastrophic breakages. Cambridge Motor Sport and Racetorations offer a front crankshaft damper which, they believe, is particularly effective.

On the other hand, Revington recommends the use of the standard dampened crank pulley we see in picture 12-20, but has made a front crankshaft washer available which is especially recessed to allow the crankshaft to poke through to the pulley.

RACE IMPROVEMENTS
Cylinder bores/piston diameters/engine capacities

You'll recall that the maximum bore/piston diameter that can be built into a racing engine is 79.5mm, which gives a capacity of 2830cc. To achieve this, it's essential to bore and sleeve the block for cylinders 2, 3, 4 and 5 so that the liners are more equi-spaced than was originally the case. You will, of course, also need to fit a special cylinder head gasket (only available from Racetorations), in order to match the different cylinder spacing. Your specialist may be able to just open the bore of cylinders 1 and 6 but, depending upon the casting, it may also be necessary to liner numbers 1 and 6 too. Any enthusiast going to the expense of equi-spaced cylinders and 79.5mm diameter pistons is very unlikely to retain the standard cast crankshaft. I have included a paragraph on billet steel crankshafts a little later, but it seems relevant to just mention here that, to my surprise, you can "get away with" using a steel crank with original journal positions even when you have changed the locations of the cylinders. The con rods will, apparently, sit off-centre on their respective gudgeon pins with no undue consequences! However, when building a top-of-the-range racing engine from scratch, Racetorations fits a correspondingly designed steel billet crank to restore the central axis of the con rod to piston.

Cam followers

Standard six-cylinder engines suffer as a result of being fitted with too small a diameter of cam follower. This is a particular weakness when high lift camshafts are used and, consequently, any engine intended for very fast road or competitive use benefits from special attention in this area.

Racetorations have two solutions. Its standard diameter followers use upgraded quality steel compared to the originals and are sold as being compatible with all its camshafts and with all but the most powerful engines.

They also offer a solution for very powerful engines but this time using a hardened sleeve pressed into the block and the larger diameter of follower we saw in photograph 12-6, which is probably better for the really high performance competition engines, but it does require that the engine have its 12 follower bores especially bored to

suit the enlarged size of follower. Not surprisingly, Revington can also supply a tuftrided cam follower.

All cam followers will come with the standard oil drain hole in place.

Low inertia steel crankshafts

These are designed to eliminate the zigzag configuration of the original crank by using 3 'dummy' main bearings in the new crank. This design makes a steel crankshaft easier to balance with less offset balancing necessary. This, in turn, has the benefit of reducing the inertia of these crankshafts. Further, if you look at Racetorations' steel crankshaft you will note that it's also bored in several places to further reduce dead weight and inertia. Not a six-cylinder example unfortunately but, nevertheless, picture 12-21 demonstrates this. That said, steel crankshafts are not significantly lighter that the cast originals they are designed to replace, although they are significantly stronger, with extra metal thickness where experience has shown additional strength is required. The response (pick-up), from any engine with a low inertia crank is improved, in exactly the same way as a lightened flywheel reduces inertia and improves response.

A few very fast road cars may elect to use steel cranks but, at £1850, they are mainly in demand for purely competitive cars where rpm in excess of 6000 will be called for. The original cast crankshafts are reasonably durable for

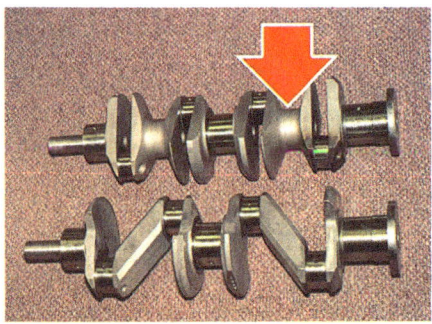

12-21. Although not pictures of six-cylinder crankshafts, these four-cylinder cranks are examples of early (bottom), and later (top), steel billet cranks and will serve to illustrate the improvements mentioned in the main text. The latest four- and six-cylinder steel cranks bring about a reduction in zig-zag via the use of the 'dummy mains' I have highlighted. This clearly improves the balance of such crankshafts.

fast road and even most ultra fast road cars. However, if one does break it tends to be where the stresses build up from each cylinder. The energy produced by the front five cylinders gets focussed towards the back of the crank, whereas the corresponding web at the front of the crank only has to handle the stress generated by one cylinder.

There is a relatively recent development in the steel crankshaft's design that is intended to reduce the turbulence within the sump. Initial thinking was to design and manufacture the improved steel crankshafts with 'knife-like' leading edges so that, it was thought, the spinning crankshaft would cut though the oil in the sump with consummate ease. Japanese GP engine design, no doubt after much research, showed this not to be true, though, and that 'bullnose' crankshaft edges generated less turbulence within the oil and were a more efficient design. Steel TR replacement crankshafts now follow this initiative.

I found a difference of opinion when it came to balancing standard and fast road crankshafts. Because a six-cylinder engine is reasonably well balanced to start with, Revington finds that neither balancing the engine nor tufriding the crankshaft is important for fast road applications, unless frequent high revolutions are likely. The other contributors, however, believe that both are very beneficial even for fast road cars. It is unanimously agreed that balancing is essential for high rpm ultra fast road or competition engines.

Several other specialists also find that the original cast iron crankshafts break relatively frequently and it too has developed a stronger steel crankshaft. Its use is recommended if you raise your six pot to racing tune or contemplate regularly using the engine at 6000rpm or above. Occasional use at 6500rpm will probably be quite in order, provided the crank has been tuftrided and carefully balanced.

Steel is inherently stronger than cast iron and, since a forged steel crankshaft is economically out of the question, we're left with little choice but to machine steel crankshafts from a billet of steel. Fortunately, modern computer controlled machinery makes this as quick as the complexity of a crankshaft allows, but it's still a time consuming operation on a large and expensive piece of machinery. Typical end results currently cost about £2500, but they are significantly stronger and more rigid than the original cast crank. Furthermore, it comes nitrided to ensure the longevity of the bearing surfaces and the oil system is fully interconnected within the crankshaft and has been improved by cross drilling the oil ways.

Although none of the original six-cylinder crankshafts have an oil feed problem, there is an advantage in choosing, if you have a choice, an early/long back one. The flywheel is shorter, lighter, and easier to lighten further still.

With the exception of the rear lip oil seal (which is very easily fitted in a standard cylinder block), most steel cranks are interchangeable with the original crank. They retain all the original bearing sizes allowing the owner to retain the standard con-rods (in the interests of cost savings), if they wish. Full race cranks with different pin sizes are available for those wishing to reduce their reciprocating weight and friction, but these require custom rods as well.

Connecting rods

There was a consensus that, if you fit a rev limiter (in order to keep your rpm generally below 6000, for example), a steel crankshaft is not a necessity. However, the point at which our various experts felt it became essential to use steel connecting rods differed. A crankshaft breakage, while not in any way desirable, of course, usually causes little peripheral damage. It will make a nasty noise, and certainly cause the engine to run rough, and will probably accompanied by severe vibration. Nevertheless, the engine will be rebuildable, albeit with a new crank and bearings and some expense, but you'll be back in business reasonably quickly. However, a broken con-rod causes catastrophic engine damage and can completely destroy every part of your engine. In short, a broken rod will bring about far more damage than a broken crankshaft, and may present you with no alternative but to start from scratch with a full replacement engine.

The six-cylinder engine's con-rods are a better design than those used for the four-cylinder engine. This is because Triumph omitted the oil holes in the later engine's con-rods (these were a major weakness in the four). However, the whole design of the six-cylinder rod is still fragile, largely due to the engine's roots. As I mentioned in *How to Restore*

Triumph TR5/250 & 6, the six-cylinder engine started life as a 1600cc four-cylinder unit producing around 75bhp (with con-rods to suit). In six-cylinder format it's not unreasonable to expect those rods to handle 110bhp ... but 200bhp? I don't think so! Racetorations' policy is that at or above 160bhp, **always** fit steel connecting rods (they're stronger and lighter than the originals).

Although the original con-rods aren't ideal in an uprated engine, they can be lightened by grinding some metal away from the five very specific places outlined in picture 12-22-1. Since the original con-rods are not regarded as indestructible, any work you do to lighten yours must be followed up by (casting) flash removal (illustrated at pictures 12-22-2 and 12-22-3), crack-testing, balancing, checking dimensions/straightness, re-hardening

12-22-1. The six-cylinder engine's con-rod is stronger than a four-cylinder rod but, nevertheless, is still susceptible to breakage at high revs. You can reduce each rod's inertia by removing some metal from the areas indicated, and ...

12-22-2. ... dramatically lessen the likelihood of breakage by also removing all the flashes and other sharp edges around each rod. Here we see a big end so treated, while ...

12-22-3. ... the little end needs just as much care and attention.

12-22-4. The safe option for high-revers, however, is the forged replacement you see at the top of this picture

(by shot-peening), and honing the big ends. However, bearing in mind the point I made about con-rods destroying an engine, home grinding/lightening of con-rods isn't something I would encourage. In the interests of safety, make fitting steel con-rods your priority before you spend cash on a steel crankshaft. Most specialists recommend forged steel con-rods if you anticipate engine rpm at or over 6500rpm.

The steel con-rods shown in picture 12-22-4 are expensive (at about £200 each) but do need to be budgeted for as the power and/or rpm increase.

Building the engine

All the specialists justifiably feel they have much to offer by way of assembly expertise. All will test run the engines on a dynamometer. However, all will also assist the home assembler in every way they can. With all this support available by 'phone, fax or email, it is possible for you to assemble a racing engine at home for possibly the first time with some confidence. However, the cost of the components for a full-race is very high indeed and, frankly, you're probably best going the extra mile and letting an experienced professional do it for you.

12-23-1. The all steel but very much lightened flywheel recommended by Racetorations has huge holes milled around the periphery of the steel billet for maximum effect, and additional holes to improve securing it to the crankshaft. I have seen as many as 12 securing holes on the most powerful six-cylinder engines.

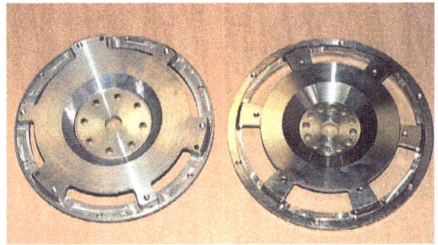

12-23-2. There are several types of steel flywheel. On the left, with eight central mounting bolt holes, is a four-cylinder flywheel for use with a standard OE clutch. On the right is a six-cylinder engine's flywheel, and we can see from the reduced diameter of friction plate face that this is intended for a 7.25in competition clutch. Neither flywheel has its starter ring gear pressed in place yet. Obviously, most of the weight reduction has been achieved by careful sculpturing of the flywheel material round the outside.

FLYWHEELS

Not surprisingly, all the contributing specialists can offer a range of flywheel options, although they don't all agree on what's the best solution. A number of specialists can supply an aluminium flywheel but feel that the essential steel facing for the clutch brings additional components, manufacturing cost and complexity since steel and aluminium have different rates of expansion. These

12-23-3. The increased power and torque from a seriously uprated engine puts unacceptable strains on the flywheel fixing bolts, regardless of the flywheel's material. However, the strain is focused on too small an area when an aluminium flywheel is used. Here we see the solution to both problems: doubling the flywheel attachment bolts. As a matter of interest, this Racetorations aluminium flywheel has a (replaceable), steel facing for the clutch.

can be avoided, however, by using a one piece, all steel flywheel. Although slightly heavier than an aluminium unit, it's light enough for use in conjunction with a four bearing six-cylinder crankshaft, and offers the reliability advantages of simplicity. Most flywheels that are available fit both standard and billet steel crankshafts. Invariably the flywheel to crankshaft securing bolts are doubled up, regardless of which type of crankshaft you use, but you're also prudent to buy a high quality flywheel bolt kit.

A selection of a small part of the huge range of flywheel options can be seen in photographs 12-23-1 to 12-23-5. Revington's and Racetorations' flywheels are all aluminium-based, albeit with steel insert options. They are available for CP and CR crank formats, respectively the long and short nose cranks, in standard and race weights (the latter having extra machined areas for reduced weight), and with and without ring gear pre-shrunk on.

12-23-4. Revington also supplies a very wide range of flywheels (here is one aluminium example for a long back six-cylinder crank). This weighs 4.4kg (a little less than 10lbs), and costs about £300. It will need a ring gear, though, adding to weight and cost.

12-23-5. Another Revington aluminium flywheel, this time for a four-cylinder engine and with a steel faceplate. In case you're wondering, Neil took this shot (I wouldn't dare), with the flywheel sitting on the bonnet/hood of a TR4A to demonstrate its light weight!

EXHAUST MANIFOLDS AND SYSTEMS

Modern cars enjoy the benefit of cast exhaust manifolds, and these can be very effective indeed. Cars of the generation we are discussing, however, will only perform well if the exhaust system generally, and the exhaust manifolds/headers in particular, are properly fabricated from tubular materials. The rest of the exhaust system must not be regarded as unimportant, but since the manifold have the greatest influence on the effectiveness of the engine, we'll look at them in a little more detail.

As far as possible the manifold design should use equal length pipes. Photograph 12-24-1 is worth a close look as it shows the exhaust makers' art very effectively. It's pretty obvious, but the less restriction within the system the better, so gradual radii are better than sharp corners and, within reason, the larger the pipe diameter the better. What might not be so obvious is that the tube's radii should be formed using mandrels (a string of brass balls), not by empty bending. A tube bent empty flattens slightly, which adds to the restriction, and should be rejected before purchase.

The material your manifolds/headers are made from is also important, not from a direct performance point of view, but with an eye on their life expectancy. Mild steel manifolds will work fine but will rust eventually, and can't really handle the temperature generated were you to wrap silicon tape around them to reduce under bonnet temperatures. Stainless steel, particularly 18/8 grade, will out-perform mild steel in every respect and handle the higher temperatures of wrapped manifolds perfectly satisfactorily.

The exhaust system itself is always a compromise between noise and performance, and it's the manufacturer's development work that sets this balance for each exhaust system. There are no rules of thumb regarding the bore

size you should select, for an increase in system bore size might increase power but move the engine's torque characteristics into a ineffective band. As a result, you're best to buy from a reputable supplier, and even better to purchase a system identical to a friend's proven set up. I would, however, always go for a system made from stainless steel, particularly if the car is going to be subjected to periods of inactivity.

For those who like the aesthetics of the six-cylinder car's twin-pipe system, Revington's offering is a definite improvement over the original

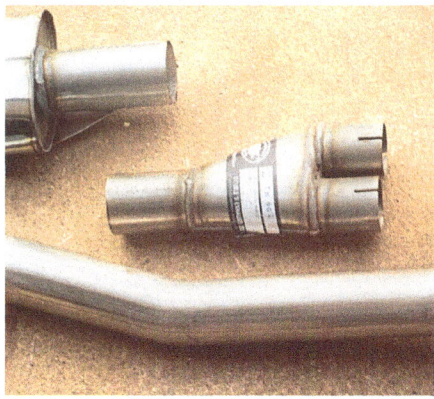

12-24-2. The six to two to one expedient is achieved via this adapter which allows standard or tubular fabricated manifolds to be married to a single large bore exhaust pipe.

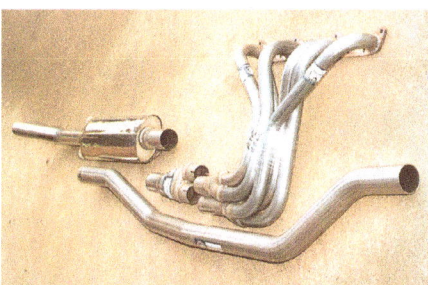

12-24-3. This is the full big bore, single box system, while ...

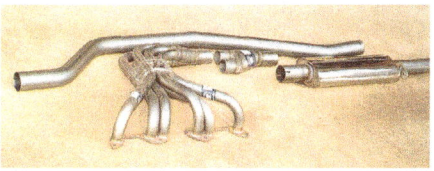

12-24-4. ... you can select the very slightly reduced bore if you want.

system since it has been specifically designed to improve ground clearance. Neil Revington has achieved this major benefit by moving the boxes forward to points in the chassis where they can sit within the chassis. The original system was 1.75in bore, but Revington's system is 2in bore, thus reducing back pressure. The system is only available in stainless steel (for longevity), but it can be fitted to a standard TR manifold, or any manifold, for which there is an adapter of the type shown in picture 12-24-2. However, most will purchase the system and fit it straight onto an extractor manifold which has two outlet pipes where the downpipe ends.

The alternative from Revington is a single pipe, big bore system with a single box and a tubular extractor manifold (picture 12-24-3). The whole arrangement is made in stainless steel, and the design of the manifold has been given particular attention in order to maximise the efficiency of the system. There's a choice of single boxes available (picture 12-24-4), the most recent design provides for a gentle 84dB exhaust note, while the earlier box, which is still available, gives what many may regard as the essential sporty exhaust note that I must confess to enjoying. The manifold part of this setup may be a shade longer than you might at first expect. The six tails from the exhaust ports culminate in a single 2.25in (57mm), pipe as far back as the bellhousing, which minimises the sharp bends within the manifold to allow for maximised gas flow. There is a downside for those with PI induction in that the manifold fouls on the standard (under-slung) throttle mechanism. Revington offers an improved throttle mechanism, which we touched upon in chapter 11, and this or a similar top-mounted mechanism is required to provide the space for the exhaust manifold. However, if your car has carburettor induction you need to check with Revington, since one inlet manifold will not marry with this particular system.

I believe that too much is made of (very) big bore exhaust systems, for it's very easy to fit a system that is too large, particularly in the primary/manifold pipes. Too large an exhaust manifold reduces the speed of gas flow out of the exhaust valves and, particularly at low revs, can even result in some exhaust gasses creeping back into the cylinder (called reversion), before the exhaust valve has

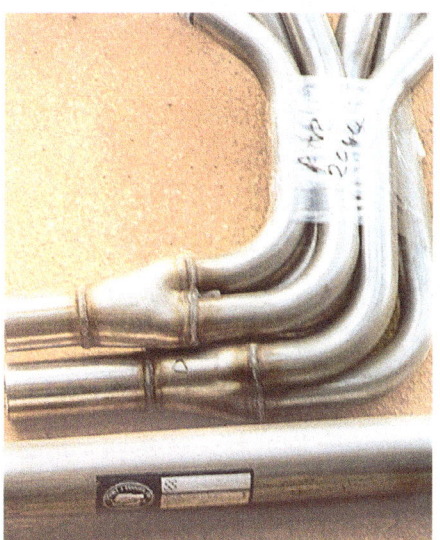

12-24-1. All mandrel-formed stainless steel pipes in this six to two system. Beautiful welding job too!

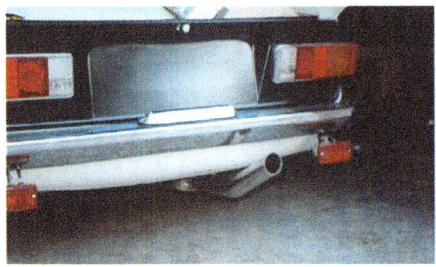

12-25. Single pipe systems, whether average or big bore, tend to turn up under the rear bumper. I found this to be good from a road-clearance point of view, but unsatisfactory as it left the exhaust gasses within the 'vacuum' behind the car, tarnishing the rear chrome work. I was anxious that this would corrode the rear lights and bumper.

had a chance to shut. Needless to say, this reduces the efficiency of the engine, its torque and ability to run sweetly at low revs. Consequently, a system with tuned pipe lengths has advantages, perhaps the biggest of which is to know that the system you are contemplating has been tested on a dyno, is free flowing, and that the pipe bores have not been enlarged just for the sake of offering a big bore system!

If you're fitting a big bore system, for example a 2¼in, it will pay you to establish whether it will come on and off the manifold studs. In fact, you may have to grind off both inner lips and reweld around the exhaust manifold in order to get the new system on and off the studs. Only buy a system that has substantial skids welded to the silencer, particularly if you have any thoughts of rallying. One experienced rally enthusiast made up a plate to fit between the two silencers

which kept the exhaust system in place. He suggests the use of caged nuts on the inner mount and accepts that the remains of the bolt will need grinding off when taking the system apart. He told me that with the skid plate the car inevitably seemed to land around the silencer area, so the exhaust enjoyed a hard life.

I would conclude this section by telling you about my own improvement to the original tailpipe exit (shown in picture 12-25), of my single pipe system. With the conventional single pipe exit I found that the rear lights and bumper were being coated in an exhaust film which I believe to be corrosive. As I had just spent several hundred pounds refurbishing the chromed parts I was unhappy about this and had the rear of the box modified to allow me to fit different tailpipes. I settled on that shown in pictures 12-26-1 and 12-26-2. It very occasionally strikes the ground but throws the exhaust fumes clear of the vortex that gathers behind the TR6's rear panel.

Silencers and noise

Noise is becoming more and more of an issue, and competitive cars are measured for noise pollution. Stage rallies normally require no more than 100dB at 0.5 metres and 45 degrees to exhaust exit, but some are now setting 98dB maximums, and this downward trend is likely to continue. A great number of tuned TR cars exceed 100dB, even with a new stainless exhaust system in place. One suggestion, which I thought potentially very helpful, was to temporarily fit an auxiliary silencer across the back of the car (mounting on the over-riders). Trevor Gilks tells me that using a stainless front box and his 'auxiliary', he got down to 95dB.

OIL AND RELATED MATTERS
Sump (oil pan)

Since an unmodified sump will allow oil to surge away from the pump on corners, it needs to be improved. The usual approach is to first cut the sump horizontally, about 3in (75mm), below the top lip, then rejoin the bottom to the top with a 1in (25mm), strip welded right round the periphery (thus increasing the depth and the capacity of the sump). Next you need to weld a baffle at the 3in cut/join line. I believe some owners then mount a second baffle on spacers about 0.5in (10mm), above the main baffle, but you'll have to experiment carefully to ensure oil pick up is not interfered with and the crank clears this added internal protrusion! Extend the oil pick up 1in lower than standard.

Alternatively, the cast alloy sump/pan shown in photograph 12-27 is available from Racetorations. These have very effective-looking fins on the external surfaces, which makes it very easy to

12-27. A cast aluminium sump, solely available from Racetorations, dramatically improves the rigidity of the bottom half of the crankcase. Note the spin-on oil-filter adapter, the aluminium flywheel and the very carefully installed brake pipes on this TR250. One of the plugs in the side of the sump is an oil drain, and one is provision for an oil temperature sender.

12-26-1. I tried a side exit, just behind the right rear wheel. That certainly cured the tarnishing problem, but did nothing for the car's aesthetics, so I tried a straight-out tailpipe ...

12-26-2 ... which I think is a good compromise. I do, very occasionally, scrape the bottom on the road, but the exit point keeps 95% of the gasses away from the rear chrome work.

jump to the conclusion that their primary purpose is to cool the oil in the sump, but we would be wrong! The primary purpose of a cast alloy sump is to provide additional rigidity to the bottom end of the engine block, and they are most effective and highly recommended for engines expected to generate over 150bhp. So, if your engine is likely to generate much above this, you should consider this route to improving the sump. You should also fit an oil cooler (a 13 row one for fast road cars and a 16 row for the big boys). The capacity of the alloy sumps is about a quarter litre (half a pint), more than standard, but they are fitted with removable alloy baffles known as windage trays. Consequently, the sump can be thoroughly cleaned, and oil gates can be attached to the underside of the baffle to help protect the oil pump from air-scavenge during very hard cornering or severe braking.

Rocker oil feeds
There is a frequently advertised non-original modification (shown in photograph 12-28), that feeds additional oil from the oil galley adjacent to the dizzy up via an external pipe to a pre-tapped, but normally plugged, hole in the cylinder head. Like many things to do with motor cars, it's very much a matter of opinion as to whether this modification should be incorporated within your engine rebuild. It can increase the oil consumption of many engines, and the rocker shaft is relatively easily, quickly and cheaply replaced. However, one's crankshaft and main

12-28. This is the optional additional oil feed pipe, looping from the oil gallery up to the rocker shaft via the rear of the cylinder head.

12-29. This is a typical oil thermostat that allows hot oil to circulate through an oil cooler when necessary, but to bypass the cooler when the oil temperature is insufficient to warrant cooling. This particular example has four ends that accept plain hoses fixed by jubilee-like clips. Some 'stats have screwed end couplings that necessitate corresponding couplings on the end of the oil lines. I think 'plain end' 'stats are easier to fit (particularly retrospectively) than those with screwed ends.

bearings are more difficult and costly to access, so I would have all the oil available to lubricate and cool the crank! In any event, use lots of engine oil when re-assembling the rocker set, and engine oil mixed with STP is even better.

Oil thermostats
Mineral oils are formulated to perform best at between 90-110 degrees C. When they become too hot they thin, and they thicken when too cold. In both events they offer less than their optimum lubricating performance. If you have elected not to have an oil cooler fitted then you need read no further since this section does not apply to your car. However, for those with or thinking about an oil cooler it seems a good idea to also consider an oil 'stat. These go in the line to your oil cooler and will route the oil past the cooler when your oil is not up to temperature. This will accelerate warming of the oil and assist initial lubrication, particularly in cold climatic conditions. They are widely available with push on or standard ⅝in threaded unions and will enable you to have an oil cooler in circuit all the time, and available when the oil temperature rises as the result of hard work or hot weather. At a stroke, overheating and overcooling your oil are eliminated. Picture 12-29 shows you what to expect.

Mineral/synthetic oils
The first stage of refining crude mineral oil is to boil it and separate the various liquefied 'fractions' by weight in a

distillation column. The lighter fractions are used to make up petrol, paraffin and diesel fuel, and leave behind the higher boiling point fraction that forms the basis for mineral lubricating oils. Lots of 'nasties' have then to be removed before the petroleum company has the starting point for a mineral lubricating oil. Synthetic base oils, on the other hand, are manufactured chemically. The molecular structure of these base lubricants can be precisely engineered to meet specific thermal or physical requirements and to possess superior viscosity characteristics at low and high temperatures.

Whether from a mineral or synthetic base, additives need to be blended to the base to provide the lubrication qualities required of each different oil. Viscosity modifiers, anti-wear additives, dispersants, anti-oxidants, anti-foam, anti-rust, and detergents, make up between 15-20% of modern engine oils. The proportions and additives would be quite different for a gear oil, and different again for a jet-engine lubricant, for example. There are differences in blend within a single category. A modern close tolerance car engine will require an oil with lots of detergent to keep everything very clean, whereas a classic engine, such as used in the TRs, with its wider tolerance components, works best with a little coke and gum to aid piston and ring sealing. Put the wrong oil in the wrong engine and neither will work well.

Oil changes
All oils regardless of their base, lose their viscosity or their protective role over time and must be changed. The more often you change the oil better the lubrication the engine receives and the longer it will last. The optimum time for changing oil relates more to the number of cold starts, ambient temperatures, the effectiveness of block scavenging, wear in the engine, accuracy of carburation (particularly during warm-up period), use of choke and the type of driving than distance travelled! So, while a mileage interval is a good indicator, use your common sense and the smell of the oil (loaded with fuel from too much use of choke?), as a guide. Once run in, I change all my classics at about 3000 mile intervals but extend that a little if I know the car has done lots of long runs, particularly to events on the Continent. The appearance of the oil should, within reason, be a secondary consideration. If

it's thick and black, change it. If it's gone black fairly quickly but still feels and smells all right, don't feel you have to change it purely because of its colour.

I spent some time in *How to Restore Triumph TR5/250/6* explaining the correct use of lubricating oils when running/breaking in your engine. In short, **never** use synthetic oils to run an engine in. I use synthetic oil for its superior lubricating properties once the engine's run in, but I use one with minimal detergent specifically marketed in the UK for 'basic' engines and have no plans to change.

Catchment tanks

The crankcase of any engine, whatever its performance level, must be allowed to breath. Often this is carried out by running a pipe from the inlet manifold (sometimes the carburettors), to the crankcase. However, as piston clearances increase and rpm increases this becomes less and less attractive. Competition and road traffic regulations prohibit venting the crankcase to atmosphere so you need a method of catching the oil mist and droplets, not to mention the water vapour that flies about. Racetorations offers the very cost-effective fibreglass solution we see in picture 12-30-1, while Revington prefers an aluminium fabricated tank

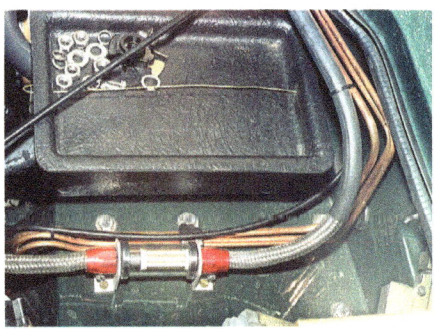

12-30-1. The fibreglass oil catch tank. Its lid is temporarily being used to hold some fastenings but the welding wire top clip is quick and easy to remove. You can just see the engine breather (in) and the tank breather (out) tubes at the top-left of the shot. Note, too, the gauze fuel filter in the foreground and the very neat mounting brackets that give a real feeling of professionalism. The glass filter is used in preference to the conventional fuel filter because its contents can be seen and the filter taken apart and cleaned when necessary.

12-30-2. Also very professionally made, this oil catch tank has a sight glass to indicate the level in the tank, and also a drain-plug!

12-30-3. My preferred catchment tank is from Cambridge Motor Sport. It combines a water header tank with, in a separate compartment of course, the oil catch.

(picture 12-30-2). However, I think the best solution to this particular problem comes from Cambridge Motor Sport, with its dual-purpose oil-catch/water-expansion tank shown in picture 12-30-3. All these tanks sit alongside the battery.

Pre-heating

For those doing circuit racing, I believe there are benefits to be had from pre-heating the oil in your sump for 10 minutes or so, even before you go out on a warm up lap. The power for a 240v electric paint stripper will be hard to come by in the middle of a cold wet paddock, but you should consider getting the oil warm before you start your race engine. Furthermore, use the oil for about 300 miles only before changing it, about 3 or 4 meetings. By all means re-use the oil in your road car, but try to keep fresh oil in your race engine.

COOLING

Electric cooling fans have several benefits and are, of course, recommended. Mechanical fans, on the other hand, work best at high rpm (just when it is not required!), consume power (estimates vary from 2 to 5bhp), and pull the crankshaft forward (against the already vulnerable crankshaft thrust washers). Although the resulting wear is minimal when compared with that from the action of the clutch, the fan's wear is constant and best dispensed with if possible.

Any problems which result from fitting an electric fan will most likely be noticed when in slow or stationary traffic. High ambient temperatures exacerbate the potential to overheat, but this can be dramatically reduced by sizing the electric fan and the radiator correctly. We'll start by looking at the fan in a bit more detail, and leave radiator suggestions until a little later.

Electric fans

There are several makes of electric fan available, but Pacet and Kenlowe spring straight to mind. Both make fans in a range of sizes, and you need to fit the biggest you can. A 16in (400mm) fan will probably suffice for most cars, but it needs to be close-coupled to the radiator to ensure maximum effect. Close-coupled fans are usually fixed by four thin rods that pass through the core of the radiator. However, before we buy the fan we need to decide whether we are pushing or pulling! Pushing fans are mounted on the front of the radiator and push the cooling air through the core of the radiator. Pulling fans are mounted behind the radiator and suck the cooling air through the matrix. Ask the retailer's advice but, although I think pushing is the more effective means of moving air, my personal choice would be to fit a puller in all but the warmest, driest climates.

Fans which are stuck out in front of the radiator get no protection from the weather, nor do they enjoy any drying warmth from the air passing through the radiator. As a result, their working lives, at least in my experience, tend to be shorter than puller fans mounted behind the radiator. Space is generally at a premium behind the radiator, however, and you may have to choose a manufacturer and/or design that is particularly thin/narrow (like the example we see in picture 12-31-1).

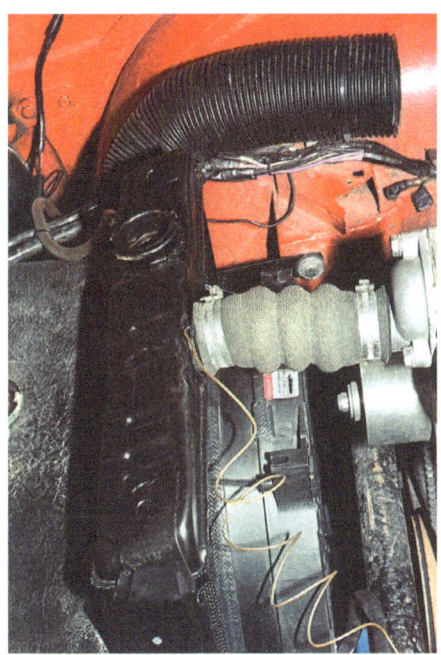

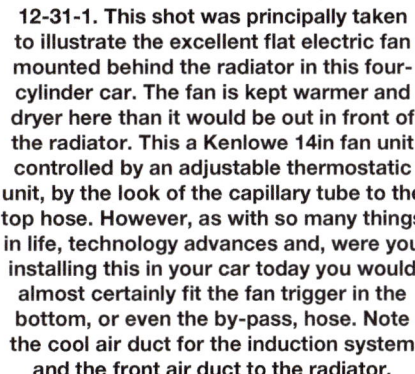

12-31-1. This shot was principally taken to illustrate the excellent flat electric fan mounted behind the radiator in this four-cylinder car. The fan is kept warmer and dryer here than it would be out in front of the radiator. This a Kenlowe 14in fan unit controlled by an adjustable thermostatic unit, by the look of the capillary tube to the top hose. However, as with so many things in life, technology advances and, were you installing this in your car today you would almost certainly fit the fan trigger in the bottom, or even the by-pass, hose. Note the cool air duct for the induction system and the front air duct to the radiator.

A relay is essential to control the fan. Most of the large fans we're thinking about will take 15 to 20amps current and, without a relay, you'll grossly overload not only the thermostatic switch that automatically controls the fan, but the manual over-ride switch too. Furthermore, you need to fit a separate fuse to the secondary power supply circuit and take the feed from somewhere that has adequate capacity. Definitely not the ignition switch and, in the case of PI cars, definitely not where you deplete the fuel pump of an adequate power supply.

You also need to ensure the fan you buy has an **adjustable** thermostatic switch included in the deal. Set the switch to trip about halfway between normal and hot in the first instance (you

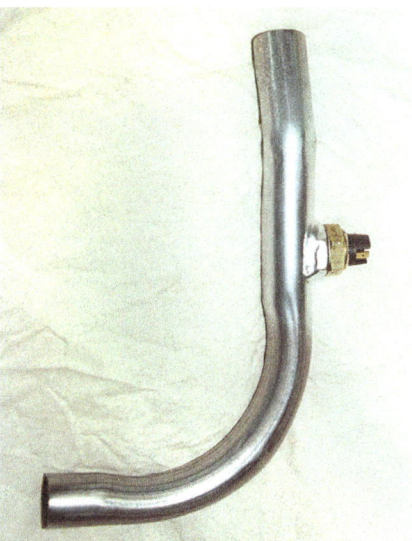

12-31-2. The bottom stainless hose can vary in shape from TR to TR, but the thermostatic switch will trigger the fan based upon the 'to-engine' water temperature.

don't want the fan to cut in too early, or too frequently). Many make the mistake of having the fan come on at normal operating temperature, but that's too early.

For non-adjustable thermostatic switches you'll need to think about a different trigger 'mechanism'. We see an example in picture 12-31-2. This is a stainless steel bottom water pipe with the 'stat switch welded in situ. The top hose has been the traditional point from which to trigger the fan, but it has to be pointed out that modern cars tend to trigger the electric fan from the cooler bottom hose. If you choose the bottom/cooler location and the fan switches on you know it really is required, whereas with the sensor in the top hose, particularly when you restart a warm car, the fan will often come on unnecessarily due to the hot water having risen to the top of the rads!

Radiators

Size matters and, if you can find a way of increasing the overall top-to-bottom length of the radiator, this will help in two ways. Firstly, you'll increase the water capacity of the system, and secondly, it will present a greater area for the cooling air to meet. You can also help your cooling by your choice of radiator core. A 'Pack' core is made differently to the

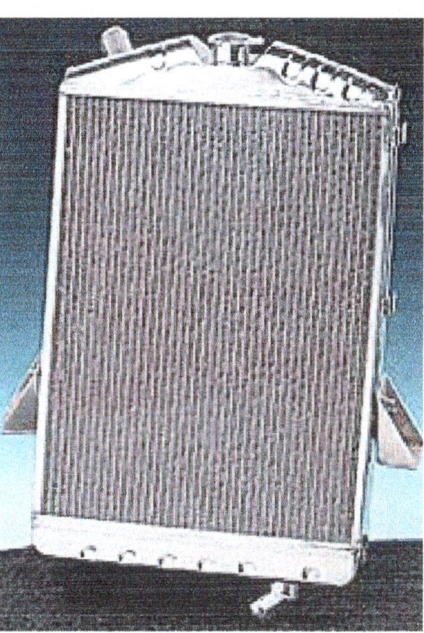

12-32-1. A wide selection are available, but this is one example of an aluminium radiator.

12-32-2. Like TR4 Rally cars, hot air finds it easier to exit the bay towards the top compartment and this vent cut into each side also aids airflow through the radiator.

normal type of core, and you are advised to pay the extra and get your radiator re-cored with this higher capacity matrix. There's also the depth of the matrix to consider. The vast majority of radiators are made from three rows, while there are some with four rows. There are some available now with five rows, though you'll have to order these specially. You might think a five row radiator would be about 60 or 70% more effective than a three row one. Unfortunately, however, that's not so, since the five row rads allows a little less air to pass though it and the 5th row is working with warmed air from the rows in front of it. Nevertheless, it's a good option to consider and it will improve the cooling.

For reduced weight, the aluminium radiator we see in picture 12-32-1 is available from Racetorations or Cambridge Motor Sport. However, you will further help the flow of air through the radiator to some extent by fitting a pair of cooling vents in a low pressure area at the rear of the engine compartment (photo 12-32-2).

Radiator ducts

As we see from picture 12-33, some of the cars we are focused on did not have a duct fitted in front of the radiator. If your car has a duct, it's worth checking that it's ducting all the air possible through the radiator. The Triumph originals were made from fibreboard and, frankly, are not very nice. You can make one yourself from 1mm thick

12-33. This TR250 doesn't have a grille to radiator duct but, frankly, even a standard car should have one fitted in order to ensure all the air entering the grille is directed through the rad.

12-34. The six- (and four-) cylinder TR water pump suffers from two disadvantages in standard form: they are heavy considering the job they do, but more importantly, the impeller only has four fins to push the water through the system and, at high rpm it cavities and is not up to the job. A Racetorations replica cast body, a turned pulley and a new water pump all made from aluminium solves the first problem by reducing the weight by some 50%. Note, too, that this weight saving will have a particularly beneficial effect because it is removed from a very high/frontal position. The solution to the cavitating is clear from this picture, the 6 profiled impeller blades in the new pump.

aluminium sheet, but the best solution is Racetorations' fibreglass example which we can see down the left edge of photograph 12-31-1.

Water flow

The largest radiator available will not cool the engine if the water pump or impeller is cavitating. This only occurs at high revolutions. Photograph 12-34 shows the standard impeller and an improved one from Racetorations. The original has four straight blades, the improved one has six which are shaped for additional effectiveness. Furthermore, the water-pump case, its impeller and the drive pulley are all made from aluminium thus reducing the weight of this vital assembly by about 50%.

Alloy rocker covers

I cannot conclude a chapter on engines without briefly pointing out that a standard pressed-steel rocker cover leaves a lot to be desired. In any case, where originality is of little consequence,

I recommend you fit a cast alloy rocker cover of the type seen in picture 12-35. The advantages are explained in the caption.

12-35. Although this picture is of a four-cylinder cast alloy cover, it serves to remind us of the aesthetic and the practical benefits of these upgraded rocker covers. They dampen the inevitable noise from the tappets, but are also stronger than the original pressed covers. Consequently they distort less and leak less oil than the original.

Chapter 13
Electrics

ALTERNATORS

There are few components more important to a TR's well being than the alternator. Consider this: When you are driving along with your Lucas electric fuel pump working away (about 10 amps), ignition system doing the business (5 amps), wipers flapping (about 5 amps), side/tail/instrument lights (3 amps), and headlamps (10 amps) illuminating the way forward, you are using about 33 amps of alternator capacity. An overdrive will need about 1 amp to hold it 'in' (and, interestly, pulls about 10 amps when you first ask it to engage). If you fit an electric fan, when that cuts in you'll need about 10-20 amps, depending upon its size, but we'll say for the purposes of this example that, in modest traffic it has a 25% duty, thus averaging 4 amps. Your stop and direction lights will want a total of 7 amps when in use but are on a low duty cycle so we will add only a further 1 amp to your average requirements. The radio will need a couple more if you have it on, bringing your total needs to *circa* 40 amps on a wet night. These figures assume you do not switch on the heater fan to de-mist the windscreen (3 or 4 more), fit any additional driving lights (probably 10 amps), and have not (yet), fitted a Bosch fuel pump to your PI system (another 3 or 4 more)! Time to consider the generating capacity of the usual TR alternators:

15AC (TR5 TR250) – 28 amps
15ACR fitted to early TR6s – 28 amps
16ACR – 34 amps
17ACR – 36 amps (ok for non-PI cars)
18ACR – 45 amps

Remember, if you have a PI system, and have retained the original fuel pump, starving it of power will decrease its efficiency and flow and, conversely to

13-1-1. The 16ACR alternator sits comfortably in the engine compartment, but its 34 amp capacity is really marginal when night driving and/or a number of short journeys are involved. Lovely car beautifully restored.

what many may think, will increase the heating within the pump and increase your likelihood of breakdown due to cavitating. And all that's before you have recharged the battery to ensure a vigorous and swift start the next time you use the car. As I say, there are few more important components on a TR, particularly a Petrol Injected TR, than its alternator, so I will start this chapter on electrical improvements with some information on improving generating capacity. Numerically, the most frequent alternator in use is the 16ACR, so let's start with a shot of one (picture 13-1-1), to aid identification.

Whatever your starting point, when assessing the size of alternator to fit to a fast road TR, you need only consider the capacity of the proposed unit. Ultra fast road cars will require just as much capacity, but you'll probably need to think about weight issues, and buy a much more compact, high output unit. Competitive cars must not entirely lose sight of capacity requirements, although they are unlikely to want to employ radios, heaters and other more luxurious refinements, and no doubt they will want to keep the size/weight issue to the fore too. Wherever you are or whatever the capacity or tune of your engine, it's essential to properly supply the electrical

13-1-2. A neat 45 amp alternator conversion kit. Also in shot is the large aluminium pulley that you will need to drop the alternator's (any alternator), rpm down to something more practical when the engine is running at the high rpm expected in competition. Note the special single mounting pivot supplied with the kit.

system with power and to recharge the car's battery. I think the majority of UK standard and fast road cars require a minimum capacity of 45 amps and, frankly, a 55 amp unit is almost essential for those, admittedly few, cars fitted with EFI.

You can get some superb small yet powerful alternators from the entire range of UK specialist TR retailers who helped me put this book together. Small, internally fanned 40 and 45 amp units are available and and can be seen in pictures 13-1-2 and 13-1-3. This size would certainly be of primary interest to owners of ultra fast road/rally cars with lots of lights, looking for generating capacity and light weight. However, this may be an unnecessarily high cost solution for some, perhaps even the

majority of cars, since UK salvage yards are well stocked with examples of the 55 amp alternator we see in pictures 13-1-4, 13-1-5 and 13-1-6, which is well suited to standard and fast road applications. At 5in (125mm), in diameter they're a bit on the chunky side and unsuited to those with one eye on the weight of the car. However, just as that you cannot overearth an engine, or any electrical component (*e.g.* a fuel pump), nor can you over-provide generating capacity. Some used alternators may need to have the front half of the alternator rotated by 120 degrees so as to present the engine mounting point with the correctly orientated alternator 'arms'. I also have an ex-Ford alternator which, although of this same diameter, is considerably shorter, and generates 45 amps. So,

13-1-4. Cheap but not small! This a 55 amp unit is salvaged from an efi Austin Montego ...

13-1-6. ... like this.

there are numerous low cost solutions worth exploring before you resort to the 65 amp examples seen in pictures 13-1-7 and 13-1-8.

If you have a TR250 or a TR5, you may have an alternator, with the suffix 'AC', which uses an external regulator mounted on the left side inner wing/fender. You can see one in picture 13-2. Modern alternators are all internally regulated (hence the suffix ACR), which necessitates two minor adjustments to the original wiring if you change to an ACR alternator. You will be supplementing the original cable to the alternator in any event so it won't be too much of an additional problem to remove the regulator from the inner wing/fender and replace it with the (official Triumph) bridge, see picture 13-5-3, or merely solder the two wires together. You'll also need to simplify the wire/plug arrangement that was originally connected to the rear of your alternator,

13-1-3. Revington's 40 amp lightweight alternator fitted with a conventional vee belt pulley.

13-1-5. ... which required the three (arrowed), fastening be undone and the front plate rotated through 120 degrees to align the pivots correctly for my mounting arrangements ...

13-1-7. This new 65 amp capacity unit is available from Revington and comes complete with an aluminium drive pulley. It will be sufficient for any car referred to in this book.

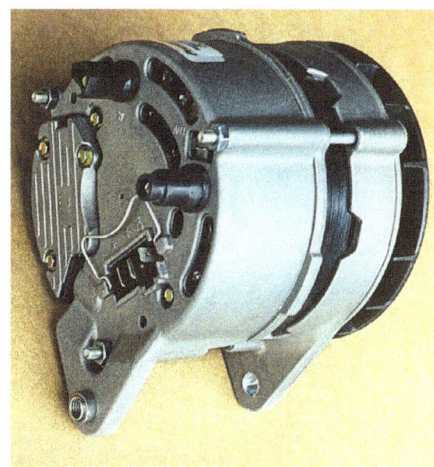

13-1-8. If you're fitting Revington's chunkiest alternator, you'll need to fit the 3 wire plug and wiring arrangement seen here. The small connection supplies the control volts via your ignition light, while either/both of the larger terminals supply the power. With 65 amps available, while you will doubtless get excellent instructions from Revington, I would recommend you use both terminals and run two power feed cables in tandem to the car's main distribution point (probably the starter).

but the wiring/diagrams for that change are well published and shouldn't prove difficult to find.

It may now be helpful to US converters to briefly look at a range of readily available (Stateside) alternators. General Motors (Delco), internally regulated alternators, called type S1, is the unit of choice for most alternator conversions or upgrades in the USA. The GM type alternators come in a range of amperage ratings and are relatively inexpensive. These are probably one of the most common alternators in the US and are, consequently, available everywhere. The S1s are manufactured in several dimensions and sizes, which aids positioning on the engine. The exact model chosen will depend on the amperage required. These are similar to the alternators shown in photograph 13-3-1. As in the UK, the output of alternators for any given size is improving. This is aided by the trend to incorporate the cooling fan inside the alternator, as can be seen in photograph 13-3-1. So, size for size, with the output of the alternator about double what it was 5 to 10 years ago, the necessity for a larger amperage alternator need not generate a space problem inside even the most crowded engine compartment.

13-3-1. Those in the USA have a wide range of alternators to chose from. This is a typical GM S1 unit, albeit not fitted to a TR.

13-3-2. This 40 amp alternator is taking place as part of a Revington efi installation. Note the stainless steel heat shield between the exhaust manifold and the alternator, and that it would be best adjusted to ensure there is some sort of air gap between manifold and shield. I would add a reflective heat blanket too, was this my car. The toothed crank positioning wheel behind the main crank pulley is the giveaway that this car is enjoying an engine management improvement. The water pump and crank pulleys are aluminium, for lightness.

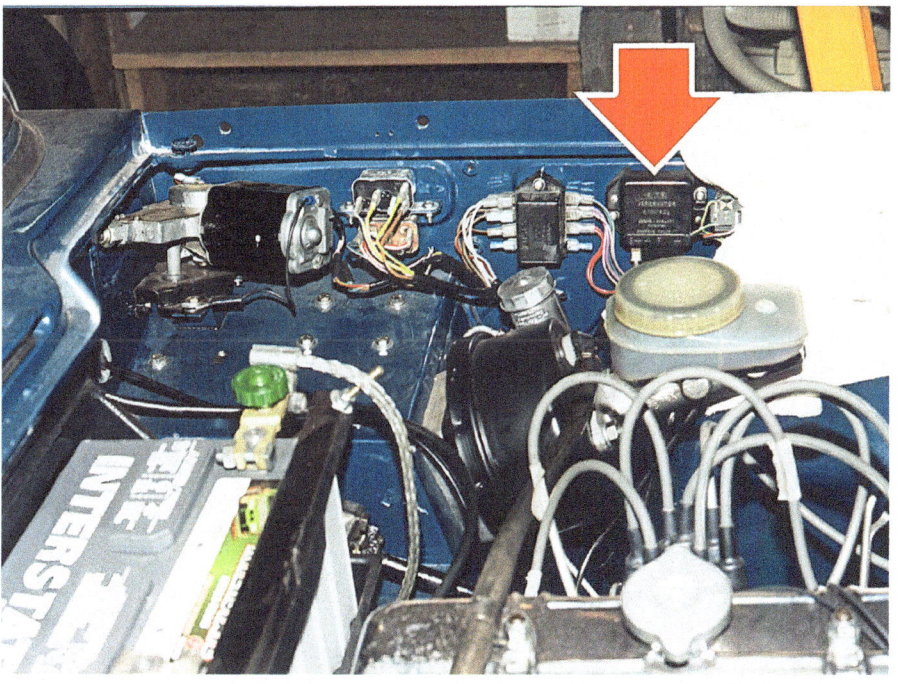

13-2. The arrow highlights the external control box on this TR250 with, out of shot of course, a 15AC alternator.

A very neat installation can be seen at 13-3-2.

However a 65-amp capacity kit is available for those in desperate need of lots of power. A super 45amp lightweight (2.8kg as compared to 3.6kg) unit is also available. These have roller bearings and twin internal cooling fans but cost circa £200. Both these last two kits are available from the TR specialists that helped with this book and are listed in Appendix 1.

CONNECTING CABLES

Note! When upgrading the output of your generator, you **must** also provide an adequate cross section (usually brown insulated), cable from the power terminals at the rear of the alternator to the battery. There is information later in this chapter about the current carrying capacity of each sized cable, and you may need to refer to this section to fit an adequate sized cable. I have not included a diagram for those upgrading a 15ACR alternator (*i.e.* a unit with internal rectification/controls), to a higher capacity ACR unit, since the wiring route, if not the cross-sectional wiring capacity, is there for you to follow. However, all larger capacity generators will need corresponding extra capacity in the wiring from the rear of the alternator (this can usually be via a second parallel cable installed alongside the original one).

If you're connecting to an ammeter, remember that the instrument must have the capacity (usually more or less the full-scale deflection of the needle), to handle the output of the alternator. There is a pair of (large), power lucar terminals in the rear of the vast majority of the ACR series of alternators, only one of which is in use. Say you have one 65/0.3 (*i.e.* a 65 strand), original cable connected to your 28 amp alternator, and you're about to increase the capacity of the alternator to 45 amps. This is an additional 17 amp capacity, and it's perfectly in order to fit a 28/0.3 cable (which has a 17 amp carrying capacity), to the unused power terminal. You must, of course, use the correct sized 'flag' terminal fitted within your rear alternator plug. However, the 28/0.3 cable has a capacity of only 17 amps, so were you to fit an even larger unit, say a 55 amp alternator, you would need to upgrade the cable still further. The original 65/0.3 strand cable has a carrying capacity of 35 amps so in this second example you need a

secondary cable that has a capacity of at least 20 amps. This requires you use a the 25 amp capacity 44/0.3 cable to supplement the original. Always over-provide capacity in cables, particularly the cable that connects the generator to the rest of the car. Failure to follow this golden rule will result in voltage drops, overheated cables and possibly fire!

MODERNISING THE DISTRIBUTION

Cars have become far more electrically orientated in the 50 years that TRs have been around. In fact, the trend has gone to the extreme of your practically needing a degree in electrical and electronic engineering to tackle today's electrics! Fortunately, that's not quite the case for most TR upgrades, although the electronics involved in an efi conversion are almost there! However, leaving that rare addition aside, most TRs these days are fitted with a number of simple electrical extras that were not fitted as standard, but which make today's motoring safer, more comfortable, or compatible with the traffic density we endure today. The problem is that every one of them consumes electrical power, and since we've just spent some time

discussing how that extra power should be generated, we'd better look at the various facets of distributing the power safely and reliably.

Electrical connectors

Like all cars of the '60s and '70s, TRs originally used soldered 'bullet' connectors and a small insulated metal sleeve for the numerous inter-wire connections. There were few relays and only four fuses in the last of the TR production run. To be fair, these types of connection have served many cars very well for many years, and you should be able to clean up the various contacts, re-solder some of the bullets and look forward to more years of continued service. However, if you're adding additional electrical components (*e.g.* an electric fan or a Bosch fuel pump), or adding additional fuses, there will be inter-harness connections to make or re-make. You can, of course, use securely mounted terminal blocks, but the modern 2, 4 and 8 way 'Multi block' wiring connections shown in photograph 13-4 are far better. They carry increased power safely and reliably, and are highly recommended. All offer male to female 6mm spade terminals housed in a

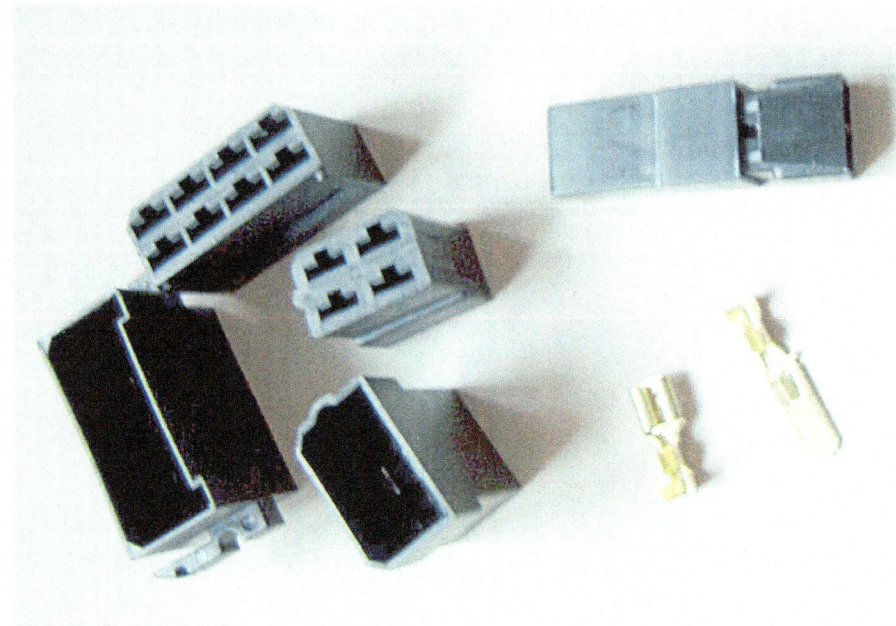

13-4. Some examples of modern multi-plug block connectors and their male and female spade terminals. The terminals are held secure within the multi-block by small 'tangs' which, in this picture, is best illustrated by the left side male where the tang can be seen clearly.

nylon moulding. Talk to your preferred electrical component supplier, of course, but it's my impression that the later spade termination provides for a bigger contact area and therefore more current capacity than the pin connectors. All these electrical connections are available from Demon Tweeks (UK), and American Autowire Systems (USA).

For maximum longevity and reliability of electrical connections old and new, crimp your electrical terminations first, then soldier the crimped termination. American improvers can buy a product called 'D5 De-Oxit' which I understand cleans and de-oxidizes old electrical terminations. A very light smear of copper slip or petroleum jelly as you push your electrical connections together will aid conductivity, and ensure corrosion is kept in check. This is particularly true of connections within the engine bay.

Wiring

Those enthusiasts who are upgrading their cars in a manner that directly or indirectly affects the wiring system should consider the extra load their modifications will impose not only on the wires themselves, of course, but also on the switches, the inter wiring connections, and the fuses. For example, a pair of 100w halogen headlamps will consume 17 amps, whereas the original 65w bulbs (and the switches, wires and connections), were only designed for 11 amps. Even though you've fitted a larger alternator to supply the additional amperage for this and several other upgrades, you've only looked after the first and last links in the electrical supply chain. Sooner or later, your car's reliability will suffer.

An electrical supply cable fitted for 11 amps (on our example), is not going to transmit 17 amps efficiently, so you must plan to duplicate or upgrade the cables to the headlights, Bosch pump, or whatever items of equipment you have added or upgraded. I have included a table of amperage to cable capacity to help you, and if you need to calculate your amperage, just divide the wattage by 12 and select the next size of cable upwards

Amperage	Cable Size	Amperage	Cable Size
5	9/0.3	25	44/0.3
8	14/0.3	35	65/0.3
17	28/0.3	42	84/0.3

Relays

Don't forget to double up the wattage when you have two units (headlights, horns and fans, for example), and also consider the load on all the related switches, particularly the ignition switch. I would suggest that all these circuits and switches will offer far more reliable long term service if they carry no more than a pilot current and that all are therefore candidates for operation via a relay. You'll also need a relay to operate any overdrive unit you have on your car, so I'd strongly recommend that high on your list of purchases for a compatible wiring and connection upgrade, should be a four-way relay holder, with a cover for added protection and reliability. These are available with four-bolt bulkhead mounting. Furthermore, I'd suggest you standardise on a five pin 30 amp relay, because this will do everything a four pin relay can, but offers you the opportunity to operate some circuits in the NC (normally closed) mode. One example that might use the fifth terminal would be a car alarm, which you would wire to the NC pin (No.5), of your ignition switch relay, and so 'arm the alarm' when you switch the ignition off.

For those hesitating about fitting a relay into an existing electrical wiring circuit, diagram D13-1 shows the before and after comparisons as a guide to how a relay could be incorporated into the one circuit to carry addition electrical load. This might be applicable were you to fit a much larger electric cooling fan, for example. A variation on my suggestion can be seen at 13-5-1.

13-5-1. Not the modern four way relay block I mention in the main text, but a very neat Revington installation of three relays in a TR. Although the mounting blocks for the relays looks a single unit, these are, in fact, the interlocking type which I have always found fitted to 1980s cars. Agents for Joseph Lucas can supply them too, no doubt! One of the relays is an ignition unit which takes the load off the ignition switch.

Fuses

The next area for consideration is key to any electrical system: the fuse box. An original four-way TR fuse box is just not adequate, for several reason, but mainly because the current passing through each fuse is too great. Also, almost everything which 'goes' through the ignition switch also goes through the fuse box. The best solution is a modern multi-fuse box, with at least 8, possibly 12, or even 16 fuse positions (especially if your car is loaded with electrical extras). A 16 way box will probably

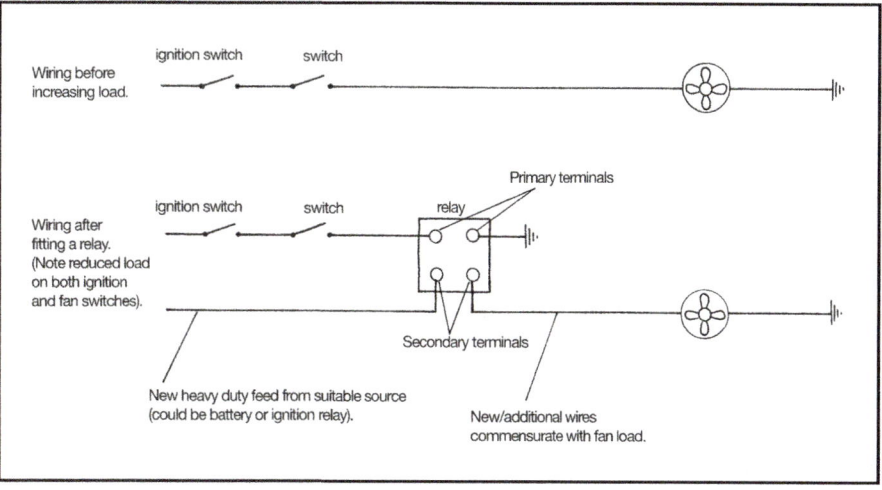

D13-1. Electrical relay – a before and after diagram.

comprise two interlocking 8 ways, but this is immaterial provided your selection enables you to fuse more cables individually. You can, for example, fuse several of the service components in the existing 'green' circuit (*e.g.* the windscreen wipers), individually. Also, you might choose to site a fuse box adjacent to or even interlocked with your relay box in order to feed each output through its own fuse.

Your selection of fuse rating must, of course, be compatible with the current associated with each circuit. My recommendation for the type of fuse and fuse holder to aim for is to fit the modern blade fuse we see in picture 13-5-2. They are available in a very wide range of capacities from 1 to 40 amps. A relatively recent innovation is the availability of 'glow' type blade fuses. These are very much more expensive than conventional blade fuses but do incorporate a small bulb that glows when a fuse blows. However, careful labelling of each fuse on the lid of the fuse holder should guide you to any problem fuse fairly quickly, so you may not need to pay over £1.00 per fuse!

Any decent fuse holder should come with a cover to help keep dirt and water out, but you'll help the reliability of your fuses if you fit them inside the car. Either side of the passenger footwell, and high enough not to get kicked, might be one possibility, if slightly inaccessible. You could make up a hardboard ceiling to the passenger footwell and sit it just under the glove compartment. This provides an excellent internal base on which to mount all your updated electrics. To really do

the job properly you could even hinge the front edge of your hardboard, and have it drop down to allow easy access to all the fuses, relays and terminal blocks in the event of trouble.

An alternative to fuses could be circuit breakers, which are easily reset. Demon Tweeks is a UK source, whilst those in the States should contact American Autowire Systems.

You may want to reduce the loading on your TR's fuses but to stop short of a major change in style. Lots of 1970's cars used a similar style of fuse-block but with more fuse positions. We see one eight-way example at 13-5-3, but if you are keen to stay with Triumph components, take a look at the twelve-way alternatives in picture 13-5-4. Note that the cable route into each block is quite different, and could govern which one you choose. The Stag fuses can only be conveniently supplied with push-on spade terminals from the other side of the mounting panel. The TR7 fuse holders are hard wired to the harness, so you need to have a short length of cable attached to the TR7 holder if it's to be of any use to you. Neither fuse holder is available new, of course, but you should have no difficulty in finding good secondhand examples.

13-5-4. Some interesting 12 way fuse installations which may be of particular interest to some since both were used in contemporary Triumph cars. The 2x6 box at the top of the picture is from a TR7, while the square hollow pressing to its right side is the neat mounting arrangement. Below is the 1x12 way arrangement used in a Stag. The Stag allows you to push Lucar spade terminals straight onto the rear of the fuse block, while the TR7 arrangement takes each wire straight to a fuse base thus allowing you slightly less flexibility. Both are about £5 secondhand.

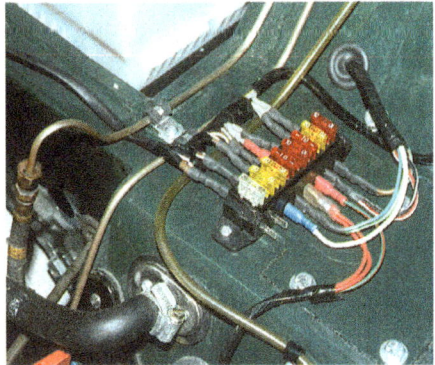

13-5-2. This is the sort of modern blade fuse block that would make such a difference to the protection and reliability of any TR. Highly recommended, every TR should have one!

13-5-3. All TRs suffered from an inadequate number of fuses. This is a traditional 8 way fuse box installed some years ago to advantage in a TR6. The box has a cover, which not only saves any accidents but also minimises corrosion of the terminal thus improving reliability. Were this installation being fitted today, a modern spade fuse box would almost certainly be used.

Supplementary harnesses

For those looking for a shortcut, Revington has designed a complete supplementary fused harness. It not only introduces modern electrical connections to at least part of your car's electrical circuit, but will increase the number of fused circuits available as well. The idea is to add one supplementary electrical harness to a TRs which has had, or is about to have, additional electrical equipment fitted. The harness has been cleverly designed to provide a variety of ignition related and ignition independent provisions, and you use those most suited to the facilities you are adding. The harness is pre-assembled, terminated and wrapped in black tape so, initially, all you need to do is to lay it as directed through the engine bay and secure it.

Only two basic electrical connections are required, one to the positive terminal on your battery or starter solenoid, and one to the ignition (white), circuit. The all-important relay to augment the ignition circuit and an 8 way fuse box are already built into the supplementary harness and these merely requires securing to the bulkhead with a couple of self-tapping screws. With the additional harness in place and connected, four of the fuses are live immediately, but as soon as you turn on the ignition switch, the other four fuses also become live via the ignition relay. A harness is available for each of the TRs and means that whatever electrical facilities you wish to add to your car, a fused and, where appropriate, switched power source is in place.

You still have to fix your fan(s), spot light(s), alarms, audio, *etc.*, and wire an appropriate individual switch into each circuit. However, I'm sure you will agree that half the job has been done for you using this harness with the added bonus that you know it has been safely and neatly completed with the correct wire sizes, and a fused supply into the bargain. I consider this a must for every new TR owner who feels nervous about wiring generally, for it simplifies the whole issue. Picture 13-6 shows a nice example.

AUXILIARIES
Higher power headlamps

In today's traffic, it's pretty much a necessity to fit higher intensity headlamps. You can get sealed beam units, but I recommend 'Quad optic'

13-6. The most important parts of Neil Revington's supplementary harness, the connection interfaces, fuses and relays. Very neat indeed and highly recommended.

replacement units. Fitted with halogen bulbs these give a slightly stronger light straightaway. Furthermore, you can also fit the blue-tinted Xenon bulbs, either immediately, or in due course, thereby increasing your illumination by a further 30% without a corresponding increase in current. It's prudent to consider additional wiring capacity and a relay at the same time, to maximise the output without straining the car's original fuse/wiring/switch capacities.

Xenon bulbs are available as replacements for H1 and H4 Halogen bulbs. They are some 30% brighter the conventional halogen bulbs, and should (for safety and legal reasons) be fitted in pairs. The Xenon gas allows the lamp to burn brighter without drawing any additional power, so cables and switches that are satisfactory for halogen bulbs need not be further upgraded. All weather, or vision bulbs are probably more suited to fog lamps, and should also be fitted in pairs. They are available as replacements for Halogen H1, H3 and H4 fittings, and have a blue tint or filter on the glass but emit a soft yellow tinted light that reduces reflective glare and gives better visibility in adverse weather conditions.

A whole new range of bulbs is starting to appear on the market, which use the performance of the long-life low consumption gas discharge units. These

units give an incredibly bright light with a defined blue tinge to the beam edges. Some of the latest bulbs claim to be able to approach gas discharge light outputs, with lower than original bulb power consumption. These bulbs cost anything up to £70 each, however, and, as all headlamps in the UK have to be matching pairs, you need two bulbs, and very often a spare!

Relay kits

These are a very good addition to your car's safety and performance. Without relays (which are pretty standard on most modern cars), the high electrical current has to be carried by the under-dash electrical wiring, the light switch and the column control stalks. This situation is only made worse by uprated headlamps which, may not perform at their best due to the relatively thin cables that feed power to the original headlamps. These thin cables act as resistors and limit the performance of your uprated headlamps. So the first step, which will probably increase the effectiveness of the existing lights, is to increase the wire thickness and fit a relay kit (available from Moss, part number is GAC40264).

To fuse or not to fuse

TR5/250 and 6s didn't employ a fuse in the headlight circuit. However, by the time the TR7 and Stag were in production, fusing the headlamps was being introduced, and today most cars have fuse protection within the headlamp circuits. There are, of course, arguments both for and against the idea, but I think on balance it's better to have some fuse protection. However, if you have only two fuses available for the headlights, I suggest you leave the full beam side unfused, but use the available fuse-places for each of the 'dipped' headlights. I think this suggestion is particularly helpful if you are upgrading your headlamp bulbs to higher wattage units. My proposal will take a worthwhile load off the original circuits and fuses, give you the added safety of independent fuses for each of the headlamps, and provide the headlamps with a higher capacity cable supply.

For those really increasing the wattage of their headlights, then there is much to be said for adding a relay into the power supply to the headlamps and upgrading the current carrying capacity of the wires leading down to the lamp units as well.

You'll hardly need me to mention the wisdom of fusing the sort of flame throwers we see in picture 13-7 separately from any of the other lights. Some auxiliary lights can be quite powerful so a relay is advisable to take the load off the switch. You should also use a cable which is more than adequate in terms of capacity.

Electric washer kits and jet mounts

Surely essential in today's motoring environment, Revington can improve all TR's ability to wash the windscreen/ windshield. An electric windscreen washer kit is available for each of the

13-7. A TR4 rally replica. You'll have problems if you fail to correctly wire these 'flame-throwers' into a car with inappropriate generating capacity and incorrect switches and relays!

Sidescreen, TR4 and TR4A cars. The later cars already enjoy electric washers, but the washer jets on the TR4s, 5s and 6s are fixed to a hard rubber ferrule which is part of the wiper wheel-box mounting. These are not very satisfactory in the long term so a welcome improvement, organised by Revington, is for the rubber ferrule to be replaced by a metal one. The replacements are indistinguishable, as they are painted black, and should hold the washer jet securely for your lifetime!

Engine cooling fans

Pacet fans are highly recommended and shown in picture 13-8. The size refers to the diameter of the fan, and 12 and 14 inch fans should fit most TRs, but if a 16 unit will fit – use it! We discussed pushing and pulling cooling fans in an earlier chapter.

If you buy a Kenlowe fan you get an adjustable thermostat switch, which is rather helpful. However, the 'bulb' has to be routed into the top hose and occasionally causes a slight weep if you fail to get the sealing boot in exactly the right place. I've taped my boot in place before using a drop of washing-up liquid to slip the top hose in place. I then used two jubilee clips on the fitting and have never had a problem! However, our contributing specialists can supply a specially-made lower water pipe in stainless steel. The unique and important detail is that the pipe incorporates a

13-8. A 14in Pacet fan ready for close-coupling to the rear of the TR radiator. It's a little hard to distinguish, but the central motor on this fan protrudes backwards into the engine compartment by an inch or so. If you are very tight for space it's possible to buy fans where the motor is virtually flush with the rear of the fan casing. Note the stainless steel bottom pipe fitted with the thermostatic switch.

thermostatic switch mounting point. A switch located here monitors the temperature of the water leaving the radiator and many say provides the ideal location for the fan control switch.

Wiring in the electric fan requires some thought. Many like to couple their fan to a constantly live (un-switched), fuse, so that the fan runs even when the engine has been turned off. I personally don't favour this method because your battery can run down. I favour wiring the fan into a fuse which is switched (via a relay), to the ignition switch.

Note! Whichever fan, and whichever type of circuit you use, the fan should be powered through a (further) relay as the 10-15 (some even need 20), amps required will significantly shorten the life of the switch. One I know lasted a couple of weeks, and the car steamed onto our show stand to the evident embarrassment of the owner!

I strongly recommend you wire in an override switch to enable the fan to be switched on when you arrive at the tail of a traffic queue on a hot day, *i.e.* before the water temperature rises!

Aftermarket starters

Revington TR and Racetorations provide aftermarket starter motors at suit all TRs (they cost around £235). Many are drawn to these, either to replace an early TR starter which can't otherwise be found, for example, or because a tiny competition battery has trouble getting a conventional starter to play, particularly if the very high-compression engine is difficult to turn over. Others are attracted by the very worthwhile weight reduction offered by these modern replacements. Average weight is 4kg (less than 9lbs), whereas a standard TR6 starter weighs 8.5kg (18.7lb). They achieve their high torque by a double gearing reduction design that generates twice the cranking power whilst drawing less current than conventional starters. One such motor can be seen in picture 13-9.

Direction indicator audible warning

It's all too easy to forget to turn the flashing directional indicator off. This is irritating to other road users and also possibly dangerous. I solved the problem with a couple of cheap (computer), buzzers wired into the flashing light circuit. The units cost about £1.50 each from Radio Spares (UK), operate at 3-18 volts and emit such a noise that even

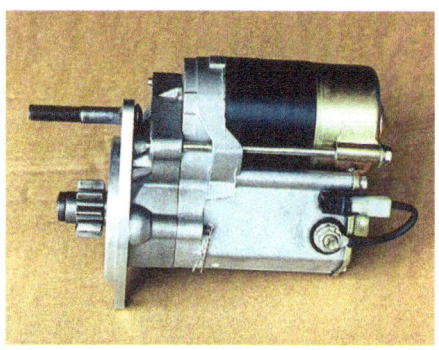

13-9. As a result of their excellent design, incorporating double reduction gearing, these modern replacement starter motors are superior in every way (except, of course, cost), to the original starter motor.

with the hood down some sticky tape was necessary to dampen them down a little. RS Catalogue Nos. 231-2793 or 295-9386, or any similar specification alternatives will get your attention. You'll need two, connected after the direction switch on the steering column, one for the left and one for the right.

Audio systems
Not everyone is aware that modern memory retaining radios draw a small constant current from the battery. Over a short time span, a few days, for example, this has no detrimental effect on a car's battery. However, if the car is left unused for three weeks, or a month, it's amazing how such a small drain can deplete the battery. There are solutions, of course, but prevention is preferable: don't buy an audio system that has a station retention memory. If you do buy one, make sure it doesn't require any battery power to retain the information. Be suspicious of radios that require the connection of two power leads (one to the ignition circuit and one to an always-live feed). If you have one already fitted, I can only suggest a battery top-up every couple of weeks with a trickle-charger, or that you disconnect the battery's earth termination whenever the car is likely to be laid-up for a while.

Immobilisers
I've already covered the subject of fitting immobilisers in *How to Restore Triumph TR5/250 & 6*. While that section doesn't warrant repetition here, as important as it is, I must mention the fact that Revington can now supply a radio controlled alarm system (made by

Eureka). This can be fitted to any classic car at home, without damaging the car's dashboard, fittings or appearance. The receiver is discretely mounted anywhere in the car, under a carpet, for example. Leads from the receiver run to and break into up to three electrical supply lines as are applicable for your car. All TRs will have starter and low tension ignition leads to interrupt, but not all will have an electric fuel pump. However, where fitted, the electrical supply line to the pump, or better yet the pump's relay, is best included in the protection offered by this device. The external trigger is about the size of a key fob. The fob is no more than a triggering device. The whole kit is available for £67 and seems very good value for money.

Incidentally, a word about installation of immobilisers, you should actually remove a length of the wire from the circuit you are protecting, say 6 or 10in (150 to 250mm). If you just cut your car's circuit and don't remove any cable, it's possible that one of the bad guys can spend a few minutes tracing the circuits through to the point that your immobiliser breaks into the car's wiring and rejoin the original wires together, thus circumnavigating your protection.

Some insurance savings are possible with a professionally fitted immobiliser. My Stag insurance is discounted but on the basis of a certificate provided by a professional installer, so be aware that the home installation route has much to commend it but you are unlikely to get an insurance discount!

Any alarm you fit must obviously be wired to a fuse that is non-switched, *i.e.* live whenever the battery is connected.

Improved switch arrangements
You can modernise your wiper controls but will need to fit the TR6 wiper motor by substituting the current stalk switches for ones that control direction indicators, overdrive, headlamp main beam control, multi-speed 'screen-wiper control, and 'screen wash. You can see the switch in picture 13-10. Furthermore, this arrangement can be augmented by an intermittent wiper function switched from the now redundant dashboard wiper switch position. The modernised arrangement also brings the wiper options right up to date in that the original twin speed wipers become augmented by a single wipe plus an intermittent wipe! The latter is achieved

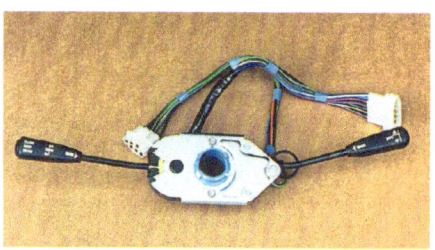

13-10. Revington have introduced this excellent steering column/stalk switching arrangement for all the TRs.

by two stalk controls. You will not be surprised to hear that the original cowlings are not suited for the stalks fitted to another car, but Revington have had special cowls moulded for most combinations of stalks/TR's.

Electronic tachometers
This upgrade is usually only applicable to those doing engine management upgrades, some of which may involve dispensing with your distributor or fitting a different one without a mechanical drive. Revington and Speedy Cables can convert your tachometer to electronic drive. This deletes the long mechanical cable connection, and is also possibly helpful to those carrying out a left hand to right hand drive conversion.

Inertia switch
The original inertia switches for PI electric fuel pumps are getting long in the tooth now, and can be unreliable. We explored ways to improve their reliability in *How to Restore Triumph TR5/250 & 6*, but even so, the highest degree of reliability will be achieved via a new/ replacement switch. Revington has a replacement inertia switch that should, like the original, operate on the primary (low current) side of a fuel-pump relay.

Courtesy lights
Revington obviously realised the impracticality of the courtesy lights in some of the TRs and has come up with a kit that puts them in a much more illuminating place: in the frame of the windscreen/windshield. I've seen numerous modern cars with the courtesy lights located either side of the rear view mirror, so Neil is basically copying a good idea. The one exception perhaps is map reading on the move when a separately wired map light is still indispensable, but for most other tasks the top of the car is a far better

place for a courtesy/interior light than that provided by Triumph. The new light can be wired to operate via door and/or dashboard switches, as you prefer, but is best fitted with the windscreen off the car (pictures 13-11-1 to 13-11-3).

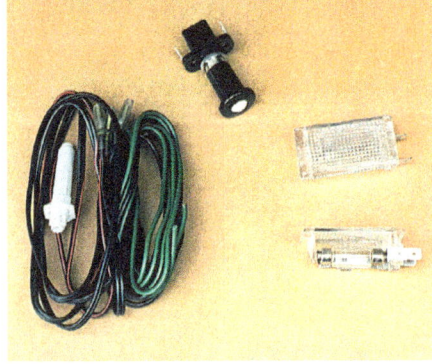

13-11-1. The interior light kit ...

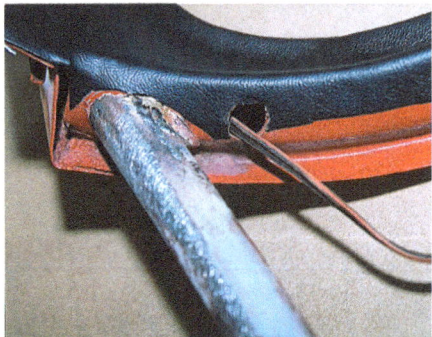

13-11-2. ... is best fitted with the screen off the car so this hole can be added to the bottom of the frame.

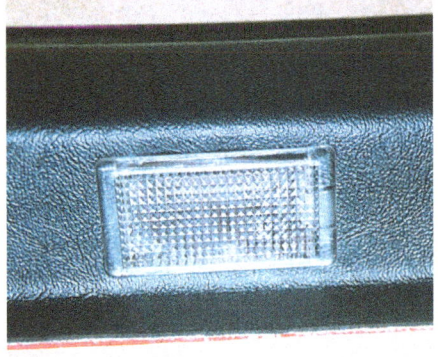

13-11-3. The end result looks absolutely 'right', and is far more practical.

Overdrive electrical improvements

We discussed the mechanics of fitting of an overdrive to your car in Chapter 6. However, some readers may well already have an overdrive fitted to their car but feel the electrics need upgrading, either by the protection of a simple line fuse or by reducing the load on the ignition circuits by fitting a relay. Drawing D13-2 shows how you might do both. Photograph 13-12 shows a neat and useful refinement for those using a warning light to signal that the overdrive is 'in' (a dimmer control that reduces the intensity of the warning light when the cars lights are on).

13-12. Revington's auto-dimmer for overdrive warning lights. Mine was fitted before Revington introduced this refinement and I think this could be very helpful when driving at night.

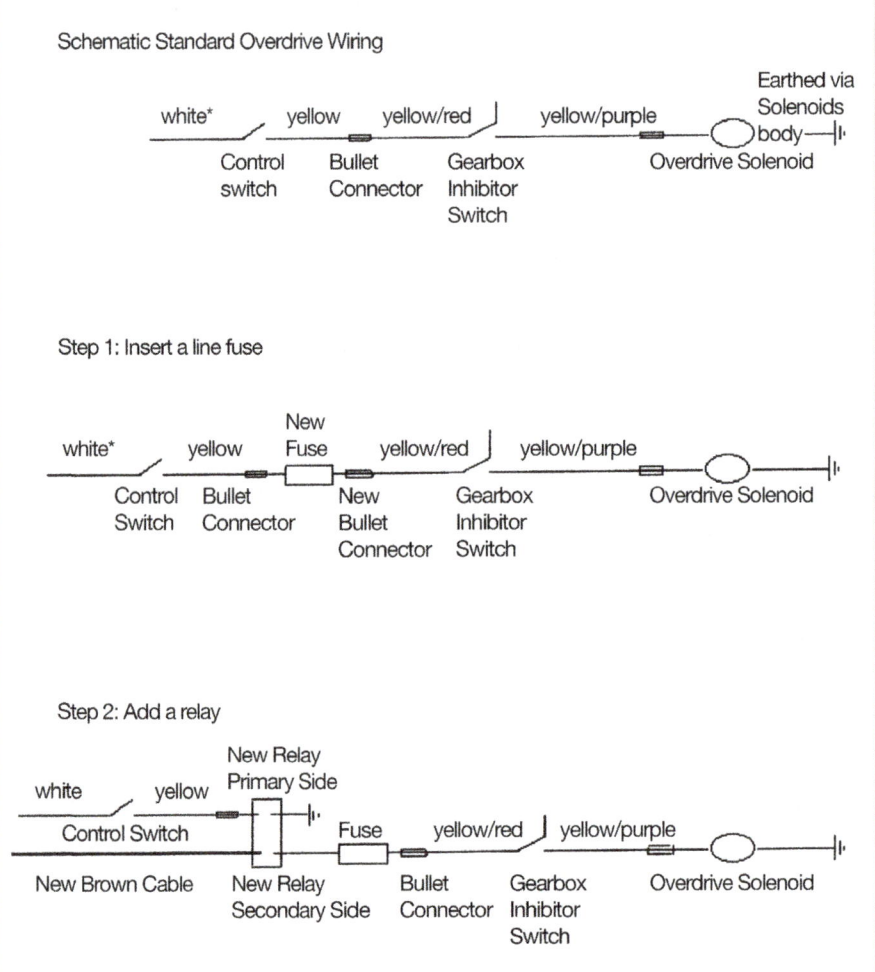

D13-2. Improving the overdrive electrics.

Chapter 14
Body & trim

BODY IMPROVEMENTS
Strengthening

The following suggestions will really only be contemplated it you're planning a competition-orientated car, or if you're separating body from chassis. If both those actions are part of your upgrading plan, you should also consider strengthening and/or altering the bodyshell in several places. Seam welding all the spot or stitch-welded panel joints (if permitted in your intended category of competition), will stiffen the bodyshell to the benefit of the car's handling, as well as increasing its longevity over a stressful period.

Firewalls are important too, for the obvious safety reasons, and they are mandatory in competitions, which may provide food for thought for owners of road going TRs. Thin aluminium firewalls are available for each of the TRs in order to meet competitive regulations with the minimum of weight penalties, and are riveted in front of the fuel tank. Although a firewall is also an excellent way of stiffening up a body tub. If this is your primary objective you are better using 18 or 20 swg mild steel sheet and welding it in position prior to painting the shell.

Severe stress cracking at the front of the body, both around the angled mountings and at the front of the bulkhead at chassis level, can be experienced in both racing and rallying. You definitely should plate the former, although a friend tells me he studiously ignored the latter without serious consequences. However, I would strengthen that too for the extra few ounces of steel involved!

Rally enthusiasts have been known to dent the body under the fuel tank, sometimes even the bottom of the fuel tank, with the back axle breather! Shorten the breather tube if your car is likely to be taking to the air.

Lightweight panels

Probably the master of lightening a motor car was Colin Chapman, whose Lotus team used its car's minimal weight to very good effect! There are three routes to reducing the weight of the body of a TR: thin steel, aluminium or fibreglass panels, or a combination of all three. Revington can build any or all panels in thin gauge steel, fibreglass or aluminium, and you'll see one such example in picture 14-1-1. Fibreglass panels are also available from a wide variety of vendors. If you're thinking of more than a few panels, provided you don't mind being restricted to steel and/or aluminium, the whole car can be constructed from lighter component

14-1-1. Here we see a front apron entirely in aluminium. Revington can supply virtually all TR panels in aluminium, saving approximately half the weight.

panels if necessary. However, the most popular route to reducing the weight of the car is to focus on the bolt on panels. As a matter of interest, each bolt on panel's weight can be roughly halved by this route, which is a considerable total saving if you consider we are talking about the bonnet, boot lid, both doors, and all four wings!

Some categories of competitive cars may be restricted as to where they use lightweight replacement panels. However, when permitted, most competitors prefer to use fibreglass replacements because they are (much) less costly and easier to repair than steel or aluminium. However, aluminium

14-1-2. This lightweight panel is actually made from fibreglass! You need to protect the underside of both aluminium and fibreglass wings, though, since they can easily be damaged from inside, so take a look at picture 14-5 too.

seems the preference amongst owners of rally cars, although bespoke lightweight steel panels will also save in the order of 50% of the original steel panel. You will not be surprised to learn that the cost for these hand prepared replacements is very high indeed. However, given the superb quality of a typical end result, few would dispute that they offer excellent value for money.

14-1-3. Fibreglass panels generally, and wings in particular, are easily adjusted at home as this shot confirms. This Michelotti front wing has been widened by about 1in (25mm), around its lip, and the extra width nicely blended into the bottom of the wing/fender which has retained its standard section.

14-1-4. At the back, the lower rear of the wing/fender has been packed out from the inner wing to give the wider wheels extra cover.

Nevertheless, an ultra fast road car may be the place for such special panelling since it will certainly not devalue the car.

On the other hand, many enthusiasts think that fibreglass panelling will devalue a road going car. It really depends upon the performance of the car and the quality of the fibreglass panels. They may not detract from a really quick car that is beautifully presented, for potential buyers will be buying the car for its performance. However, a standard performance car poorly presented may attract so few buyers if/when the time comes to sell that indeed the value could be lower than a conventional steel panelled car. If I was seeking a TR, I would always choose one that had been restored with steel panels. Nevertheless, fibreglass panels certainly have a place in improving TRs, and not just for competitive cars either. Firstly, they do look good, indeed they're undetectable, as you will see from Neil Brown's car shown in picture 14-1-2. Secondly, they can be (easily), repaired or modified at home with equally good results, as photos 14-1-3 and 14-1-4 show. Neil wanted to widen his wheelarches by an inch or so and simply sawed the edge off, fibreglassed the appropriately widened piece back in place, and then filled and finished the end result!

Special panels

You may wish to customise the apprearance of your car for aesthetic reasons, or to overcome a practical problem. The bonnet louvres in picture 14-2-1 may be a case in point. I'll return to bonnet louvres in the next section. Racetorations, for example, brought a nice touch of individuality to the TR6 shown in photograph 14-2-2. The modification had practical overtones and would, therefore, be quite acceptable to the TR world at large. However, I would sound a cautionary note about changing your TR's shape too radically. You could spend a lot of money devaluing your car! In general, most body shape changes are unlikely to enhance the value of any TR. There are exceptions, though, and properly converting a TR250 to a TR4 Rally (picture 14-3) replica would offend very few, and would probably

14-2-1. Modifying or adjusting steel panels is not out of the question, of course, but you do need bodybuilding skills, experience and equipment to make a nice job of it. Here we see some full length bonnet louvres on a Sidescreen bonnet. The same company will be able to produce an equally good set of louvres in any of the TR bonnets/hoods.

14-2-2. A TR6 with a difference. Bespoke bodywork by Racetorations enabled this owner to enjoy enhanced illumination by night and a unique appearance by day.

enhance the value of the car. Revington can help with the supply of some less popular panels you might want if you're planning a replica rally car or upgrading your own vehicle. Side vents, big-hinged ally panels, light bars, extra capacity fuel tanks and perspex side and rear windows are all available from Revington for the TR4, 4A, 5 and 250 - although I would give changing a TR5 a **great** deal of thought!

Under bonnet ventilation
Bonnet louvres need to be done nicely, since they are very visible. A press and

14-3. 6VC, one of the original TR4 rally cars in its heyday. We will look at the detail of creating a couple of TR 'replica' cars in the companion volume to this book (How to Improve Triumph TR2 to 4A). However, all the removable panels on this car were handmade in aluminium.

experience are essential, of course, and they need to have their openings facing the windscreen/windshield. Since hot air rises, louvres do help to extract air from the engine bay, particularly in heavy traffic as the air finds it easier to go up than under the car when there is little forward movement. However, remember that the windscreen/windshield creates a high-pressure area in front of it when travelling at speed, and this will negate the effect of any louvres positioned in the rear one-third of the bonnet. In fact, it's possible to have air entering any louvres positioned in the high-pressure area (*i.e.* too far back in the bonnet), when travelling at speed. Therefore, rather than cover the whole of the bonnet in louvre slots, it's a very good idea to plan them with some care.

In addition to leaving the rear of the bonnet plain, it's quite a good idea not to louvre areas above the ignition equipment (dizzy, plug leads and coil, in particular), and the carburettors. If you

feel that you are left with too little bonnet to effectively reduce your under-bonnet temperatures, bear the following points in mind. The front of the bonnet is the area of lowest pressure, so it has the greatest potential to extract air when moving at speed. Furthermore, it's just behind the radiator where a large part of the hot air you want to remove while stationary builds up. Finally, carburettors and/or high-tension electrics are rarely positioned towards the front of the engine so, in short, choose an area behind the radiator but in front of the vulnerable engine components.

Cockpit ventilation
You'll improve the flow of air through the fresh air system no end if you fit a scoop over the air inlet. The design doesn't have to be traditional to be effective. You could fold up a 45 degree 'flap' in aluminium or thin steel and get the improved cooling and heating benefits I mention. However, pictures 14-4-1 and 14-4-2 show the design which Triumph used for the TR4 rally cars. These are available from Revington and possibly other specialists too.

Preservation
The obvious method of preservation your TR is by injecting wax into the body

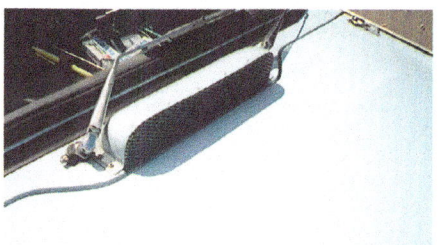

14-4-1. First used on TR4 rally cars, these additional air scoops really do increase airflow into the cockpit at speed.

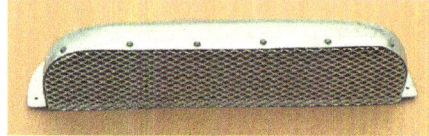

14-4-2. Here is the individual bolt-on unit in closer detail. Fitting it need not involve significant body damage, although as designed it requires four self tapping screws to secure it. I think I might try double sided sticky tape initially, and take it slowly for a week or two until I was sure it was holding securely.

14-4-3. You may find this 'in line' heater control valve more convenient but more effective too.

and chassis cavities. We discussed that subject in *How to Restore Triumph TR5/250 & 6,* so nothing more than a brief *precis* is necessary here. There is a misconception, though, namely that a car of the TR variety, once treated, is good for years. This is not so. TRs need a regular application of protective wax treatment. I don't feel it's essential to treat a low mileage closeted car annually, but any TR used almost daily in all weathers would benefit from an annual top up, certainly in the UK! Therefore, for the small cost involved, it's worth buying a compressed air injection gun, long reach tube and flexible hose (Machine Mart is one possible source). You must close all injection holes with a plastic bung, and be prepared to go through the underside/box section protection exercise every couple of years.

Revington has reintroduced a set of inner wing liners that afford some extra protection for TR4 to TR6 cars. Originally conceived by Jerry Vincent, the

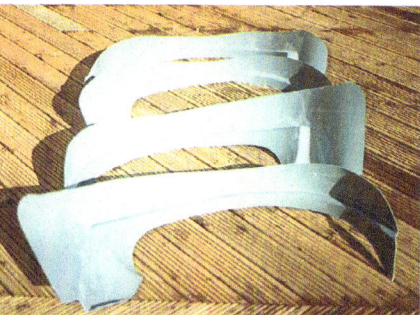

14-5. These are a set of fibreglass under wing liners. They are available for all models of TR. Some form of under wing protection is important if you're using lightweight panels, but more than one owner has successfully made some from old PVC barrels.

Revington products use Jerry's moulds to make these thin fibreglass panels. They come with an outer sealing rubber, which fits against the wings/fenders. At £200 for the set, these sound expensive but are a good idea provided you don't have to drill holes in your wing to secure them.

If you've purchased a nice rust-free, dry-state car, you may not appreciate that you'll need to remove all four wings/fenders to seal the joint against the ingress of water (assuming it hasn't been done already). I covered this important detail in *How to Restore Triumph TR5/250 & 6*, but it deserves a mention again here. In the interests of longevity, all four wings must be removed. No paint was ever applied to the mating surfaces, and even the most generous application of wax preservatives won't find the joints. If the wings are in good shape, and many are indeed superb, you might get away without repainting the whole wing, or indeed its mating panel, if you tackle the job early and carefully enough.

Mask the existing paintwork each side of each joint and as near the wing/body joint-line as practical. Remove the wings in pairs (if only because you need to remove the respective bumper/fender), and rub down the mating faces until they are bright and rust free. This is where great care is required for you need to get the corrosion out without damaging your masking tape and the visible paint beneath. The choice of paint and its application is down to you but, for this sort of prevention, brushing on a rust-preventative paint seems essential. Let the paint dry and harden for several days before removing your masking tapes and rebolting the wings in place. Use a generous coating of Dumdum sealant between the mating faces. Give the sealant a couple of days to squeeze

out, retighten the fastenings and use a plastic spatula to remove the surplus sealant. Picture 14-6 will give you a little more information.

TR4/6 plenum drain
Another modification that it's wise to make sooner rather than later is to improve the two drains from the plenum chamber on TR4 to 6 cars. The front wings/fenders need to be removed so if you have to carry out the above improvement, this is an ideal opportunity to simultaneously effect this upgrade, if only because three-quarters of the job is removing and replacing the wings! This was also a detail we covered in *How to Restore Triumph TR5/250 & 6* but this is an important and very worthwhile change, particularly if your feet and the floor of the car are getting wet. Photograph 14-7 shows how the plenum drain can be improved to stop water flowing over the inner wing and the front part of the sills.

Clearly it's tempting, and certainly does no harm, to remove the tubes off each end of the (two), plenum drains and

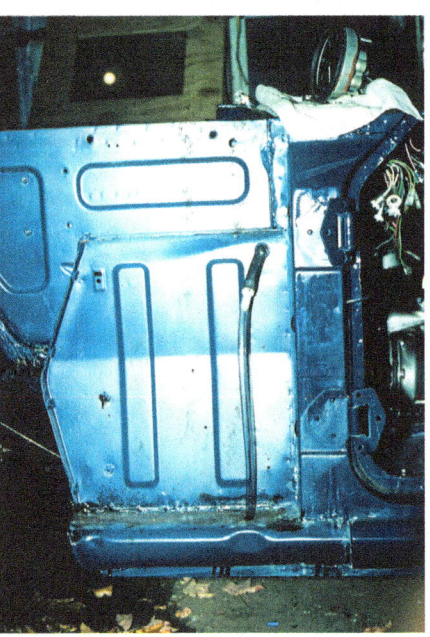

14-7. The reasons and details appear in the text, but this is the recommended revised drain for the plenum chamber that passes an extended tube down through the top of the outer sill and out through the inside of the inner sill. This would be a logical time to make these changes and to finalise the front right side.

push a flexible piece of wire up into the plenum chamber and down into the inner wing to clear any blockage. However, that's a short term solution for you're still letting water run down the (probably unpainted), inner wing and front sill. So, before the rot gets a hold, it really is best to take both front wings off, clean and paint the inner wing, and fit one of the alternative drain improvements. Moss does a kit that takes the drain out through the splash plates but, since air pressure can then restrict the outflow of water, the better solution is to exit through the top of the sills, as detailed in my earlier book.

You can still get damp feet, though, since the seam between the front and rear of the plenum chamber can leak, even a new one needs sealing. A liberal dose of waxoyl after a long dry spell is probably your best bet if you are not into the restoration work required to fit a new plenum!

Paint protection
A clear stone repellent film that can be applied to the exerior paintwork. This is invaluable if you're going rallying and want to keep at least the most vulnerable areas of your paint work protected. The film can be stuck to vulnerable areas and pealed off as and when appropriate. It's available from TR Enterprises as well as, no doubt, the other TR specialists listed in the Appendix.

INTERIOR/EXTERIOR TRIM AND FITTINGS
Gearbox cover
There are several options for you to choose from when it comes to fitting a replacement gearbox cover, but I have to tell you that the two piece fibreglass one we see in picture 14-8 impressed me. Getting to the fastenings at the front of a conventional one piece cover is difficult, or at least my back found it difficult. If the gearbox has to come out it makes little difference, the whole cover has to come out. If it is only the speedo, overdrive or oil level that needs attention then the detachable rear on this Racetorations product makes life so much easier.

Uprated tops
Originally only applicable to the TR4/4A, since we've thrown originality constraints aside, you can now also consider the Surrey top. Revington can now supply Surrey tops with some

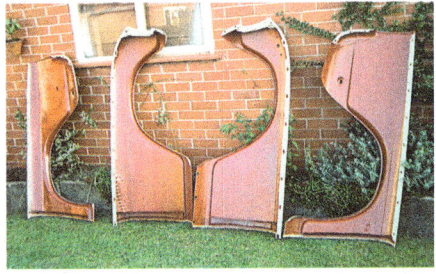

14-6. It's vital that you remove all four wings/fenders and properly prepare, paint and seal between them and the body tub (if it hasn't already been done).

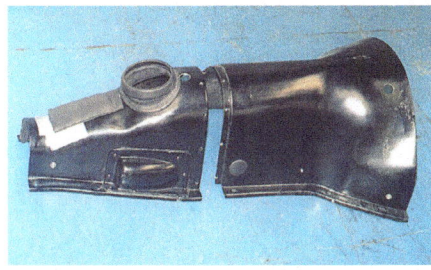

14-8. As anyone who has fitted an original or moulded plastic gearbox cover knows, it's a bit of a nightmare. This Racetorations improvement is very welcome on two counts. Firstly, it's made much more accurately in fibreglass, and secondly, it's made in two parts, so any minor attention at the rear of the box (i.e. overdrive, speedo cable, universal joint, etc.), can be accomplished without removing the whole cover. If you are planning a gearbox change, of course, then the whole thing still has to come off but in one piece, but you'll enjoy the benefits of the more accurate fibreglass construction when it comes to re-assembly.

14-10. The aftermarket burr walnut dashboards/fascias are very unlikely to lift car's performance but, to my mind at least, they sure lift its appearance particularly when ...

interesting improvements. First, let's get our nomenclature correct! The main constituent parts should be called:

• The assembly should be called a 'hard top' with removable central panels.
• The rear window should be called a 'back light'.
• The cloth top is what Triumph refered to as the 'Surrey top'.

If you're looking to upgrade your Michelotti car's weather protection, Revington makes two types of fibreglass back light frame. The first is a reproduction standalone unit that

14-9. A very pretty and very competitive car with the hard top in place. This picture has some interesting features. Did you spot the cooling vents cut into the side windows, or those in the lower part of the back light?

is undistinguishable from the original aluminium one. The alternative is a slightly lighter fibreglass one that is strengthened by an integral roll-over protection bar. This carries on down to the floor of the car. Revington also supply several types of central sections (lids), one piece ones in fibreglass or aluminium, for example, or you can also buy a central section made from aluminium in two halves. This is rather nice since it can be popped in the boot in two halves. The back light is available, too, and here you have to make a decision between perspex or glass. Some excellent hard tops are also available - an example from Racetorations is shown in photograph 14-9.

Dashboards
If you're fitting a full roll cage, two of the members will have to go through the dashboard, which will wreck a standard one. The solution is to fit an Revington alloy dashboard around the roll cage members, and keep the car's original dash for another day. This actually has a more immediate benefit in that you can position your instruments just where they are convenient and most easily seen.

Picture 14-10 shows a burr walnut veneer alternative to the standard wood dash/fascia. You may care to consider this, purely for aesthetic reasons, of

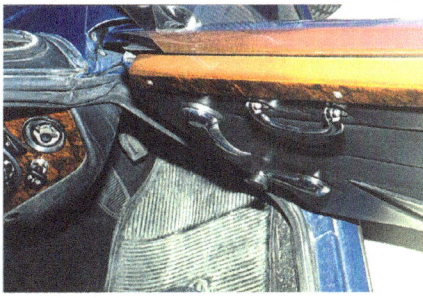

14-11. ... coupled to matching door cappings.

course, when your instruments are next out for maintenance or repair.

Door cappings
I'm not sure what the current situation is but, when I was refurbishing our TR6, the original moulded door cappings (the ones with the moulded-in door pulls) were not available. I fell upon the idea of fitting the wooden/veneered ones shown in photograph 14-11 and a TR4 internal pull handle. I had heard that the original style cappings were always pulling off the top of the door frame and, since the TR4 handle mounting holes were already *in situ* in my TR6 frames, I felt the modification was 'meant to be'. It's actually proved to be a blessing in disguise, for the TR6's new furflex door

seals initially made the closing the door difficult, unless you gave them a really good slam, so the TR4's handles proved invaluable!

The new arrangement doesn't look out of place (at least to my eyes), although I must tell you I made one mistake. I bought the dash from one source and the cappings from somewhere else at a later date and, in spite of my best efforts, they didn't match. I ended up buying a second dash/fascia. A nice dashboard/fascia doesn't make the car go quicker, but we make progress very elegantly I think you'll agree! Take care who you buy your dashboard from, my first one was definitely inferior and wouldn't fit. BH Veneered Fascias (UK telephone number 01270 883933), provided a matched pair of cappings and dash/fascia that fitted perfectly.

Back draft deflectors

Long, high speed, hood down runs are much less tiring if you've got a back-draft deflector in place. The proprietary ones are constructed from welded steel angle and are usually fastened via a flat plate sandwiched between the hood frame and the B post. You can make them yourself, although most of the larger DIY superstores sell 3mm perspex, however you are advised to look for 4mm thick material since extra thickness is more robust and well worth searching for. Although perspex cuts easily with a jigsaw, it also scratches easily, so you should cover the cutting area with masking tape (onto which you can draw your cut line), before attempting your cut. The edges can then be cleaned up , de-burred and polished with a fine file. Rivet it to the angle from the metal side but use a largish washer to spread the stresses on the perspex side.

I doubt you'll be able to erect the hood with a back deflector in place, unless you've been very clever with the design of the angle frame.

Upgraded hoods

We explored fitting a new hood in *How to Restore Triumph TR5/250 & 6* so I don't propose to do more than touch on the subject here. I did feel that I should draw your attention to the pros and cons of a mohair hood upgrade. Mohair hoods are heavier, bulkier and attract more dirt than a vinyl hood. However, they are stronger, flexible in all temperatures and do deaden wind noise, so take a

14-12. A hood is a hood ... to be raised only when static in traffic in pouring rain? Well, that's as may be, but when it's up, it's good to have one that does keep the water out. This is my blue mohair one from TR Bitz, which does just that.

look at some hoods when next you need to replace yours. You can see mine in picture 14-12.

IMPROVING THE SEATING

Many drivers, particularly the taller owners or those who have had back problems, find that the TR seats aren't as comfortable as they would like. Standard and fast road cars, for example, would

14-13-1. Mazda MX-5 seats are very comfortable and don't look out of place in a Michelotti or Karmann bodyshell.

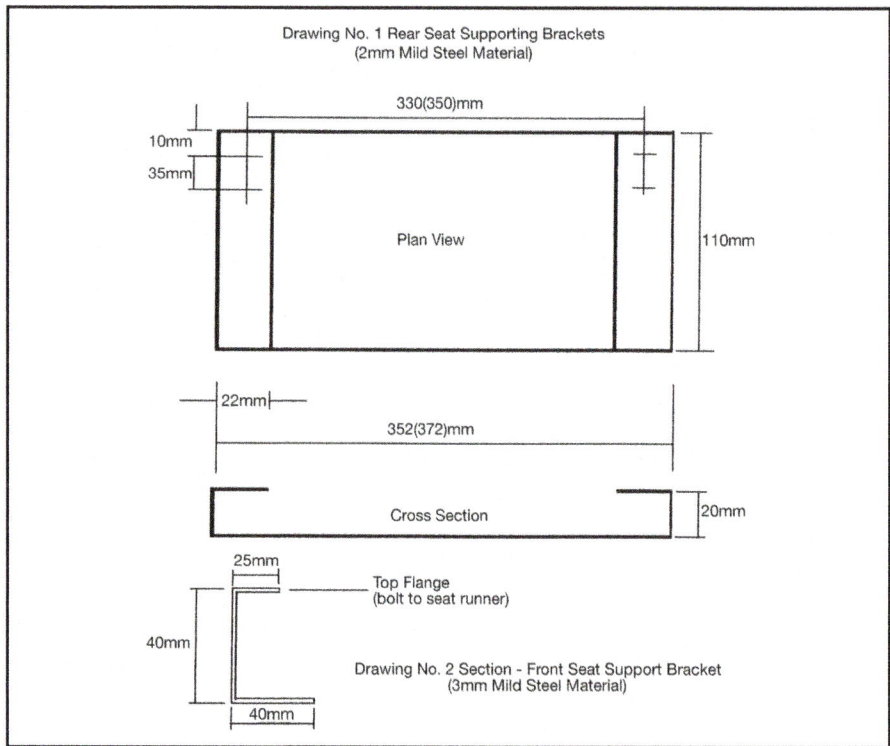

Drawing No. 1 Rear Seat Supporting Brackets
(2mm Mild Steel Material)

330(350)mm

10mm

35mm

Plan View

110mm

22mm

352(372)mm

Cross Section

20mm

25mm

Top Flange
(bolt to seat runner)

40mm

Drawing No. 2 Section - Front Seat Support Bracket
(3mm Mild Steel Material)

40mm

D14. A pair of mounting brackets for MX5 seats.

benefit from improved seating (which ideally doesn't necessitate modifying any original TR parts). Owners of ultra fast and competitive cars, on the other hand, are looking for something quite different, of course. They need to be held much more securely by the seat(s) than would be practical in every-day use, for example, and also require provision for a four point safety harness.

14-13-2. The Mazda seats come with four mounting feet that need to be removed. This shot shows one (arrowed) gone, and one (arrowed) to go.

14-13-3. The drawing opposite actually shows a slightly different mounting bracket to my first attempt shown here. However, there is no right or wrong method, just make sure your seats are very secure and use these ideas and your own to achieve that objective.

Standard and fast road

For TR4 to TR6 owners, the suggestion shown in picture 14-13-1 will get you sitting much more comfortably. It's also much cheaper than many alternatives. You'll have to make the special brackets shown in drawing D14, but the car won't need to be altered. As a bonus, the suggestion offers the choice of modern cloth covering in black/charcoal or tan leather material. Safety is also enhanced. These replacement seats are MUCH cheaper than having your existing TR seats refurbished, and also save you the cost of replacing your TR seat runners if they're tired or rusty. The replacement seats adjust easily, and the tilt-forward facility is retained. No welding is required to effect the change. The seats I'm refering to, of course, are from a Mazda MX-5/Miata/Eunos Roadster. I'm pretty sure that Mazda 323 saloons/sedans use the same seats, if getting hold of genuine MX-5 seats proves difficult.

TR5s, TR250s and the TR6 all use the same seat mounting/adjusting frame and fitting the new seats can be summarised in two parts. You need to make or buy some bespoke mounting brackets. However, note that the Mazda seats have different hole centres between the left side pair of seat runners and the right side seat runners, which accounts for the extra dimensions shown in brackets in my drawings. You need to use the un-bracketed dimensions for the narrower left side rear bracket. You can order a set of pre-formed brackets (4 pieces), from RMR Engineering Ltd (telephone number (UK) 01303 253166), if you prefer.

You'll need to remove the four original Mazda mounting feet and two locating dowels from each end of the seat runners, as per picture 14-13-2. Fasten your new rear mounting brackets to the Mazda seats using four 5mm diameter high tensile bolts, nuts and the largest possible washers. Picture 14-13-3 gives you some idea as to the shape of the rear bracket I initially used, although the drawings show a later design that I think you will find easier to fit. Bolt the back bracket to the seat and position the open part of the front channel facing forward, and the narrower 'leg' uppermost. Secure the front channel to the seat using 5mm high tensile bolts, nuts and washers.

Position the seat in the car and persuade a partner to sit in the seat. Crawl under the (safely elevated) car

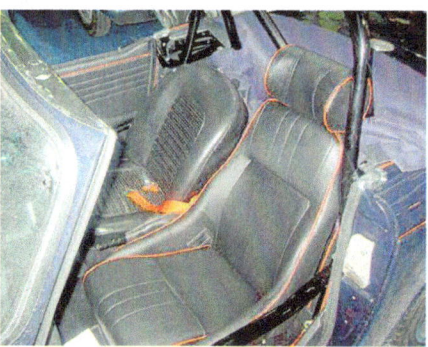

14-14-1. Racetorations seats are unique to the best of my knowledge, in that they can be ordered in (almost) any colour you like, and any width, too. They are designed for long distance comfort and support, so can be used for racing/rallying and fast-road driving. Adaptable for use with a single seat belt or full race harness, they are available in (so Darryl Uprichard tells me) narrow, medium & 'comfort' widths. The headrest is detachable, so a tonneau cover can still be used.

14-14-2. Another view of Restorations' bucket seats.

and scribe the positions of the four fixing holes up through the floor before removing the seat and drilling all four mounting bolt holes in the new brackets.

Competition bucket seats/belts

Racetorations offers the very comfortable bucket seats you see in pictures 14-14-1 and 14-14-2. You get a further view of DKU's seats in a superb TR5 in pictures 14-14-3 and 14-14-4. Revington has Corbeau make the seats shown in picture 14-14-5 in any colour you choose!

Needless to say, both Racetorations and Revington TR are experienced in competition, and their seats improve hold, provide excellent lumbar support and incorporate headrests, as and when required. All these factors make the seats safer and more comfortable which

indirectly, of course, also improves safety.

Both companies can also supply belts, harnesses and mountings, *etc.,* to

suit your car, seat and intended use. On the subject of safety harnesses, Safety Devices' 'ASM' system is designed to prevent 'submarining', *i.e.* the wearer slides forwards under the seatbelt in a head on collision. An inertia reel rally harness, made by German specialists Schroth, is also available. It is used by several Formula One teams and is marketed within the UK by Safety Devices. Called 'Autocontrol', this is a three point full harness with Sensor Modulated Automatic Restraint Technology (SMART). The system incorporates an inertia reel fitted with an electro sensor that constantly monitors abnormal movements and forces inside the vehicle. During normal driving, the Autocontrol's sensor allows the inertia reel to 'relax', enabling the wearer to move freely in the harness. However, if the sensor detects rapid deceleration or acceleration, a high G-force turn, quick side movement or inclines of over 25%, it instantly locks.

14-14-3. Racetorations superb bucket seats in situ in a very fast TR5. The narrowing of the roll cage tells us this owner wanted to be able to raise the hood frame from time to time. The harnesses speak for themselves.

14-14-4. The same TR5 with the removable access bars on the roll cage in view. The gearlever has the overdrive control button just in view and, of course, the very comfortable thigh support built into the bucket seat.

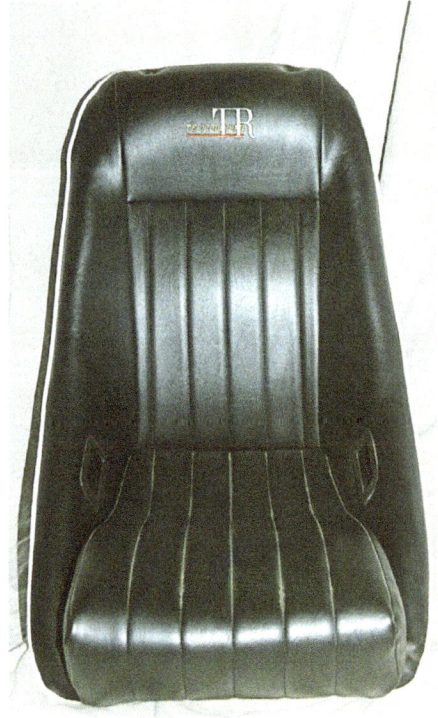

14-14-5. An equally effective, but perhaps less plush, Revington bucket seat. This is one of a range that Neil has especially made for his distribution.

Chapter 15
Engine transplants

WHAT ENGINE?

There tends to be considerable restraint when it comes to modifying TRs in the UK and in Europe. European owners actually need to ensure that any modifications are reasonably easily reversed lest they devalue their cars while trying to improve them. On the other hand, I don't believe owners in the USA are quite so conservative and, as a result, this is where you'll find quite a number of exciting engine transplants. Although most readers will be fairly relaxed about originality issues, many stop short of considering an engine transplant.

However you view engine transplants, I hope at least that this chapter will be of interest.

Although any engine can be considered for transplanting, the majority favour the grunt of a V8, though the initial criteria must be size, weight and ease of fitting. The accompanying table covers the vast majority of transplants that have taken place.

My personal favourite is the Buick/Rover V8, ideally the 4000cc version for its power, tunability and smoothness. However, any of these Rover's V8 power plants could be a candidate due to the reduced weight and length. Its extra 4in (100mm) width should not present too

many problems. Its overall length varies depending upon the donor vehicle but, if the one you acquire is too long, you can usually reduce the length of the front crank pulley by fitting an early one

15-1-1. This is the development of what started life as Buick's 215ci aluminium engine and, in view of its low weight, would be the automatic choice for most UK based transfers. It can now be obtained in a very nice 4000cc version, with even larger, if slightly less smooth, versions also available.

(ex-Buick or Rover P6). The all aluminium Rover/Buick engine in picture 15-1-1 has been around for what seems like a lifetime and, because of its light weight and high power to weight ratio, is the

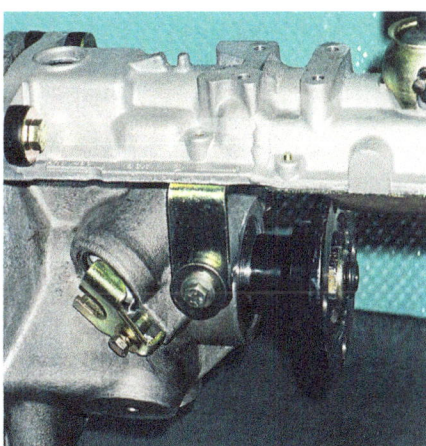

15-1-2. The natural choice of any one fitting a Rover V8 is the mating Rover LM77 5-speed gearbox. The gear change extension will be 3 or 4in too long which necessitates this sort of cut and weld alteration. Richard Tudor located his Rover engine a bit further back and, as we'll see shortly, had to fit a very short extension indeed.

	Width (inches)	Length (inches)	Height (inches)	Approx weight (lb)	Key points
TR6 2500cc cast iron block and head	22	29.5	25	460	Original engine
Buick-Rover P6 3500 to 4600cc alloy V8	26	28	27	355	Lightest alternative
Ford 302 iron V8 4900 to 5600cc	24	29	27.5	475	Same weight, more capacity
Ford with alloy heads	24	29	27	424	Shortlist but watch sump
Chevrolet 350 with alloy heads.	26	28	27	525	Possible, but only just
All iron Chevy 350 (5700cc) V8	26	28	27	575	Much too heavy
Triumph Stag 3000cc V8	22	28	24	460	Good match with 'box

usual engine of choice for kit-cars, replicas and engine upgrades. It's also generally regarded as ultra reliable. Capacity can vary from 3500cc up to 4600cc in standard trim, depending upon the year of manufacture and the donor vehicle, and the larger capacities are achieved without any material weight increment from that shown in the table. Furthermore, the Triumph gearbox is heavy, largely because it has an overdrive unit fitted, and the Rover engine offers a further weight saving of 30 to 40lb if you switch to Rover's five-speed gearbox. The combination is actually very attractive from a weight reduction point of view since the contribution is 100 to 150lb lighter than the original Triumph six-cylinder engine, Triumph gearbox and overdrive.

Be advised, however, that fitting the Rover combination into the car may have two, relatively minor, complications. Firstly, you'll probably need to shorten the gear change remote casting by cutting and welding (this is not difficult for the right specialist), and you can see the end result at 15-1-2. Secondly, the Rover's cylinder heads have vertical faces to the exhaust flanges requiring that the exhaust manifold/headers loop away from the heads. We'll discuss this point and the solutions a little later.

The second shortlisted engine should be the Ford 302 which offers about twice the capacity of the original for no significant weight (when fitted with alloy heads), or size penalty. Picture 15-1-3 show the principal alternative US power plant almost ready to go. The Ford 302 motor is usually mated to a Borg Warner T5 gearbox and provides 320bhp and a modest (!) 360 ft-lb of torque. The resulting car weighs little more than the original TR6 but has over twice the power! It does necessitate some sheet metal modification around the gearbox bellhousing that some may find daunting, and we will explore this

15-1-3. This is a 302ci Ford crate motor with B303 high performance roller cam, GT40 aluminium cylinder heads, Edelbrock inlet manifold and dual Edelbrock 1404, 500cfm carbs, both fitted with vacuum operated secondaries.

and the engine in a little more detail when we look at Dan Master's superb TR6 project shortly.

The Ford's main competitor in the US is, of course, the ever popular Chevy 'small block'. To my mind it is too heavy for use in a TR, even with alloy heads, although it would seem to be the most frequently selected transplant! What about the 327 Chevy? The capacity may be a little down on the 350, but I think there is a small weight reduction. However, even at 500lb it's still a bit heavier than the original Triumph power plant and, although I think this is a step in the wrong direction, I guess the increment is manageable. You can see a Chevy 350 in photographs 15-1-4 and 15-1-5.

The Stag V8 is available in the UK, though you may not find one at every breaker's yard you visit. There are plenty available through the numerous Stag used spares specialists. This 3000cc V8 engine has the same overall dimensions as the original engine yet provides a couple of extra pots and some 20% more capacity. The exhaust system may be easier to fabricate for a Stag engine, as you may be able to see in picture

15-1-4. Chevrolet 350 in Ted Lathrop's TR6 V8. The fairly chunky air cleaner necessitates a fairly large power-bulge in the bonnet/hood.

15-1-5. I wonder where the small-block Chevy engine we see here would stand in a most-engines-made list. I think it would be well placed!

15-1-6, since the cylinder head flanges are actually angled towards the ground, making a tighter-fitting exhaust manifold/ header more practical. The engine is relatively easy to fit if you retain the original Stag gearbox but unfortunately the combination offers little by way of weight savings.

Drawing D15-1 will give you an idea as to whether a particular engine will fit into your particular car.

I have made much of the weight issue of potential transplanted engines and we are best to complete this outline by exploring why weight is important to engine transplants. All cars, but particularly sportscars, drive nicely or badly as the case may be as a result of numerous design features. The frontal area of a car, for example, determines wind noise and wind resistance. Not every reader will have thought about the stability of the car in a crosswind, though, and that the profile of the body will, in part, determine how a car drives in a straight line. These are important considerations for any car, but particularly for quick cars, and these days designers spend hours in a wind tunnel to get it right. However, of equal importance to the handling is the front to rear weight balance. This not only affects the cornering capabilities of the car, but also the car's reaction to a crosswind. If the side profile gives a fairly neutral reaction to a crosswind, consider what effect you will bring about were you to alter that ideal weight distribution by fitting a heavier engine. Not only would the centre of gravity move (forward if the new engine is heavier, backward if lighter), thus affecting the car's reaction to a crosswind, but all sorts of handling characteristics change just by altering the front/rear distribution. The six-cylinder TRs are already a shade front heavy, so a slightly lighter engine will be the ideal option. A heavier engine will only accent the current (roughly 55/45), weight distribution situation, unless you are able to position the engine a little further back in the chassis than is strictly necessary from a pure 'fit' point of view. A heavier engine will also have a multiplying effect

15-1-6. The Stag V8 engine provides 3000cc capacity. It was designed by Triumph by putting two four-cylinder engines together. Generating 150bhp in standard tune, it can be tuned to provide more power, however it requires regular servicing & an effective cooling system for reliability.

on the car's acceleration and its braking, since the car's inertia will be increased.

Our next consideration must be how much metalwork is involved in each transplant. Every transplant will require some sheet metal carving, but the chassis construction of these TRs makes the internal bodywork alterations relatively simple for most. A modification to the gearbox mounting on the chassis will often be required, but this should be relatively minor. Obviously, any engine transplant that minimises cutting and carving of the body panels has to start favourite. The battery tray is usually the first casualty and it usually requires the front half to be removed and compensatory sheet metal modifications made to the top of the body above

the bellhousing. Some may even need to find an alternative location for the battery, although the first project we will study has managed to retain enough of the battery tray to allow a smaller battery to be fitted there.

Depending upon the engine (the spread of the heads in particular), and how far back you position it, you are also likely to have to modify the inner edges of both footwells to provide clearance for the gearbox bellhousing. These changes may extend to your having to alter the arc above the bellhousing too. Pictures 15-1-8 and 15-1-9 show a superbly

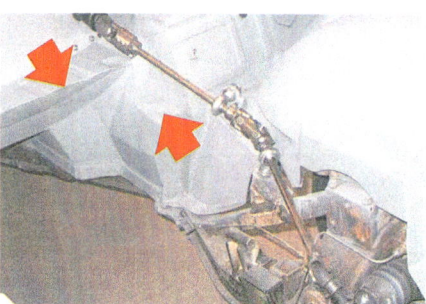

15-1-8. I have highlighted the sort of body alterations you can more or less expect when carrying out a big engine transplant. The extent will vary from engine to engine and indeed from car to car but this shot should prepare you for the sort of changes required. Note the steering shaft arrangement, which is also pretty routine, and that in this case, the front turret brace has been temporarily removed, no doubt to get the engine in and out. The brace must be replaced once the engine is back in the car.

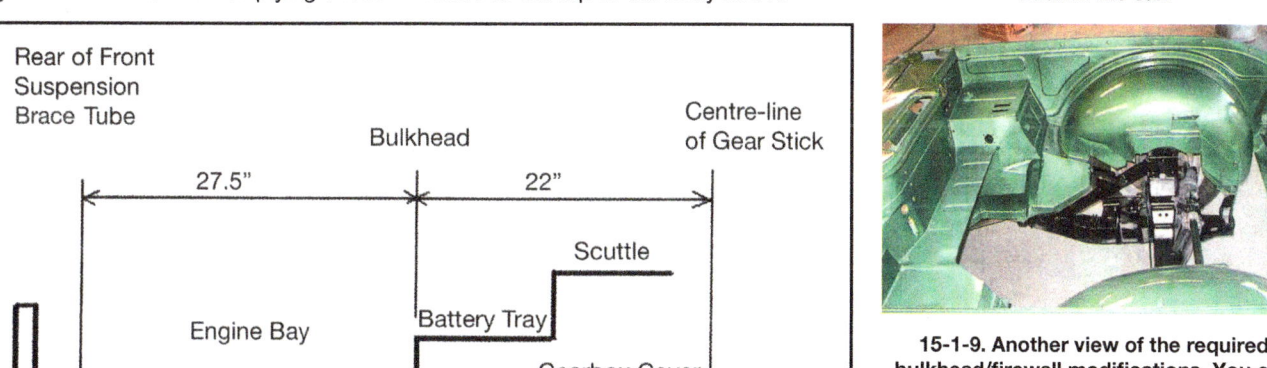

D15-1. Schematic outline of TR250/5/6 engine bay.

15-1-9. Another view of the required bulkhead/firewall modifications. You can clearly see that about half the battery tray has been sacrificed, and note the angled cutaway of the inside of each footwell. We cannot see where the battery is to be relocated in this shot, but above the passenger footwell is popular.

modified TR4 ready to accept a Chevy small block. Owners transplanting the Triumph Stag engine probably have the least amount of sheet metal alterations to carry out and, if they also use the Stag's gearbox, no gearbox/chassis alterations should be required.

In every case, fitting a V8 engine generates steering linkage problems. This is probably the largest obstacle to the transplant. There is no universal solution (other than a cranked steering column), as per picture 15-1-10 and we'll look at each case individually. You may rotate the rack without generating problems, but I do advise against moving the steering rack as there is a real danger you will introduce bump steer. If you do plan to relocate the steering rack, I urge you to seek suitable, experienced professional advice beforehand.

Most cars require some minor throttle linkage changes, but if you adopt a cable operated throttle, this usually poses little difficulty.

15-1-10. Steering shaft mock-up using wooden dowels, to verify functionality. After everything was determined, dimensions were transferred to the Burgeson steering shafts.

PROJECT 1
TR6/FORD 302 V8/T5 GEARBOX

Dan Masters, to whom I am indebted for the following explanation and pictures, is an electrical engineer (clearly one with a wide range of skills). He's an author specialising in TRs too, and you may be familiar with his electrical repair manuals. Initially prepared for TR250/6, the interest generated led him to follow up with sister volumes on the earlier TRs. As well as his literary and electrical skills, Dan has obviously loads of patience, for this engine transplant required numerous trial fits and test mock ups. Mounting the Ford 302 engine and T5 gearbox (pictures 15-2-1 and 15-2-2), which we will talk about in a bit more detail

as we go, was a matter of trial, error and patience, resulting in the bespoke mountings we see at 15-2-3, 15-2-4-1 and 15-2-4-2. We've already seen that it was necessary to trim a little off the front of the battery tray, but Dan tells me that he set the engine as low as possible without having the oil pan drop below the chassis/frame rails. Consequently, a bulge in the bonnet/hood, about 1½in max, is necessary.

Some minor changes were decided upon to the 302's dual sump arrangement in order to reposition one of the drain plugs. A fabricated centre section was let in which increased the oil capacity by a litre/quart or so. Never a bad thing. Dan thinks that the engine

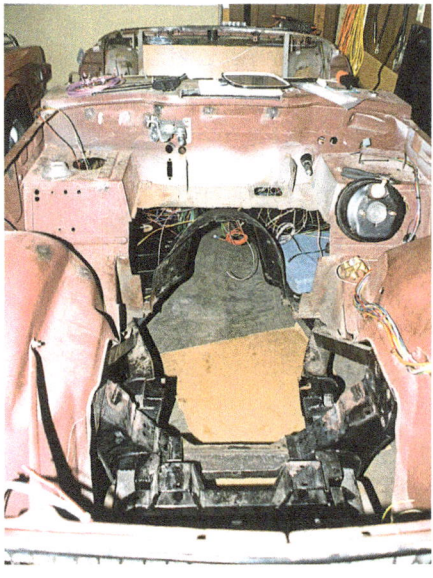

15-2-1. The only cutting required (except for hood scoop), was to the bulkhead/firewall where the battery tray and the 'wings' on each side were cut away. The cross-member was also notched.

15-2-2. That was quick, the 302 is in the TR6 already and looking good!

could have been dropped another inch or so by further modifying the oil pan and redoing the oil pickup. This, and using a single carburettor with a small air cleaner, would have eliminated the need for the bonnet/hood bulge.

Like so many transplants, the exhaust manifolds/headers were a headache. Ford 'Shorty' manifold/headers were no use since they exit to the rear of the engine, right where the bulkhead/firewall is! Dan tried a set of 'Block huggers' but they didn't hug the block close enough, and he ended up cutting them off, leaving 1in stubs. He'll

15-2-3. Dan's home made engine mounts - nice job!

15-2-4-1. The stock TR6 'box/trans mount bolts right up to the T-5 gearbox. Even the bolt holes lined up!

15-2-4-2. Access holes bored into the new gearbox cross-member to aid removing/replacing the mounting.

have a bespoke/custom system made when the car is nearer completion. His silencers/mufflers should fit in the usual spot behind the rear axle, but he's not yet sure how the exhaust pipes will run from the headers to the mufflers. Probably a little low at the front until they clear the engine, but thereafter he thinks they'll be routed within the central chassis/frame as per a standard car.

For clutch actuation Dan has fitted one of the Tilton hydraulically operated throw-out bearings we discussed in Chapter 6. The T5 gearbox/transmission is a late model with high torque capacity. Dan comments that it's larger (no doubt!), than the stock gearbox, but is actually lower than the Triumph unit. Nevertheless, the Borg Warner T5 necessitated significant alterations to the area beneath the battery tray too. We get some idea from picture 15-2-5. Dan progressed the modification by fitting the pedals next, as we see from picture 15-2-6, in order to be sure he had room

15-2-5. Only a minimum of leg room was lost as the result of the larger bellhousing on a T5! The engine and gearbox are in their final position in this shot.

15-2-6. When seen at its worst, the situation can look pretty drastic, but in fact the sheet metal fabrication and welding to repair the bulkhead/firewall should be easy and quick ...

for the pedals and his feet! His next step was to relocate the firewall (15-2-7), and finally to ensure the 'H' casting that supports the dashboard still fitted (picture 15-2-8).

When it came to the steering, Dan found it necessary to increase the number of steering universal joints to four, and to add additional steadies to each shaft. He explained that he had to shorten the outer steering column so that it only protruded about an inch forward of the bulkhead/firewall. The inner column is in two parts: a smaller diameter inner shaft, and a larger diameter hollow outer shaft. The line of the shaft necessitated a double universal joint in the middle of the shaft. This required Dan to fit the two Heim steadies

15-2-7. ... there we are, much of the original bulkhead is tacked back in place. Dan tells me he plans to fit a 'Street rod' gas pedal once the bulkhead repairs are finished. It will mount to a bracket welded to the top of the footwell and sits to the other pedals perfectly.

15-2-8. Modification of the dash support and the transmission tunnel proceed apace. Note that the top of the tunnel could be lowered since the T-5 is lower than the original TR6 'box. The gear change leaver will come a short way back from the original location so the hand brake is to be moved back by about 3in.

I mentioned earlier; the first of which needed a particularly secure mount since there are shock loads transmitted to the steering gear when you hit a bump, and unsupported sheet metal just wouldn't stand up to the pounding. With a plan established, the original outer shaft was cut in two at the point of the steering lock. Using a Borgeson steering shaft with splines on one end and the other end plain, Dan cut (the plain end!) to the correct length. The plain end was now turned down to fit inside the hollow shaft, as we see from picture 15-2-9-1, and had it professionally welded. The result to this point can be seen at picture 15-2-9-2. At the rack end, a Borgeson universal joint was bought with matching splines for the standard steering rack.

At this point it seemed a good idea to try the bonnet/hood, and I doubt anyone is surprised to hear that it didn't quite close. The piece that was cut out of the bonnet/hood was used to form the top of the bubble, as Dan calls it. By this method he ensured that the contour of the power bulge, as we might call it, follows the original bonnet line. Picture 15-2-10 shows the original bonnet/hood section sitting on wooden mock-ups of the new up stands that will require fabricating and welding in place.

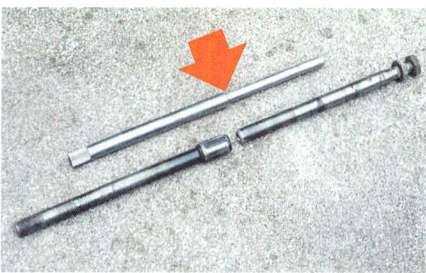

15-2-9-1. Note the shoulder where the new Burgeson steering shaft at the top of this picture has been turned down. The original shaft is on the bottom, cut into two. The Burgeson was inserted into the stock shaft and welded ...

15-2-9-2. ... like this. The weld still required a little more grinding and polishing.

15-2-10. The initial mock-up for the bonnet/hood power bulge. Dan plans to plenish the sides, weld it together and dress it so the bonnet/hood flows smoothly into the bulge.

Turning his attention the to the rear axle, Dan felt something 'bullet proof' was needed to put all this power on the road and that neither the original Triumph differential nor the IRS drive shafts stood a chance of standing the pace. I am quite sure Triumph's engineers would have agreed, given the 360ft-lb in mind! Dan's solution was a live rear axle, a Ford 9in crown wheel one, in fact, since it comes with a very wide range of gear ratio options, it has an impressive reputation for robustness, and is widely available. We see a nice comparative shot at picture 15-2-11-1. The Ford axle's track has been reduced to that of a TR6, and it's currently fitted with a 3.7:1 ratio crown wheel. The usual US Triumph rear axle ratio is, of course, 3.7 to 1, so basically Dan is opting for no change. He will have a huge increase in

power and torque with the transplanted engine, and since his T5 gearbox/transmission will have a 0.63:1 ratio fifth gear, so it's not wise to increase the rear axle ratio too high or he will rarely get the trans into 5th gear! This combination will give about 70mph at 2000rpm, just barely into the torque curve! Dan tells me that he doesn't really know if that's the best choice or not, but points out that if it proves to be the wrong ratio, it's very easy to change. An easy afternoon job for a good mechanic (he assures me!). The rear brakes have to be part of the planning, and we can see a comparison at picture 15-2-11-2 between the original TR rear drum (that looks positively tiny), and those that come with the Ford axle. Toyota 4-pot calipers will be fitted to the front to match the rear braking power. Except for changing the hydraulic fittings the calipers just bolt-on!

The suspension and mounting the rear axle are currently planned, but not finished. At least one torque control arm each side is essential, since Dan is going to use a US style TR4A leaf spring to locate and suspend the rear upon. Without a torque arm each side, the rear springs will 'wind up' under engine torque, and rear axle steering will be dramatic, especially when Dan comes off the gas! Although you may have regarded the TR4A as an IRS car with coil springs, a surprising number of '4A's went Stateside with leaf sprung TR4 live rear axles. The chassis was very similar to the TR4A shape, but the front of the leaf spring was secured to the chassis legs that UK enthusiasts picture

as carrying the IRS trailing arms by the brackets we see at 15-2-12-1. Picture 15-2-12-2 depicts a spring assembled to one of these brackets.

The rear of each road spring needs to be accommodated, of course, and that's also fairly easily achieved by cutting the pair of rear spring hangers we see at 15-2-13-1 from an old TR4 or US '4A chassis. The remains of the cross-tube needs to be drilled out and the resultant bracket welded over the cross-tube in the '6's chassis, as per 15-2-13-2. I think the centre of the cross-tube also needs strengthening by a fitting thick inner reinforcing tube each side, and even adding some extra gussets. It's then a matter of fitting a TR4's shackles and fixing the road spring in place!

Dan is at the stage of making another wooden mock-up of a new, larger fuel tank. We can see this preparatory work at pictures 15-2-14-1 and 15-2-14-2.

15-2-12-1. These are the brackets (from a US TR4A) that secure the front of the rear spring. They simply bolt in place to the TR6 since, on a '6, the holes are still in place along with the internal supports in order to mount the outboard trailing arm bracket.

15-2-12-2. Here we see the front brackets in place, with the leaf spring installed. There is an extra set of holes in the TR6 frame in this area, which you can see between the hangers and the frame in this shot.

15-2-11-1. Ford 9in 'bullet proof' differential versus the TR6 original is, in fact, a no-contest when 360lb-ft of torque has to be handled! The Triumph diff might cope with 200ft-lb but will last no time at all with the power Dan will have at his disposal.

15-2-11-2. An original 9in TR6 drum placed over the 11in Ford drum. It must fit comfortably inside!

15-2-13-1. The rear spring hanger/body mount from a US TR4A. The tubular cross-member was cut off just outboard of the chassis frame. The original tube was then ground and drilled away and the mount positioned on the TR6's equivalent cross-member. The only real difference between the TR6 original and the US TR4A mounts is the presence of the second hole for the spring hanger on the latter.

15-2-13-2. Here we see the TR4A mounts installed on the TR6, along with the spring shackle and, of course, the unloaded road spring. Expect the shackle to be more or less straight up and down when the car is standing on its wheels.

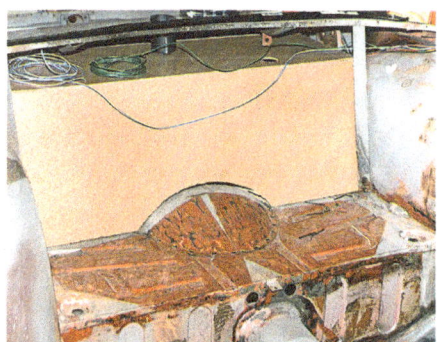

15-2-14-1. Front view of the fuel tank mock-up. It will be a close fit when finished.

15-2-14-2. Masonite/hardboard mock-up of the 19.5 US gallon fuel tank, which will now be properly fabricated in steel. Dan plans a flat boot/trunk floor in place of the originally raised one as he has given over some of the space for his fuel tank. A 'space saver' spare will, however, go in. In Europe we use Saab space savers but Dan has a 15 x 3in wide wheel/tyre that is normally used on the front of dragsters. I think Dan's car may give some dragsters a run for their money!

15-2-14-3. It takes up every bit of space and reduces the spare wheel storage area but, to my mind, it's for the best for I think the fuel capacity of a normal TR is too small. A great piece of fabrication too, but probably best to have a welded rear firewall between you and nearly 20 US gallons of fuel!

15-2-15-1. Both alternator support brackets were hand made by Dan. They have since been polished and chromed.

I hear that Dan hates to stop even for fuel, so his tank will hold 19.5 US gallons (about 15 Imperial gallons) and can be seen at picture 15-2-14-3.

The electrics are a routine matter for Dan but we can see the installation progressing in the sequence of pictures at 15-2-15-1 to 15-2-15-4. The photo texts will tell more!

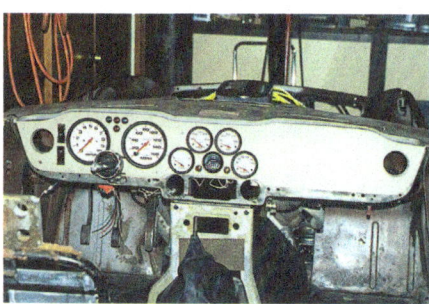

15-2-15-2. Autometer gauges are looking very good in this plywood mock-up dash/fascia. The 5in tach and speedo are supplemented with 2⅝in oil, water, etc., instruments. In due course a matching clock will be fitted.

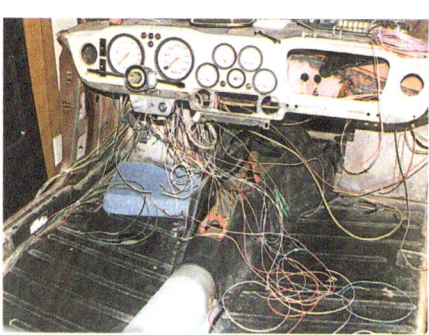

15-2-15-3. I think the wiring is Dan's favourite part of the whole job.

15-2-15-4. Home made fuse/relay/flasher panel, mounted to the pedal assembly. When the wiring is finished, it'll be tucked up out of sight.

Cooling any engine is a key detail, of course, but again Dan has 'triumphed' by settling on a design that will certainly keep even his beast cool, yet won't require any cutting of the frame, or add any weight penalty. Photographs 15-2-16-1 to 15-2-16-3, along with the associated texts, are the best method of describing the preparatory work. The $200 cross-flow aluminium Griffin radiator can be seen installed at picture 15-2-16-4 (http://griffinrad.com/). It's 19in tall x 22in wide, and has two rows of 1in x ⅜in tubes. Inlet/outlet fittings are 1½in ID.

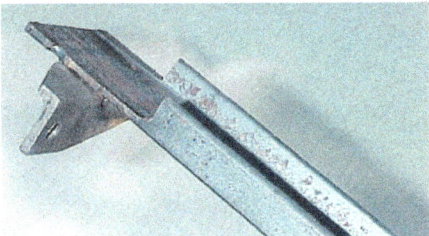

15-2-16-1. Here is a piece of steel U-channel with the lips removed and a tab welded in place at each end to provide a mounting for the (aluminium), fan support. The steel channel will be welded to a slightly altered skid pan, and the channel fitted with a rubber strip or similar for the bottom of the radiator to sit on.

15-2-16-2. The reasons for the alterations to the bottom channel become clearer with this view of the left bottom corner of the radiator. A pair of vertical aluminium angles bolt to the radiator as can be seen in the next picture, while the fan is fixed to the angles by counter sunk fastenings to prevent the screw heads from touching the radiator fins.

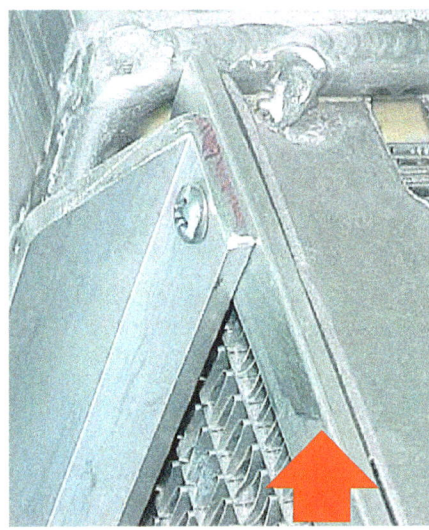

15-2-16-3. A flat section of aluminium (arrowed), was required to space the angles out from the radiator for added clearance for the fan fixings.

15-2-16-4. You will note from this installation shot that the radiator is not fastened at the top, by design, thus allowing for expansion. Securing is by the bottom channel and the braces that run forward from the turret braces. A front shroud will be required to ensure all the air coming through the grille will go through the radiator. The whole assembly, fan and all, only weighs 4 pounds more than the original radiator (19 as compared to 15)! The fan is a 16in diameter 2900cfm unit, it pulls 18-20 amps and necessitates the significant alternator upgrade we discussed in Chapter 13.

PROJECT 2
TR250/STAG V8/TR GEARBOX

You can't beat the sound of a V8. The 'burble' is fantastic, and is enough to turn heads even when the car is being driven modestly. Of course, it really gets people's attention at speed! However, in the car, the exhaust note from the twin pipes of Neil Browns Stag powered TR5 (picture 15-3-1), is surprisingly refined. Certainly less wearing than a six-cylinder TR6 with the wrong exhaust. Clearly, it's easy to change the exhaust system to a slightly less wearing one, but Neil thought there were other benefits to be had from a V8 engine and decided to change the engine instead. Having now been in the car, I think he was right!

Neil farms in Staffordshire but clearly has a wide range of skills beyond, as he puts it, making cows eat grass. He has welded steel, stainless and aluminium, grafted an efi system's electronics to a TR5, made his own dashboard/fascia, and sorted it all to produce an exhilarating drive. Like most UK enthusiasts, Neil's initial thoughts turned to an ex-Buick/Rover 3500cc engine. I must confess that I would never have given an ex-Stag 3-litre engine a thought until I saw Neil's car and discussed fitting the 8 cylinder steel block/alloy headed engine with him.

The relative ease of fitment was what persuaded Neil to focus on the Stag engine. The similarity between an original TR gearbox and that of the Stag also makes fitting this combination the easier. There are, of course, very few differences between the two

15-3-1. The V8 engine, regardless of size and manufacturer, has a very special sound. A burble on tickover/idle, rising to a wonderful but indescribable noise at mid-revs. At full chat, however, they can become a scream! To my mind a good enough reason for fitting a V8, not that I am biased.

transmissions, as we were discussing at length in Chapter 6. I learned that there is a slight complication, though, in that the Triumph 'box sits at the back of the Stag's engine on a slight angle. As a result, the gearlever tends to twist to one side, and requires a compensatory sideways shift. How's it done? Cut the gearlever off just above the ball, weld a plate to the, now foreshortened, top, and then re-weld the gear stick to the plate.

Re-using a Triumph 'box would, perhaps, have been a missed opportunity to lose some weight. The Stag engine and Triumph gearbox with its overdrive weighs no less than the original engine/gearbox/overdrive combination, but there are, of course, other considerations apart from weight to think about when effecting an engine transplant.

As you will see from picture 15-3-2, there really is not a lot of room between the cylinder heads and the inner wings/fenders. You do have the option of cutting holes in the inner wing through which to exit the exhaust manifold/headers. Such holes need strengthening with a ring of 16swg/1mm thick mild steel, which is hardly a major disadvantage, and the engine compartment temperatures are dramatically reduced via an outflow of

15-3-2. Unfortunately, Neil's fuel filter obscures the very best of views in this shot. Nevertheless, you'll see that the right side cylinder head is close to but clear of the car's original bulkhead and that this has been achieved without any bulkhead alterations! The clutch master cylinder is mounted on the (almost), vertical face of the footwell. This being an ex-USA TR250, Neil will have transferred straight across when doing the LHD to RHD conversion. He would have given himself a little more room had he put the master cylinder atop the footwell, as I suggest in How to Restore TR250/5/6.

hot air into the low pressure area within the front wheelarches. So there is, on balance much to be said for taking the exhaust out through the inner wing, and I include picture 15-3-3, to help those thinking about which route to choose. However, exhaust flanges on the Stag engine's cylinder heads are angled (downwards), which makes it far easier to take the pipes away close to the block without altering the inner wing. We can just catch a glimpse of the Stag's exhaust/headers in picture 15-3-4 and, although hard to see, we do get an impression of how little they protrude from the face of the cylinder head before dropping straight down between block and chassis rails.

Before we move completely away from matters concerning the weight of the power unit, I would just pass on one partly valid, but possibly subjective, point from Neil: the Stag's aluminium cylinder heads lower the centre of gravity as compared to the original six-cylinder engine. Neil feels this has contributed to improved road holding. I must tell you his car holds the road very well indeed, so perhaps he has a point. Indeed, we will look at weight disposition in the next chapter.

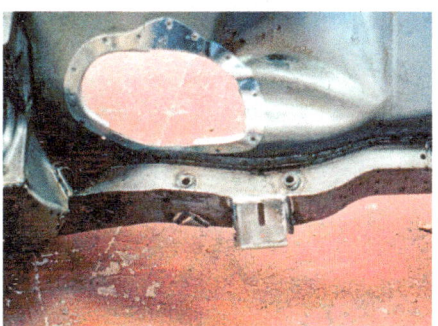

15-3-3. This MGR V8's exhaust is routed through the inner wing/fenders primarily to get the manifold/headers away from the engine in a smooth efficient arc. However, this route has the significant supplementary benefit of keeping the water, engine oil and engine bay cooler too. The exhaust system gets away from the engine quickly and thus the effect of radiated heat on the engine generally, and its oil in particular, is minimised. Furthermore, the wheel wells are low pressure areas and, as a result, there is a ready flow of air from the engine bay into the wheel wells which reduces water (more air through the radiator), and engine bay temperatures. Not very pretty perhaps, but very effective.

15-3-4. The arrow highlights the very difficult to see right hand exhaust manifold/header. The shaft that traverses the picture is the steering column. The exhaust, made from 1.5in o/d stainless tube to a 'block hugger' design, just slips down besides the inner wing/fender and chassis rail.

Essentially, it's the ease with which the Stag engine fits into the TR's engine bay that is really its key advantage. We have covered the minor exhaust/inner wing issue, but it's the fact that you can fit a Stag engine into a TR with negligible bulkhead carving that is the real advantage. You'll probably have to bias the engine away from the driver's side of the car (by about 25mm), to give the steering column a little room while leaving sufficient space to get the exhaust pipe down the side of the block, however this can be achieved with hardly any metal carving, certainly none worth talking about. The real test is whether the engine sits clear of the car's unchanged bulkhead and, as photographs 15-3-5 and 15-3-6 show, indeed it does!

15-3-5. There is a lot of equipment in the engine bay, as this shot clearly shows. However, the ancillary gear made getting a shot showing the head/bulkhead clearance very difficult ...

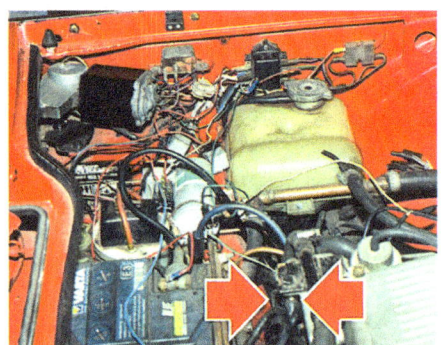

15-3-6. ... so I had another try and have resorted to a pair of arrows to show how well Neil has judged the clearance without any bulkhead alterations.

Anyone interested in Triumph cars has to have heard that the Stag engine's reliability is questionable. Back in the 1970s the car sadly developed an entirely deserved reputation for overheating, warped cylinder heads and some doubt as to what car you would come home in when you left in a Stag! The fact of the matter is that Triumph neither developed the excellent basic design sufficiently nor paid adequate attention to quality controls during manufacture. A bad situation was made worse by dealers failing to appreciate the importance of servicing the engine properly. Today, the development has taken place, albeit by the aftermarket industry rather than Triumph engineers. No-matter who found out, it's now generally understood that there are several key re-build and maintenance issues to look after and that properly attended to, the Stag power plant can be a super mode of transport. I have a Stag and am delighted with the car generally and the engine in particular. However you **must** have the crankshaft tufride hardened after a re-grind, put an oil baffle in the sump and fit an inter-head cross-tube at the rear of the cylinder heads to balance water temperatures and flow. You **must** re-torque the cylinder heads after the engine has cooled following the first time it has run and then re-torque the heads after 1000 miles (many run a torque wrench over the heads annually thereafter). You **must** change the engine oil and filter regularly every 3000 miles to aid the longevity of the timing chains. You will also need to change the timing chains about every 30,000 miles, sooner, if they get noisy earlier than that, which also tells you

that you are not changing the engine oil frequently enough.

You'd be wise to ensure that the water pump stays submerged by providing an enlarged header tank (picture 15-3-7), and the automatic bleed from the top of the radiator to that header tank shown in picture 15-3-8. Furthermore, although it adds to the complications of plumbing the engine in, I recommend you fit the old-fashioned but far more accurate mechanical water temperature and oil pressure gauges shown in photograph 15-3-9. Nothing to it really! Before you start to say something along the lines of 'what a list that is', consider the shortcomings of the

15-3-7. There are two important changes that need to be made to the Stag engine's cooling system. The first one is shown here, a nice big header-tank, in this case an ex-Ford Granada one, while secondly ...

15-3-8. ... you need to allow any air to escape from the water pump which was mounted too high up to be truly safe. As a result, a bleed tube back to the header tank from atop the radiator or its top hose is required and is shown here.

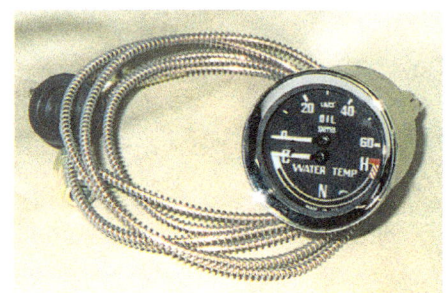

15-3-9. This is actually an ex-MGB dual water temperature/oil pressure gauge. You can get them with a variety of calibrations and full scale deflections, so don't be put off if you see something you don't like the appearance of. The important point is that both gauges work mechanically and give a much more accurate reading than the Triumph electrically transmitted instruments. This is particularly important with regard to the Stag engine's water temperature. Fit the sensing bulb in the left/hotter head.

trusted six-cylinder engine and, indeed, almost any engine of the era. They all had their foibles and weaknesses; the Stags were publicised a shade more than most others. Pictures 15-3-10 to 15-3-14 and their associated captions illustrate some of the other details involved with fitting this engine.

The trailing arms are basically as you would expect, with hard polyurethane pivot bushes, and have given Neil no problems. However, I understand that the significant extra torque from the V8 is showing up the numerous universal joints in the drive train as being inadequate. Neil has fitted the best greasable standard size units that are available, but now recognises that an upgraded size is essential. I would upgrade the hubs and drive shafts too, as explained in Chapter 3. Neil finds the 3.45 ratio differential is great, and it certainly seemed right to me too.

Neil puts the power on the road with 70-spoke centre lace wire wheels with 6in rims and 195x60 Yokohama tyres. They certainly look the business as you can see in picture 15-3-15. Centre laced wires are apparently much easier to clean than the usual rim laced wires, which gave me food for thought!

The Stag's usual method of induction is a pair of 1.75in Stromberg carbs, although many Stag owners use a specially adapted Stag inlet manifold and Holley 390 four-barrel carburettor.

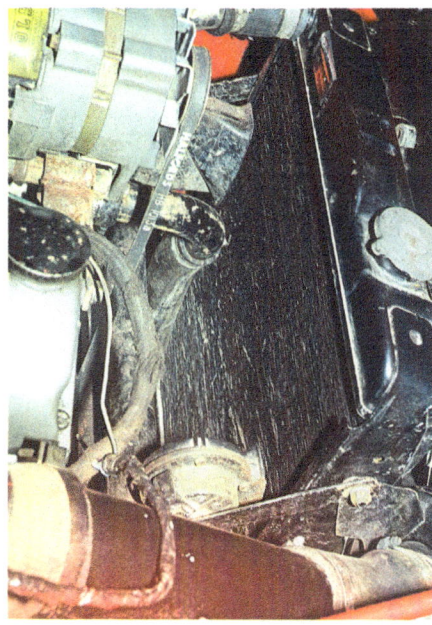

15-3-10. A standard copper TR radiator is perfectly satisfactory for the Stag's 3-litre engine size, although you should duct the front side of the radiator to ensure all the air entering the front grille has no option but to pass through the radiator.

15-3-11. A front air dam/spoiler was required, but not to help keep the engine cool as you are bound to think. Neil felt the car steered better when the front wheels were in contact with the road!

Neil and I both found, albeit on different engines, that the Holley had several flat spots and it was interesting to compare notes. However, neither of us managed to resolve the problem while retaining the Holley and I switched to a Weber/Edelbrock four barrel 500cfm carb (see picture 15-3-16). A 400 cfm would have been ideal but they are no longer made. Neil switched to the ex-Rover efi system you see in photographs 15-3-17 to 15-3-19. There is no objective way of saying which is best, other than for

15-3-12. As I mentioned earlier, it proved to be very difficult to get pictures of details that were down in the bottom of a pretty crowded engine bay, but this was my best shot of the lowest steering universal joint fixed next to the steering rack.

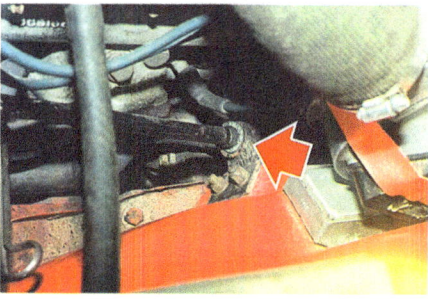

15-3-13. This is the steady that Neil added to the bottom of the main steering column.

15-3-14. The alternator nestles between the cylinder banks

15-3-15. The centre laced 70 spoked wire wheels set off this excellent car very well indeed.

15-3-16. There are all sorts of induction options available, and most readers will think Holley when it comes to induction for this size of engine. I have two 3500cc Rover V8s, one with efi, and one with an aluminium four barrel (AFB) Weber marketed under the Edelbrock name.

15-3-17. Neil used an ex-Rover efi system ...

me to assure you both go very well, but that for ease of fitting I think the Weber route is quickest, easiest and presents most readers with the most reliable of induction systems.

In summary then, a great car, a super installation and a wonderful exhibition of Neil's many skills. I for one feel both grateful and privileged to have witnessed it. Thank you Neil, and allow me to conclude this short overview where I started; at the exhaust note (see picture 15-3-20).

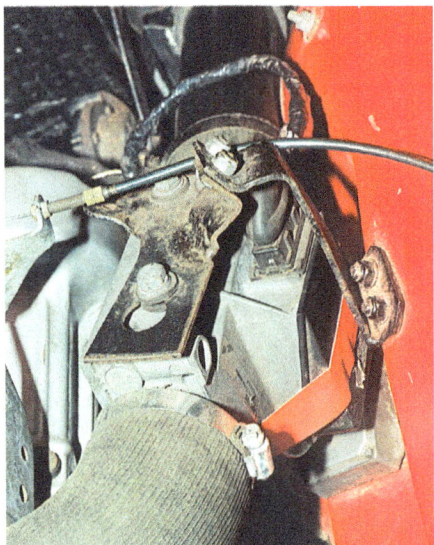

15-3-18. ... with an air-flow meter, which is best mounted turned through 90 degrees, and ...

15-3-19. ... a Bosch fuel pump that seems very effective, though I would have mounted it a bit lower.

15-3-20. You can just catch sight of Neil's very well adapted six-cylinder silencers, which give the perfect balance of throatiness and noise level.

PROJECT 3
TR6/ROVER V8/ROVER LM77

Richard Tudor is a project manager for a multi-national telecom company, so he's used to handling big projects. However, I think he found squeezing a Buick/Rover 4-litre into his TR6 a bit of a handful! He told me that he had experience of putting V8 engines into MGBs but, it's my impression, underestimated this project slightly. However, to his credit, not only did he finish the job, but he did so very professionally, and the car looks, sounds, handles and goes absolutely beautifully. His task was made slightly the more difficult by the fact that he had bought an ex-US left-hooker, so he had the left to righthand drive conversion to handle too.

Richard started with an ex-Range Rover 4000cc engine, efi system and 5-speed gearbox. After lots of measuring up he decided his project wouldn't benefit from shortening the front of the engine by fitting a Rover P6 crankshaft pulley, water pump and water pump pulley. Instead, the exhaust manifolds would dictate the engine position, not the distance in front of the timing chain cover, as picture 15-4-1 shows. However, he did alter the feed from the oil pump by replacing the lower half of the oil pump with an MGB GT V8 one. The MG half pump had the added bonus of incorporating the take-off and return pipes for a remote oil filter and cooler.

Richard's next step was to offer the engine and gearbox to their new home. It was clear that the engine would have to move backwards and that, in due course, the bulkhead would require reshaping. Richard debated whether to remove the body in order to fit the engine (and gearbox), to the chassis, or whether to

15-4-1. This picture is deceptive in that the water pump spindle is not actually in line with the turret brace. There are a couple of inches (50mm), available at the front of the engine if other constraints were resolved and the engine moved forward.

leave the body on the chassis and carry out the modifications to chassis and body simultaneously. He chose the latter route and confirmed that even with hindsight he felt he had gone about the changes via the best route and would follow that course in the very unlikely event of him ever repeating the exercise!

Richard's MGB GT V8 'block-hugger' tubular exhaust manifolds/ headers needed the extra space to clear

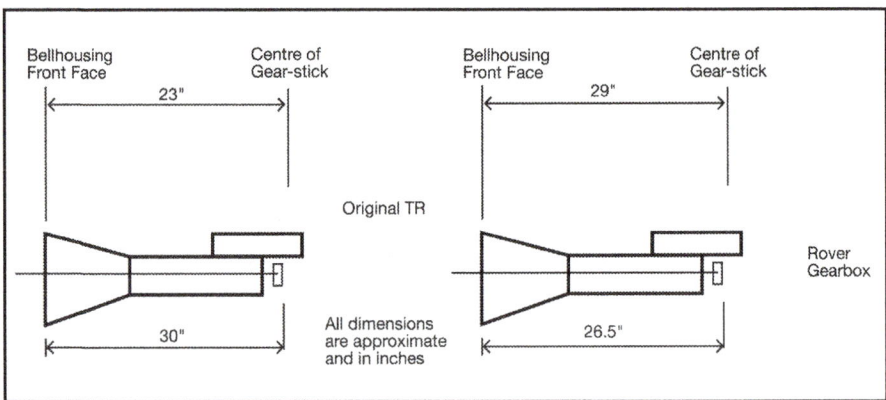

D15-2. Main dimensions compared, TR/Rover gearboxes.

the chassis rails around the TR's front crossmember area. There was certainly plenty of room for them down the side of the sump, and this engine location also allowed him to select the position of the engine. He decided to have the bottom of his sump about 0.5in below the front crossmember, which was a good position in that he subsequently can close his unbulged bonnet without any difficulties. Once the engine and gearbox were positioned to his satisfaction, the respective mountings clearly required sorting. The flexible rubber mounts he used for the engine are standard Rover SD1, positioned in the normal TR6 position on the chassis. He had to fabricate a pair of special side plates for the engine, with three bolt fixings to the side and front of the block. The gearbox crossmember was standard SD1, with the usual SD1 'cotton reel' rubber mounts. The SD1 crossmember required the small but specially fabricated chassis locating plates we see in picture 15-4-2, the original ones cut off and the replacements positioned to suit the SD1 gearbox. The SD1 gearbox crossmember can be seen in picture 15-4-3. Since the body would not go over the cylinder heads, the engine and gearbox needed to come out so that the body could come off the chassis, enabling the usual chassis strengthening improvements to be carried out once the engine location had been fixed.

Richard tells me that he was only able to work on the car in his spare time, so the engine spent about three weeks suspended over the front of the car, going in and out of the engine bay while he worked out what bulkhead/firewall changes were required. After

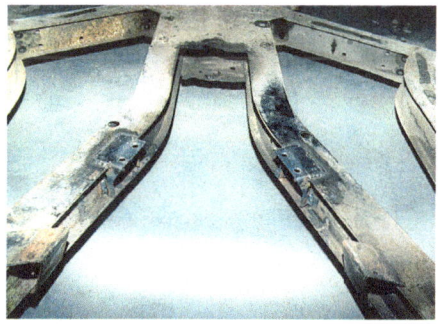

15-4-2. The original gearbox mounting position can just be seen, but, the main point of the picture is the new welded brackets and their strengthening gussets awaiting ...

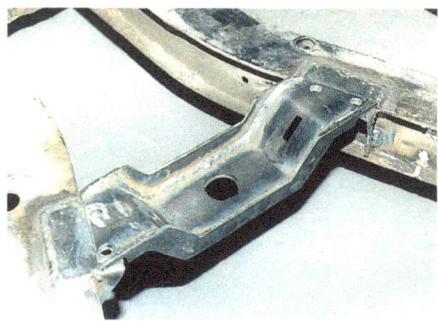

15-4-3. .. the Rover gearbox crossmember. The vertical slots are for the rubber Rover mountings.

much trial and error, about 4in (100mm), was removed from the front of the battery tray (see picture 15-4-4), which meant that the battery had to move to the boot/trunk (picture 15-4-5). The larger diameter of the Rover bellhousing necessitated changes to the radius of the front of the gearbox tunnel, while the inside faces of both footwells had to be altered to clear the exhaust manifolds. Moving inside the car, the

15-4-4. The altered inner 'walls' to the footwells and increased radius to the front of the gearbox tunnel.

15-4-5. The foreshortened battery tray required the battery to be relocated and secured in the boot.

use of a fibreglass gearbox cover was invaluable since this could be altered to accommodate the larger bellhousing and the altered bulkhead fixings we can see at picture 15-4-6.

I've already mentioned the fact that the steering column had to be raised at the bulkhead end, and a new hole cut in the bulkhead about 1in (25mm), higher than normal. You can perhaps see that in picture 15-4-7. The wider bellhousing and resulting slightly narrower footwells brought Richard to fit the brake/clutch pedal box about 1in (25mm), outboard from its original location. With regard to the steering, Richard was forced to fit a 12in (300mm), lower steering shaft with a universal joint on each end, and to have the main steering shaft especially fabricated around a bottom rose joint/steady, as shown in picture 15-4-8.

15-4-6. From inside the car we can see changes were also required to the front inner lips of the floors where, they meet the altered sides to the footwells. Note that the gearbox cover will require altering too if it's to marry with the change to the bulkhead.

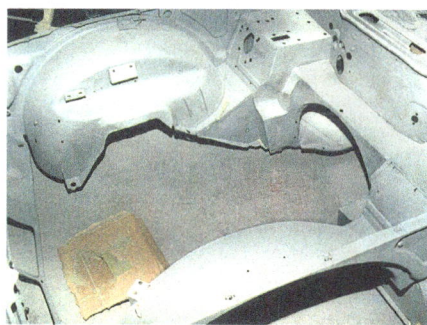

15-4-7. With all the fabrication and welding complete, a light sand blast effectively hides the changes, making everything look quite uniform. Note that the absence of the usual radiator mounting on the far inner wing/fender is offset by different radiator and oil filter mounting brackets.

15-4-8. The steering support can be adjusted, slightly, but even so, it's all a bit 'tight' here!

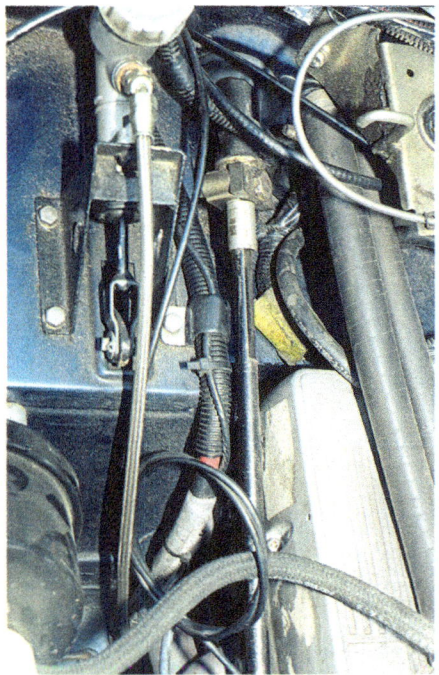

15-4-9. It's not much more spacious towards the top of the column either.

15-4-10. The remote oil filter and the oil cooler (integral with the radiator), might have been designed for Richard's car.

A shot of the top part of the steering column, photo 15-4-9, doesn't look all that different until you realise that the top rubber 'doughnut' has been omitted.

There were some important details to get right and brackets to make and weld in place before Richard could contemplate having the body painted. The first mounting bracket was for the remote oil filter mounting. This is a standard MGB GT V8 casting and filter, and you can see the filter arrangement in picture 15-4-10. The radiator mounting arrangements also needed to be resolved. The standard cross-flow Range Rover radiator was too wide, even for the TR's cavernous radiator area. Richard retained its end tanks (and the integral oil cooler at one end), as we can see from picture 15-4-11, but had it re-cored to give the maximum number of rows and the maximum width the car and end-tanks would accommodate. Richard tells me that the cooling effect is absolutely fine even on the hottest Mediterranean day, so long as the car is moving. However, in static traffic the 16in pusher fan is not quite up to the job, and the water temperature gradually rises. As a result, a more powerful fan looks on the cards. The left and right side radiator mounting arrangements can be viewed at pictures 15-4-12 and 15-4-13 respectively.

Richard had the car (beautifully) painted Jaguar Sapphire Blue Metallic once all the changes had been resolved, whereupon putting the car together started. The Rover's gearbox has a very long remote-gear-change that would need to be shortened, unless you like changing gear using your left elbow! Cobra kit-cars have exactly the same problem and use the ultra-shortened

15-4-11. Note the thick multi-core radiator, the feeling of space at the front of the engine and, just in shot, the alternator that Richard found very hard to locate.

15-4-12. The air intake and filter for the engine are nicely placed in the cool airstream.

15-4-13. Right side radiator mounting and oil cooler inlet.

extension we see in picture 15-4-14. This resolved most of Richard's problem. However, he still had to extend his 'H' dashboard/fascia support by about 2.5in (60mm), to accommodate the gearlever's location, and you can see the end result in shot 15-4-15. To Richard's delight, not only did the standard prop-shaft flange marry perfectly to the Rover gearbox's rear flange, but the length of the standard prop-shaft proved ideal too!

As picture 15-4-16 shows, the modifications to the bulkhead and battery tray proved absolutely correct, and the 'Hot-wire' mass meter (picture 15-4-17), efi went in nicely too. The engine swap was part of a total rebuild, so Richard had the usual rewiring task, as we see at 15-4-18, but he also had to get the tachometer converted to electronic pulse activation. Richard had the front end of the exhaust system buttoned up (MGB GT V8), and used a pair of 2.25in bore silencers and tailpipes from a conventional 'big-bore' single pipe system at the back end. He married the two ends together, threading the connecting pipes through the middle of the chassis rails and cruciform. The

15-4-14. The Rover gearchange 'remote' - ultra-shortened for Cobra kit-cars and Buick/Rover TRs!

bore feed pipe for the usual external Bosch efi fuel pump. You may have noticed the efi fuel filter in picture 15-4-16.

Vented 24mm thick discs/rotors were used, along with Wilwood 4-pot calipers, to provide the major stopping power, but the rear drums were augmented with the Alfin drums we see illustrated at 15-4-19. This same picture also gives us a clue that the car has had lowering road springs fitted which, along with his other suspension improvements, contribute to the terrific ride, handling and road holding that I hear (from the very good authority of John Sykes), is absolutely first class. Richard fitted Nylatron polyurethane suspension bushes throughout, while Avo shocks and a ⅞in rose-jointed roll/sway-bar were used at the front. The standard steering rack is fixed via the 'solid' mountings we discussed in Chapter 3.

After some experimenting, Richard has settled on Spax adjustable gas shocks at the rear. The standard rear hubs and drive shafts have been used since the car was re-commissioned along with a 3.45 differential. The differential is secured to boxed and strengthened diff pins with yellow polyurethane bushes. None of these features have caused Richard any concern whatsoever. The grip is provided by 205/60/15 Yokohama A520s, fitted

result sounds a perfect blend of eight cylinder burble, authority and muted power. Absolutely great!

Richard used a standard TR6 fuel tank, modified by fitting an ex-Ford Granada internal swirl-pot and a 0.5in

15-4-15. In fact, it sits very naturally in the TR, although as I explain in the main text, the 'H' casting has been lengthened and very nicely retrimmed.

15-4-16. As the engine installation progresses, we can see how close the head/bulkhead gap is. The fuel filter sits nicely on the curtailed battery tray.

15-4-17. The hot wire mass meter efi is in the centre of the picture, with the all-important air tight air hose linking it to the plenum chamber (just out of shot).

15-4-18. The wiring for any restoration is an important task if the car is to provide reliable transportation. I note that Richard has very wisely run the new thick main battery cable inside the car.

15-4-19. The Alfin rear drums are plain to see, but can you just spot the rear half of the Bosch fuel pump mounted on the chassis to the right of this wheel?

15-4-20. The whole car has a feeling of balance that nicely hides the true extent of the pretty extensive changes that ...

to 7J Compomotive Minilites. They look very much in keeping with the car as you can see from picture 15-4-20.

Along with Richard Tudor, we see his Racetorations' front spoiler in picture 15-4-21. Richard tells me the spoiler was really fitted purely for aesthetics and certainly it adds something to this otherwise standard looking '6. There is absolutely nothing standard about this car, though, and I not only thank him for sharing his impressive car with us, but also for his time and trouble. Thanks Richard, it was a great pleasure, and it's a stunning car.

CONCLUSIONS

I have been privileged to explore in some detail three great cars. If an engine transplant is on your mind it has to be with the object of enhancing your car's performance, so I thought it might be helpful to conclude this chapter with comparison figures for each of our projects. I thought we would look at front to rear weight balance, which is ideal at 50/50, and also the car's sprightliness, which is traditionally expressed as a power to weight ratio. Without going into the individual assumptions I made, I think the cars will be something like:
• A standard TR6 has 55% of the weight on the front axle and has a power to weight ratio of about 130bhp/ton.
• I believe Dan's Ford-engined TR6 will

be heavier than an original TR6, but with much of the increase at the rear, the front axle will probably be carrying 54% of the weight and the car should have a power/weight ratio of about 270bhp/ton.
• Neil's Stag-engined TR5 will have lost a little weight but the distribution will be about the same as a standard car. However, his reduced weight and increased power will raise his power to weight ratio to about 180bhp/ton.
• Richard's Rover/TR6 will also have lost weight and, with the battery transferred to the rear, will be very nicely balanced with 51% on the front wheels. I think his power/weight ratio must be about 230bhp/ton.

15-4-21. ... Richard Tudor has brought about.

Chapter 16

Weight reduction

I have already referred to the highly acclaimed performance demonstrated by Lotus cars; performance achieved not so much by very powerful engines, but more by superb handling and very light weight. A lighter car allows a high power to weight ratio, with the added benefit that the handling is optimised too (there being less weight and therefore inertia when changing direction or speed). Every car on the road will enjoy improved acceleration, braking, cornering, responsiveness and the opportunity for greater fuel economy, if its weight is reduced. You don't need me to go through the whole car, component by component, suggesting weight reductions as so many are obvious.

However, there are some particularly crucial areas where weight reductions are doubly important:

• Unsprung weight - *i.e.* lightweight brake calipers, alloy front hubs and alloy wheels.
• Weight outside the wheel base - *i.e.* the radiator.
• Weight located high in the car - *i.e.* the cylinder head.
• There are also some within the engine which will have the double benefit of slightly reducing the weight of the engine but significantly reducing its internal inertia too.

It's possible get very pedantic about reducing the weight of a car. I have no doubt that this is how Lotus Cars, for example, operate. As I have said, I don't intend to adopt that approach, and will leave that level of detail to you. Consider that in an aircraft, for example, you'll rarely find a steel lever or pulley (they will all be made from aluminium). Unfortunately, aluminium is significantly more expensive than steel. Furthermore, in your TR most of the parts you consider will have been made from iron and steel and, if you plan to have one made from aluminium it will have to be a bespoke/custom job, further increasing your costs.

It all depends upon how important improved performance is to you. If you're leading the TR Register championship with a couple of races to go and can see a 5lbs weight reduction available, for example, you may be prepared to pay for it. If you only go on a couple of track days each year, I doubt you'll see that expense in the same light! This why I intend to leave the detail to each individual.

All the specialists which have contributed to this book have invaluable experience and special products specifically intended to reduce the weight of your car. My focus will be on those reductions which I think offer a dual benefit.

UNSPRUNG WEIGHT

Items on the road side of the springs represent unsprung weight. If these are light, then the car weighs less. However, the double benefit of minimising unsprung weight is that it dramatically affects the behaviour of the suspension. The work the shock absorber has to do, the extent to which the tyres stay in contact with the road, and the car's roadholding all benefit. Unsprung weight, therefore, refers to the wishbones, shock absorbers, hubs, brake calipers and discs, wheels and tyres and drive shafts. The greater the combined weight of these components the higher the inertia of every movement of the suspension. That's one reason why the IRS cars are likely to have better roadholding than the live axle cars, the unsprung weight of a live axle is greater than the hubs and drive shafts of an IRS car. At the rear of an IRS TR it is the wheels that offer the greatest single opportunity to reduce unsprung weight, although picture 16-1-1 and 16-1-2 may be informative. The trailing arms are already made from alloy, the drive shafts are likely to become unreliable if their size is reduced although alloy

16-1-1. These Racetorations Cosworth hubs not only couple to the TR drive shaft seen here but ...

16-1-2. ... increase the diameter of the stub-axle (Cosworth on the right). They reduce unsprung weight too.

Wheel	approx weight (lb)
5x15 steel	16
5.5x15 alloy	14
6x15 Minilite	12.5
7x15 Minilite	17
7x15 Magnesium	12.5

Weight comparisons for a range of wheels.

16-2-1. These Alloy Alfin brake drums reduce unsprung weight and increase the heat dissipation on any TR with 9" diameter rear brakes.

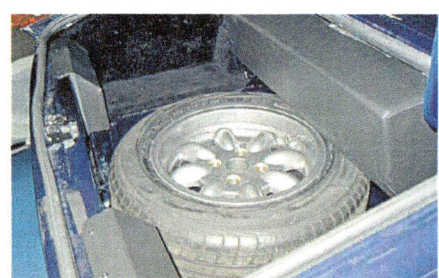

16-2-2. Racetorations magnesium alloy wheels reduce unsprung weight outside the wheelbase. The 15in diameter wheels come in gun-metal or silver powder coating and with two rim widths – 6in and 7in. Apart from their aesthetics, the main advantage of these wheels is their 5.5 and 6kg (12-13lb) respective weights coupled to their strength. They will not crack or shatter like aluminium wheels can from time to time. The 70-litre (about 19 imperial gallons) fuel tank has obvious range advantages and sits mostly within the wheelbase.

16-3-1. Racetorations alloy hubs not only reduce the unsprung weight, but also increase the track width via a thicker flange. They increase the load capacity using a bigger outside bearing and ...

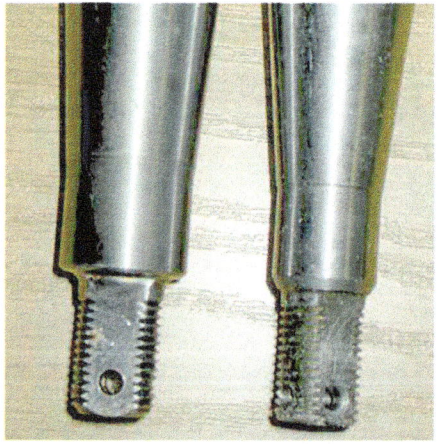

16-3-2. ... stronger (ex Dolomite Sprint) stub axles. The thicker Dolly stub axle is on the left.

brake-drums, pictured at 16-2-1, might be a useful opportunity.

The heaviest single unsprung component at the front is also going to be the wheel/tyre. The trade-off, however, is between a largish wheel with the capacity for powerful brakes, and a small lighter wheel with possibly insufficient space for adequate brakes. Then there is the compromise of tyre width. Obviously, the wider the tyre the heavier it is, but the more rubber it puts to the road and the better it grips. Generally speaking, from a roadholding point of view, wide is good, so forget the weight penalty with that one! However, there is one wheel/tyre issue we can do something about, the material the wheel is made from. There has been a huge increase in the number of alloy wheels on the market in recent years and for very good reason, as I trust you'll agree when you study picture 16-2-2 and carry out some weight comparisons.

Staying with weight reduction opportunities at the front, if you've ever carried a pair of cast/original brake calipers home from the salvage yard, you'll know straightaway that there has to be an opportunity for unsprung weight reduction here. I've not got a spare TR one to weigh but a similar one weighed 15lb. It's not surprising that there are numerous alloy calipers available, as I detailed in Chapter 5. They will save 50 to 60% of the cast units' weight, and are to be very much encouraged since, not only is the unsprung weight saved, but the heat dissipation is usually better too!

The hubs to which your front wheels bolt are weighty items and again, a 50% weight saving opportunity awaits you. Pictures 16-3-1 and 16-3-2 may be of interest.

WEIGHT OUTSIDE THE WHEELBASE

The wheelbase is that distance between the centres of the front and rear wheels. Anything outside that distance is overhanging the wheelbase and, from a roadholding point of view is most undesirable. Technically, it's the Polar Moment of Inertia you wish to minimise by keeping all the weight you can within the wheelbase, avoiding long overhangs outside the wheelbase, and keeping the weight outside the wheelbase to an absolute minimum. Not important? Well, lots of motor manufacturers think it is and go to great lengths to design cars with a 'wheel at each corner'. You can't redesign your TR, although you will appreciate that a lightweight boot/trunk lid and/or bonnet/hood will both fall into the double benefit category of weight saving.

The front and rear bumpers are best removed, from a weight saving/outside the wheel base point of view. The water radiator is 'way out there' and no lightweight. An aluminium radiator saves about 40%, and is outside the wheelbase, furthermore reducing the current front/back imbalance of most TRs. You can help a little by not carrying heavy spares items in the boot (like a starter motor, for example, or a jack).

WEIGHT LOCATED HIGH IN THE CAR

I mentioned in my pre-amble that the cylinder head was both heavy and high in the car, certainly well above the centre of gravity, and therefore contributes to body roll. My easy solution with a four-cylinder engine is to suggest you fit an aluminium head and save a doubly important 30lb. It's not quite so simple when it comes to reducing the weight at the top of a six-cylinder engine. It all depends upon your objectives, of course, but you may recall that I mentioned in the previous chapter how Neil Brown improved his car's road holding by lowering the centre of gravity by fitting the Triumph Stag engine. The Stag engine fits and has aluminium heads!

Many an alternator is heavy and certainly does not help the height issue, but lighter versions are available. Do not overlook the savings you might achieve using alloy mounting components too.

The water pump housing, pulley and impeller are and located very high and right on the wheelbase. They are made from cast iron and I would guess they total some 9 - 10lb. Replacing these with alloy components gives you the chance to reduce the car's weight by about half that total, but to benefit by much more than just saving 5lb because of the high/frontal location.

The battery is relatively high in the car, and a weighty item. I use a small Ford Escort (compact sedan), battery for cost saving reasons. That weighs about 30lb, but I think a full size TR designated battery might weigh in at 40lb. So my first suggestion is to fit a smaller battery.

Weight distribution is an issue, too, and the TRs are front heavy, as I mentioned in Chapter 15. You'll achieve a double benefit if you relocate the smaller battery somewhere to the rear of the car but within the wheelbase. Anyone who has to have a bespoke/custom fuel tank made up could give some thought as to whether a slot could be found for the battery alongside the new fuel tank.

ENGINE

There are two types of components within the engine which can be looked at in the context of weight reduction: rotating (*e.g.* flywheel, crankshaft, clutch and pulleys, *etc.*), and reciprocating (*e.g.* con-rods, pistons, gudgeon pins, pushrods and rockers). Any weight saving within the engine is welcome, but the savings from rotating parts have the triple benefits of reducing the weight of the engine, improving the front/rear balance and reducing the inertia of the engine, thereby improving the engine's responsiveness. However, while reciprocating weight offers little by way of actual weight savings (we are dealing in ounces saved), they are nevertheless very important, although reciprocating weight reductions will reduce your bank balance even more severely than the rotating reductions!

Rotating weight losses are easiest to deal with first. I've mentioned some of the pulleys earlier, but to emphasise the point, did you appreciate that the front crank pulley weighs about 5lb, and offers a 50% reduction opportunity in alloy? Flywheels and clutches offer the greatest single weight reduction opportunity within the engine. However, it needs to be approached carefully, for too light a flywheel for your application can make driving the car a misery. The early sixes with a long back crank have a (roughly), 20-22lb flywheel, whilst the later cars with a short back crank have a 25-27lb flywheel. Lightening the flywheel makes a huge difference to the responsiveness of the engine because less weight has to be accelerated up to speed by the engine. You can't swap a late flywheel for an early one unless you change the crankshaft/flywheel assembly, but you can lighten both flywheels by turning off the 'excess' metal. An experienced machinist should be able to get about 4lb off the early flywheels (to *circa* 16-18lb), and 8lb off a later one, reducing that to about 17-19lb, depending upon whether you count the ring gear or not. Try the car with the lightened flywheel, but bear in mind that there is scope for milling out slots between the clutch bolt holes to remove a further 3lb. This is especially valuable since removing weight from the outer edge of the flywheel has the greatest benefit. Cost for all these operations is *circa*

£125-150, and for the majority of fast road cars offers good value for money. For the fastest cars, an aluminium flywheel can be fitted. These can weigh as little as 10lb, including the ring gear, but at nearly £400, they are costly.

There are no material weight reduction opportunities in changing the crankshaft. The steel replacements are much stronger, of course, but offer no attraction from a weight watchers point of view.

Time to consider reciprocating weight savings to con-rods and pistons. I feel gudgeon pins to be part of the piston and, while pushrods and rockers do offer opportunities, it has to be the major reciprocating parts where we must focus our attention. The con-rods are very important components in any engine but particularly in an engine likely to be used at high-revolutions. Steel con-rods are the key, and Carillo forged steel rods, marketed under a variety of brand names, are about 0.5lb lighter per rod than original Triumph ones. They are much stronger too, and offer an amazing opportunity particularly when you think of the rod flashing up and down within each bore of your engine at unimaginable speeds. However, you do need to think of a (very), positive benefit before you order a set for they are about £150 per rod!

Pistons flash up and down too, and are equally, possibly more, important from a reciprocating weight point of view. The method of manufacture (cast or forged), has a major bearing on their strength, forging being a stronger manufacturing method than casting. Surprisingly perhaps this also affects the weight of the piston. The design also affects the weight of each piston (material thickness being obvious, but skirt lengths also differ from piston to piston). Some pistons have cut-outs in the base of the skirt, and any one of these variations can easily make one piston an ounce or two heavier or lighter than a competitive product. Sure, a couple of ounces is going to make no difference to the overall weight of an engine, but it makes an enormous difference to the inertia of that piston as it tries to break free of its con-rod and fly though your cylinder head. So, you can't judge your success at weight reduction entirely by weight alone, strength counts too! Have fun planning what's right for you, your car and your bank balance, but get that weight off!

Chapter 17
Conclusion

Whatever your car and whatever the category you're aiming at, two 'rules' apply. Firstly, you don't need to carry out all your proposed changes simultaneously, but secondly, buy all 'related' parts from one supplier simultaneously. With regard to the first rule, providing you carry out the upgrades in the correct order, there's no reason why you can't spread the cost of the whole improvement programme over a number of years. The order you tackle the improvements requires your careful consideration, however, and I trust this book has helped in this respect. However, safety related modifications need to take priority over speed and power.

Moving on to my second rule, buy the parts you need to upgrade the car in 'kits', and buy each kit from the same supplier. For example, don't buy brake calipers from one source, brake discs from another, brake lines from somewhere else, *etc*. Buy the lot in one go from one reliable retailer. This may cost a little bit more, but believe me, this policy will be very worthwhile. You don't have to use the same specialist every time, indeed there are good reasons for selecting someone who you think is the most advanced technically and/or competitively when it comes to brakes, for example, but another retailer when it comes to engine parts. However, to emphasise my point, when it comes to the clutch and related parts, do go to one source for all flywheel, clutch and clutch release components.

With regard to suspension packages, I consider it important that you fit the same manufacturer's gear to the back and the front, even if you fit these upgrades 12 months apart, don't forget that you should always carry out the front improvements first.

There are some places where this 'one supplier' situation becomes less straightforward, though. The engine is a case in point. In an ideal world, the wise approach may be one supplier for all your engine bits. However, you may find the cost, or technical solution, not to your liking and find it preferable to split the engine into top and bottom. However, I really would not split it down further than that, and strongly recommend that, for example, you buy all your camshaft, followers, valves, valve springs, cylinder head, rocker assembly, *etc*., from one supplier in one go. This method makes it most unlikely that you will suffer problems but, if you later find the valve springs are binding, there is but one source that will, normally, readily accept responsibility and take corrective action. If you have bought the parts separately and/or from different suppliers you will be without recourse.

Appendix

CLUBS & ASSOCIATIONS

TR Register, 1B Hawksworth, Southmead Industrial Park, Didcot, Oxon, OX11 7HR. England.
Tel: 01235 818866. www.tr-register.co.uk.
Email: office@tr-register.co.uk

Vintage Triumph Register, 15218 West Warren Avenue, Dearborn, MI 48126, USA. www.vtr.org.

Motor Sport Association. Tel: 01753 765000. www.msauk.org.

Historic Sports Car Club. Tel 01327 858400. www.hscc.org.uk.

Hillclimb and Sprint Association. www.hillclimbandsprint.co.uk.

PERFORMANCE SPECIALISTS

Moss Europe, Unit 16, Hampton Business Park, Bolney Way, Feltham TW13 6DB, England.
Tel: 020 8867 2020. www.moss-europe.co.uk.

Protek Engineering, Unit 13, Bushells Business Estate, Wallingford, Oxfordshire, England.
Tel: 01491 832372. www.protek-engineering.co.uk.

Racetorations, Caldicott Drive, Heapham Road Industrial Estate, Gainsborough, Lincs, DN21 1FJ, England.
Tel: 01427 616565. www.racetorations.co.uk.

Revington TR, Thorngrove Barns, Middlezoy, Somerset, TA7 0PD, England.
Tel: 01823 698437. www.revingtontr.com.
Email: info@revingtontr.com.

Rimmer Bros, Sleaford Rd, Bracebridge Heath, Lincoln, JN4 2NA, England.
Tel: 01522 568000. www.rimmerbros.co.uk.
Email: sales@rimmerbros.co.uk.

The Roadster Factory, PO Box 332, Armagh, PA 15920, USA.
Tel 800 234-1104. www.the-roadster-factory.com.

TR Bitz, Swine Yard Lane, High Legh, Knutsford, Cheshire, WA16 0SD, England.
Tel: 01925 756000. www.trbitz.com.

TR Enterprises, Dale Lane, Blidworth, Mansfield, Nottinghamshire, NG21 0SA, England.
Tel: 01623 793807. www.treenterprises.com.
Email: info@trenterprises.com.

OTHER SPECIALISTS

Brakes

EBC, EBC Buildings, Countess Road, Northampton, NN5 7EA.
Tel: 01604 583344.

EBC, 806 Buchanan Blvd., Unit 115-256, Boulder City, Las Vegas, NV89005.

Hi Spec Motorsport, Unit 5 Parker Ind. Centre, Watling St, Dartford, Kent, DA2 6EP. Tel: 01322 286850

Injection parts and service

Jenvey Dynamics Ltd, Building 2, Stanmore Ind Estate, Bridgenorth, WV15 5HP England. www.jenvey.co.uk (throttle-bodies and efi equipment).

Prestige Developments and Injection, 77 Box Lane, Wrexham, Clwyd, LL12 8DA, England.
Tel: 01978 263449. www.prestigeinjection.net.

Safety cages, harnesses and other related equipment

Safety Devices International Ltd, Cambridge House, Holborn Avenue, Mildenhall, Suffolk, IP28 7AN.
Tel: 01638 713606. www.safetydevices.com.

Gearbox adaptation kits

Autogear Transmissions Ltd, Leeview Farm, Hawkswood Road, Downham, Essex CM11 1JZ England.
www.autogear.co.uk (Sierra 5-Speed Gearbox kits)

Dellow Automotive Pty. Ltd., 37 Daisy St, Revesby, NSW 2212, Australia. Tel: (02) 9774-4419. www.dellowconversions.com.au.

Conversion Components, 316 Pencarrow Road, Tamahere, RD3 Hamilton, New Zealand 3283. www.conversioncomp.com.

Cylinder head modifications

Bailey and Liddle, 16-17 The Shipyard, Upper Brents, Faversham, ME13 7DZ. Tel: 01795 535068. http://www.baileyandliddle.co.uk

Peter Burgess Automotive Performance Engineering, Unit 1, Amber Buildings, Meadow Lane, Alfreton, Derbyshire, DE5 7EZ, England. Tel: 01773 520021. www.mg-cars.org.uk/peterburgess. Email: peter@burgesstuning.free-online.co.uk

Index

Printed and bound by CPI Group (UK) Ltd, Croydon, CR0 4YY

22/04/2026

02095412-0008